Health Care Policy and Practice

In *Health Care Policy and Practice: A Biopsychosocial Perspective*, Moniz and Gorin guide students through the development of the American health care system: what it is, what the policies are, and how students can influence them. Part I focuses on recent history and reforms; Part II examines the system's structure and policies; and Part III explores policy analysis and advocacy, and disparities in health based on demographics and inequities in access to care. The book concludes with a discussion of the impact of social factors on health and health status.

This new, fifth edition has been fully updated to include the Trump administration's efforts to "repeal and replace" the Affordable Care Act (ACA) and to integrate content throughout the text on the impact of the ACA in recent years. In addition, new content on health disparities for the LGBTQ community has been added.

Cynthia D. Moniz is Professor Emeritus of Social Work at Plymouth State University in New Hampshire.

Stephen H. Gorin is Professor Emeritus of Social Work at Plymouth State University in New Hampshire.

Health Care Policy and Practice

A Biopsychosocial Perspective

Fifth Edition

Cynthia D. Moniz and Stephen H. Gorin

Routledge
Taylor & Francis Group

NEW YORK AND LONDON

Fifth edition published 2019
by Routledge
52 Vanderbilt Avenue, New York, NY 10017

and by Routledge
2 Park Square, Milton Park, Abingdon, Oxon, OX14 4RN

Routledge is an imprint of the Taylor & Francis Group, an informa business

First edition published by Allyn and Bacon 2002
Fourth edition published by Routledge 2014

Library of Congress Cataloging-in-Publication Data
Names: Moniz, Cynthia, author. | Gorin, Stephen H., author.
Title: Health care policy and practice : a biopsychosocial perspective /
    Cynthia D. Moniz and Stephen H. Gorin.
Other titles: Health and mental health care policy
Description: Fifth edition. | New York, NY : Routledge, 2019. | Includes
    bibliographical references and index. |
Identifiers: LCCN 2018037839 (print) | LCCN 2018038635 (ebook)
    | ISBN 9781315114163 (Master Ebook) | ISBN 9781351626507
    (Web pdf) | ISBN 9781351626491 (ePub) | ISBN 9781351626484
    (Mobipocket) | ISBN 9781138079953 (hardback) | ISBN
    9781138079960 (pbk.)
Subjects: LCSH: Medical policy—United States. | Medical policy—
    Social aspects—United States. | Medical policy—Psychological
    aspects—United States. | Mental health policy—United States. |
    Mental health services—Social aspects—United States. | Medical
    care—United States.
Classification: LCC RA395.A3 (ebook) | LCC RA395.A3 M662 2019
    (print) | DDC 362.10973--dc23
LC record available at https://lccn.loc.gov/2018037839

ISBN: 978-1-138-07995-3 (hbk)
ISBN: 978-1-138-07996-0 (pbk)
ISBN: 978-1-315-11416-3 (ebk)

Typeset in Stone Serif
by Swales & Willis Ltd, Exeter, Devon, UK

TABLE OF CONTENTS

CONTENTS

PREFACE

Our aim in writing this book was to create a health policy and policy practice text for undergraduate and graduate students in social work education. It is written from a social determinants of health perspective, which is compatible with social work's biopsychosocial perspective. The social determinants of health perspective demonstrates the impact of the social environment on individual and population health, and provides insight into prospects for the future of not just health care policy, but *health* policy as well.

The text focuses on both health and health care policy and considers broader social issues and public policies that impact the health of the U.S. population. It suggests the need to go beyond health care policy to health policy. During the 10 years that passed after the publication of the first edition of this text (published in a different format by a different publisher), the problem of access to health insurance and health care in the U.S. actually worsened; policy-makers struggled and battled to address the widening gap in coverage and escalating health care costs, and finally passed the Affordable Care Act (ACA) in 2010. During this period, at-risk populations including low-income individuals and families, people of color, children, women, and older adults continued to experience significant disparities in health. With the historic presidential election of Barack Obama in 2008 and 2012, the nation considered a new direction in health care policy for the first time since the Clinton era, and enacted legislation with the promise of getting the U.S. closer to providing access to care for everyone. More recently, with the election of Trump to the White House in 2016 and a conservative Republican-controlled Congress, the gains made with the passage of the ACA have been threatened. The need to advocate for health and health care policies consistent with the values of social work are perhaps as great as ever.

CHAPTERS 1 AND 2

The first two chapters provide a historical overview of the politics of health care policy in the U.S., the enactment of major health care policies from 1865 to the present, with emphasis on the ACA, and a discussion of the failure of the U.S. to enact universal health insurance. The first chapter focuses on the "where we are now" in the changing landscape of health care policy.

CHAPTER 3

With the enactment of the ACA, public, community, and mental health have received the greatest attention in public policy since the 1990s. This chapter examines efforts to renew the role of public health during the Clinton and Obama administrations and current efforts to strengthen community and mental health, and the efforts of the Trump administration to reverse some of these gains.

CHAPTER 4

This chapter examines the cost of health care in the U.S. from an international perspective and provides a historical overview of strategies to contain costs including managed care and the new ACA. Health care inflation has plagued the U.S. health care system for decades and was one of the driving forces behind enactment of health care reform in 2010.

CHAPTERS 5, 6, AND 7

These three chapters provide a comprehensive overview of the structure and funding of the U.S. health care "system" today, including employment-based health insurance, Medicare, Medicaid, and the Children's Health Insurance Program (CHIP). Chapter 5 examines the important but declining role of private employment-based health insurance, Chapter 6 examines the Medicare program, and Chapter 7 examines the Medicaid/CHIP program. Medicare evolved as an employer-/employee-financed federal insurance for older retired and disabled workers. Medicaid evolved as a publicly financed insurance for low-income individuals who meet the government's standards for eligibility. Overall, however, the system remains dominated by the private sector. The impact of the ACA (Obamacare) is integrated throughout these chapters, as well as the potential impact of the Trump administration's efforts to reduce spending on Medicare, Medicaid, and CHIP.

CHAPTER 8

This chapter provides a transition from Parts I and II of the book by focusing on the role of social workers in affecting policy and engaging in policy practice. It provides an overview of the stages of policy practice in social work, and examines values and standards for assessing policy.

CHAPTERS 9, 10, AND 11

These three chapters apply concepts and skills of policy practice to health and mental health care policy. Chapter 9 examines the problem of access in the U.S., including concepts of access and trends in coverage; Chapter 10 examines the problem of disparities in health for people of color, including concepts of risk and disparity, and examines explanations for inequities in health status; Chapter 11 applies the basic policy practice questions raised in analysis of the problem of disparities in health for women, children, older adults, and the LGBTQ community in the U.S. With poverty and inequality as essential determining factors in health status and access to health care, these chapters are essential to understanding health disparities in major health outcomes such as infant mortality, cardiovascular disease, HIV/AIDS, cancer, diabetes, and infectious diseases. Risk factors particular to specific groups, such as violence against women, and the role of federal health and welfare policies, such as CHIP or child welfare legislation, in prevention, health promotion, or access to care are examined. Charts and graphs are used to highlight disparities in health status and access to health care; selected websites are provided to help the reader update this information. Major social welfare policies that address abuse and neglect, violence, substance abuse, and other social problems that impact and shape health status are also discussed.

CHAPTER 12

The final chapter introduces the reader to the concept of social determinants of health and the relationship between social determinants of health, such as poverty and inequality, and health care policy. It invites the reader to consider new directions in health and health policy by considering the implications of this perspective not only for health *care* policy, but also for *health* policy. It also examines implications for advocating for health policy in the U.S. in this context.

ACKNOWLEDGMENTS

Now that this text is in its fifth edition, we would like to acknowledge those individuals who originally helped to make this book a reality through their support: Alice Lieberman, Kevin Corcoran, and Sam Flint, longtime friends and colleagues, who generously shared their insights into writing and publishing in social work and health care reform; and Michael Rachlis and Debby Copes, who gave us insight into the Canadian health care system, introduced us to the social determinants of health, and provided warm hospitality in Toronto. We owe a special debt to Richard Wilkinson for his path-breaking research and his generous friendship and support. We *still* (so many years ago now) have fond memories of our walk through a sheep pasture overlooking Brighton, England, as we discussed the complexities of a social perspective of health.

PART I

Where We Are and How We Got Here

CHAPTER 1

Efforts to Achieve Universal Health Care
From Clinton to Trump

THE FOCUS OF THIS FIRST CHAPTER IS THE CURRENT SYSTEM of health care in the U.S.—where we are and how we got here. In 2010, after more than a year of contentious debate, Congress enacted the Obama Administration's Affordable Care Act (ACA). The ACA marked a significant step forward in a very long struggle to achieve national health insurance. It was not as ambitious as the Clinton administration's Health Security Act of 1993 which failed to be enacted, but it positioned the U.S. to move toward universal health care and brought significant reforms in access, quality, and cost. However, in 2017, President Donald Trump was elected on a promise to "repeal and replace" the ACA. As noted by one of the leading health economists, "the U.S. has never experienced a sea change in national health policy like that which occurred in early 2017" (Jost, 2017b).

THE RISE AND FALL OF THE HEALTH SECURITY ACT: 1988–96

To begin, let us review the Clinton administration's effort to reform health care in the U.S. and the events that led up to this historic legislation. During the late 1980s, as health care costs continued to accelerate, national health insurance (NHI) emerged once again as an important policy issue. In 1988, as part of the Medicare Catastrophic Coverage Act, Congress created a Bipartisan Commission on Comprehensive Health Care (Rolde, 1992). The chair of the commission was Representative Claude Pepper (D-FL), a longtime advocate for older adults. When Pepper died, Senator Jay Rockefeller (D-WVA) became chair and the commission was renamed the Pepper Commission.

In its final report, released in September 1990, the Pepper Commission warned that the "American health system" was "approaching a breaking point" (Pepper Commission, 1990, p. 2): 32 million people (including 9 million children) lacked any health care coverage, and 20 million more had inadequate coverage. Moreover, due to "continuously escalating health care costs," anyone relying "on job-based coverage face[d] an increasing risk of joining the ranks of the uninsured" (Pepper Commission, 1990, p. 5). The commission also called attention to the need for long-term care coverage, noting that between 9 million and 11 million people "of all ages" had chronic disabilities, and 4 million were "so severely disabled that they cannot survive without substantial help from others" (Pepper Commission, 1990, p. 10).

The Pepper Commission went beyond analysis and considered ways to expand coverage for health and long-term care. By a narrow vote, the commission recommended a step-by-step approach that would eventually require all employers to provide coverage to their workers (Pepper Commission, 1990). Unemployed people and individuals in poverty would receive coverage through a public plan. The commission also endorsed managed care to reduce costs and the enactment of legislation that would prevent insurers from refusing to cover high-risk individuals (Pepper Commission, 1990). Finally, the commission recommended "social insurance for home and community-based care and . . . three months of nursing home care, for all Americans, regardless of income" (emphasis in original) (Pepper Commission, 1990, p. 120).

Although Congress largely ignored the Pepper Commission's report, the Commission's work strengthened the hand of reformers and helped frame debate in the years ahead. The Commission's employment-based model of universal coverage formed the basis of the "play or pay" approach that emerged, which would require employers to either insure their workers (play) or contribute to a national plan (pay) for individuals who did not have coverage (Marmor, 1994). George Mitchell (D-ME), the Senate majority leader, introduced such a bill (Rolde, 1992).

PROPOSALS FOR A SINGLE-PAYER PLAN

The Pepper Commission also considered, and eventually rejected, a Canadian-style, single-payer plan. Under a single-payer plan, "health insurance is paid for by the government, out of funds it collects from individuals (and, possibly, employers)" (Marmor, 1994, p. 11). With such a plan, Canada succeeded in covering its entire population at much less cost than the U.S. could under its current system (Rachlis and Kushner, 1994). In the early 1970s, Senator Edward Kennedy (D-MA) proposed a plan based on the Canadian system (Marmor, 1994) and, in the late 1980s and early 1990s, the single-payer plan was resurrected as a possible model for the U.S. by labor unions, advocacy groups, and others, including Lee Iacocca, president and CEO of Chrysler and one of the world's best known business leaders (Marmor, 1994). David Himmelstein and Steffie Woolhandler (1989), from Physicians for a National Health Plan, published numerous articles demonstrating the relative efficiency of the Canadian health care system and arguing in favor of a single-payer plan.

The National Association of Social Workers (NASW) supported a single-payer plan. In 1979, the NASW formally went on record in favor of NHI (National Association of Social Workers, 1991) and, in 1990, the Delegate Assembly identified NHI as the profession's chief policy priority (National Association of Social Workers, 1991). Senator Daniel Inouye (D-HI) introduced the National Health Care Act (S. 684) in 1993, NASW's proposal for a single-payer system (Mizrahi, 1995).

By 1990, national health expenditures had risen to 12.1 percent of gross domestic product (GDP) (up from 8.9 percent in 1980), and per capita health expenditures stood at $2686 (versus $1068 in 1980) (Levit et al., 1994). Backing for reform now reached a 40-year high (Skocpol, 1995). A year later, with the unexpected election of Harris Wofford, an advocate of NHI, to the Senate, health care reform assumed center stage (Smith et al., 1992). Despite this, President George Bush adamantly opposed fundamental reform. Although the Democratic presidential candidates criticized Bush, they hesitated to propose solutions of their own. When Senator Bob Kerrey (D-NE) announced support for a single-payer system, the other candidates also faced pressure to become more specific (Johnson and Broder, 1996).

Bill Clinton, then the governor of Arkansas, promised to reform "the health-care system to control costs, improve quality, expand preventive and long-term care, maintain consumer choice, and cover everybody" (cited in Skocpol, 1997, p. 37). Clinton developed a plan that required employers to contribute to the cost of insuring their employees; the government would cover individuals without jobs (Starr and Zelman, 1993). To control costs, Clinton advocated "'competition within a budget'" (cited in Starr and Zelman, 1993, p. 9).

An Election Day exit poll showed that voters preferred Clinton's approach to health care to George Bush's by a wide margin. A quarter of Clinton's supporters identified his position on health care as the chief reason why they had voted for him. When the pollsters asked voters to choose among Clinton's plan, Bush's plan (which relied on tax incentives and health maintenance organizations [HMOs]), and a single-payer proposal, Clinton's plan finished last. According to Robert Blendon, an expert on public opinion, these findings showed that, although Clinton had support for a plan to "'expand coverage and contain costs,'" he did not "have a mandate for a particular plan" (cited in Johnson and Broder, 1996, p. 91).

CLINTON'S PROPOSAL: THE HEALTH SECURITY ACT OF 1993

Bill Clinton introduced the Health Security Act (HSA) (H.R. 3600, 103d Congress, 1st Session) on September 22, 1993. The fundamental goals of the act were to ensure universal coverage and control costs (Zelman, 1994). To achieve universal coverage, the HSA required employers to pay 80 percent of the cost of insuring their employees; the government guaranteed coverage for low-income and unemployed people (Zelman, 1994). To control costs, the HSA relied on a combination of competition and regulation (Zelman, 1994).

The HSA built on the work of several theorists, particularly Alain Enthoven, a Stanford economist (Reinhardt, 1994; Starr, 1994). The RAND Health Insurance Experiment found that staff-model HMO) could deliver high-quality, low-cost care (Newhouse and the Insurance Experiment Group, 1993). Enthoven and Kronick (1991) proposed a system of managed, or government-regulated, competition among prepaid plans. Small businesses and self-employed people would join purchasing cooperatives, which would negotiate with HMOs for discounted prices (Roberts and Clyde, 1993). Consumers, who annually would choose the group to which they wished to belong, would drive this system (Starr, 1994). As rational actors, they would presumably opt for the best combination of cost and quality (Enthoven and Kronick, 1991).

Managed competition did not go unchallenged (Starr, 1994). Some observers questioned whether it would really contain costs (Schwartz and Mendelson, 1992, 1994). Others worried that managed care would have an adverse impact on the quality of health care (Davis et al., 1994). Even supporters of managed competition acknowledged that it would not work in areas with few providers (Kronick et al., 1993).

In response to this criticism, the Clinton administration expanded Enthoven's framework (Starr, 1994). The most significant change was around cost control. As a "backstop," in case competition did not reduce costs, the administration proposed capping the rate of growth of insurance premiums (Enthoven and Singer, 1994; Kronick, 1994; Zelman, 1994). The act also included a comprehensive benefit package, which would force providers to compete based on quality, not withholding care, and prevent cost shifting (Zelman, 1994). Comprehensive benefits would prevent development of a two-tiered system.

Mental Health Parity

The HSA also addressed mental health needs. Tipper Gore, the wife of the vice-president and a leading advocate for people with mental illness, headed a Working Group on Mental Health and Substance Abuse. No other specialty area received this level of attention. As a result of the group's work, the HSA offered a wide range of mental health and substance abuse services, including hospitalization and nonresidential care, prescription drug coverage, therapy and counseling, and case management (Aaron, 1994). Copayments and deductibles were similar to those for other health services. Although Congress failed to pass the HSA, the Act's emphasis on parity, or equity between health and mental health treatment, helped set the stage for more limited reforms.

WHY THE ACT FAILED

Clinton's speech introducing the HSA received wide acclaim, and for a time it seemed possible that the U.S. might finally achieve universal coverage. Before long, however, public opinion turned against the act (Johnson and Broder, 1996; Skocpol, 1997). The HSA provoked opposition from both the left and the right. Many on the left supported a single-payer plan and criticized Clinton's bill for preserving the employer-based system of health care coverage and relying on insurance companies. On the right, insurers and pharmaceutical companies, along with conservative interest groups, engaged in a massive campaign aimed at defeating the bill. The administration was unable to respond effectively, which resulted in widespread confusion among the public. Although polling showed that the public supported specific parts of the HSA, they strongly opposed the "Clinton Plan" (Bok, 1998), similar to more recent efforts from conservatives to instill opposition to "Obamacare".

In July 1994, leading Democrats declared the HSA "officially dead" without ever bringing it to a vote and attempted to develop a proposal of their own (Johnson and Broder, 1996). On September 26, a year and four days after Clinton's original speech, George Mitchell (D-ME), the Senate majority leader, announced an end to efforts for "comprehensive" reform (Johnson and Broder, 1996). By rejecting the HSA, the public opened the door to an unregulated system, without consumer protections (Johnson and Broder, 1996). This may explain why, in 1996, with the benefit of hindsight, 58 percent of the population said they would have been "better off" had the HSA been enacted (Skocpol, 1997).

HEALTH INSURANCE PORTABILITY AND ACCOUNTABILITY ACT

The failure of the HSA contributed to the Republican sweep of Congress in 1994 (Johnson and Broder, 1996). For many voters, the Act represented both the threat of government bureaucracy and the inability of the Democratic Congress to govern effectively. According to Bill McInturff, a leading Republican pollster, "the collapse of the health care plan . . . fed the voters' sense that Washington was in gridlock and that the Democrats . . . were to blame" (cited in Toner, 1994).

The election led many observers to conclude that NHI was dead (Aaron, 1998). Attention increasingly focused on incremental reform as a path to universal coverage (Gorin and Moniz, 1997).

In 1996, in an effort to demonstrate their commitment to compromise, Republicans joined with Democrats and Clinton in supporting PL 104-191, the Health Insurance Portability and Accountability Act (HIPAA) (Atchinson and Fox, 1997). The primary aim of HIPAA was to "eliminate health status from health insurance consideration" (Patel and Rushefsky, 1999, p. 296). In a sense, it was the culmination of the 1993–94 effort for health care reform. An evaluation of the HIPAA by Pollitz and associates (2000, p. 8) concluded that despite "early implementation challenges, HIPAA's successes have been significant, although limited by the law's incremental nature." Although the HIPAA had expanded protections for individuals belonging to group plans, it had done little to help people with individual coverage (Pollitz et al., 2000).

Title I of the HIPAA protects health insurance coverage for workers and their families when they change or lose their jobs, and allows for coverage even with preexisting conditions. However, Title II of the bill has become the source of controversy and concern among providers and consumers. Title II includes Administrative Simplification provisions which regulate issues of privacy and confidentiality in both private and public settings; these went into effect in 2003. As noted by Kuczynski and Gibbs-Wahlberg (2005, p. 283), providers were "plunged into a mire of federal definitions, acronyms, regulations, and procedures that spiked the jargon meter. A veritable compliance melee erupted as a result of struggles to comply with the . . . law."

More importantly, patients' rights advocates have argued that the HIPAA has actually threatened patients' rights and reduced confidentiality as a result of regulations that mandate the use of electronic billing and sharing of client information.

The HIPAA regulations have also broadened public access to private medical information without patient knowledge or consent. By 2005, the federal government received about 10,000 complaints of violations of the Privacy Rule (Appeal for Patient Privacy Foundation 2005). In 2009, as part of the economic stimulus bill, new rules were passed to establish goals for meaningful use of electronic health records, incentives to providers, including Medicare and Medicaid using e-records, and penalties for Medicare providers who did not use e-records by 2015. Efforts to create a national health database are still under way. Managed care has changed considerably as a result of HIPAA, and yet much still remains unknown about the impact of this policy on health and mental health practice (Corcoran et al., 2005).

STATE CHILDREN'S HEALTH INSURANCE PROGRAM

Congress and the White House also addressed the problem of children without insurance (Rosenbaum et al., 1998). The Balanced Budget Act of 1997 created Title XXI of Social Security, also known as the State Children's Health Insurance Program (S-CHIP). Title XXI provides funds for states to expand coverage for children by either expanding Medicaid or creating new programs (Rosenbaum et al., 1998). Although S-CHIP has been successful in expanding coverage to uninsured children, the program's capped financing system has also created challenges for the states, including inequities among states and projected federal funding shortfalls. In recent years, many states have taken actions that reduce access to coverage for eligible children and families. S-CHIP came up for reauthorization in 2007 and, although Congress passed bills that would have expanded the program, they were vetoed twice by President Bush (Gorin and Moniz, 2007) and were finally reauthorized by President Obama in 2009 when he took office.

The economic recession and subsequent financial meltdown of 2008 imposed severe constraints on state spending, forcing many states to reduce expenditures for Medicaid and S-CHIP (Families USA, 2008). At the end of 2008, advocacy groups, legislators, and governors urged President-elect Obama to include funds for these programs as part of a financial stimulus package (Calmes and Hulse, 2009). With the passage of the ACA in 2010, the Obama Administration extended CHIP (formerly referred to as S-CHIP) to 2015, and required states to maintain current income eligibility levels for Medicaid and CHIP through September 30, 2019. Congress extended CHIP for two additional years to 2017. However, the Republican-controlled Congress, under President Trump, failed to fully reauthorize CHIP when it was scheduled for renewal in September 2017; instead they authorized a six-month extension until they could agree on how to fund the program, which covers nine million children.

MENTAL HEALTH PARITY ACTS (1996 AND 2008)

In addition to the HIPAA and S-CHIP, Congress also enacted the Mental Health Parity Act in 1996. This act took effect on January 1, 1998, and was extended through December 2005. It "imposed new federal standards on mental health coverage offered under most employer-sponsored group health plans" (U.S. General

Accounting Office, 2000, p. 3). Under the Act, employers who offered mental health benefits to their workers could not "impose annual or lifetime dollar limits on mental health benefits that [were] less than those applied to medical/surgical benefits" (Hennessy and Goldman, 2001, pp. 59–60). The National Association of Social Workers (1996) called the act a "significant [legislative] win" and a "first step" toward mental health parity.

Although the aim of this legislation was to address long-standing discrimination against people with mental health disorders, its impact was limited. The Act did not require employers to provide mental health benefits, and it did not prevent plans from imposing other restrictions, "such as differential cost sharing or day and visit limits," on mental health benefits (Hennessy and Goldman, 2001, p. 60). It also did not apply to benefits for substance abuse treatment.

Despite its limits, the Act did raise parity as an issue and gave impetus to state efforts to enact "more-comprehensive parity provisions" (Gitterman et al., 2001, p. 68). As a result, in most states, plans may not "place a greater financial burden on access to diagnosis or treatment for mental health conditions than for other health conditions" (Gitterman et al., 2001, p. 69). Yet, as Gitterman et al. (2001) note, these state laws were limited by the federal Employment Retirement Income Security Act (ERISA), which prevents states from regulating health plans financed by employers. To address this, Senators Paul Wellstone (D-MN) and Pete Domenici (R-NM) introduced legislation (Gitterman et al., 2001, p. 70).

After the unexpected death of Wellstone in a plane crash in 2002, Senator Edward Kennedy (D-MA) co-sponsored the Paul Wellstone Equitable Mental Health Treatment Act of 2003, renamed in Wellstone's memory, but new legislation was not enacted until 2008. Opponents of the legislation argued that it would prohibitively increase health care costs, even though President Bush's New Freedom Commission on Mental Health, which released its report on the state of the U.S. mental health system in 2003, strongly recommended enactment of full parity on the federal level, and the Congressional Budget Office said that parity legislation would not significantly raise costs.

In an unlikely turn of events, the Paul Wellstone and Pete Domenici Mental Health Parity and Addiction Equity Act was passed by Congress and signed into law by President Bush on October 3, 2008, as part of the $700 billion economic "rescue" plan to address the nation's financial market crisis. The legislation, which applies to group health plans of 51 or more employees, built on the original parity bill by banning differences in co-payments, deductibles, and other treatment limitations. It extended parity protection to millions not protected by state laws (Medicaid and S-CHIP plans) (Mental Health America, 2008), but the 2008 legislation did not cover everyone with insurance and offered little to those without insurance. Through the passage of President Obama's Affordable Care Act, parity has been expanded to a much wider population.

HEALTH CARE IN THE 2004 AND 2008 ELECTIONS

Health care did not completely disappear from the policy agenda during George W. Bush's two-term presidency (2001–9). In 2002, Bush appointed a New Freedom

Commission on Mental Health to examine the nation's mental health service delivery system. In 2003, with Bush's support, the Republican-controlled Congress enacted the Medicare Prescription Drug, Improvement, and Modernization Act of 2003 (MMA, see www.ssa.gov/OP_Home/comp2/F108-173.html), which created a new Medicare Part D (Kaiser Family Foundation, 2003), which is detailed in Chapter 6. In the 2004 presidential campaign, health care reform did not assume the importance it held in previous elections, but the issue of coverage did begin to resurface (Blendon et al., 2005, p. W5–87). President Bush offered proposals for tax credits for low income workers to use to buy insurance, health savings accounts, and the creation of association health plans, which would allow small businesses to purchase insurance through large insurance pools to help reduce administrative costs. Senator John Kerry (D-MA), the Democratic candidate, advocated expanding coverage under Medicaid or S-CHIP and the Federal Employees Health Benefits Program (FEHBP) (Gorin and Moniz, 2004).

By 2008, health care reform had not fully emerged as a focal point of the presidential campaign but the three leading primary candidates, Barack Obama (D-IL), Hillary Clinton (D-NY), and John McCain (R-AZ), each emphasized health care reform in their campaigns (Flint and Gorin, 2008). Obama supported expanding Medicaid and S-CHIP, coverage for all children, and a "play or pay" approach, which would require all but the smallest employers to cover their workers or contribute to a publicly funded plan for individuals without insurance (Flint and Gorin, 2008). In the aftermath of the election, President-elect Obama appointed former Senator Tom Daschle as Secretary-designate of Health and Human Services, and charged him with overseeing the process of health care reform. Daschle promised "Health reform . . . from the grassroots up" and initiated a series of town hall meetings and community discussions (Flint and Gorin, 2008).

AFFORDABLE CARE ACT 2010

In March 2010, after more than a year of contentious debate, Congress enacted the Affordable Care Act (ACA) (see Figure 1.1, p. 17, for a summary of the major provisions related to the discussion in this chapter). As mentioned earlier, the ACA was a compromise bill that nearly failed enactment. Progressives supported a "public option," which would force private insurers to compete based on cost and quality, but Republicans and some Democrats seriously opposed this component and it was removed from the bill (Gorin, 2009). Despite this, the ACA represented a significant advancement in achieving national health insurance and moving toward universal coverage.

Individuals and families in the U.S. obtain health insurance through a disconnected patchwork of programs, including employment-based insurance, Medicare, Medicaid, CHIP, the Veterans Health Administration, the Indian Health Service, the Public Health Service, and community mental health centers. But millions of individuals who are ineligible for these programs lack insurance coverage and therefore lack access to affordable health care services. In 2010, when the bill was enacted, an estimated 52 million people were without coverage for all or part of the year, and an additional 29 million were underinsured (Schoen et al., 2011).

The ACA addressed the lack of **coverage** for millions of Americans in a variety of ways. Starting in 2014, the ACA prohibited insurers from imposing lifetime limits on "most benefits" (U.S. Department of Health & Human Services, 2011), most young adults became eligible to remain on a parent's health insurance plan until age 26, and employers with at least 50 employees were required to provide coverage (or pay a penalty for noncompliance). By expanding coverage, the ACA also helped ameliorate long-standing racial and ethnic disparities in access to coverage and care. In 2015, for the first time in more than 50 years, the uninsured rate in the U.S. dropped below 10 percent; almost 16 million more people were insured in 2015 than in 2013 (Cohen and Martinez, 2015).

Cost and financing have been central issues in the nation's debate over health care reform for decades; both are addressed by the ACA. The ACA is funded through (1) increased taxes on individuals earning more than $200,000, (2) the elimination of "overpayments" that were established during the Bush Administration for private Medicare Advantage insurance companies designed to encourage them to add managed care, and (3) the introduction of new fees in sectors of the health care industry, such as tanning salons (Mahar, 2011). Mahar (2011) estimated that these measures would create $750 billion in revenues and savings and an additional $196 billion in other savings. Orszag (cited in Mahar, 2011) and others also estimated that the ACA could bring about billions more in savings through structural changes in the health industry (which are too complex for the Congressional Budget Office [CBO] to project savings). Although still too early to know if the ACA is responsible for reducing health care costs, it seems fair—based on economic analyses—to identify the ACA as a contributing factor. Per capita health costs are still rising, but the *rate of growth* in health care costs has dropped significantly; much of the role of the ACA in this trend is likely due to reforms in Medicare payments (Annenberg Public Policy Center, 2014).

The ACA also addressed issues of **quality** in the delivery of health care, which emerged as a separate and distinct concern over the past two decades. During the Clinton Administration's efforts to address health care, his 1998 Commission on Consumer Protection and Quality in the Health Care Industry found variability in the quality of care delivered to patients, including avoidable errors and both the underuse and overuse of treatments and services (U.S. President's Advisory Commission on Consumer Protection and Quality in the Health Care Industry, 1998). Many studies bear this out. Classen et al. (2011) found that "adverse events" were at least ten times more common than previously thought and occurred in one-third of hospital admissions. For the past 20 years, with funding from the National Institutes for Health, researchers at the Dartmouth Institute for Health Policy and Clinical Practice (see the *Dartmouth Atlas of Care* – www.dartmouthatlas.org) have been examining variations in the delivery of health care around the country; Skinner and Fisher (2010, pp. iii)) suggest the need for "new models of payment that reward providers for improving quality, managing capacity wisely, and reducing unnecessary care."

To address the issue of quality, the ACA called for the development of a national plan for improving health care delivery, patient outcomes, and the general health of the population (The Interagency Working Group for Health Care

Quality, 2011). The ACA also (1) provided incentives for hospitals to reduce readmission rates for chronically ill patients, and (2) encouraged the development of voluntary accountable care organizations under Medicare, which would enhance communication, collaboration, and coordination among providers (Centers for Medicare and Medicaid, 2011). Eventually, the intent of these reforms was to move the health care system from traditional, fee-for-service medicine, which allows for duplicative, unnecessary and wasteful care, to one that focused on quality and efficiency (Wennberg, 2010, p. 266). In addition, as mentioned earlier, the ACA also focused on the need to address racial and ethnic health disparities (Koh et al., 2011). (See Figure 1.1, p. 17, for a summary of the ACA.)

One of the more controversial aspects of the ACA was its creation of an Independent Payment Advisory Board (IPAB) with members *appointed* by the President for six-year terms and approved by the Senate. The IPAB was scheduled to take effect in 2013 and take responsibility for monitoring Medicare spending and making recommendations to reduce spending if it exceeded a determined "target growth rate" (Health Affairs, 2011). However, the IPAB could not make "major . . . changes that directly affect beneficiaries" and its recommendations would need either approval from Congress or to be substituted with provisions of its own. Aaron (2011) described the IPAB as an effort to avoid "executive inactivity" (not using the leverage of Medicare to negotiate costs and effect reforms), on the one hand, and "legislative intrusiveness" (decisions motivated by campaigning politicians), on the other. IPAB's "Congress's 'Good Deed'" (Aaron, 2011, p. 2379) could harness all the principles and regulations of the ACA to "mobilize the power of the country's largest health care buyer to effect health system change." However, the IPAB has been politically controversial. Congress introduced bills to repeal it, dozens of medical associations including the AMA asked for its repeal, and President Obama never appointed any members to the panel. In 2018, the IPAB succumbed to health care politics and was eliminated by Congress during the passage of the federal budget (Spatz, 2018).

CHALLENGES TO THE ACA DURING THE OBAMA ADMINISTRATION

The fundamental tenant of the ACA is the "mandate" that everyone purchase health insurance or pay a penalty. This requirement was challenged by a number of conservatives and states and brought to the Supreme Court for a decision. As noted by Liptak (2012), "the [June 28, 2012] court ruling was the most significant federalism decision since the New Deal and the most closely watched case since Bush v. Gore in 2000. It was a crucial milestone for the law . . . allowing almost all—and perhaps, in the end, all—of its far-reaching changes to roll forward." The court upheld the individual mandate and, in doing so, it essentially upheld the ACA.

However, the court did strike down the law's expansion of Medicaid to approximately 17 million people by requiring that all states participate in the expansion with substantial subsidies from the federal government. Instead, the court revised the law to give states the option to participate in the expansion (while receiving additional federal payments) or to choose not to participate (and maintain existing federal payments). The percentage of individuals without coverage decreased dramatically from 18.4 percent in 2013 to 10.6 percent in the first three months of 2015 in states that participated in Medicaid expansion; although the percentage without coverage decreased in states that did not expand Medicaid, individuals in these states were more likely to be uninsured than in states that did expand Medicaid coverage (Cohen and Martinez, 2015).

A second challenge to the ACA was brought to the Supreme Court in 2014 which claimed that certain tax credits should be available only to states where the state government set up the health exchange (as opposed to the federal government setting up the exchange). Although conservatives thought the court would uphold this challenge, the court ruled (June 25, 2015) that the clear intent of the ACA was to make the tax credits available nationwide (Gorod, 2015). This was a truly significant ruling. Without nationwide tax credits to the states, "insurance markets in states with federal exchanges would have been in chaos, meaning disaster not just for Americans receiving the tax credits, but for all Americans living in those states" (Gorod, 2015).

CHALLENGES TO THE ACA UNDER THE TRUMP ADMINISTRATION

The surprise election of Donald Trump (R) in the presidential election of 2016 brought enormous uncertainty for the ACA. Unlike the Democratic nominee, Hillary Rodham Clinton, who promised to improve the ACA by addressing some of its flaws, candidate Trump promised to eliminate the ACA and replace it with "something better." On his first day in office (January 20, 2017) Trump signed an executive order to begin the process of repealing the ACA. Republicans in Congress in support of the reform focused on two ideas: pursuing "universal access" rather than "universal coverage," and shifting responsibility from the federal government to the states.

The Republicans' first reform bill, the Patient Freedom Act of 2017 (PFA), was introduced (January 23, 2017) by Senators Cassidy (R-LA), Collins (R-ME), Isakson (R-GA), and Capito (R-WV), to partially repeal and replace the ACA. The bill would repeal federal mandates such as the individual and employer mandates, among others, and preserve consumer protections, including prohibitions on annual and lifetime limits, preexisting condition exclusions, and discrimination. It would also preserve the guarantee of issue and renewability, allow young adults to stay on their parents' plan until age 26, and preserve coverage for mental health and substance use disorders. Last, the bill would give options to the states to maintain or change federal state funding and insurance market arrangements including tax credits, cost-sharing subsidies, and Medicaid dollars (Jost, 2017a).

The concept of "universal access" is challenging, however, because it presupposes affordability. The major challenge with access is the ability to afford coverage either as an individual or as an employer. The challenge for the Republican Congress is to come up with a plan that will reduce costs; under the ACA:

> the vast majority of individuals who purchase coverage through the marketplaces receive premium tax credits that reduce the cost of coverage dramatically, making it affordable for most. Nevertheless, individuals with incomes above 400 percent of the federal poverty level are ineligible for tax credits, as are purchasers outside the marketplaces. Almost half of the remaining uninsured cite cost as the reason they remain uncovered. So how could insurance be made more affordable?
>
> (Jost, 2017a)

Jost (2017a) suggested that there are only a few ways to reduce costs (discussed further in Chapter 5), most of which were debated during the deliberations over the ACA.

Two other strategies for lowering costs considered by Republicans in Congress are (1) allowing the sale of insurance across state lines, which is already allowed under the ACA and by several states, and (2) imposing limits on malpractice litigation. In an unregulated market, however, permitting the sale of insurance across state lines could simply create a "race to the bottom" for the sale of cheap, but limited, insurance plans. Given that medical malpractice accounts for a small fraction of health care costs, placing further restrictions on malpractice litigation would likely have little impact on the cost of premiums (Jost, 2017a).

The second strategy, shifting responsibility from the federal government to the states by repealing the ACA and permitting the states to develop their own plans, is also challenging. Some legislative proposals allow the states to stick with the provisions of the ACA as an option. Most legislative proposals include the block granting of Medicaid to the states. Although shifting responsibility to the states is popular with Republicans, most states, before the enactment of the ACA, found it extremely difficult to provide affordable, accessible coverage to low- and moderate-income individuals and families. A state-based approach also does not address the variability of health insurance costs across the states (Jost, 2017a).

In early 2017 (January), several additional replacement plans were introduced in Congress by Republican leaders, including Speaker Paul Ryan (R-WI), Health and Human Services (HHS) secretary-designee Rep. Tom Price (R-GA), Senator Rand Paul (R-KY), and others. Although different in approach, all shared similar key components, as summarized below, and incorporated a philosophy similar to the Patient Freedom Act (Jost, 2017b):

- Preserve access to coverage despite preexisting conditions by
  (1) establishing a continuous coverage requirement by allowing enrollees to transition from one form of coverage to another without underwriting or preexisting condition exclusions, and creating an initial open enrollment period (however, this would still exclude from coverage

those who did not purchase at the outset); and (2) encouraging the states to offer high-risk pools (the ability of these pools to provide quality, affordable coverage would depend, however, on the degree of federal support provided).

- Repeal the individual mandate.

- Repeal the ACA's ban on health status underwriting in individual and small-group markets.

- Repeal the ACA's variable income-based premium tax credits and cost-sharing reductions and replace them with fixed-dollar tax deductions or credits (this would make it more difficult for low-income recipients to afford the premiums).

- Expand the role of health savings accounts (this too would be problematic for low-income people); and

- Include provisions designed to lower the cost of premiums, such as reducing or eliminating health benefit requirements and allowing higher cost sharing, giving states the responsibility for defining required coverage, and allowing the sale of insurance across state lines in an effort to promote competition and increase the number of insurance providers in states.

- Provisions to limit access to abortion services also appear in these proposals.

By March 2017, the Republicans felt under pressure to get one compromise bill introduced in Congress and presented the American Health Care Act to the American public. It was immediately met with opposition from Democratic leaders, doctors, hospitals, insurers, the American Medical Association, AARP, and others arguing that the reform measure would offer fewer protections than the ACA; it was also met with opposition from conservative Republicans who felt that it was essentially "Obamacare light" (Eilperin and DeBonis, 2017). The legislative proposal would eliminate the individual mandate that requires everyone in the U.S either to obtain coverage or to pay a tax penalty, and the mandate for businesses with at least 50 employees to provide insurance. The bill would replace income-based subsidies with refundable tax credits based on age and income (larger subsidies for older age groups and lower income groups), create a 30 percent surcharge for individuals who obtain coverage after allowing it to lapse, and, perhaps most significantly, decrease support to the states for Medicaid coverage. The insurance industry seemed to signal concern when its trade association, America's Health Insurance Plans, indicated that the proposed changes to Medicaid "could result in unnecessary disruptions in the coverage and care beneficiaries depend on" (Eilperin and DeBonis, 2017, paragraph 12).

The CBO weighed in with its analysis of the impact of the proposed reforms and reported that 14 million people would lose insurance coverage within a year of enactment, and, by 2020, 21 million more people would be uninsured than under the ACA (Families USA, 2017). Although the House voted to pass the bill, the Senate voted on its on own version, the Better Care Reconciliation Act of 2017 in July 2017, but the bill failed.

The final threat to the ACA in 2017 came under the major tax reform legislation (permanently reducing the corporate tax rate), led by the White House and the Republican-controlled Congress in the form of a repeal of the individual mandate. In November 2017, the CBO estimated that repeal of the mandate would cause 13 million individuals to lose coverage by 2017; other estimates were much lower (S&P Global). In 2018, the Urban Institute released a report (Blumberg et al., 2018) showing that eliminating the individual mandate, combined with other Trump administration reforms to the ACA, would lead to 8.9 million fewer Americans with health insurance. All agreed, however, that repeal of the individual mandate would increase premiums for individual health plans (Mangan, 2017). The Urban Institute (Blumberg et al., 2018) found that premiums would increase dramatically nationwide by 16.4 percent and by as much as 18.2 percent in 2019 in 42 states. Overall, elimination of the individual mandate cuts at the heart of the ACA's structure, which pools together both healthy and unhealthy enrollees, thus driving down the cost of insurance and allowing for coverage of preexisting conditions. In December 2017, Congress passed Trump's tax reform bill and repealed the ACA's penalty for noncompliance with the individual mandate, effectively undermining the authority of the mandate.

HIGHLIGHTS

- Before the enactment of the Affordable Care Act (2010), the Clinton Administration's Health Security Act of 1993 was the only significant policy reform effort to establish a national universal system of health insurance since the 1950s. This bill was designed to expand coverage by guaranteeing insurance for low-income and unemployed people. To control costs, the HSA relied on a combination of competition and regulation. Congress failed to enact this legislation.

- In the aftermath of this failed attempt, the nation's will to address national health care reform was weakened. Incremental reforms were supported. Congress passed the Health Insurance Portability and Accountability Act, the State Children's Health Insurance Program (S-CHIP), and the Mental Health Parity Act. It also overhauled the Veterans Health Administration and made efforts to renew the Public Health Service.

- With the election of President Obama, the Democrats turned their attention once again to health care reform and passed the Affordable Care Act (ACA). The ACA represents a significant advancement in achieving national health insurance and moving toward universal coverage.

FIGURE 1.1

Title I. Quality, Affordable Health Care for All Americans

Immediate Insurance Reforms (effective 2010):
- Eliminates lifetime and unreasonable annual limits on benefits
- Prohibits rescissions of health insurance policies
- Provides assistance for those who are uninsured because of a pre-existing condition
- Bans pre-existing condition exclusions for children
- Requires coverage of preventive services and immunizations
- Extends dependent coverage up to age 26
- Develops uniform coverage documents so consumers can compare policies
- Caps insurance company nonmedical, administrative expenditures
- Ensures consumers have access to an effective appeals process and provide a means for consumer assistance with appeals and accessing coverage
- Creates a temporary re-insurance program to support coverage for early retirees
- Establishes an internet portal to assist with identifying coverage options
- Facilitates administrative simplification to lower health system costs

Insurance Reforms by 2014:
- Establishes an "individual mandate," which requires nearly all individuals not already covered by an employer or public insurance to buy an approved private insurance policy or pay a penalty for noncompliance
- Requires employers with 50 or more full-time-equivalent employees to provide coverage or pay a penalty for noncompliance
- Provides subsidies to low-income individuals to help purchase the mandated coverage
- Bans pre-existing condition exclusions for adults
- Expands access to mental health services by increasing funding for community health centers

Title II. The Role of Public Programs

- Expands Medicaid and essentially assumes federal responsibility for cost (all children, parents, and childless adults up to 133% FPL covered by 2014)
NOTE: The Supreme Court ruled (June 2012) that states could not be *required* to expand eligibility, but instead could *opt* to expand coverage

- Increases federal support for the Children's Health Insurance Program (CHIP)
- Simplifies Medicaid and CHIP enrollment
- Improves Medicaid services
- Provides new options for long-term services and supports
- Improves coordination for dual-eligibles
- Improves Medicaid quality for patients and providers

Title III. Improving the Quality and Efficiency of Health Care

- Payment for services will be linked to better quality outcomes
- Funding for research to inform consumers about treatment and patient outcomes
- New Center for Medicare & Medicaid Innovation to disseminate new patient care models
- Improvements for rural patient care
- Improvements in payment system
- Enhancements to Medicare Part D prescription drug benefit
- Reductions in Medicare coverage gap, or "donut hole"
- Independent Medicare Advisory Board to address long-term fiscal stability

Title VI — Transparency and Program Integrity

- New requirements to provide information to the public about providers in the health system including physician owned hospitals; nursing homes; Medicare, Medicaid, and CHIP suppliers and providers and protect consumers from high-risk providers
- Enhanced requirements to combat fraud and abuse in public and private programs
- Establishes a private, nonprofit Patient-Centered Outcomes Research Institute governed by a public-private board to conduct comparative clinical outcomes research

Title VII – Improving Access to Innovative Medical Therapies

- Price competition and innovation in generic drugs
- More affordable medicines for children and underserved communities
- Extends drug discounts to hospitals and communities that serve low-income patients

Title VIII – Community Living Assistance Services and Supports (CLASS)

- Establishes new, voluntary, self-funded long-term care insurance program, the CLASS Independence Benefit Plan
NOTE: Congress repealed CLASS (January 2013). A new bi-partisan Commission was established to propose policy solutions to address the nation's long term care needs.

TITLE IX – Revenue Provisions

- New excise tax of 40 percent on insurance companies for charging annual premium that exceeds established thresholds
- New tax credits for families with incomes below $250,000 to help reduce premium costs and purchase insurance

REFERENCES

Aaron, H. J. (1994, Winter). Thinking Straight about Medical Costs. *Health Affairs*, 13(5), 7–13.

———. (1998). Less Is More: After the Clinton Plan, Let's Think Small. *Health Affairs*, 12, 204–215.

———. (2011, June 23). Perspective: The Independent Payment Advisory Board— Congress's "Good Deed". *New England Journal of Medicine*, 364, 2377–2379. Retrieved from www.nejm.org/doi/pdf/10.1056/NEJMp1105144

Annenberg Public Policy Center. (2014, February 2014). ACA Impact on Per Capita Cost of Health Care. Retrieved from www.factcheck.org/2014/02/aca-impact-on-per-capita-cost-of-health-care

Asch, S. M., McGlynn, E. A., Hogan, M. M., Hayward, R. A., Skekelle, P., Rubinstein, L. et al. (2004). Comparison of Quality of Care for Patients in the Veterans Health Administration and Patients in a National Sample. *Annals of Internal Medicine*, 141(12), 938–945. Retrieved May 13, 2006 from www.annals.org/egi/content/full/141/12/938

Atchinson, B. K. and Fox, D. M. (1997, May/June). The Politics of the Health Insurance Portability and Accountability Act. *Health Affairs*, 16(3), 146–150.

Blendon, R. J., Brodie, M., and Benson, J. (1995, Summer). What Happened to America's Support for the Clinton Health Plan? *Health Affairs*, 14(2), 7–23.

Blendon, R. J., Brodie, M., Altman, D. E., Benson, J. M., and Hamel, E. C. (2005, March 1). Voters and Health Care in the 2004 Election. *Health Affairs*, Web Exclusives, 24, 1, W5-86–5-95.

Blumberg, L. J., Bueltgens, M., and Wang, R. (2018, February). *The Potential Impact of Short-Term Limited-Duration Policies on Insurance Coverage, Premiums, and Federal Spending*. Urban Institute. Retrieved from www.urban.org/sites/default/files/publication/96781/2001727_0.pdf

Bok, D. (1998). *The Great Health Care Debate of 1993–94*. Retrieved from www.upenn.edu/pnc/ptbok.html

Calmes, J. and Hulse, C. (2009, January 3). Obama Considers Major Expansion in Jobless Aid. *The New York Times*. Retrieved June 9, 2009 from www.nytimes.com/2009/01/04/us/politics/04stimulus.html?hp.

Centers for Medicare and Medicaid Services. (2011, November 14). Prospective Payment Systems - General Information: Overview. Retrieved December 11, 2011, from www.cms.gov/ProspMedicareFeeSvcPmtGen/

Classen, D., Resar, R., Friffin, E., Federico, F., Frankel, T., Kimmel, N., and James, B. (2011, April). Global Trigger Tool Shows That Adverse Events In Hospitals May Be Ten Times Greater Than Previously Measured. *Health Affairs*, 30(4), 581–589.

Cohen, R. A. and Martinez, M. E. (2015, August 15). Health Insurance Coverage: Early Release of Estimates from the National Health Interview Survey, January–March 2015. U.S. Department of Health and Human Services, Centers for Disease.

Corcoran, K., Gorin, S., and Moniz, C. (2005). Managed Care and Mental Health. In S. A. Kirk (Ed.), *Mental Disorders in the Social Environment*. New York: Columbia University Press.

Davis, K., Collins, K. S., and Morris, C. (1994, Fall). Managed Care: Promise and Concerns. *Health Affairs*, 13(4), 178–185.

Eilperin, J. and DeBonis, M. (2017, March 8). Doctors, Hospitals and Insurers Oppose Republican Health Plan. *Washington Post.* Retrieved from www.washington post.com/powerpost/doctors-hospitals-and-insurers-oppose-republican-health-plan/2017/03/08/d9f0f5c2-0426-11e7-ad5b-d22680e18d10_story.html?utm_term=.e7cfec5cf6c6

Enthoven, A. C. and Kronick, R. (1991, May 15). Universal Health Insurance through Incentives Reform. *Journal of the American Medical Association,* 265(19), 2532–2536.

Enthoven, A. C. and Singer, S. J. (1994, Spring [I]). A Single-Payer in Jackson Hole Clothing. *Health Affairs,* 13(1), 81–95.

Families USA. (2008, November). A Painful Recession: States Cut Health Care Safety Net Programs. Washington, DC: Families USA. Retrieved February 16, 2012 at www.familiesusa.org/assets/pdfs/a-painful-recession.pdf

_____. (2017, March). Talking Points: CBO's Score of The American Health Care Act. Retrieved from http://familiesusa.org/product/talking-points-cbo-score-american-health-care-act

Flint, S. S. and Gorin, S. H. (2008, May). Health Care Reform in the 2008 Presidential Primaries. *Health & Social Work,* 33(2), 83–86.

Gitterman, D. P., Sturm, R., and Scheffler, R. M. (2001, July–August). Toward Full Mental Health Parity and Beyond. *Health Affairs,* 20(4), 68–76.

Gorin, S. H. (2009). Health Care Reform: The Importance of a Public Option. *Health & Social Work,* 34(2), 83–85.

Gorin, S. H. and Moniz, C. (1997, August). Universal Health Care Coverage in the United States. *Health & Social Work,* 22(3), 223–230.

_____. (2004, November). Will the United States Ever Have Universal Health Care? *Health & Social Work,* 29(4), 340–345.

_____. (2007, November). Why Does President Bush Oppose the Expansion of SCHIP? *Health & Social Work,* 32(4), 243–246.

Gorod, B. (2015, June 25). Supreme Court upholds ACA, Defies Partisanship: Column. *USA Today.* Retrieved from www.usatoday.com/story/opinion/2015/06/25/supreme-court-affordable-care-act-column/29267183

Health Affairs. (2011, December 15). *Health Policy Brief: The Independent Payment Advisory Board.* Retrieved December 21, 2011 from www.healthaffairs.org/healthpolicybriefs/brief.php?brief_id=59

Hennessy, K. D. and Goldman, H. H. (2001, July–August). Full Parity: Steps toward Treatment Equity for Mental and Addictive Disorders. *Health Affairs,* 20(4), 58–67.

Himmelstein, D. and Woolhandler, S. (1989). A National Health Program for the U.S. *New England Journal of Medicine,* 320, 102–108.

The Interagency Working Group for Health Care Quality. (2011, March 21). *Report to Congress: National Strategy for Quality Improvement in Health Care.* HealthCare.gov. Retrieved December 21, 2011, from www.healthcare.gov/law/resources/reports/quality03212011a.html

Johnson, H. and Broder, D. S. (1996). *The System: The American Way of Politics at the Breaking Point.* Boston: Little, Brown.

Jost, T. (2017a, January 24). ACA Replacement Bill From Cassidy And Colleagues Offers State Options, Roth HSAs. Health Affairs Blog. Retrieved from http://healthaffairs.org/blog/2017/01/24/aca-replacement-bill-from-cassidy-and-colleagues-offers-state-options-roth-hsas

———. (2017b, February). *First Steps of Repeal, Replace, and Repair*. Retrieved from http://content.healthaffairs.org/content/early/2017/02/10/hlthaff.2017.0165.full

Kaiser Family Foundation. (2003, December 10). Prescription Drug Coverage for Medicare Beneficiaries: A Summary of the Medicare Prescription Drug, Improvement and Modernization Act of 2003. Retrieved July 22, 2005, from www.kff.org/medicare/loader.cfm?url=/commonspot/security/getfile.cfm&PageID=28710

Koh, H. K., Graham, G., & Glied, S. A. (2011). Reducing Racial and Ethnic Disparities: The Action Plan From the Department of Health And Human Services. *Health Affairs*, 30(10), 1822–1829.

Kronick, R. (1994, Spring). A Helping Hand for the Invisible Hand. *Health Affairs*, 13(1), 96–101.

Kronick, R., Goodman, D. C., Wennberg, J., and Wagner, E. (1993, January 14). The Marketplace in Health Care Reform: The Demographic Limitations of Managed Competition. *New England Journal of Medicine*, 328(2), 145–148.

Kuczynski, K., and Gibbs-Wahlberg, P. (2005, July). HIPAA the Health Care Hippo: Despite the Rhetoric, Is Privacy Still an Issue? (Commentary). *Social Work*, 50(3), 283–287.

Levit, K. R., Cowan, C. A., Lazenby, H. C., McDonnell, P. A., Sensenig, A. L., Stiller, J. M., and Won, D. K. (1994, Winter). National Health Spending Trends, 1960–1993. *Health Affairs*, 13(5), 14–31.

Liptak, A. (2012, June 28). Supreme Court Upholds Health Law, 5-4, in Victory for Obama. *New York Times*. Available at www.nytimes.com/2012/06/29/us/supreme-court-lets-health-law-largely-stand.html?pagewanted=1&ref=policy

Mahar, M. (2011). Better Care for Less: How the Affordable Care Act Pays for Itself and Cuts the Deficit (Rep.). Retrieved December 21, 2011, from http://tcf.org/publications/pdfs/Mahar_BetterCareforLess.pdf/++atfield++file

Mangan, D. (2017, November 17). Killing Obamacare mandate won't cut number of insure—or budget deficit—as much as predicted, analysis says. Retrieved from www.cnbc.com/2017/11/17/effects-of-obamacare-mandate-repeal-seen-as-less-dramatic-than-cbo-says.html

Marmor, T. (1994). *Understanding Health Care Reform*. New Haven, CT: Yale University Press.

Mental Health America. (2008, October 3). *Mental Health America Hails Approval of Federal Parity Legislation* (press release). Available at: www.marketwatch.com/news/story/mental-health-americahails-approval/story.aspx?guid=%7BC653BF6F-BFCB-4A33-A657-AC4132467F35%7D&dist=hppr

Mizrahi, T. (1995). Health Care: Reform Initiatives. In R. L. Edwards (Ed.-in-Chief), *Encyclopedia of Social Work*, 19th edn. (pp. 1185–1198). Washington, DC: National Association of Social Workers.

National Association of Social Workers. (1991). National Health. In *Social Work Speaks: NASW Policy Statements* (pp. 178–180). Silver Spring, MD: NASW Press.

———. (1996, October 4). Health Insurance Portability and Accountability Act, Mental Health Parity. Government Relations Update. Washington, DC: NASW.

Newhouse, J. P. and the Insurance Experiment Group. (1993). *Free for All? Lessons from the RAND Health Insurance Experiment*. Cambridge, MA: Harvard University Press.

Patel, K. and Rushefsky, M. E. (1999). *Health Care Politics and Policy in America*, 2nd edn. Armonk, NY: M. E. Sharpe.

Pepper Commission (U.S. Bipartisan Commission on Comprehensive Health Care). (1990, September). *A Call for Action*. Washington, DC: U.S. Government Printing Office.

Pollitz, K., Tapay, N., Hadley, E., and Specht, J. (2000, July–August). Early Experience with "New Federalism" in Health Insurance Regulation. *Health Affairs*, 19(4), 7–22.

Rachlis, M., and Kushner, C. (1994). *Strong Medicine: How to Save Canada's Health Care System*. Toronto: HarperCollins.

Reinhardt, U. E. (1994, Spring [II]). Lineage of Managed Competition. *Health Affairs*, 13(12), 290.

Roberts, M. J. and Clyde, A. (1993). *Your Money or Your Life: The Health Care Crisis Explained*. New York: Doubleday.

Rolde, N. (1992). *Your Money or Your Health*. New York: Paragon House.

Rosenbaum, S., Johnson, K., Sonosky, C., Markus, A., and DeGraw, C. (1998, January–February). The Children's Hour: The State Children's Health Insurance Program. *Health Affairs*, 17(1), 75–89.

Schoen, C., Doty, M., Robertson, R., and Collins, S. (2011, September). Affordable Care Act Reforms Could Reduce The Number Of Underinsured US Adults By 70 Percent. *Health Affairs*, 30(9), 1762–1771.

Schwartz, W. B. and Mendelson, D. N. (1992, Summer). Why Managed Care Cannot Contain Hospital Costs—Without Rationing. *Health Affairs*, 11(2), 100–107.

———. (1994, Spring [I]). Eliminating Waste and Inefficiency Can Do Little to Contain Costs. *Health Affairs*, 13(1), 224–238.

Skinner, J. and Fisher, E. (2010). *Reflections on Geographic Variations in U.S. Health Care*. Dartmouth Institute for Health Policy and Clinical Practice. Retrieved February 15, 2012 from www.dartmouthatlas.org/downloads/press/Skinner_Fisher_DA_05_10.pdf

Skocpol, T. (1995, Spring). The Rise and Resounding Demise of the Clinton Plan. *Health Affairs*, 14(1), 66–85.

———. (1997). *Boomerang: Health Care Reform and the Turn against Government*. New York: Norton.

Smith, M. D., Altman, D. E., Leitman, R., Moloney, T. W., and Taylor, H. (1992, Winter). Taking the Public's Pulse on Health System Reform. *Health Affairs*, 11(2), 124–133.

Spatz, I. (2018, February 22). IPAB RIP. Health Affairs. Retrieved from www.healthaffairs.org/do/10.1377/hblog20180221.484846/full

Starr, P. (1994). *The Logic of Health Care Reform: Why and How the President's Plan Will Work*. New York: Whittle Books in association with Penguin Books.

Starr, P. and Zelman, W. (1993, Supplement). Bridge to Compromise: Competition under a Budget. *Health Affairs*, 7–23.

Toner, R. (1994, November 16). Pollsters See a Silent Storm That Swept Away Democrats. *New York Times*, p. 12.

U.S. Department of Health & Human Services. (2011). *Patient's Bill of Rights*. HealthCare.gov. Retrieved December 18, 2011, from www.healthcare.gov/law/features/rights/bill-of-rights/index.html

U.S. General Accounting Office. (2000). Mental Health Parity Act: Despite New Federal Standards, Mental Health Benefits Remain Limited (HEHS-00-95). Washington, DC: U.S. Government Printing Office.

U.S. President's Advisory Commission on Consumer Protection and Quality in the Health Care Industry. (1998). *Improving Quality in a Changing Health Care Industry*. Retrieved December 21, 2011, from www.hcqualitycommission.gov/final/chap01.html

Wennberg, J. E. (2010). Tracking Medicine: A researcher's Quest to Understand Health Care. New York: Oxford University Press.

Zelman, W. A. (1994, Spring [I]). The Rationale behind the Clinton Health Reform Plan. *Health Affairs*, 13(1), 9–29.

The Early Years
The Road to Employer-Based Coverage, Medicare, and Medicaid

CHAPTER 2 EXAMINES A CRUCIAL PERIOD IN THE DEVELOPMENT of health care policy in the U.S. from the end of the Civil War through World War II to the Great Society (1865–1965). Unlike other western nations, which established systems of universal health care, the U.S. rejected national health insurance. Instead, it pursued a path of voluntary employment-based insurance. Although efforts to achieve a national health care system were defeated, two significant health insurance programs, Medicare and Medicaid, were enacted.

INITIAL REFORM EFFORTS (1865–1912): THE BEGINNINGS OF SOCIAL WORK AND PUBLIC HEALTH

After the Civil War ended in 1865, the nation entered into an era (1865–1920) of enormous industrial growth and expansion. This period brought rapid social and economic change to the U.S., including massive immigration from Europe and severe poverty among the poor and working classes. On the one hand, it enhanced national wealth, raised the general standard of living, speeded up urbanization, and had many other constructive effects. On the other hand, it produced, among other things: Periodic cycles of depression and unemployment, a small group of men who controlled the nation's resources and modes of production, wretched living and working conditions, a high incidence of industrial accidents and fatalities, and numerous other unfortunate results that affected every segment of American society (Trattner, 1999, p. 82).

Both social work and the public health movement emerged in the U.S. in response to these social conditions and human needs. In a period fueled by Herbert Spencer's ideology of Social Darwinism ("survival of the fittest"), the government played little role in meeting the needs of children and families ravaged by the severe economic depression of 1870. Voluntary charity was acceptable, while public relief was discouraged: "Orthodox Social Darwinists found no place in their general scheme of things for public support of education, or for sanitary regulation, a public mail system, regulation of business or trade, or, least of all, for public assistance to the needy" (Trattner, 1999, p. 88).

Charity organization societies (COSs) and settlement houses took on the role of providing assistance to poor and needy children and families. These societies originated in England and were replicated in the U.S. during the 1870s. As the name implies, the COSs aimed at organizing, or rationalizing, the delivery of private charities. These societies wanted to deter the fraudulent receipt of aid and the duplication of private, charitable services offered by churches and other religious groups, labor unions, mutual aid societies, women's clubs, fraternal associations, ethnic and immigrant associations and clubs, and other philanthropic groups.

England gave birth to the settlement house movement during this period, which spread quickly to the U.S. Settlement houses and brought together "people of different socioeconomic and cultural backgrounds to share knowledge, skills and values for their mutual benefit" (Barker, 1999, p. 436). From the beginning, settlement house workers focused on the relationship between poverty—including poor sanitation, substandard housing, malnutrition, disease and illness, and high mortality rates—and poor work conditions, crowded and unsafe housing, low wages, child labor, and industrial accidents. Initially, settlement house workers tried to improve neighborhood conditions by working to improve sanitation, garbage collection, and public health facilities. However, as Trattner (1999) states, they soon realized that to improve living and work conditions they would have to become involved in reforms at the local, state, and national levels.

Although the COSs and settlement house movements are often depicted as representing opposing, conservative and liberal, approaches to poverty, their differences should not be exaggerated. According to Brieland (1995), settlement house workers "often" worked "in COS programs," and "some" COS workers "lived in settlement(s)." Bertha C. Reynolds (1963, p. 28), an influential social work pioneer and a self-described Marxist, credited the Boston COSs with playing "a major part in creating the responsiveness to human need for which the city was famous."

In 1905, Jane Addams, founder of Hull House in Chicago, perhaps the most famous of the settlement houses, became the first president of the National Conference of Charities and Correction, which was established in 1874 by the State Boards of Charities; but it quickly came under the control of the COS movement (Axinn and Levin, 1997). Between 1905 and 1914, activists from the COSs and settlement house movements increasingly became allies in their efforts for social reform. As noted by Trattner (1999, p. 183), reformers in both movements seemed in agreement that "poor people were . . . an oppressed lot . . . and that social reform was more important than the elevation of personal morality."

However, both groups had white European immigrants in mind in their social reform efforts. COSs and settlement houses generally ignored the needs of people of color. Some settlement leaders, such as Jane Addams and Lillian Wald, cofounder of New York's Henry Street Settlement, helped establish settlements for African–Americans. They were also instrumental in founding the NAACP (National Association for the Advancement of Colored People), a lobbying group for African–Americans (Iglehart and Becerra, 2000). On the other hand, Addams seems to have underestimated the significance of white supremacy as a barrier to social reform. Like many, she urged reformers to postpone confronting white supremacy until they had a broader following (Lasch, 1982). Others, such as W. E. B. Du Bois, argued that, until reformers directly challenged white supremacy, they would not have a broader following (Lewis, 1993).

The National Conference of Charities and Correction proposed and advocated for legislation to establish fair standards of employment and workers' compensation, prohibit child labor, and improve public health. In 1912, the Conference's "platform of 'minimum standards' for well-being . . . included a federal system of accident, old-age, and unemployment insurance" (Trattner, 1999, p. 226 n. 5). The Conference worked with the American Association for Labor Legislation (AALL) to support and establish a system of social insurance in the U.S. (Trattner, 1999). The AALL, which was established in 1906 by economists from the University of Wisconsin, represented a broad group of social reformers and progressives, including "social workers," physicians, lawyers, political scientists, historians, labor leaders, business leaders, and politicians (Feingold, 1966).

Social workers were also instrumental in the creation of the U.S. Children's Bureau, which played a central role in promoting maternal and child health (Jaros and Evans, 1995). During the early 1900s, Florence Kelley (1859–1932), Lillian Wald (1867–1940), and Edward Devine (1867–1948) raised concerns about the condition of children in the U.S. (Trattner, 1999). In 1906, the National Child Labor Committee, whose board included Wald and Kelley, arranged for a bill to establish a Children's Bureau to be introduced in Congress. Three years later, in 1909, President Theodore Roosevelt hosted the first White House Conference on Dependent Children.

At the request of the conference delegates, Roosevelt urged Congress to enact the bill to create a Children's Bureau. In public hearings, reformers noted that the federal government devoted more resources to the study of animals than children, and "young animals" had a "lower mortality rate" than "young children" (Trattner, 1999). In 1912, Congress established the Children's Bureau to "investigate and report" on "all matters" concerning "the welfare of children and child life among the classes of our people" (U.S. Children's Bureau, 1914, p. 2). The bureau's first director was Julia Lathrop (1858–1932), a settlement house worker from Illinois and the first woman to run a federal agency (Edwards, 1995; Trattner, 1999).

THE NEED FOR PUBLIC HEALTH SERVICES

Industrialization and urbanization created sanitation and health issues in all major industrial cities. As urban centers grew rapidly with poor controls for water quality and sewage disposal, they exposed families and neighbors to the risk of communicable diseases. Increased trade between seaports contributed to the spread of disease from one region of the country to another, while overcrowded, unsanitary living conditions made it easy for infectious diseases to spread. For example, in 1849, cholera spread from New Orleans to Chicago, killing almost 3 percent of

Chicago's population (Turnock, 1997). "The Chadwick and Shattuck reports of the 1840–1850 period documented the relationship of poverty, bad sanitation, housing, and working conditions with high mortality, and ushered in the idea of social epidemiology" (Tulchinsky and Varavikova, 2000, p. 62).

In 1848, Britain's Parliament enacted the Health of Towns Act and the Public Health Act based on the work of Edwin Chadwick. This legislation established state and local health departments responsible for sanitation efforts, control of communicable diseases, data collection on vital statistics, and maternal and child health services. In the U.S., Lemuel Shattuck replicated Chadwick's work, which led to the development of state boards of health, most of which were created after 1870. However, unlike Britain, boards of health in the U.S. initially limited their role to the control of infectious diseases (Turnock, 1997).

Although members of the upper class could escape overcrowded cities by moving to rural areas, members of the emerging urban middle class did not enjoy this luxury (Baltzell, 1964). They "paid taxes, supported cleanliness and public education, recognized and abhorred corruption, and, as home owners, had an investment in their cities" (Garrett, 2000, p. 284). Thus, the middle class took the lead in advocating a wide range of reforms, including the enactment of health and safety regulations (Garrett, 2000). During the 1890s, many cities "instituted new public works sanitation projects (such as piped water, sewer systems, filtration and chlorination of water) and public health administration" (Haines, 1991, p. 105).

Until the end of the nineteenth century, the sanitation movement in Britain and the U.S. was driven by the theory that disease was caused by "infectious mists or noxious vapors emanating from filth in the towns" and that the best way to prevent the spread of disease was "to clean the streets of garbage, sewage, animal carcasses, and wastes that were features of urban living" (Tulchinsky and Varavikova, 2000, p. 27). By the turn of the twentieth century, however, it was scientifically proven that microscopic germs were responsible for communicable diseases.

With the development of vaccines against rabies and diphtheria, many communities, particularly in the east, required their citizens to be immunized (Garrett, 2000). In New York City, Hermann Biggs, a leading public health figure, asserted that health authorities could resort to any measure that was "designed for the public good" and "beneficent" in its "effects" (cited in Garrett, 2000, p. 297). Authorities "routinely deployed police officers and zealous nurses or physicians to the homes of those suspected of carrying disease . . . . In some cases, police officers pinned the arm of those who refused while a city nurse jabbed it with a vaccination needle" (Garrett, 2000, p. 299). These efforts seemed to pay off. Between 1900 and 1915, death rates (among children) from measles, whooping cough, scarlet fever, and diphtheria declined in the U.S. (Garrett, 2000).

THE MENTAL HYGIENE MOVEMENT

Public hospitals for the mentally ill also emerged during this period of industrial and urban change. Since the early 1800s, hospitalization served as the primary means of caring for people with problems of mental health. The approach used was known as "treatment" or "moral management" and was based on the work of a

French theorist, Philippe Pinel (Grob, 1994). Pinel opposed the common practice of confining the "insane" to asylums and relying on seclusion and physical restraint to control deviant social behaviors. Pinel believed that the hospital could employ psychological treatments to help patients recover from their mental disease. In fact, Pinel's use of the French word "moral" did not refer to ethical or moral reforms, but rather to an institutional setting that could create order and promote recovery through psychological therapy (Grob, 1994).

From 1800 to roughly 1825, small privately funded hospitals were established in wealthy urban communities. Examples include the McLean Asylum in Boston (1818), the Hartford Retreat (1824), and the Friends Asylum in Philadelphia (1817). Initially, these institutions were designed to serve the entire community, yet they accepted few patients and remained rather exclusive. With patients expected to pay for their own treatment, these new hospitals found it increasingly difficult to live up to their ideal of serving everyone in the community (Grob, 1994).

Attention shifted to the need to establish and fund public hospitals for the mentally ill. According to Grob (1994), public hospitals emerged first in the rural south. These hospitals did not adopt the new therapeutic approach of moral treatment; they were essentially custodial in nature. The pioneer of the public mental health hospital movement was Worcester State Hospital, established in 1830 in Massachusetts. As noted by Mechanic (1999), in its early history, Worcester State Hospital "practiced moral treatment and offered its patients an optimistic and humanitarian climate" (Mechanic 1999, p. 90). Reformers, such as Dorothea Dix, encouraged state legislatures to build new hospitals for the mentally ill.

However, with the huge wave of immigration that occurred between 1830 and 1850, and the industrial and urban growth that followed, Worcester State Hospital and others began to retreat to custodial care: "In densely populated areas insane people were more visible, and public concern about security increased" (Grob, 1994, p. 24). Overcrowding, insufficient funding, and other problems made it impossible to provide humane care.

The mental hygiene movement was a response to the inhumane treatment of patients in public hospitals and, initially, an effort to improve conditions. The National Conference of Charities and Corrections challenged asylum psychiatry and suggested the need for alternatives to institutional care. The National Association for the Protection of the Insane and the Prevention of Insanity was formed in 1880, and asylum physicians found it difficult to defend their practices. The bond between psychiatry and asylums began to break as younger psychiatrists turned away from asylums and wanted to be viewed as general practitioners. Some psychiatrists took up the task of redefining mental illness, whereas others joined the mental hygiene movement (Grob, 1994). Clifford W. Beers, a former mental patient diagnosed with manic depression, wrote an exposé of his hospitalization, *A Mind That Found Itself*, in 1908 and became the leader of the mental hygiene movement.

Initially, Beers was concerned with the deplorable conditions of mental hospitals, but by the early 1900s the mental hygiene movement had shifted its attention to outpatient care and the prevention of mental illness (Grob, 1994). During this period, social workers participated in educational campaigns to broaden public understanding of mental illness and participated in the development of "free child guidance clinics, dispensaries, outpatient centers, and hospitals for early detection, diagnosis, and treatment of mental disorders" (Trattner, 1999, p. 198).

COMPULSORY HEALTH INSURANCE EFFORTS (1912–20)

By 1912, Germany, Austria, Hungary, Norway, Britain, and Russia had all created compulsory health insurance programs. The U.S., in keeping with its decentralized government and its limited role in regulating the economy or social welfare, had not pursued this path. However, between 1912 and 1920, social and political events made compulsory health insurance an issue for public debate, both at the national level and in many states. Workers' compensation laws were enacted in 42 states between 1910 and 1920 (Skocpol, 1992). During this period, advocates for health care reform were encouraged by this step toward social insurance.

Presidential candidate Theodore Roosevelt advocated compulsory health insurance in 1912 as part of a broad package of social insurance programs (Starr, 1982; Rolde, 1992). Jane Addams and other social workers active in the settlement house movement played leading roles in Roosevelt's campaign (Jansson, 2001). That same year, the American Association for Labor Legislation (AALL) established a Social-Insurance Committee to study various proposals for health care reform.

AMERICAN ASSOCIATION FOR LABOR LEGISLATION

AALL leaders from the business and private insurance industry visited Europe to study the national health insurance systems in Germany and England. Their findings were discussed at social work meetings and conferences amid optimism for reform (Mizrahi, 1995). AALL developed model legislation that mandated health care coverage for workers and their dependents. Proposed benefits included physician, nurse, and hospital services, pay for sick days, maternity benefits, and death benefits. AALL proposed shared financing for the program from employers, employees, and state governments (Starr, 1982).

Between 1916 and 1919, believing that a movement for health insurance would prove as successful as the drive for workers' compensation, AALL launched a major campaign to enact its model legislation in the states. AALL leaders had identified a strong interrelationship of work-related accidents, sickness, and dependence on workers' compensation. Providing coverage for medical expenses, they argued, would help eliminate the poverty caused by sickness and injury, and help reduce employers' costs for compensation.

The reformers' optimism soon waned, however. With the entry of the U.S. into World War I, social insurance, which had originated in Germany, fell into disrepute (Rolde, 1992). The Bolshevik Revolution and the subsequent "red scare" also placed reformers on the defensive. "Superpatriots" accused the National Welfare Council and the Federation for Social Service of the Methodist Church of "leaning towards Bolshevism," while Jane Addams and others faced blacklisting (Levin, 1971). At a "social work conference" held in 1917, a leading insurance executive described compulsory health insurance as a "communistic system . . . repugnant to American minds and destructive of American initiative and individuality" (Rolde, 1992, p. 20).

Opposition from labor leaders was also damaging to their cause. Samuel Gompers and other prominent labor leaders opposed compulsory health insurance. In 1920, the American Medical Association (AMA), which had initially supported compulsory health insurance, reversed its position and launched its opposition to reform (Rolde, 1992). Fifteen states introduced compulsory health insurance bills, and nine created commissions to study the problem of access to health insurance. However, no state actually enacted health insurance legislation (Rolde, 1992). After the failure of these efforts, compulsory health insurance was not considered again until the 1930s.

ESTABLISHMENT OF THE U.S. PUBLIC HEALTH SERVICE

The public health movement, on the other hand, continued to gain strength between 1912 and 1920. Despite the success of vaccines and treatments in lowering death rates from communicable diseases, a number of diseases, including tuberculosis, were still a serious threat to public health. Poor children and families in urban settings were particularly vulnerable. In the early 1900s, city health departments began the practice of sending public health nurses into communities to conduct home visits, and local schools began to establish health clinics. By 1915, there were more than 1000 health clinics administered by city health departments for the treatment of tuberculosis and to address the problem of infant mortality (Institute of Medicine, 1988).

In 1912, the Marine Hospital Service, established by the federal government, was renamed the U.S. Public Health Service. When the Marine Hospital Service was first established in 1798, it created a network of hospitals along the eastern and southern seaboard to treat merchant seamen, and thereby prevent the spread of infectious diseases. By the end of the nineteenth century, the Marine Hospital Service was responsible for public quarantines and the health inspection of immigrants to the U.S. (Moroney, 1995). In 1912, the surgeon general of the U.S. Public Health Service was granted more authority and the agency took steps to address rural health and the control of venereal diseases (Institute of Medicine, 1988); however, the "federal government [still] could not act directly in health matters; it could only act through states as the primary delivery system" (Turnock, 1997, p. 123).

FEDERAL–STATE REFORMS AND PRIVATE INSURANCE (1920–32)

Despite the opposition to compulsory health insurance, Congress addressed the problem of maternal and child health care in 1921. Julia Lathrop and Grace Abbott, both of whom had worked at Hull House, the Chicago settlement house founded by Jane Addams, were advocates of this reform (Simon, 1994). Under Lathrop's direction, the Children's Bureau studied the problem of infant mortality; the findings were sobering. The U.S. had "a shockingly high infant mortality rate" and one of the highest maternal death rates in the world (Trattner, 1999, p. 219). Poverty and lack of prenatal care were identified as primary causes.

SHEPPARD–TOWNER INFANCY AND MATERNITY BILL

At Lathrop's urging, Jeanette Rankin, a former social worker and the first female member of Congress, introduced the Sheppard–Towner Infancy and Maternity Bill (or Act) in 1921. The legislation was designed to provide grants-in-aid to the states for prenatal and child health centers to help reduce maternal and infant death rates (Starr, 1982; Trattner, 1999). The Sheppard–Towner Act was passed in 1922 and was administered by the Children's Bureau, which disseminated more than 20 million pieces of literature, sponsored more than 100,000 conferences, created thousands of prenatal care centers, and facilitated millions of home visits between 1922 and 1929 (Skocpol, 1995). The Sheppard–Towner Act established the Federal Board of Maternity and Infant Hygiene and was the first federal legislation to give funds to the states to establish programs in nursing, home care, health education, and maternal care (Institute of Medicine, 1988).

The Sheppard–Towner Act was also the catalyst for government involvement in the establishment of federal guidelines for public health programs administered by the states. The expansion of federal–state efforts to improve public health increased the demand for public health experts and leaders (Institute of Medicine, 1988). As early as 1916, the Rockefeller Foundation, which had played a central role in the development of medical education, expressed concern that "insufficient attention was being paid to environmental and social factors in disease" (White, 1991, p. 2). To rectify this imbalance, the foundation advocated the creation of independent schools of public health, which would address "the determinants of health and disease in populations" (White, 1991, p. 2).

Whatever the foundation's intentions, the creation of schools of public health reinforced, indeed codified, a growing separation between efforts to prevent disease and efforts to cure it, and the Sheppard–Towner Act faced growing opposition from political conservatives and the medical profession. Physicians were particularly alarmed by the expansion of public health, viewing it as a threat to their authority. After New York City required physicians to report the names of patients who had been diagnosed with tuberculosis, the president of the County Medical Society accused the city of overstepping its bounds (Starr, 1982). Similarly, when the city health department started manufacturing and distributing serum for diphtheria and rabies, it was accused of engaging in "'municipal socialism' and unfair competition with private business" (Starr, 1982, p. 186).

The AMA called the Sheppard–Towner Act "a form of federal bureaucratic interference with the sacred rights of the American home" (Rolde, 1992). The Illinois Medical Society published a pamphlet referring to the staff of the Children's Bureau as "endocrine perverts [and] derailed menopausics" and warning that the Sheppard–Towner Act would make the bureau "the ruling power in the United

States" (Trattner, 1999, p. 220). A prominent senator asserted that, under the Sheppard–Towner Act, "female celibates would instruct mothers on how to bring up their babies" (Trattner, 1999, p. 220). In 1929, Congress discontinued funding for the Sheppard–Towner Act. A number of factors, including opposition from the Hoover administration and the stock market crash and economic crisis of 1929, led to its demise. However, the most significant factor was the concerted opposition by organized medicine (Trattner, 1999).

Efforts to establish compulsory health insurance were also waning. In 1928, a group of professionals, with funding from several foundations, established the Committee on the Costs of Medical Care (CCMC). The Committee engaged in a comprehensive study of the economics of compulsory health insurance and in 1932 released a final report, which opposed compulsory health insurance (Abbott, 1966). The CCMC recommended a group practice and payment system, and the use of private insurance and local revenues to establish group health plans for low-income consumers. However, the AMA opposed the idea of group practices and any form of government involvement (Starr, 1982).

Given the political and economic obstacles facing advocates of prevention and public health, it is not surprising that physicians increasingly focused on biomedical research and clinical practice. Public health was also a victim of its own success. With the discovery that microorganisms caused many diseases, researchers lost interest in studying the environmental causes of disease: "Such was the specificity of the diseases associated with the growing number of microorganisms that every 'disease' was considered to have a single 'cause'; and that cause was thought to be a microorganism" (White, 1991, p. 2). As it turns out, the development of vaccines (as well as improvements in sanitation) played a relatively minor role in reducing mortality from infectious disease; however, this was not evident a century ago (Sagan, 1987). By the 1930s, public health had been relegated to "a secondary status: less prestigious than clinical medicine, less amply financed, and blocked from assuming the higher-level functions of coordination and direction that might have developed had it not been banished from medical care" (Starr, 1982, p. 197).

THE CREATION OF BLUE CROSS AND BLUE SHIELD AND THE VETERANS HEALTH ADMINISTRATION

The Great Depression made it even more difficult for individuals and families to pay for hospital care and medical services, and sustained the social pressure to reform the health care system. In 1927, the president of the American Hospital Association (AHA) noted the difficulty faced by "the great bulk of people of moderate means" in meeting hospital bills (Kotelchuck, 1976, p. 84). With hospital occupancy rates falling and deficits spiraling, hospitals began to develop their own insurance plans under the name of Blue Cross (Kotelchuck, 1976). In 1930, Congress created a new agency, the Veterans Administration (VA), to coordinate all the veteran programs in place since World War I. From 1931 to 1941, the bed capacity at VA hospitals doubled (Veterans Administration, 2005). In 1932, the AHA sanctioned prepaid group hospital plans, as long as they were nonprofit, covered hospital care only, did not interfere with private practitioners, and allowed patients a free choice of hospitals. In 1939, Blue Shield, which offered coverage for physicians' services, was created (Edinburg and Cottler, 1995) and, by 1940, 39 Blue Cross plans were providing group hospital services to more than six million people (Starr, 1982). The establishment of Blue Cross and Blue Shield insurance plans laid the foundation for a third-party payment system, completely changed health care financing, and paved the way for employment-based insurance.

THE NEW DEAL REFORMS (1932–40)

As hospitals and physicians struggled to control the medical system, President Franklin D. Roosevelt, elected in 1932, began to develop his administration's program for economic and social reform, the New Deal. Among Roosevelt's advisers was a social worker named Harry L. Hopkins. Hopkins' first job out of college had been as a camp counselor for Christadora House, a New York settlement. Radicalized by this experience, he "plunged into social work on the lower East Side" (Schlesinger, 1959, p. 265). Hopkins later worked for the Association for Improving the Condition of the Poor, the Board for Child Welfare, the (New Orleans) Red Cross, and the New York Tuberculosis and Health Association.

In 1931, when Roosevelt was governor of New York, he made Hopkins director of New York's Temporary Emergency Relief Administration (TERA) (Freidel, 1990). TERA spent millions of dollars to assist unemployed New Yorkers and provided both "a model" and "personnel for New Deal programs and agencies" (Trattner, 1999, p. 280). Hopkins was a friend of Roosevelt's wife, Eleanor, who was also "strongly influenced" by the settlement house movement. Eleanor Roosevelt was a tireless advocate for the Children's Bureau, the Sheppard–Towner Act, and other progressive causes, including the rights of African–Americans (Davis, 1991; Cook, 1992; Goodwin, 1994).

In 1933, Hopkins, along with William Hodson, a former president of the American Association of Social Workers, met with Frances Perkins, Roosevelt's secretary of labor, to discuss plans for a federal relief program (Schlesinger, 1959). Perkins, known as "Madam Secretary," was another veteran of the settlement house movement and the first social worker appointed to a federal cabinet position. Perkins arranged for Hopkins to meet with Roosevelt, who hired Hopkins to run the newly established Federal Emergency Relief Administration (FERA) (Schlesinger, 1959). By 1936, Hopkins, a strong supporter of compulsory health insurance (Starr, 1982), had become one of Roosevelt's close advisers and a confidant (Goodwin, 1994).

In 1934, Perkins became chair of the Committee on Economic Security, which was given the task of developing a plan for old-age retirement, unemployment, and health care insurance. When Perkins suggested that the committee consider compulsory health insurance, the AMA organized physicians to flood Congress with telegrams and letters of protest (Marmor, 1973). Roosevelt feared that this controversy would doom plans for retirement and unemployment insurance. On advice from close advisers, including Hopkins, Roosevelt removed health insurance from the final version of the bill (Moniz, 1990).

MATERNAL AND CHILD HEALTH SERVICES

When Congress enacted the Social Security Act in 1935, it chose not to introduce compulsory health insurance. However, it did enact Title V, which established Maternal and Child Health Services, a federal–state program administered by the Children's Bureau "to extend and improve" maternal and child health and other services, particularly in rural and other underserved areas (Axinn and Levin, 1997). When the Sheppard–Towner Act was discontinued in 1929, the states struggled to continue their health promotion activities and infant mortality began to rise again (Jaros and Evans, 1995). Title V also provided funds for services for crippled children and child welfare services, and gave the states resources to establish "prenatal care, well baby clinics, school health services, immunization, public health nursing and nutrition services, and health education" (Lesser, 1985, p. 1683).

THE FAILURE TO ENACT COMPULSORY INSURANCE

Compulsory health insurance was excluded from the Social Security Act, but it remained a focus of public debate. In 1935, Roosevelt established an Interdepartmental Committee to Coordinate Health and Welfare Activities to monitor the programs enacted by the Social Security Act and to study the feasibility of compulsory health insurance (Abbott, 1966). That same year, the first large-scale study of health conditions, the National Health Survey, was conducted. In 1937, a subcommittee of the Interdepartmental Committee, the Technical Committee on Medical Care, recommended a National Health Program, including the possibility of compulsory insurance. However, Roosevelt, again fearing opposition from conservatives, offered only lukewarm support for its plan (Starr, 1982). Frustrated by Roosevelt's ambivalence, Senator Robert Wagner (D-NY) introduced his own proposal for a national health plan in 1939 (Dewhurst and associates, 1947). The AMA, the AHA, and the American Dental Association testified in opposition to Wagner's bill and, as the nation's attention shifted toward the start of World War II, interest in national health insurance waned.

Most historians and policy analysts agree that the New Deal launched the welfare state in the U.S. The Social Security Act of 1935 established a strong role for federal government and laid the foundation for national social insurance programs. However, as noted by Trattner (1999) and others, it also had many shortcomings, particularly the failure to include national health insurance. Moreover, Social Security and other New Deal programs primarily benefited white people. Social Security's insurance programs excluded farmworkers and domestic servants, positions largely held by African–Americans (Quadagno, 1994). Although African–Americans were, in theory, eligible for Aid to Dependent Children (ADC) and other public assistance programs, given the racism of southern officials they were highly unlikely to receive the same benefits as whites. With good reason, many African–Americans were ambivalent about the New Deal (Hamilton and Hamilton, 1997).

The exclusion of African–Americans during this period should be placed in social and political context, however. To enact his legislative agenda, Roosevelt needed support from the southern Democrats, who strongly opposed extending rights and benefits to African–Americans (Goldfield, 1997). Roosevelt's wife, Eleanor, was a strong advocate for African–Americans and, through her, he helped "convey to blacks that the administration was on their side" (Goodwin, 1994, p. 165). She also helped convince him to issue an executive order banning discrimination in the Works Progress Administration, an important New Deal program. African–American social workers were hopeful that the federal government was starting to "care" about "Negro men and women" (Goodwin, 1994, p. 163).

FEDERAL HEALTH AND MENTAL HEALTH POLICY AND SERVICES (1941–46)

World War II (1941–45) provided a major catalyst for efforts to expand and reform the health care system in the U.S. The system's deficiencies were brought to light when men from across the country were recruited to join the military. Between 1940 and 1941, half of the potential inductees were found to be physically or mentally unfit to serve. Although the military later eased its standards, eight to nine million young males were still deemed unfit for service. "Mental and nervous disorders" accounted for almost a third of the rejections; moreover, studies suggested that early intervention "might have prevented or remedied" half "the disqualifying defects" (Dewhurst and associates, 1947, p. 247). Other studies found similarly high, and preventable, rates of illness and debilitation in other segments of the population.

Not surprisingly, the health of African–Americans was much worse than that of whites. For example, in 1940 the infant mortality rate for African–Americans was almost twice the infant mortality rate for whites (Newman et al., 1978). In addition, African–Americans had a far greater likelihood of dying from diabetes, flu and pneumonia, hypertension, and tuberculosis than did whites. African–Americans also faced discrimination in the health professions. In the late 1940s, a third of the nation's medical schools refused to admit African–Americans, and only 14 hospitals admitted African–American patients (Newman et al., 1978).

EMERGENCY MATERNAL AND INFANT CARE PROGRAM

In an effort to address the nation's pressing health care needs, in 1943 Congress created the Emergency Maternal and Infant Care Program (EMIC), a federal–state program to provide free health care and social services to the wives and infants of servicemen (Simon, 1994; Axinn and Levin, 1997). Before the war, most of these women and children had limited access to care. Katherine Fredrica Lenroot (1891–1982), head of the Children's Bureau and former president of the National Council of Social Work, was a major catalyst for EMIC (Syers, 1995). During its 2 years of existence, EMIC provided care to 1.25 million women and 230,000 children (Simon, 1994). At the end of the war, the federal government established the Veterans Administration, which provided health care to millions of veterans through a network of hospitals.

PUBLIC HEALTH SERVICES ACT

World War II also gave impetus to medical research (Starr, 1982). In 1944, Congress enacted the Public Health Services Act, which gave the Public Health Service (PHS) responsibility for the National Institutes of Health (NIH). The NIH had been created in 1930 as successor to the National Hygienic Laboratory. In 1937, it was expanded to include the National Cancer Institute (Starr, 1982). Although the 1937 legislation also allowed the NIH "to make grants to outside researchers," funds for this purpose remained "quite limited" (Starr, 1982, p. 340).

With the advent of the war, however, the importance of research became abundantly clear. In 1941, the Roosevelt administration established an Office of Scientific Research and Development to address war-related medical problems. Roosevelt also commissioned a report on postwar government aid to science, "including what could be done to aid 'the war of science against disease'" (Starr, 1982, p. 341). Between 1945 and 1947, NIH research funding increased dramatically (Starr, 1982). Even "[o]pponents of national health insurance could display their deep concern for health by voting generous appropriations for medical research" (Starr, 1982, p. 343).

NATIONAL MENTAL HEALTH ACT

The most significant contribution of the mental hygiene movement occurred during the early years of World War II. Selective service boards throughout the country tried to evaluate the mental health status of millions of draftees, but were forced to rely on an insufficient supply of psychiatrists and inadequate screening tools. Psychiatrists were supposed to spend at least 15 minutes conducting individual examinations, yet reports indicated that an average evaluation lasted only 2 minutes, and an individual psychiatrist might examine 200 men in a single day (Mechanic, 1999). To assist selective service boards, State Committees on Mental Hygiene across the country enlisted thousands of volunteer social workers from 1941 to 1946 to conduct social case histories of men drafted for the war effort (Trattner, 1999).

During this period, conventional beliefs about the hereditary nature of mental "disease" were being challenged by the impact of environmental stress. Combat and the "realities of war," not personality, seemed to be the defining cause of mental breakdown and illness for many soldiers. To treat nightmares, sleep disturbances, anxiety, and other conditions that soldiers experienced, psychiatrists experimented with "rest periods, rotation policies, and measures encouraging group cohesion and social relationships" at battalion aid stations. From these experiments they found that the alleviation of stress brought positive results (Grob, 1994).

This finding led psychiatrists to the belief that similar approaches could help other mental patients, and that government and other social institutions could play a role in reducing mental health problems. To help realize this goal, in 1946 Congress passed the National Mental Health Act, which established a Mental Hygiene Division in the U.S. Public Health Service, and a research center, which, in

1949, became the National Institute of Mental Health (NIMH). The purpose of the NIMH was to pursue research on war-related problems such as "battle fatigue," as well as "child development, juvenile delinquency, suicide prevention, alcoholism, and television violence" (Starr, 1982, p. 346). It was the first national effort supported by federal funding to promote mental health through research, education, and training.

The NIMH encouraged each state to find supplements and alternatives to hospitalization for mental health care. It explicitly promoted the development of a broader scope of services to a wider population of consumers which included children and adults with both acute and chronic needs. It also encouraged the development of follow-up clinics to serve patients as they left the hospital and to assist with reintroduction to the community. By the 1950s, community-based programs could be found in every state (Grob, 1994).

The mental hygiene movement had little impact on the prevention of mental illness, but it was influential in decreasing the central role of hospitals in the delivery of mental health care. Other contributing factors to this change were the discovery of pharmaceutical drugs, which allowed individuals to function independently in the community, and the expanded role of the federal government. As noted by Grob (1994), the NIMH funded not only the establishment of community clinics, but also close ties between the government and mental health professionals. The NIMH founded regional offices across the country and employed consultants in psychiatry, psychology, social work, and nursing.

HILL–BURTON HOSPITAL SURVEY AND CONSTRUCTION ACT

In 1946, in an effort to expand access to care, Congress enacted the Hospital Survey and Construction Act of 1946. This legislation, also known as Hill–Burton, enjoyed support from both the AMA and the AHA (Mizrahi, 1995). Hill–Burton provided federal grants and loans (approximately $4 billion between 1946 and 1975) for the construction of hospitals (Patterson, 1996). The policy encouraged states to survey their medical facilities and develop plans to ensure an adequate number of hospital beds, particularly in low-income areas (Starr, 1982).

Although funds from Hill–Burton were used to increase the number of hospital beds available in the poorer states, the policy did not have the impact many of its supporters intended. "Within states . . . funds went disproportionately to middle-income communities" (Starr, 1982, p. 350). Hill–Burton also failed to protect African–Americans. In 1949, a federal official noted that, out of 218 new hospitals, only 4 were not "operated on a policy of segregation" (Newman et al., 1978, p. 198). The courts did not prohibit "separate but equal" hospitals until 1963 (Starr, 1982). Although Hill–Burton required hospitals to offer "a reasonable volume of . . . service to persons unable to pay," it created no mechanism to enforce this (Starr, 1982, p. 350). It also created no mechanism for cost control and thus contributed to subsequent health care inflation (Kotelchuck, 1976).

POLITICAL OPPOSITION AND THE DEFEAT OF NATIONAL HEALTH CARE LEGISLATION (1943–50)

During the 1940s, voluntary, employment-based coverage became the primary means of financing and accessing health care services. This occurred largely as a result of World War II. Facing a shortage of qualified workers and government-imposed wage controls, some employers began offering health insurance to their employees (Starr, 1982). In 1943, the government's War Labor Board ruled that health insurance did not violate wage and price controls. After the war, workers "gained the right to bargain collectively for health benefits," and employment-based insurance emerged as a "functional substitute for social insurance" (Starr, 1982, p. 311).

The growth of employment-based insurance was accelerated by political developments within the labor movement and society. During the 1930s, in its efforts to organize workers, the Congress of Industrial Organizations (CIO) had pursued a "popular-front" (or center-left) strategy, which united moderates and radicals (Bartley, 1995). Between 1935 and 1940, Roosevelt also pursued a center-left strategy, uniting "radicals, liberals, and moderates in support of a broad reform program" (Bartley, 1995, p. 45) (Wencour and Reisch, 1989). Although most leftists felt that the New Deal reforms were limited, they also believed Roosevelt was preferable to the Republicans (Baltzell, 1966; Wencour and Reisch, 1989). This popular front was replicated internationally when the U.S. and the Soviet Union collaborated against the Axis powers during World War II.

As the war ended and the alliance between the U.S. and the Soviet Union began to crumble, the domestic alliance also ended. In 1948, the popular-front liberals broke with Truman over the Cold War and supported the presidential candidacy of Henry Wallace, the vice-president during Roosevelt's third term (Patterson, 1996). Truman and other conservative liberals attacked Wallace and his supporters as Communist sympathizers and a threat to national security (Caute, 1978; Bartley, 1995). The struggle between Truman and Wallace put liberals at war with themselves, and by 1950 liberalism had "sharply narrowed" its focus and the energy and excitement of the 1930s had waned (Bartley, 1995).

In 1949, the CIO expelled its left-wing unions, which had been the strongest advocates of race and gender equality (Bartley, 1995). As it moved to the right, the CIO began to emulate the "job-conscious business unionism" of the American Federation of Labor (AFL). The prewar CIO had advocated for its members and workers as a whole (Bartley, 1995). The postwar CIO downplayed this broader, class perspective and increasingly focused on obtaining "contracts with welfare, health, and retirement provisions" (Bartley, 1995, p. 44).

The split within the CIO also weakened progressives and strengthened conservatives. When the CIO embarked on Operation Dixie, a postwar effort to organize workers in the south, its efforts were hindered by the "absence of the dedicated and tireless organizers of the left who had contributed to so many previous drives" (Foner, 1974, p. 277). The failure of Operation Dixie and a related effort by the AFL ensured the continued dominance of the southern Democrats, who had played such a prominent role in blocking social welfare legislation, including NHI (Bloom, 1987; Quadagno, 1994). During the 1960s, the southern Democrats helped create the modern Republican Party, which continues to oppose NHI.

DEFEAT OF THE WAGNER–MURRAY–DINGELL BILL

In 1943, Senators Robert F. Wagner (D-NY) and James Murray (D-MT), and Representative John Dingell (D-NY) introduced a new national health care bill, which was more comprehensive than the one introduced by Wagner in 1939. The expanded bill included medical, hospital, dental, and nursing home provisions (Starr, 1982; Rolde, 1992). One author of the Wagner–Murray–Dingell Bill was Wilbur Cohen (1913–87) (Berkowitz, 1989). Well known in social work circles, Cohen had helped write the Social Security Act and later played a central role in the development of Medicare and Medicaid. He also served as secretary of health, education, and welfare under President Lyndon Johnson (Guyotte, 1995).

African–American organizations, such as the NAACP and the National Urban League, tried unsuccessfully to include antidiscrimination clauses in the Wagner–Murray–Dingell Bill (Hamilton and Hamilton, 1997). They knew that, even if Congress enacted the bill, its implementation in the south would be subject to segregationist policies. Although organized labor supported the Wagner–Murray–Dingell Bill, the AMA opposed it, and, like Wagner's original bill, it died in committee (Moniz, 1990). President Roosevelt did not support the Wagner–Murray–Dingell Bill because he wanted to wait until the end of the war to seek compulsory insurance.

In 1944, Roosevelt proposed an "economic bill of rights" which included "a right to adequate medical care" (Starr, 1982, p. 280). However, Roosevelt died in 1945 before he could reveal his plan to campaign for compulsory insurance as part of his reelection platform. His successor, Harry Truman, took up the mantle and advocated "a single health insurance system that would include all classes of the society" (Starr, 1982, p. 281). Again conservatives reacted strongly (Ball, 1995). Senator Robert Taft (R-OH) derided Truman's bill as "the most socialistic measure this Congress has ever had before it," and the AMA warned that it would turn doctors into "slaves" (Starr, 1982, pp. 282–283).

Although Truman denied that his plan was "socialized medicine," which he defined as a system in which "all doctors work as employees of the government," the Republicans were able to block the bill (Rolde, 1992, p. 25). When Truman tried unsuccessfully to resurrect it a few years later, the AMA and its allies engaged in a high-powered propaganda campaign which convinced many, including even some of the Bill's supporters, that it would bring about "socialized medicine" (Starr, 1982, p. 285). Once again, NHI came to naught.

THE ENACTMENT OF MEDICARE (1950–65)

The defeat of Truman's proposal led many supporters of NHI to seek a more limited goal (Ball, 1995). During the early 1950s, the Truman administration, under the leadership of Wilbur Cohen and others, developed a plan to provide Social Security recipients with 60 days of hospital coverage (Marmor, 1973). This allowed the government to expand an existing program, as opposed to creating a new one, and to insure older adults against financial catastrophe (Moniz, 1990). However, the 1952 elections brought victory for the Republicans and derailed efforts to extend hospital coverage to older adults (Ball, 1995).

Although the Eisenhower administration acknowledged that seniors faced difficulty in affording health care, it opposed compulsory insurance. AMA leaders and staff had figured prominently in Eisenhower's campaign and, as president, he relied on them for advice. Eisenhower encouraged state efforts, rather than national reforms, and recommended subsidies to private insurers to expand coverage for people with low incomes (Moniz, 1990).

During the 1950s, support for Medicare came largely from organized labor, which was concerned about its retirees. Through collective bargaining, unions had gained private health insurance benefits for their members while they were employed. However, these workers often lost this coverage when they retired (Moniz, 1990).

In 1955, the newly created AFL–CIO targeted disability insurance as its first legislative effort. According to Nelson Cruikshank, the labor federation's department of Social Security focused on disability insurance because it wanted a "foot in the door" toward compulsory health insurance (Moniz, 1990, p. 69). In 1956, with labor's encouragement, Congress amended the Social Security Act to provide income assistance to totally and permanently disabled workers over age 55. Wilbur Cohen worked actively to support this legislation (Marmor, 1973).

Between 1957 and 1959, Representative Aime Forand (D-RI) introduced legislation for compulsory health insurance. This was the first legislative effort to build on the Social Security Act by providing health insurance to retired beneficiaries (Moniz, 1990). According to Marmor (1973, p. 13), the Forand bill was motivated by a need to "resurrect health insurance in a dramatically new and narrower form." The Forand bill faced strong opposition from the AMA and the conservative coalition of southern Democrats and northern Republicans. In 1959, the House Ways and Means Committee held hearings across the country, raising awareness of the health care problems of older adults. Nevertheless, the committee rejected the social insurance approach to health care policy (Moniz, 1990).

The Democrats renewed their commitment to Medicare at their 1960 national convention, at which they endorsed a plan to expand Social Security by adding compulsory health insurance for older adults. In response, the Republicans proposed voluntary, state-administered programs that would be limited to low-income older adults. In 1960, as a compromise, Congress enacted the Kerr–Mills Bill, a means-tested, optional grant-in-aid program to the states for poor elderly citizens (Trattner, 1999). The Kerr–Mills Bill did not adequately address the growing concern for reform, however, and by 1963 "only thirty-six states had 'joined' the system" and "only some (states) paid physician fees" (Trattner, 1999, p. 326).

With the election to the presidency of John Kennedy, a strong supporter of Medicare, the AMA launched a new effort against "socialized medicine" (Bernstein, 1991, p. 253). Despite this, Kennedy immediately appointed a task force on health and Social Security (chaired by Wilbur Cohen), which recommended expanding Social Security to provide hospital and nursing home coverage for older adults (Bernstein, 1991). Kennedy sent this proposal to Congress, where it was introduced as the King–Anderson Bill (Feingold, 1966). After several days of hearings, the House Ways and Means Committee, headed by Wilbur Mills (D-AK), who was lukewarm about Medicare, decided not to act on the legislation (Marmor, 1973). Although Kennedy died before Medicare passed, Bernstein (1991) argued that, by the time of his assassination, Kennedy had come to an agreement with Mills that resulted in the Bill's enactment in 1965.

To the surprise of many, Kennedy's successor, Lyndon Johnson, became a strong supporter of Medicare (David, 1985). Between 1963 and 1965, Johnson and the Democrats, along with the National Council of Senior Citizens (formed in 1961) and organized labor, mobilized support for the bill (Moniz, 1990). In the November 1964 elections, several congressional opponents of Medicare, including three members of the House Ways and Means Committee, were defeated (Moniz, 1990).

Despite a final effort by the AMA to enact a means-tested plan, Wilbur Mills recognized the need for a compromise. In March 1965, he proposed a "three-layer cake" comprising: Compulsory insurance for hospital, nursing home, and home health care (Medicare Part A); voluntary insurance for physicians' services (Medicare Part B); and a means-tested insurance plan for people with low incomes (Medicaid). In July 1965 the Senate approved Mills' proposal and, with Harry Truman looking on, President Johnson signed Medicare and Medicaid into law as Titles XVIII and XIX of the Social Security Act of 1935 (Marmor, 1973).

HIGHLIGHTS

- Unlike other industrialized nations, the U.S. has not established a national health care system that guarantees access to health care services for all its citizens. Efforts to achieve compulsory health insurance failed to survive ideological and political opposition.

- From 1912 to 1920, the American Association for Labor Legislation, supported by the National Conference of Charities and Correction, led the initial drive for compulsory health insurance. It advocated a broad system of social insurance programs that included public health and proposed legislation for mandatory health insurance. By 1920, however, prominent labor leaders and organized medicine (American Medical Association) opposed compulsory insurance and played a key role in defeating reform efforts under way in many of the states. On the other hand, efforts to establish a system of public health during this period were more successful. The U.S. Public Health Service was established in 1912.

- The Children's Bureau, also established in 1912, was highly influential in the promotion of maternal and child health and was the catalyst for the Sheppard–Towner Bill, which provided grants-in-aid to the states to establish child health centers to help reduce infant mortality.

The Sheppard–Towner Bill also gave rise to the development of federal public health guidelines for the states, which once again incensed the AMA. Congress discontinued funding for the Sheppard–Towner Bill in 1929.

- A final effort to establish compulsory health insurance during the 1920s was led by the Committee on the Costs of Medical Care in 1928 and was opposed by the AMA.

- The Great Depression of 1929 and the 1932 New Deal administration of President Roosevelt were major turning points in the development of health and social welfare legislation. However, when Congress enacted the Social Security Act of 1935, it chose not to include compulsory health insurance. Instead, it enacted Title V, the Maternal and Child Health program, to reestablish funding to the states; Title V also created Child Welfare Services. In 1937, Roosevelt's administration considered the possibility of compulsory insurance, but offered little support for it. Senator Robert Wagner introduced a bill in 1939, but the nation's attention had already shifted to World War II.

- Entry into World War II highlighted the nation's pressing health care needs. Millions of young male potential inductees were physically or mentally unfit to serve. In 1943, Congress established a federal–state system of free health care and social services, the Emergency Maternal and Infant Care Program, for the infants and wives of servicemen. It was clear from the recruitment process that many of these families had little or no access to health care.

- At the end of the war, Congress established a nationwide network of government hospitals to address the medical needs of returning veterans. In 1946, Congress also established a Mental Hygiene Division in the U.S. Public Health Service and a research center, which became the National Institute of Mental Health (NIMH) in 1949. Many World War II veterans returned with battle fatigue and psychological disorders that challenged conventional beliefs about mental disease. The NIMH was successful in promoting state-level, community-based care as an alternative to mental asylums, while Congress enacted legislation, the Hill–Burton Act of 1946, to provide billions of dollars in funding for the construction of hospitals, particularly in poor, underserved areas.

- The economic crisis of the 1930s and the demands of World War II dramatically increased the role of the federal government in health care policy. However, in both cases the government addressed immediate, pressing needs that were created or exposed by these events, and it did so by providing funds to the states to establish facilities and services. By the end of World War II, the federal government had taken major steps to help build the nation's medical system and to expand access to care to segments of the population, but the nation was no closer to a social insurance model of health care.

- Although the federal government's role in the delivery of health and mental health services grew substantially during the 1940s, efforts to establish national health insurance were unsuccessful. From 1943 to 1950, the Congress of Industrialized Organizations (CIO) became increasingly narrow in its goals and significantly undermined earlier efforts by organized labor to legislate national health insurance. At the same time, the American Medical Association (AMA) escalated its opposition to national health insurance and lobbied against government intervention in health care.

- With the defeat of the Wagner–Murray–Dingell Bill in 1943 and President Truman's efforts in 1949, many advocates of national health care concluded that compulsory insurance could be achieved in the U.S. only in stages (Ball, 1995). Accordingly, they turned their attention to one of the most needy segments of the population: Older adults over age 65 (Ball, 1995).

- Between 1900 and 1950, the number of older adults in the U.S. quadrupled; only one in eight had private health insurance (Bernstein, 1991). The Democratic Party supported Medicare and introduced legislation as early as 1952, but the bill languished in Congress until 1960. The political battle for Medicare was tedious and costly, but it was finally enacted in 1965.

- Medicare established a mandatory, federal health insurance system for retired adults. Congress also enacted Medicaid in 1965, a voluntary federal–state system of health insurance for poor adults and children. Today, these are still at the core of the nation's health care system and health care policy.

REFERENCES

Abbott, G. (1966). *From Relief to Social Security*. New York: Russell & Russell.

Axinn, J., and Levin, H. (1997). *Social Welfare: A History of the American Response to Need*, 4th edn. New York: Longman.

Ball, R. M. (1995, Winter). Perspectives on Medicare: What Medicare's Architects Had in Mind. *Health Affairs*, 14(4), 62–73.

Baltzell, E. D. (1964). *The Protestant Establishment*. New York: Vintage Books.

——. (1966). *The Protestant Establishment: Aristocracy and Caste in America*. New York: Vintage Books.

Barker, R. L. (1999). *The Social Work Dictionary*, 4th edn. Washington, DC: National Association of Social Workers.

Bartley, N. V. (1995). *A History of the South*, Vol. XI, *The New South 1945–1980*. Baton Rouge, LA: Louisiana State University Press.

Beers, C. W. (1908). *A Mind that Found Itself*. Oxford: Longmans.

Berkowitz, E. D. (1989). Wilbur Cohen and American Social Reform. *Social Work*, 34(4), 293–303.

Bernstein, I. (1991). *Promises Kept: JFK's New Frontier*. New York: Oxford University Press.

Bloom, J. M. (1987). *Class, Race, and the Civil Rights Movement*. Bloomington, IN: Indiana University Press.

Brieland, D. (1995). Social Work Practice: History and Evolution. In R. L. Edwards (Ed.), *Encyclopedia of Social Work*, 19th edn. (pp. 2247–2257). Washington, DC: National Association of Social Workers.

Caute, D. (1978). *The Great Fear: The Anti-Communist Purge under Truman and Eisenhower*. New York: Simon & Schuster.

Cook, B. W. (1992). *Eleanor Roosevelt*, Vol. I, *1884–1933*. New York: Viking.

David, S. I. (1985). *With Dignity: The Search for Medicare and Medicaid*. Westport, CT: Greenwood.

Davis, A. F. (1991). Settlement Houses. In E. Foner and J. A. Garraty (Eds.), *Reader's Companion to American History* (pp. 983–984). Boston, MA: Houghton Mifflin.

Dewhurst, J. F. and associates. (1947). *America's Needs and Resources*. New York: Twentieth Century Fund. Retrieved from www.foreignaffairs.com/reviews/capsule-review/1947-10-01/americas-needs-and-resources

Edinburg, G. M. and Cottler, J. M. (1995). Managed Care. In R. L. Edwards (Ed.), *Encyclopedia of Social Work*, 19th edn. (pp. 1635–1642). Washington, DC: National Association of Social Workers.

Edwards, L. M. (1995). Lathrop, Julia Clifford (1858–1932). In R. L. Edwards (Ed.), *Encyclopedia of Social Work*, 19th edn. (pp. 2596–2597). Washington, DC: National Association of Social Workers.

Feingold, E. (1966). *Medicare: Policy and Politics*. San Francisco, CA: Chandler.

Foner, P. S. (1974). *Organized Labor and the Black Worker 1619–1973*. New York: International.

Freidel, F. (1990). *Roosevelt*. Boston: Little, Brown.

Garrett, L. (2000). *Betrayal of Trust: The Collapse of Global Public Health*. New York: Hyperion.

Goldfield, M. (1997). *The Color of Politics*. New York: New Press.

Goodwin, D. K. (1994). No Ordinary Time—Franklin and Eleanor Roosevelt: The Home Front in WWII. New York: Simon & Schuster.

Grob, G. N. (1994). *The Mad Among Us: A History of the Care of America's Mentally Ill*. New York: Free Press.

Guyotte, R. L. (1995). Cohen, Wilbur (1913–1987). In R. L. Edwards (Ed.), *Encyclopedia of Social Work*, 19th edn. (p. 2579). Washington, DC: National Association of Social Workers.

Haines, M. R. (1991). Birthrate and Mortality. In E. Foner and J. A. Garraty (Eds.), *Reader's Companion to American History* (pp. 103–105). Boston, MA: Houghton Mifflin.

Hamilton, C. D. and Hamilton, C. V. (1997). *The Dual Agenda: The African American Struggle for Civil and Economic Equality*. New York: Columbia University Press.

Iglehart, A. P. and Becerra, R. M. (2000). *Social Services and the Ethnic Community*. Prospect Heights, IL: Waveland Press.

Institute of Medicine. (1988). *The Future of Public Health*. Washington, DC: National Academy Press.

Jansson, B. S. (2001). *The Reluctant Welfare State*, 4th edn. Belmont, CA: Wadsworth.

Jaros, K. J. and Evans, J. C. (1995). Maternal and Child Health. In R. L. Edwards (Ed.), *Encyclopedia of Social Work*, 19th edn. (pp. 1683–1689). Washington, DC: National Association of Social Workers.

Kotelchuck, D. (Ed.). (1976). *Prognosis Negative: Crisis in the Health Care System*. New York: Vintage Books.

Lasch, C. (Ed.). (1982). *The Social Thought of Jane Addams*. New York: Irvington.

Lesser, A. J. (1985). The Origin and Development of Maternal and Child Health Programs in the United States. *American Journal of Public Health*, 76(6), 590–598.

Levin, M. B. (1971). *Political Hysteria in America*. New York: Basic Books.

Lewis, D. L. (1993). *W. E. B. Du Bois, Biography of a Race*. New York: Henry Holt.

Marmor, T. R. (1973). *The Politics of Medicare*. Chicago: Aldine.

Mechanic, D. (1999). *Mental Health and Social Policy: The Emergence of Mental Health*, 4th edn. Boston, MA: Allyn & Bacon.

Mizrahi, T. (1995). Health Care: Reform Initiatives. In R. L. Edwards (Ed.), *Encyclopedia of Social Work*, 19th edn. (pp. 1185–1198). Washington, DC: National Association of Social Workers.

Moniz, C. M. (1990). *National Council of Senior Citizens: The Role of the Elderly in the Enactment of Medicare*. Ann Arbor, MI: UMI Dissertation Services.

Moroney, R. M. (1995). Public Health Services. In R. L. Edwards (Ed.), *Encyclopedia of Social Work*, 19th ed. (pp. 1967–1973). Washington, DC: National Association of Social Workers.

Newman, D. K., Amidei, N. J., Carter, B. L., Day, D., Kruvant, W. J., and Russell, J. S. (1978). *Protest, Politics, and Prosperity: Black Americans and White Institutions, 1940–75*. New York: Pantheon.

Patterson, J. T. (1996). *Grand Expectations: The U.S. 1945–1974*. New York: Oxford University Press.

Quadagno, J. (1994). *The Color of Welfare*. New York: Oxford University Press.

Reynolds, B. (1963). *An Uncharted Journey: Fifty Years of Social Work by One of Its Great Teachers*, 2nd edn. Hebron, CT: Practitioners Press.

Rolde, N. (1992). *Your Money or Your Health*. New York: Paragon House.

Sagan, L. A. (1987). *The Health of Nations: Two Causes of Sickness and Well-Being*. New York: Basic Books.

Schlesinger, A. Jr. (1959). *The Age of Roosevelt: The Crisis of the Old Order*. Boston, MA: Houghton Mifflin.

Simon, B. L. (1994). *The Empowerment Tradition in American Social Work: A History*. New York: Columbia University Press.

Skocpol, T. (1992). *Protecting Soldiers and Mothers*. Cambridge, MA: Harvard University Press.

——. (1995). *Social Policy in the United States*. Princeton, NJ: Princeton University Press.

Starr, P. (1982). *The Social Transformation of American Medicine: The Rise of a Sovereign Profession and the Making of a Vast Industry*. New York: Basic Books.

Syers, M. (1995). Lenroot, Katherine Frederica (1891–1982). In R. L. Edwards (Ed.), *Encyclopedia of Social Work*, 19th edn. (pp. 2596–2597). Washington, DC: National Association of Social Workers.

Trattner, W. I. (1999). *From Poor Law to Welfare State*, 6th edn. New York: Free Press.

Tulchinsky, T. H. and Varavikova, E. A. (2000). *The New Public Health*. San Diego, CA: Academic Press.

Turnock, B. J. (1997). *Public Health*. Gaithersburg, MD: Aspen Publishers.

U.S. Children's Bureau. (1914). *First Annual Report of the Chief, to the Secretary of Labor for Year Ended June 30, 1913*. Washington, DC: Government Printing Office.

Veterans Administration. (2005). *A Brief History of the VA*. Retrieved from www.va.gov/opa/publications/archives/docs/history_in_brief.pdf

Wencour, S. and Reisch, M. (1989). *From Charity to Enterprise: The Development of Social Work in a Market Economy*. Urbana, IL: University of Illinois.

White, K. L. (1991). *Healing the Schism: Epidemiology, Medicine, and the Public's Health*. New York: Springer-Verlag.

CHAPTER 3

Public, Community, and Mental Health

CHAPTER 2 HAS ALREADY PROVIDED AN OVERVIEW OF THE nation's earliest efforts to address public health in the U.S. by summarizing historical events and policies from the mid-1800s to 1920 when the U.S. Public Health Service was established. It also examines the importance of public health policy initiatives during the New Deal and World War II. Here we examine more recent efforts to renew and strengthen the role of public and community health during the Clinton and Obama administrations, and the Trump administration's efforts to move in a very different direction.

With the absence of a universal health care approach in the U.S. until recently, both public health and community health (community health centers and community mental health centers) have played and continue to play a special role in promoting health and providing public access to care. With the enactment of the Affordable Care Act (ACA) in 2010, both have received the greatest attention since the 1990s. As noted by Bovbjerg et al. (2011, p. 1), "President Barack Obama . . . made prevention and public health a cornerstone of his approach to health policy." The ACA allocated millions of dollars to advance the nation's public health infrastructure through improved information technology, workforce training, regulation and policy development, and improved laboratory facilities. Millions of dollars were also allocated to help community mental health centers play a significant role in the provision of coordinated health and behavioral health care for individuals with serious chronic health and behavioral health conditions, and to help states improve their heath center infrastructure. For the first time, the ACA also put mental health on a par with health insurance coverage by eliminating discriminatory policies on insurance coverage and benefits.

However, with the election of President Trump in 2016 and the administration's determination to "repeal and replace" the ACA and make cuts to environmental and prevention programs, the government's commitment to community and public health is unclear at best. As noted by the Center for American Progress, the Trump administration has "set their sights on gutting the Clean Air Act, Clean Water Act, and other cornerstone protections" (Alexander-Kearns, 2017, paragraph 1). The failed American Health Care Act proposed by the Republican-controlled Congress would have eliminated the prevention and public health fund (Jost, 2017).

PUBLIC HEALTH

Efforts to Renew Public Health (1990–2010)

In the late 1980s, the Institute of Medicine, Committee for the Study of the Future of Public Health, Division of Health Care Services (1988) stated that our public health system was in disarray. The Clinton administration took some strides to address serious public health issues. With the enactment of the Vaccines for Children Act (VCA) in 1993, child immunization rates have improved dramatically, and the VCA remains the primary source of childhood vaccinations. The Office of Minority Health, in the U.S. Department of Health and Human Services, actively sought to expand immunization among racial and ethnic minority groups (Thurm, 1998) as part of Clinton's 1998 Initiative to Eliminate Racial and Ethnic Disparities in Health.

Despite these efforts, in 1994 a group of experts noted that budget restrictions had severely limited the ability of public health departments to respond to infectious disease (cited in Ryan, 1997). In 2000, the U.S. General Accounting Office (2000) raised doubts about the nation's ability to respond adequately to infectious diseases, especially influenza, and the Institute for the Future (2000, pp. 8–9) found that during the past 30 years the public health system had been operating under the pressure of resource scarcity, limits in leadership, and organizational fragmentation. Similarly, a massive study of the public health system by Garrett (2000), a Pulitzer Prize-winning journalist, described the U.S. system as being in a shambles, in light of the "nightmare of bioterrorism."

The attack on the World Trade Center in New York City on September 11, 2001 reinforced the importance of having a public health infrastructure in place to respond to a public health crisis. The anthrax scare that followed also signaled the importance and limitations of our public health system and raised questions about the nation's ability to face threats of bioterrorism. For scientists, the worst-case scenario would be an outbreak of smallpox, which is a highly contagious virus (Brownlee, 2001). The World Health Organization (WHO, 2001, p. 1) has called it "one of the most devastating diseases known to humanity." Although a vaccine can prevent or delay the development of symptoms in individuals exposed to the virus, smallpox has no known cure.

With much effort, the WHO, under the leadership of Dr. Donald Henderson, successfully eradicated smallpox in 1977 (Garrett, 2000). However, the former Soviet Union and the U.S. preserved laboratory samples of the virus, and the precise location of the Soviet sample is unknown. With the demise of the Soviet Union, tens of thousands of scientists who had been engaged in bioweapons research were forced to find new employment. This raised the chilling possibility that some scientists might have sold their expertise, and perhaps biological agents, to other countries (Garrett, 2000). Governments stopped immunizing against smallpox years ago, and the world has a short supply of the vaccine; if unleashed, the virus could spread quickly (Altman, 2001). Although a smallpox attack is unlikely, after September 11, scientists felt it could not be ruled out (Brownlee, 2001). The Centers for Disease Control and Prevention (CDC) has a plan to protect against the use of smallpox as a biological weapon (CDC, 2016a).

A 2008 report by the Trust for America's Health and the Robert Wood Johnson Foundation found that "budget cuts and the economic crisis" threatened to reverse "progress made to better protect the country from disease outbreaks, natural disasters, and bioterrorism." Hurricane Katrina in New Orleans and along the Gulf coast demonstrated how vulnerable the nation is to large-scale disaster (Redlener, 2006). Concern about infectious disease is not limited to bioterrorism, however, and remains a serious and growing problem (Hamburg et al., 2008). In January 2000, the government's National Intelligence Council (NIC, 2000) described infectious disease as an emerging threat to international stability and national security. Since 1973, older diseases, such as tuberculosis and malaria, have reappeared in more virulent forms, and newer incurable diseases, such as HIV and hepatitis C, have appeared. The deadliest infectious diseases are respiratory infections, HIV, diarrheal diseases, tuberculosis, malaria, measles, and hepatitis B and C (NIC, 2000). In 1998, infectious diseases accounted for a quarter of the 53.9 million deaths worldwide (WHO, 1999). This number may underestimate the total, because some forms of heart disease, cancer, and other diseases may be linked to infections. Between 1980 and 2000, the U.S. mortality rate from infectious disease almost doubled (NIC, 2000). Redlener (2006) estimated that avian flu alone could kill 50,000 people in New York City.

Several factors have facilitated the spread of infectious disease: Population growth and urbanization, economic development (which brings humans closer to animal and insect carriers of disease), climate change, and a worldwide collapse of public health systems (NIC, 2000). International travel and tourism and the "global movement of goods and services" also play a role (Kassalow, 2001, p. 6). With growing numbers of U.S. citizens traveling abroad and citizens of other countries entering the U.S., the likelihood of exposure to infectious disease has increased. The growth of imports, including food, adds to this problem (Kassalow, 2001). For example, the Asian tiger mosquito, which carries eastern equine encephalomyelitis, first came to the U.S. in 1982 in a shipment of used tires (Morse, 1999).

Microbial resistance is another factor. From one angle, this is a natural process because, "under the pressures of Darwinian evolution," microbes develop an ability to resist "the drugs commonly used to treat them" (Ryan, 1997, p. 133). However, microbial resistance is also a social phenomenon. One cause has been the widespread dissemination and indiscriminate use of antibiotics throughout the world. In the case of tuberculosis, failure (usually for reasons of cost) to treat new cases, particularly among people in poverty, facilitated the development of "multidrug-resistant" forms of the disease (Farmer, 1999). In addition, because of the "enormous increase in international travel in recent years," individuals may "be exposed to resistant microbes in one country and carry them to other countries, where resistance can then spread" (WHO, 1999).

The aging of the population could also exacerbate the problem of infectious disease. As Garrett (2000) noted, aging results in a natural reduction in immunity, which explains why "influenza and pneumonia, for example, are often lethal infections in elders, while the identical microbes may produce little more than a few days discomfort in young adults" (Garrett, 2000, p. 553). At the same time, unless a significant segment of a population is immunized, "disease-causing microbes" will "continue to lurk and kill vulnerable individuals" (Garrett, 2000, p. 553). In a society composed of a large number of older adults whose "childhood vaccinations" may have "waned," infectious diseases, particularly if drug resistant, could "claim millions of lives" (Garrett, 2000, p. 553).

At first glance, the spread of infectious disease and the events of September 11 seem to have little to do with each other. However, both can be viewed as products of globalization and the increasing interdependence of nations. International travel and commerce, essential elements of globalization, facilitated the entry of terrorists and infectious diseases into the U.S. Garrett (2000) noted that in the twenty-first century the fate of public health is closely linked to "the ultimate course of globalization" (Garrett, 2000, p. 582). To ensure our own safety, we must address not only our own health, but also the health needs and concerns of other countries (Kassalow, 2001).

Public Health and the ACA

The ACA enacted by the Obama administration began anew a national effort to tackle the challenge of public and community health (Figure 3.1). The ACA allocated $70 million to advance the public health infrastructure in the states through improved information technology, workforce training, regulation and policy development, and with grants to the states to improve laboratory facilities (U.S. Department of Health and Human Services [HHS], 2012a, 2012b). As noted by the American Public Health Association (2011, p. 13), "many [state] public health departments struggle to maintain a sufficient and adequately trained laboratory and epidemiological workforce, and functional, up-to-date equipment."

In addition to taking on the need for an improved and enhanced infrastructure, the ACA also provided support for traditional public health initiatives in prevention and health promotion. As noted by the Urban Institute (Bovbjerg et al., 2011, p. 1), "the ACA's emphases on prevention and population health illustrate how far public health has advanced as federal policy," particularly when compared with the "unsuccessful early-1990s push for health reform." A National Prevention Council chaired by the Surgeon General was created by the ACA to develop national strategy to promote health across all agencies and policies that play a substantial role in health. The Council provides "coordination and leadership among 20 executive departments and agencies with respect to prevention, wellness, and health promotion activities" (National Prevention, Health Promotion, and Public Health Council, 2014, p.3) by advancing the nation's National Prevention Strategy.

In addition, the ACA created the nation's first Prevention and Public Health Fund ($16 billion over 10 years) to provide "expanded and sustained" annual funding "in place of the shifting and uncertain funding of annual appropriations at all levels of government" (Bovbjerg et al., 2011, p. 3) to promote healthy living and reduce the disease rate. The initial focus was on improving the effectiveness of community-based prevention (diet, physical activity, obesity, tobacco prevention and cessation, etc.), but the ACA also funded a variety of state initiatives such as healthy aging, nutritional labeling in chain restaurants, and research on public health services. From 2010 to 2016, the fund accounted for 12 percent of the CDC's

FIGURE 3.1

Public Health and Community Mental Health Provisions: Affordable Care Act

TITLE IV. PREVENTION OF CHRONIC DISEASE AND IMPROVING PUBLIC HEALTH

- Health promotion initiatives

- New interagency prevention council

- Increases access to clinical preventive services

- Support for prevention and public health innovation to develop healthy communities

TITLE V. HEALTH CARE WORKFORCE

- Innovations in health workforce training, recruitment, and retention

- Establishes a new workforce commission

- New workforce training and education infrastructure to support increased supply of health care workers (including mental and behavioral health education and training grants to schools for the development, expansion, or enhancement of training programs in social work)

- Funds the expansion, construction, and operation of community health centers across the country

Source: U.S. Department of Health and Human Services (2012b).

programming and included support for its immunization program, Preventive Health and Health Services Block Grant, support to the states to address infectious disease threats, childhood lead poisoning prevention, and preventing health-care-associated infections (CDC, 2016b).

COMMUNITY HEALTH: HEALTH CENTERS

The Creation of Community Health Centers (1965–68)

The first community health centers (initially named neighborhood health centers) were established in Massachusetts and Mississippi in 1965 as part of the Johnson administration's War on Poverty in connection with the Economic Opportunity Act of 1964. "Two young doctors turned space at a Boston housing project [in Columbia Point] into the nation's first community health center . . . to bring care to people where they live" (Kong, 1990). The center was opened with a $1 million grant to Tufts Medical School from the Office of Economic Opportunity (OEO) (dismantled in 1968) to start the first center as a demonstration project through the Community Action Program (CAP). Dr. Jack Geiger was an activist physician who brought his 1950s' experience in South Africa with primary health care delivery in community-based settings to a vision of community health centers in the U.S. In addition to the Boston health center, he gained support from the OEO to bring a health center to rural Mississippi; this health center opened in 1967 in Mound Bayou, and operates today as the Delta Health Center.

Geiger's vision was part of a community-oriented primary care model that connected social and economic issues with health and disease. As part of the OEO anti-poverty program, the neighborhood health center model empowered local communities with federal resources to establish affordable, accessible neighborhood centers. Today, community health centers remain the only health care system that is controlled in partnership with consumers. One of the statutory requirements of federally qualified community health centers (FQHCs) is that a community board must govern each with a patient majority; these patient-controlled boards have full authority to oversee the operations of the facility. As Kotelchuk et al. (2011) note, this model of prevention, accessibility, and patient-centered care "has a surprisingly modern resonance as . . . professionals incorporate these principles into current health policy and practice" (Kotelchuk et al., 2011, p. 2091).

Health Center Reforms (1975–2002)

Before Congress dismantled the OEO, the health centers program was moved to the Department of Health, Education, and Welfare (HEW), and was combined with President Kennedy's early migrant health centers' initiative. In 1975, Congress authorized neighborhood health centers as "community and migrant health centers," and in later years added primary care for residents of public housing and homeless individuals. With the passage of the Health Centers Consolidation Act of 1996 under the Public Health Services Act, all of these components (community, migrant, homeless, and public housing) were combined to establish one authority for all of these programs (Taylor, 2004).

Today, the (renamed) Geiger Gibson Community Health Center continues to provide care and delivers medical, dental, and behavioral health services as an FQHC. FQHCs are public and private, nonprofit, health care organizations that meet U.S. Department of Health and Human Services criteria under Medicare and Medicaid, and receive funding through the Health Center Program (under the Public Health Service Act) (HHS, 2012a). The FQHC program was created in 1989 in response to concerns that health centers were using their Public Health Service grants—called (section) 330 grants—to compensate for low Medicaid reimbursement rates; the FQHC program allowed consolidated health centers to receive full compensation from Medicare and Medicaid for treatment costs.

This policy became contentious in the 1990s when Medicaid-managed care was introduced. In 1997, to preserve their special cost-based reimbursement rate, Congress required state Medicaid programs to cover the difference in lost revenue from managed-care reimbursement rates. To respond to the financial difficulties created by this policy at the state level, some health centers created their own managed-care plans in an effort to receive reimbursement in a more timely fashion. This policy changed again in 2001, when Congress created a Medicaid prospective payment plan for FQHCs that was less generous and based on a different formula for reimbursement. None the less, today, Medicaid is the largest revenue source for community health centers (Taylor, 2004; Shin et al., 2015). Within the HHS, the Health Resources and Services Administration (HRSA), the Bureau of Primary Health Care (BPHC) operates community health centers.

Bush's Health Centers Initiative (2002–7)

In a climate of rising health care costs, the Bush administration took note of the health centers' track record of providing cost-efficient care to underserved populations. President Bush set an initial goal of adding 1200 new and expanded health center sites over 5 years as part of his effort to address the rising rates of those medically uninsured in the U.S. However, as a result of budget constraints and reductions in social spending, this goal was changed to one that would increase the number of patients served by these facilities; federal funding for community health centers was increased through 2008 (Whelan, 2010). To achieve this goal, grant funds were made available to focus on three objectives: Create new access points, expand medical capacity, and expand services (Taylor, 2004).

President Bush's initiative almost doubled federal health center funding by increasing funding from about $1 billion in 2000 to more than $2 billion in 2002 (Shi et al., 2010). According to Shi et al. (2010), health centers experienced a 58 percent increase in total number of patients served compared with 10 percent for centers receiving no funding at all; thus public funding is critical to expanding services to medically underserved communities. Health centers located in rural areas had much more difficulty expanding services and actually had negative patient growth. The authors speculate that this was likely due to understaffing and difficulties in recruiting health care personnel to rural communities. Health centers serving homeless patients also found it difficult to expand their services due to the complexity of serving this population, which has multiple, co-occurring medical, substance abuse, and behavioral health problems, difficulty recruiting personnel, and the transient nature of homeless individuals' lives. Overall, however, the expansion of federal funds to community health centers significantly increased access to care for underserved populations.

Obama's Recovery Act (2009) and the ACA (2010)

The Obama administration also focused on strengthening the nation's community health centers as part of its efforts to address the recession of 2007–9. Through the American Recovery and Reinvestment Act of 2009, the administration provided about $2 billion in one-time funding for operating costs and new construction, which doubled the federal community centers' budget. Over two million new patients were served in the first year of funding while thousands of new jobs were created with the stimulus funds. Much of the funding for community health centers from the stimulus act went to states with the highest unemployment rates (Whelan, 2010).

Today there are about 1375 community health centers in more than 9750 communities serving 24.3 million people in both rural and urban areas and in every state in the country (Paradise et al., 2017). These centers play a vital role in the delivery of preventive and primary care, particularly for low-income individuals, who are often uninsured or publicly insured, homeless, migrant and seasonal workers, and medically underserved. Approximately half of the patients are treated in poor, rural communities, while the other half are from poor inner-city neighborhoods. The care received at health centers is ranked among the most cost-effective and, unlike the health centers of the 1960s, today's community health centers provide a full array of medical, pharmaceutical, dental, and behavioral health care (Bureau of Primary Care, 2009). More than half of the patients are members of racial and ethnic minorities, which is one of the reasons these centers demonstrate success in reducing racial and ethnic health disparities (Shin et al., 2015).

According to Kotelchuk et al. (2011), community health centers play three important roles in the delivery of health care to low-income communities: Vital clinical care, the creation of jobs, and community development by promoting education, healthier lifestyles, and addressing social determinants of health. Through the ACA, the Obama administration built on these strengths by further expanding the role of community health centers. The ACA provided $11 billion to expand services over 5 years (2010–15), including major construction and renovation projects, and $1.5 billion to expand the National Health Service Corps (NHSC), from which health centers recruit many of their clinical staff. The number of patients served increased to 20 million in 2012 (Sebelius, 2012) and almost 22 million in 2013 (Shin et al., 2015).

Federal allocations from the ACA Health Center Trust Fund continued to fund health centers through 2015. These funds, along with regular Congressional allocations, allowed health centers to grow and help meet the health care needs of communities, including the uninsured. In addition, "increased awareness of health coverage options due to ACA-related outreach efforts, and modernized and streamlined Medicaid eligibility and enrollment systems required of all states under the ACA" (Shin et al., 2015) increased participation in Medicaid and generated increased patient revenues for health centers. With the expiration of the trust fund in 2015, Shin et al. (2015) estimated that the number of patients served by health centers in the nation's most vulnerable communities would drop by one-third or 7 million people. Despite bipartisan support, Congress missed the September 2017 deadline to reauthorize funding for the Community Health Center Fund. President Trump's 2018 fiscal year budget request includes $3.6 billion for the Community Health Center Fund in each of the 2018 and 2019 fiscal years.

COMMUNITY HEALTH: MENTAL HEALTH CENTERS

The Creation of Community Mental Health Centers (1963–92)

Although President Kennedy did not live to see the enactment of Medicare in 1965, he succeeded in transforming the nation's mental health policy. The president was sensitized to the issues of mental retardation[1] and mental health through the experience of his sister, Rosemary. While hospitalized for mental retardation, Rosemary Kennedy underwent a lobotomy, which significantly worsened her condition. The reform of mental health services became one of Kennedy's personal legislative priorities.

The first efforts to provide community-based mental health services to hospitalized patients occurred in the states. New York led the way in 1954 by passing the Community Health Services Act. This bill allowed local communities to establish mental health boards, which could use state funds to partially support the delivery of community-based inpatient and outpatient care. Other states, including California, soon enacted similar legislation (Grob, 1994).

The structure and funding of state mental health services slowly began to shift from state mental hospitals to local community-based care (Grob, 1994). In 1955, Congress enacted the Mental Health Study Act, which established the Joint Commission on Mental Illness and Mental Health to examine effective approaches to treating mental illness. In 1961, the commission proposed a new community-based mental health system, which would come about through the gradual transformation of large state mental hospitals (over 1000 beds) into chronic community care centers and the construction of new smaller hospitals. The community centers would facilitate access to social supports and reduce the need for hospitalization (Grob, 1994; Mechanic, 1999).

MENTAL RETARDATION AND COMMUNITY MENTAL HEALTH CENTERS CONSTRUCTION ACT (1963)

In 1963, after establishing several committees to study the needs of those with mental illness and mental retardation, Kennedy introduced a federal plan for the construction of comprehensive community mental health centers (Grob, 1994; Mechanic, 1999). The final bill, the Mental Retardation and Community Mental Health Centers Construction Act, was enacted in 1963. It provided funds for grants to states between 1965 and 1967 to construct community mental health centers. The Act established approximately 2000 catchment areas, with populations ranging in size from 75,000 to 200,000 (Karger and Stoesz, 2002). The intent was that a clinic, or mental health center, would serve each catchment area. By 1980, however, there were still only 754 centers, far short of the goal of 2000 (Grob, 1994).

According to Grob (1994), the failure to establish community mental health centers was largely due to disagreements over their purpose. Some professionals believed the centers should focus on *treatment*, whereas others argued that they should focus on *prevention*. A third group saw the centers as providing an opportunity to focus on larger social reforms that would promote *community mental health*. There was disagreement about the organizational structure and staffing of the centers and even the kind of clients they should serve (Grob, 1994).

The shift away from hospitalization toward community care also raised policy issues for planners and administrators, given the lack of agreement on the mental health centers' purpose and function: Should the centers be substitutes for hospitals? If so, what should be the future of mental health hospitals? If not, what should be the relationship among hospitals, centers, and other community resources? Who should administer the mental health centers? How should they be staffed? How should the operating costs be financed (Lin, 1995)?

As mental health professionals grappled with these issues, mental health centers found it harder and harder to function as substitutes for mental hospitals and provide truly comprehensive care, as the legislation required. For example, how could mental health centers ensure food, clothing, housing, and safety for patients with severe and chronic mental illness? What kind of aftercare programs could they offer to support and maintain patient health?

Medicaid's Role in Deinstitutionalization of Mental Hospitals (1960s–1970s)

While community mental health centers struggled to become alternatives to mental hospitals, the passage of Medicaid in 1965 added to the growing trend to release patients from state mental hospitals. In fact, Medicaid played an even more significant role in the deinstitutionalization of mental hospitals during the 1960s and 1970s than the community mental health center movement, and it fueled the growth of nursing homes (U.S. General Accounting Office, 1977). Medicaid extended coverage for psychiatric hospital care to poor people, and created incentives for states to place elderly recipients with behavioral problems in nursing homes. The nursing home population doubled during the 1960s as a result of Medicaid (Grob, 1994). In addition, Medicaid provided support for community residential care for former mental patients who were eligible for Aid to the Permanently and Totally Disabled, which was changed to Supplemental Security Income (SSI) in 1972 (Segal, 1995).

These Medicaid policies contributed to the decline of hospital admissions and the increase in patient discharges from mental hospitals during the 1960s. They also contributed to the emerging division of care in mental health services. Public mental health hospitals were becoming institutions for the treatment of severely and chronically mentally ill patients, whereas community mental health centers were becoming counseling and crisis intervention centers for individuals with acute problems.

Alcohol and Drug Abuse Services (1968)

In 1968, the Community Mental Health Centers Construction Act was amended to include funding for alcohol abuse treatment and programs. This amendment came on the heels of congressional action in 1966 to expand NIMH to create the Center for the Studies of Narcotic Addiction and Drug Abuse and the National Center for the Prevention and Control of Alcoholism. With national attention shifting toward alcohol and drug abuse and much-needed additional funding, community mental health centers began to focus on alcohol and drug abuse counseling.

President Nixon advocated curtailing the federal government's role in mental health policy. Between 1970 and 1972, Nixon considered serious reductions in funding for NIMH programs, and in 1973 he recommended the termination of federal funding for community mental health centers. The Watergate scandal prevented Nixon from implementing these proposals.

Nevertheless, the Nixon administration set the stage for Congress to examine the problems of community-based mental health care and reconsider the federal role in mental health policy. In 1973, Congress reorganized the Public Health Service (PHS) and moved NIMH back to the National Institutes of Health (NIH). Congress also created the Alcohol, Drug Abuse, and Mental Health Administration (ADAMHA) as an umbrella organization to administer the PHS, NIMH, the National Institute on Alcoholism and Alcohol Abuse (NIAAA), and the National Institute on Drug Abuse (NIDA). NIDA had been created in 1972 in response to increased concern about substance abuse (Grob, 1994).

In 1975, Congress decided against termination of funding for community mental health centers. Instead, it required the delivery of seven new services, including screening and aftercare, which were considered essential to a comprehensive continuum of community-based care. However, mental health centers across the country were already struggling to meet the needs of patients discharged from mental hospitals that had been closed or reduced in size. Most centers were unprepared to expand their services (Grob, 1994).

Consumer Protection Efforts: Patients' Rights (1970s)

In the 1970s, states also faced the need to protect the civil rights of people identified as mentally ill. For example, in *Wyatt v. Stickney<AQ6>*, a district court required the state of Alabama to treat patients still living in state hospitals (Karger and Stoesz, 2002). The Supreme Court (D*onaldson v. O'Connor<AQ7>*) ruled that states could not "confine" individuals unless they were a danger to themselves or to the community or were being treated during confinement (Karger and Stoesz, 2002, p. 363). These rulings led the states to accelerate efforts to empty hospitals and, as much as possible, limit new hospitalizations. "Thus, legal decisions favoring the mentally ill often proved illusory," in many instances, offering "nothing more than the right to be insane" (Karger and Stoesz, 2002, p. 363).

A few years later, President Jimmy Carter established a Commission on Mental Health, which developed recommendations for coordinating existing federal, state, and local services and protecting the rights of patients (Grob, 1994). In 1979, families of the mentally ill founded the National Alliance for the Mentally Ill to advocate these protections. In 1980, Congress enacted the Mental Health Systems Act, which included a model bill of rights for patients that the states were expected to enact (Grob, 1994; Mental Health Policy Resource Center, 1996). As noted by Mechanic (1999), the process was "long and tortuous" and "substantially modified" to satisfy opponents of the legislation. By the time the bill was signed by President Carter, Ronald Reagan was only a month away from winning the 1980 presidential election and embarking on a new direction for mental health policy.

Community Support Program (1977)

In 1977, the NIMH established a new Community Support Program in an effort to respond to policy issues that surfaced during the congressional review of mental health centers. The purpose was to facilitate a federal–state partnership to encourage state initiatives to target the needs of people with severe mental illness. The program focused on issues of daily living, such as housing, income, and the many support services needed to sustain community-based care for the mentally ill, especially those with severe or chronic disorders. The "Madison Model," or Programs of Assertive Community Treatment (PACT), pioneered by Marx, Test, and Stein in 1973 at the Mendota State Hospital in Madison, Wisconsin, served as the model for the Community Support Program. PACT was designed to teach life skills to patients in the community, rather than in a state hospital (Hughes, 1999).

The Community Support Program also recognized the need to integrate the funding and delivery of services provided by Medicare, Medicaid, Supplemental Security Income (SSI), and Social Security Disability Insurance (SSDI) with community-based services provided by the mental health centers. During the late 1970s, NIMH promoted changes that enabled recipients of public assistance and entitlement programs to receive community-based care. For example, changes in Medicaid allowed for reimbursement of specialized case management services and services offered by the mental health centers (Grob, 1994).

The community service programs initiated by NIMH had a positive effect on the lives of many severely and chronically mentally ill patients (Grob, 1994). However, these improvements received little public attention in light of the emerging problems of homelessness that dominated the social landscape of the 1980s. For example, between 1980 and 1990 the size of the homeless population increased fivefold (Jencks, 1994). Many of those living on the streets and in shelters were severely mentally ill, substance abusers, or both.

The Decline of Community Mental Health (1980–92)

The Reagan administration was determined to reverse the expanding federal welfare state that first emerged during the New Deal in the mid-1930s. In 1981, the Omnibus Budget Reconciliation Act (OBRA) was passed as a way to reduce the federal role in social welfare and federal funding for social programs. A primary strategy used to achieve this was the creation of block grants, which shifted the responsibility for many social programs from the federal government to the states.

OBRA collapsed 57 separate programs and their funding into 7 block grants. Federal funding appropriated for specific legislated programs within a given policy area was consolidated, reduced by 20 percent, and then granted to the states to spend as they saw fit. In doing this, the federal government relinquished its responsibility for regulating and monitoring these individual categorical programs. Instead, each state was given the freedom to decide on its priorities. Many states struggled to find ways to maintain the same programs and services with reduced funds; some succeeded, but many failed.

Mental health programs were not spared from this process. Several NIMH categorical programs for mental health and substance abuse were collapsed into one

Alcohol, Drug Abuse, and Mental Health block grant available to the states and, like other block grants, overall funding was reduced by 20 percent. By making these changes, the Reagan administration in essence repealed the provisions of the Mental Health Systems Act (1980) and the Community Mental Health Centers Construction Act (1963).

In addition to the block grants, the Reagan administration used OBRA to make changes in a number of public assistance programs. These changes were designed to reduce eligibility and thereby decrease the number of recipients. By redefining disability, thousands of disabled SSI and SSDI recipients were denied coverage by the Social Security Administration. Many of these recipients were mentally ill and their benefits were denied until 1983, when the Supreme Court reinstated their benefits. To make matters worse, other programs that served low-income, mentally ill individuals, such as Medicaid, housing, and social services, were also reduced by OBRA.

The NIMH role in directing national mental health policy was clearly altered during the Reagan–Bush era (1980–92). In fact, by 1992, Congress no longer provided funding to NIMH for direct services; instead, NIMH was reorganized to focus primarily on research. A new agency, the Substance Abuse and Mental Health Services Administration (SAMSHA), was created and made responsible for training and services. SAMSHA managed three separate centers: The Center for Substance Abuse Treatment (CSAT), the Center for Substance Abuse Prevention (CSAP), and the Center for Mental Health Services (CMHS).

State Comprehensive Mental Health Services Plan Act (1986)

However, the Community Support Program gained legislative support from Congress in 1984 during the Reagan administration, and in 1986 Congress encouraged the federal–state partnership approach by enacting the State Comprehensive Mental Health Services Plan Act. This legislation allowed states to use federal block grant funds to expand their community-based mental health services, and, as noted earlier, these efforts had a positive impact on the recipients of these services (Grob, 1994).

Stewart B. McKinney Homeless Assistance Act (1987)

In 1987, Congress passed the Stewart B. McKinney Homeless Assistance Act, which was renamed the McKinney–Vento Homeless Assistance Act in 2000. This Bill established a new federal block grant, the Community Mental Health Services Block Grant, available to the states to provide assistance and services to homeless individuals, including emergency food and shelter, housing, health and mental health services, alcohol and drug abuse treatment, and prevention services such as education and job training. The programs were "inadequately funded, fragmented, and extremely diverse," however (Johnson, 1995, p. 1343). Most of the funds were spent on building emergency shelters, and little was done to provide outreach to mentally ill people and others who avoided shelters (Jansson, 2001).

The President's New Freedom Commission on Mental Health (2002)

During the 1990s, proposals for mental health reform were part of the failed Health Security Act of the Clinton administration. It fell to President George W. Bush in April 2002 to create a New Freedom Commission on Mental Health, which was charged with undertaking a "comprehensive study" of the nation's "mental health service delivery system" and making recommendations that would "enable" children and adults with "serious mental illnesses" and "emotional disturbances" to "participate fully in their communities" (Executive Order 13263—see www.whitehouse.gov/news/releases/2002/04/20020429-2.html). In an interim report in October 2002, the commission acknowledged that the current system was "fragmented and in disarray" (cited in President's New Freedom Commission on Mental Health, 2003, p. 4). The Commission's final report in July 2003 urged a transformation of "mental health care in America" and the creation of a system that would recognize the importance of mental health, reflect the interests of consumers and families, eliminate cultural and geographical "disparities in mental health services," and offer "early mental health screening, assessment, and referral to services" (President's New Freedom Commission on Mental Health, 2003, pp. 24–25).

Community Health and the Affordable Care Act (2010)

With the passage of the ACA, mental health services, in general, underwent a fundamental change. By 2014, insurance coverage had to include treatment for mental health and substance use. Funds ($20 million) were targeted to help communities coordinate and integrate primary care services into publicly funded community mental health and other community-based behavioral health settings. Additional funds ($11 billion) were targeted to communities to expand and construct community health centers, which would also be able to provide behavioral health and substance abuse services.

According to the Bazelon Center for Mental Health Law (2012), people with serious mental illness have especially high rates of chronic health conditions (such as cardiovascular disease, diabetes, cancer, asthma, and obesity). This combination of serious physical and mental health conditions leads to worse health outcomes for these individuals, as well as higher health care costs. The Bazelon Center for Mental Health Law (2012) study found that "individuals with serious mental illnesses served by the public mental health system die, on average, 25 years earlier than people in the general population," and that the ACA "encourages the development of a variety of chronic care strategies to achieve better health outcomes for all individuals with chronic conditions" (Bazelon Center for Mental Health Law, 2012, p. 2) (Figure 3.2). Community mental health centers, which often serve as the only source of care for individuals with severe mental illnesses, can play a promising role in the provision of coordinated health and behavioral health care.

FIGURE 3.2

*Chronic Care
Strategies:
Affordable Care
Act*

COLLABORATIVE CARE MODELS

- Medical or health homes (including a new state option for Medicaid)

  Responsible for overseeing health of an individual with at least two chronic conditions, one chronic condition and one at-risk chronic condition, or a serious mental health condition; community mental health centers encouraged to serve as health homes

- Co-location of primary care and mental health services

  Grants to community mental health agencies to co-locate primary care services in mental health agency to provide a specialized health home for adults with serious mental illness

- Community health teams

  Grants to states and others to develop teams to support a patient-centered medical home model

- Accountable care organizations (ACOs)

  Physician groups, networks of practices, nurse practitioners, and physician assistants and others affiliated with a local acute care hospital to provide coordinated and collaborative care

- Medicare special needs plans

  Federal government will create a shared-savings program to reward ACOs that become accountable for the quality, cost, and overall care of their Medicare fee-for-service beneficiary patients

- Pediatric ACO demonstration (2012–16)

- Medicare special needs plan program

  A Medicare managed care plan (Advantage plan) for individuals residing in an institution (including a psychiatric facility) or in need of institutional care, eligible for both Medicare and Medicaid (dua-leligibles), or with one or more specific chronic or disabling conditions (such as diabetes, HIV/AIDS, schizophrenia)

- Other Chronic Care Strategies

  – Specialized services, including home-based services and medication management

  – Preventive services

  – Research and outcomes and quality of care measurement

  – Testing of new innovations

  – Expansion of the workforce

Source: Bazelon Center for Mental Health Law (2012).

Mental Health and the Affordable Care Act (2010)

The ACA fundamentally changed the landscape for mental health care in the U.S. For the first time, the ACA included mental health coverage on a par with health insurance coverage by eliminating annual and lifetime caps on coverage, higher deductibles, and, in some cases, no coverage at all by building on the Mental Health Parity and Addiction Equity Act (MHPAEA) of 2008. Friedman (2012) predicted that the ACA would have an enormous impact on the treatment of mental illness:

> Surveys show that only about 50 percent of Americans with a mood disorder had psychiatric treatment in the past year—leaving the rest at high risk of suicide, to say nothing of the high cost to society in absenteeism and lost productivity.
>
> (Friedman, 2012, p. D6)

Friedman (2012) also pointed out that, due to the onset of psychiatric illness, including depression, anxiety disorders, and substance abuse during adolescence and typically before age 25, most adults with mental illness have (by definition) preexisting disorders. Until the passage of the ACA, such preexisting conditions made these adults ineligible for coverage. Moreover, the new policy to require coverage of young adults until age 26 on their parents' insurance would help to identify these conditions during these at-risk years and allow for early intervention.

The ACA would also help older people with mental illness who would no longer be subject to the gap in Medicare drug coverage known as the "donut hole" (discussed in Chapter 6). The law required drug companies to provide a 50 percent discount on brand-name drugs and gradually provide subsidies until the gap closed in 2020 (Friedman, 2012). All patients receiving treatment for mental illness would benefit from the elimination of lifetime limits on treatment, because chronic mental disorders are often characterized by remission, relapse, and the need for lifetime treatment (Friedman, 2012).

Indeed, the ACA was "one of the largest expansions of mental health and substance use disorder coverage in a generation" and reached an estimated 62 million people (Beronio et al., 2013). The ACA required individual and small employer health insurance plans (effective January 2014), and all plans offered through the health exchanges to cover mental health and substance use services. Large-group plans were not required to provide mental health coverage, but, if they did offer it, it had to be on a par with health coverage. The ACA, post-2014, also made prescription behavioral drugs more accessible. New individual and small-group plans included behavioral drug prescriptions, although some carriers still restricted their covered drug lists. Other benefits of the ACA for mental health care included prevention. All health plans (individual, small group, and large group) were required to include a range of preventive services; these include screenings for depression and alcoholism, and behavioral assessments for children.

Finally, the expansion of Medicaid under the ACA also impacted access to mental health care. According to the WHO (2007), mental health, addiction and poverty are positively correlated. "By 2020, up to 32 million people will have gained access for the first time to mental health and addiction treatment coverage as a result of Medicaid expansion" (Norris, 2016).

Efforts to "repeal and replace'" or undermine the structure of the ACA under the Trump administration would be detrimental to mental health care, especially for those helped most by the ACA. A *USA Today* story (O'Donnell and DeMio, 2017, p. 1) noted that:

> nearly 30 percent of those who got coverage through Medicaid expansion have a mental disorder, such as anxiety or schizophrenia, or an addiction to substances, such as opioids or alcohol, according to the federal Substance Abuse and Mental Health Services Administration. That compares to the more than 20% of the overall population—68 million people—who experienced a diagnosable mental health or substance abuse disorder in the past year, the American Psychiatric Association says.

With the Supreme Court decision that allowed states to decline to expand Medicaid to millions without insurance, poor people have remained at most risk for lack of access to mental health treatment even with the ACA in place.

To date, the Trump administration's focus in mental health policy has been on the most seriously mentally ill. The Trump administration's Interdepartmental Serious Mental Illness Coordinating Committee (ISMICC) issued its first congressionally mandated report, *The Way Forward: Federal Action for a System That Works for All People Living with SMI and SED and Their Families and Caregivers*, in December 2017. The report offers findings and recommendations to address improvements for providing care; the primary recommendations include expanding the Community Behavioral Health Clinic (CCBHC) program, addressing the shortage of psychiatrists working in federally supported programs by improving payment rates, and increasing criminal justice system diversion programs and early identification and intervention services for children and young adults (Pellitt, 2017).

HIGHLIGHTS

- **Public health**: During the Bush years, public health concerns were raised after September 11, 2001 about bioterrorism and the spread of infectious disease. The Bush administration created the New Freedom Commission on Mental Health, added prescription drug coverage and health savings accounts to Medicare, and continued to expand the role of the private market in the structure of Medicare.

- The Affordable Care Act enacted by the Obama Administration allocated millions of dollars to advance the nation's public health infrastructure through improved information technology, workforce training, regulation and policy development, and improved laboratory facilities.

- **Community health**: The first community health centers (initially named neighborhood health centers) were established in Massachusetts and Mississippi in 1965 as part of the Johnson Administration's War on Poverty, in turn part of the Economic Opportunity Act of 1964. As part of the OEO anti-poverty program, the neighborhood health center model empowered local communities with federal resources to establish affordable, accessible neighborhood centers. Today, community health centers remain the only health care system that is controlled in partnership with consumers.

- The Federally Qualified Health Center program was created in 1989 in response to concerns that health centers were using their Public Health Service grants—called (section) 330 grants—to compensate for low Medicaid reimbursement rates; the FQHC program allowed consolidated health centers to receive full compensation from Medicare and Medicaid for treatment costs, but this policy became contentious in the 1990s when Medicaid-managed care was introduced. In 1997, to preserve their special cost–basis reimbursement rate, Congress required state Medicaid programs to cover the difference in lost revenue from managed care reimbursement rates. This policy changed again in 2001 when Congress created a Medicaid prospective payment plan for FQHCs that was less generous and based on a different formula for reimbursement.

- Bush's Health Centers Initiative (2002–7) almost doubled federal health center funding. In a climate of rising health care costs, the Bush administration took note of the health centers' track record of providing cost-efficient care to underserved populations. President Bush set a national initial goal to significantly increase the number of patients served by community health centers. Grant funds were made available to focus on three objectives: Create new access points, expand medical capacity, and expand services.

- The Obama administration also focused on strengthening the nation's community health centers, first as part of its efforts to address the recession of 2007–9 through the American Recovery and Reinvestment Act of 2009. The administration provided about $2 billion in one-time funding for operating costs and new construction, which doubled the federal community centers' budget.

- With the enactment of the ACA, the community health centers' budget increased by $9.5 billion to expand services over 5 years (2010–15) and included $1.5 billion to support major construction and renovation projects. The number of patients served increased to 20 million in 2012 and was expected to double to 40 million annually by 2015.

- **Community mental health**: Significant mental health legislation was enacted between 1963 and 1992. The Mental Retardation and Community Mental Health Centers Construction Act of 1963 provided funds to the states to close psychiatric hospitals and replace them with community-based services. This shift in policy led to problems of deinstitutionalization with insufficient care at the community level. Congress was increasingly disheartened by the approach and threatened to terminate funding in 1975, but introduced new regulations in an effort to improve the system. During the Reagan administration in the 1980s, funds were dramatically reduced, however, and the system underwent further decline.

- With the passage of the ACA, mental health services will change dramatically in that all insurance coverage must include treatment for mental health and substance use by 2014.

- The ACA also allocates millions of dollars to help community mental health centers play a significant role in the provision of coordinated health and behavioral health care for individuals with serious chronic health and behavioral health conditions.

- **Mental health policy**: For the first time, under the ACA, mental health coverage will be on a par with health insurance coverage by eliminating annual and lifetime caps on coverage, higher deductibles, and, in some cases, no coverage at all.

- Younger adults will be able to receive coverage during vulnerable years of onset of mental illness, older adults will not be susceptible to gaps in prescription drug coverage, and all mental health patients will be able to receive lifetime coverage on a par with health coverage.

- The Trump administration's efforts to "repeal and replace" the ACA threaten the advances made by the Obama administration to establish mental health parity, especially for low-income Medicaid recipients.

NOTE

1 Please note that the phrase "mental retardation" was used widely during this period. However, the term "mental retardation" has been criticized by disability advocacy groups as derogatory and carries a negative stigma. In 2010, President Obama signed legislation to replace this term with "intellectual disability" in federal policy. Many state and local agencies and school systems made this change.

REFERENCED LEGAL CASES

Wyatt v. Stickney – see https://disabilityjustice.org/wyatt-v-stickney
Donaldson v. O'Connor – see https://caselaw.findlaw.com/us-supreme-court/422/563.html

REFERENCES

Alexander-Kearns, M. (2017, February 7). The Trump Administration's Two-pronged Assault on Public Health. *Center for American Progress*. Retrieved from www.americanprogress.org/issues/green/news/2017/02/07/298183/the-trump-administrations-two-pronged-assault-on-public-health
Altman, L. K. (2001, November 4). U.S. Sets up Plan to Fight Smallpox in Case of Attack. *New York Times*, pp. A1, B8.

American Public Health Association. (2011, June). *The Affordable Care Act's Public Health Workforce Provisions: Opportunities and Challenges.* Retrieved from www.apha.org/NR/rdonlyres/461D56BE-4A46-4C9F-9BA4-9535FE370DB7/0/APHAWorkforce2011_updated.pdf

Bazelon Center for Mental Health Law. (2012). *How Health Care Reform Can Improve Care for People with Chronic Health Conditions.* Retrieved from www.bazelon.org/LinkClick.aspx?fileticket=Tf8iX-DlvaQ%3D&tabid=218

Beronio, K., Po, R., Skopec, L., and Glied, S. (2013, February 20). *Affordable Care Act Expands Mental Health and Substance Use Disorder Benefits and Federal Parity Protections for 62 Million Americans.* Retrieved from https://aspe.hhs.gov/report/affordable-care-act-expands-mental-health-and-substance-use-disorder-benefits-and-federal-parity-protections-62-million-americans

Bovbjerg, R. R., Ormond, B. A., and Waidmann, T. A. (2011, November). *What Directions for Public Health Under the Affordable Care Act?* The Urban Institute. Retrieved from www.urban.org/UploadedPDF/412441-Directions-for-Public-Health-Underthe-Affordable-Care-Act.pdf

Brownlee, S. (2001, October 28). Clear and Present Danger. *Washington Post Magazine,* pp. 8–23.

Bureau of Primary Health Care. (2009). *Uniform Data System (UDS) Report 2009.* Washington, DC: Health Resources and Services Administration, U.S. Department of Health and Human Services.

Centers for Disease Control and Prevention. (2016a, January 15). *What You Should Know About a Smallpox Outbreak.* Retrieved from https://emergency.cdc.gov/agent/smallpox/basics/outbreak.asp

———. (2016b, May 4). *Accomplishing CDC's Mission with Investments from the Prevention & Public Health Fund, FY 2010–FY 2016.* Retrieved from www.cdc.gov/funding/documents/cdc-pphf-funding-impact.pdf

Farmer, P. (1999). *Infections and Inequalities: The Modern Plagues.* Berkeley, CA: University of California Press.

Friedman, R. A. (2012, July 9). Good News for Mental Illness in Health Law. *New York Times.* Retrieved from www.nytimes.com/2012/07/10/health/policy/health-care-law-offers-wider-benefits-for-treating-mental-illness.html?_r=1&ref=health

Garrett, L. (2000). The Nightmare of Bioterrorism. *Foreign Affairs,* 80(1), 76–90.

Grob, G. N. (1994). *The Mad Among Us: A History of the Care of America's Mentally Ill.* New York: Free Press.

Hamburg, M. A., Levi, J., Elliot, K., and Williams, L. (2008, October). *Germs Go Global: Why Emerging Infectious Diseases Are a Threat to America.* Trust for America's Health. Retrieved from http://healthyamericans.org/assets/files/GermsGoGlobal.pdf

Hughes, W. C. (1999). Managed Care, Meet Community Support: Ten Reasons to Include Direct Support Services in Every Behavioral Health Plan. *Health and Social Work,* 24, 103–111.

Institute for the Future. (2000). *Health and Health Care 2010: The Forecast, the Challenge (Report).* San Francisco, CA: Jossey-Bass.

Institute of Medicine, Committee for the Study of the Future of Public Health, Division of Health Care Services. (1988). *The Future of Public Health* (Report). Washington, DC: National Academy Press.

Jansson, B. S. (2001). *The Reluctant Welfare State,* 4th edn. Belmont, CA: Wadsworth.

Jencks, C. (1994). *The Homeless.* Cambridge, MA: Harvard University Press.

Johnson, A. K. (1995). Homelessness. In R. L. Edwards (Ed.), *Encyclopedia of Social Work*, 19th edn. (pp. 1705–1711). Washington, DC: National Association of Social Workers.

Jost, T. (2017, March 14). CBO Projects Coverage Losses, Cost Savings From AHCA: Administration Signals Flexibility To Governors On Waivers. *Health Affairs*. Retrieved from http://healthaffairs.org/blog/2017/03/14/cbo-projects-coverage-losses-cost-savings-from-ahca-administration-signals-flexibility-to-governors-on-waivers

Karger, H. J. and Stoesz, D. (2002). *American Social Welfare Policy*, 4th edn. New York: Longman.

Kassalow, J. S. (2001). *Why Health is Important to U.S. Foreign Policy*. New York: Council on Foreign Relations and Milbank Memorial Fund.

Kong, D. (1990, October 28). 25 Years of Intensive Caring. *Boston Globe*, pp. 29, 32.

Kotelchuk, R., Lowenstein, D., and Tobin, J. (2011, November). Community Health Centers and Community Development Financial Institutions: Joining Forces to Address Determinants of Health. *Health Affairs*, 30(11), 2090–2097.

Lin, A. M. P. (1995). Mental Health Overview. In R. L. Edwards (Ed.), *Encyclopedia of Social Work*, 19th edn. (pp. 1705–1711). Washington, DC: National Association of Social Workers.

Mechanic, D. (1999). *Mental Health and Social Policy: The Emergence of Mental Health*, 4th edn. Boston: Allyn & Bacon.

Mental Health Policy Resource Center. (1996, April). *Themes and Variations: Mental Health and Substance Abuse Policy in the Making. Policy in Perspective*. Washington, DC: Mental Health Resource Center.

Morse, S. S. (1999). Factors in the Emergence of Infectious Diseases. In B. DeSalle (Ed.), *Epidemic: The World of Infectious Disease* (pp. 53–60). New York: New Press (published in conjunction with the American Museum of Natural History).

National Intelligence Council. (2000, January). *The Global Infectious Disease Threat and Its Implications for the United States* (Report). Washington, DC: NIC.

National Prevention, Health Promotion, and Public Health Council. (2014). *Annual Status REPORT*. Retrieved from www.surgeongeneral.gov/priorities/prevention/2014-npc-status-report.pdf

Norris, L. (2016, Feb 16). *How Obamacare Improved Mental Health Coverage*. Retrieved from www.healthinsurance.org/blog/2016/02/16/how-obamacare-improved-mental-health-coverage

O'Donnell, J. and DeMio, T. (2017, January 8). *Obamacare Repeal Jeopardizes Mental Health, Addiction Coverage*. Retrieved from www.usatoday.com/story/news/politics/2017/01/08/obamacare-repeal-jeopardizes-mental-health-addiction-coverage/96199628

Paradise, J., Rosenbaum, S., Markus, A., Sharac, J., Tran, C., Reynolds, D. and Shin, P. (2017, January 18). *Community Health Centers: Recent Growth and the Role of the ACA*. Kaiser Family Foundation. Retrieved from http://kff.org/report-section/community-health-centers-recent-growth-and-the-role-of-the-aca-issue-brief

Pellitt, S. (2017, December 17). *Interdepartmental Serious Mental Illness Coordinating Committee Releases Report to Congress*. National Council for Behavioral Health. Retrieved from www.thenationalcouncil.org/capitol-connector/2017/12/interdepartmental-serious-mental-illness-coordinating-committee-releases-report-congress

President's New Freedom Commission on Mental Health. (2003, July). *Achieving the Promise: Transforming Mental Health Care in America, Final Report*. Washington, DC: U.S. Government Printing Office.

Redlener, I. (2006). *Americans at Risk*. New York: Albert A. Knopf.

Ryan, F. (1997). *Virus X: Tracking the New Killer Plagues*. Boston, MA: Little, Brown.

Sebelius, K. (2012, May 1). *Healthcare Blog: Strengthening Health Centers in Communities Across the Country*. Retrieved from www.healthcare.gov/blog/2012/05/healthcenters 050112.html

Segal, S. P. (1995). Deinstitutionalization. In R. L. Edwards (Ed.), *Encyclopedia of Social Work*, 19th edn. (pp. 704–712). Washington, DC: National Association of Social Workers.

Shi, L., Lebrun, L., and Tsai, L. (2010, March–April). Assessing the Impact of the Health Center Growth Initiative on Health Center Patients. *Public Health Reports*, 125(2), 258–266.

Shin, P., Sharac, J., Barber, Z., Rosenbaum, S., and Paradise, J. (2015, May 17). *Community Health Centers: A 2013 Profile and Prospects as ACA Implementation Proceeds*. Kaiser Family Foundation. Retrieved from www.kff.org/report-section/community-health-centers-a-2013-profile-and-prospects-as-aca-implementation-proceeds-issue-brief

Taylor, J. (2004) *The Fundamentals of Community Health Centers*. National Health Policy Forum. Retrieved from www.nhpf.org/library/background-papers/BP_CHC_08-31-04.pdf

Thurm, K. (1998, November). *Adult Immunizations Save Lives. Office of Minority Health Resource Center*. U.S. Department of Health and Human Services. Retrieved from www.omhre.gov/assets/pdf/checked/Adult%20Immunizations%20Save%20Lives. pdf

Trust for America's Health. (2008). *Ready or Not? Protecting the Public's Health from Diseases, Disaster and Bioterrorism*. Retrieved from https://pdfs.semanticscholar. org/0bcf/7df6e83514d65efac050659d4153fd54248f.pdf

U.S. Department of Health and Human Services. (2012a). *The Health Care Law and You*. Retrieved from www.healthcare.gov/law/full/index.html

——. (2012b). *Primary Care: The Health Center Program*. Retrieved from www.american progress.org/issues/2010/08/community_health_centers.html

U.S. General Accounting Office. (1977). *Returning the Mentally Disabled to the Community: Government Needs to Do More*. Washington, DC: U.S. Government Printing Office.

——. (2000). *Global Health: Framework for Infectious Disease Surveillance*. Washington, DC: U.S. Government Printing Office.

Whelan, E. M. (2010). *The Importance of Community Health Centers. Center for American Progress*. Retrieved from www.americanprogress.org/issues/2010/08/pdf/chc.pdf

World Health Organization. (1999). *Removing Obstacles to Healthy Development* (Report). Retrieved from www.who.int/infectious-disease-report/index-rpt99.html

——. (2001). *Smallpox*. Media Center. Retrieved from www.coursehero.com/ file/18276194/WHO-Smallpox

——. (2007). *Breaking the Vicious Cycle Between Mental Ill-health and Poverty*. Retrieved from www.who.int/mental_health/policy/development/1_Breakingviciouscycle_ Infosheet.pdf

CHAPTER 4

The Cost of Health Care in the U.S. and Strategies for Containment

FROM THE MID-1960s TO THE EARLY 1990s, BOTH HEALTH CARE inflation and the number of people without coverage grew dramatically in the U.S., particularly in comparison to other western industrialized nations with universal coverage. At the root of these problems was the nation's failure to regulate health care costs. Health care inflation continues to plague the U.S. health care system and was one of the driving forces behind enactment of the Affordable Care Act (2010) under the Obama administration. This chapter provides an overview of private insurance, managed care, the inflationary nature of health care in the U.S., and efforts to contain the escalating cost of providing health care in the U.S. through the Affordable Care Act (ACA). It also examines the impact of the Trump administration's efforts to "repeal and replace" the ACA on cost. The length of this chapter reflects the extent of the problem of health care inflation in the U.S. health care system; it includes a history of past efforts to contain costs and the continuing need for significant reforms.

U.S. HEALTH CARE COSTS IN INTERNATIONAL PERSPECTIVE

The U.S. has the most expensive health care system in the world. Many observers believe that technology is the decisive factor in the growth of health care inflation; however, something more must be at work. This becomes clear when we compare health care costs in the U.S. to those in other countries. In 2013, per capita health care spending in the U.S. was $9086 compared with $4361 in France, the second-highest-spending country (Squires and Anderson, 2015). The U.S. figure represents more than 17.1 percent of its gross domestic product (GDP), which is far higher than the percentage of GDP spent on health care in any of the other 33 countries in the Organisation for Economic Co-operation and Development (OECD), including the wealthiest nations such as Norway. Squires (2011; Squires and Anderson, 2015) suggests that the high cost of health care in the U.S. cannot be attributed to an aging population or a greater supply or utilization of hospitals and doctors. The study shows that, although more readily accessible technology may contribute to higher spending, the primary cause seems to be higher prices for pharmaceuticals, hospital stays, and physician services. The lowest-spending countries, United Kingdom, which covers every resident through a public system (Squires and Anderson, 2015), and Japan, which has a similar fee-for-service (FFS) system, control costs by "aggressively controlling health prices" (Squires, 2011, p. 11) (Squires and Anderson, 2015).

Studies from the last two decades show a number of contributing factors to the high cost of health care in the U.S. In a review of the literature, Mahar (2008) attributed high health care costs to the inefficient use of technology, which results in "excess capacity and low productivity." At a more fundamental level, the problem seems to be lack of planning and regulation. Excess capacity and low productivity are linked with the spread of technology to geographical areas where it is not needed and facilities that "run 'well below capacity'" (Ginsburg, cited in Mahar, 2008). According to Berwick (cited in Mahar, 2008), much "of the waste and delay in health care comes from mismatches between supply and demand . . . we tend to maintain high capacities in order to meet sporadic demands." Lack of planning and regulation also contribute to the spread of technologies of questionable or unproven value.

A related issue is the widespread variation in practice patterns and costs among and even within regions that was first reported in the seminal report of Jack Wennberg et al. in 1973. Wennberg et al. (2008, p. i) "found a 2.5-fold variation in Medicare spending in different regions of the country, even after adjusting for differences in local prices, and the age, race, and underlying health of the population." Interestingly, individuals in higher-spending areas had no "better health outcomes" than individuals in lower-spending ones. They concluded that controlling these variations is necessary if we wish "to extend coverage to America's uninsured without inducing a major increase in health care spending" (Wennberg et al., 2008). More recently, the American Hospital Association's (2011) Task Force on Variation in Health Care Spending found "that a significant portion of variation is under the control or influence of hospitals and other providers, and that the time for action is now" (American Hospital Association, 2011, p. 1). Garber and Skinner (2008) argued that "the very high level and rate of growth of U.S. health spending" are linked with "a combination of high prices for inputs, poorly restrained incentives for overutilization, and a tendency to adopt expensive medical innovations rapidly, even when evidence of effectiveness is weak or absent" (Garber and Skinner, 2008, p. 28). To control health care costs, we need to regulate them (White, 2008; Ikegami and Anderson, 2012).

The Institute of Medicine (IOM) was asked to independently evaluate geographic variation in health care spending in the U.S.—Medicare, Medicaid, private insurance, uninsured populations—and to make recommendations for changes in Medicare payment systems under the ACA. The report (IOM, 2013) released Wennberg's core findings: geographic variations in spending are substantial, pervasive, and persistent over time; adjusting for individuals' age, sex, income, race, and health status modifies these variations, but substantial variations remain; and there is little or no correlation between spending and health care quality.

Quality of Health Care in the U.S.

Concerns have also been raised about the quality of health care in the U.S. (Leape, 2000; Mullan, 2001; Singer, 2000). The Commonwealth Fund study (Squires and Anderson, 2015) shows that, despite higher spending, the U.S. has poor population health as measured through several important determinants of health. In 1998 President Clinton's Commission on Consumer Protection and Quality in the Health Care Industry showed that both managed care and FFS medicine are "plagued" by overuse and underuse of services and "errors in health care practice." The prestigious IOM drew attention to these issues in two landmark studies, *To Err is Human: Building a Safer Health System* (Kohn et al., 2000) and *Crossing the Quality Chasm: A New Health System for the 21st Century* (Committee on Quality of Health Care in America, 2001).

Although some critics have claimed that the IOM exaggerated the scope of the problem, Wachter (2004) argued that the problems are deep-seated and rooted in archaic and outmoded beliefs and systems that "created a milieu in which patient safety was quite naturally ignored" (Wachter, 2004, p. W4–536). Although providers, institutions, and policymakers now take safety seriously, "there is still a long way to go" (Wachter, 2004, p. W4–534). Berwick (cited in Galvin, 2005), an author of *To Err is Human: Building a Safer Health System*, struck a similar note. Although welcoming increased awareness of the issue, he lamented that the "pace and improvement of care itself are still very disappointing" (Galvin, 2005, p. W5–1). Three years later, Wennberg et al. (2008, p. i) noted that the quality of our care "is inconsistent and often poor, rates of errors and other adverse events are unacceptably high, and costs are higher than anywhere else in the world." The challenge to establish high-quality health care in the U.S. that is "safe, effective, patient-centered, delivered on a timely basis, and devoid of disparities based on race or ethnicity" is "herculean" (Dentzer, 2011, pp. 554–555).

The most recent IOM report (2013) offered the following recommendations:

- More and better public and private health care data is needed and should be made available;

- Congress should not adopt a geographically based value index for Medicare payments because it "would unfairly reward low value providers in high-value regions and punish high-value providers in low-value regions" (p. xxv). (In 2010, Congressional members from regions with lower costs argued for a "Value Index" in Medicare that would reward low-spending regions with higher Medicare reimbursements, at the expense of high-spending regions, but the committee found that this would not provide the kind of incentives needed to reduce costs and improve quality);

- The Centers for Medicare & Medicaid Services (CMS) should continue to test new payment models that encourage clinical and financial integration;

- CMS should evaluate these new models as they are implemented so that improvements can be made to the models; and

- Congress should grant CMS the flexibility to accelerate the transition to value-based payment models that prove successful.

As a result, the CMS (2017) established four original value-based programs and several others, as well. The aim is to link quality measures of provider performance to provider payment. The following value-based payment models were scheduled for implementation, as follows:

- Hospital Value-Based Purchasing (HVBP) Program (2012);

- Hospital Readmission Reduction (HRR) Program (2012);

- Value Modifier (VM) Program (also called the Physician Value-Based Modifier or PVBM) (2015);

- Hospital Acquired Conditions (HAC) Program (2014);

- End-Stage Renal Disease (ESRD) Quality Initiative Program (2012);

- Skilled Nursing Facility Value-Based Program (SNFVBP) (2018);

- Home Health Value-Based Program (HHVBP) (2012).

Transitioning from provider reimbursement for "fee-for-service" care to "managed care" and most recently, to "value-based care" has brought changes and challenges to the provider market. Value-based care is discussed in Chapter 6, but first we need to introduce how we got to this point in our health care system, because the U.S. is unique in its approach to health care delivery and is still grappling with how best to achieve universal access and coverage.

THE ROLE OF PRIVATE INSURANCE

From the beginning, health care in the U.S. was organized on an individualistic and private basis. The earliest physicians were entrepreneurs who learned their craft by apprenticing with established physicians (Patel and Rushefsky, 1999). As medicine developed and became more professional, physicians remained committed to this individualistic approach and jealously guarded against encroachment from "private corporations" and "agencies of government" (Starr, 1982, p. 200). Physicians also strongly supported an FFS approach, which reimburses providers for each service (Patel and Rushefsky, 1999).

The result was what Dranove (2000) calls "Marcus Welby medicine" (*Marcus Welby*, MD TV series, 1969–1976). General practitioners working in individual offices dominated the health care system. Individuals visited the physician of their choice, who diagnosed the problem and prescribed a course of care (Dranove, 2000). The physician billed the patient directly for this treatment, based on the number of services provided. If a patient required hospital care, this was available as well. Although hospitals were generally independent institutions, "physicians held the strings to the hospital purse, since they influenced the patient's choice of facility" (Robinson, 1999, p. 20).

This system was reinforced by the insurance industry, which generally offered coverage on an indemnity basis. In exchange for a premium, individuals were reimbursed specific amounts for the cost of various services (Robinson, 1999). Blue Cross offered a slightly different arrangement, reimbursing physicians directly (Robinson, 1999). Regardless of the approach, insurers did not intervene between physician and patient and reimbursed physicians retrospectively, "on the basis of their usual charges" and the prevailing fee structure "in the community" (Robinson, 1999, p. 22).

Although this Marcus Welby model was the dominant one, there were exceptions. During the 1800s, fraternal organizations, unions, and some industrialists contracted with physicians to offer services on a prepaid basis to their members or employees (Friedman, 1996). During the 1930s, Henry J. Kaiser, a leading industrialist, began offering prepaid health care to his workers (Starr, 1982). "For the first time, workers' families were given full medical coverage, wives for seven cents a day and children for twenty-five cents a week" (Kotelchuck, 1976, p. 365). A decade later, Kaiser built ships for the war effort and again established clinics for his workers (Kotelchuck, 1976).

After the war, Kaiser opened his plan to the public, calling it the Kaiser-Permanente Plan; by 1969, Kaiser-Permanente had two and a half million subscribers (Kotelchuck, 1976). Kaiser-Permanente contracted with groups of physicians to offer services to its members, and owned the facilities in which these physicians worked; for this reason, Kaiser became known as a group-model health maintenance organization (HMO) (Davis et al., 1994).

Kaiser-Permanente was not the only type of prepaid group practice. During the early postwar years, a group of Seattle farmers and workers created the Group Health Cooperative of Puget Sound (GHCPS) (Starr, 1982). By the 1980s, GHCPS had grown to 320,000 members and was "run by a community board elected by its consumer members" (Rachlis and Kushner, 1989, p. 224). GHCPS was known as a staff-model HMO, because physicians were employees of the organization. The American Medical Association (AMA) strongly opposed prepaid group practices and went to great lengths to suppress them (Starr, 1982). In 1938, the federal government indicted the association and its affiliates for violating antitrust laws. Although the Supreme Court upheld these charges, the AMA succeeded in convincing state legislatures to enact laws hindering the development of prepaid group practices (Starr, 1982).

HEALTH CARE INFLATION (1970–80) AND HMOS

During the late 1960s, health care analysts and political leaders became concerned about a new phenomenon: health care inflation (Rolde, 1992). Inflation was not *completely* new, of course, "[b]ut what had been a steady rise during the 1950s and early 1960s took a sharp turn upward after 1966" (Kotelchuck, 1976, p. 17).

What caused this increase in health care costs? Much of the problem was related to the peculiar reimbursement structure adopted by Medicare. To ensure the bill's enactment, Lyndon Johnson made extraordinary concessions to the American Hospital Association. The administration not only agreed to reimburse hospitals retroactively, for their costs, but also agreed to allow them to include in these costs expenditures for new equipment and facilities (Starr, 1982, p. 375). Hospitals were also able to choose "fiscal intermediaries," in most cases Blue Cross, to oversee and regulate billing and payments (Starr, 1982): "Since the elderly are the medically neediest members of society and require the most invasive procedures, Medicare clients immediately constituted more than 75 percent of all hospitalized patients" (Garrett, 2000, p. 347). Hospital expenditures and incomes grew dramatically between 1966 and 1970 (Garrett, 2000).

Johnson also sought to placate physicians. The law itself explicitly prevented the government from exercising "any supervision or control" over "compensation" to institutions or individuals "providing health services" (Starr, 1986, p. 110). Instead, physicians were reimbursed on the basis of their "customary" fee structure and were even allowed to balance bills, or charge patients more than Medicare paid (Starr, 1986). In short, as Garrett (2000, p. 346) notes, Medicare effectively placed "hospitals and physicians, as well as Blue Cross, in the driver's seat of cost control."

Between 1966 and 1970, when the consumer price index increased by 19.1 percent, health care costs increased by 29.1 percent (Kotelchuck, 1976). Physicians' fees and hospital charges grew even more rapidly. In July 1969, President Richard Nixon warned that the nation faced "a breakdown in our medical system" (cited in Starr, 1982, p. 381). In an effort to bring costs under control, the Nixon administration turned to Paul Ellwood, a physician from Minnesota. Ellwood had long criticized the FFS system, which he believed promoted inefficiency and waste by encouraging doctors to provide too much care (Starr, 1982). Ellwood argued that the government should encourage new incentives through the development of prepaid group practices, which, in exchange for an annual fee, would provide "comprehensive" health care services to their members (Ellwood et al., 1976). These prepaid group practices, or HMOs, as Ellwood called them, would reward physicians for preventing illness and keeping "people healthy" (Ellwood et al., 1976, p. 348).

According to Friedman (1996), the "roots" of prepaid health care may lie in mutual aid societies created by immigrants during the 1800s. Later, mining companies, railroads, and other corporations also offered health care services to their workers on a prepaid basis (Friedman, 1996).

The AMA strongly opposed prepaid heath care, and the approach spread slowly. In 1929, in California, physicians, working through the Ross–Loos Clinic, began providing medical services to public employees in exchange for "a fixed monthly payment" (Dranove, 2000, p. 37). Prepaid plans also developed in Texas, Oklahoma, Wisconsin, and elsewhere (Starr, 1982). During the 1930s, Henry J. Kaiser organized perhaps the best-known prepaid health plan when he contracted with a physician named Sidney Garfield to provide health care to Kaiser's employees engaged in building the Grand Coulee Dam (Starr, 1982). During World War II, Kaiser hired "prepaid physicians to provide medical care in group practice settings" to 200,000 workers in his west coast shipyards (Dranove, 2000, p. 38). After the war, Kaiser's plan reopened as the Kaiser Foundation Health Plan and allowed members of the public to join. Prepaid health plans developed in other areas as well (Dranove, 2000).

With encouragement from Nixon and others, support for HMOs began to grow. Rothfeld (1976, p. 352) noted that in 1973 *Fortune* magazine observed, "HMOs have expanded and proliferated throughout the nation at an unprecedented rate." He estimated that, by "the mid-1980s," 50 million people might belong to HMOs and noted, "Blue Cross alone" hoped "to have 280 HMOs in operation by then" (Rothfeld, 1976, p. 353). In 1971, the Nixon administration created an office to distribute funds for the "planning and development" of HMOs (Rothfeld, 1976).

Nixon also redefined the nature of prepaid health care. In the traditional prepaid plans, physicians generally worked "exclusively" for the organization, either as salaried employees (GHCPS) or as part of a group such as Kaiser (Dranove, 2000). The term "health maintenance organization," however, referred not only to this type of plan, but also to independent practice associations, which reimbursed "independent physicians" on a FFS basis (Starr, 1982). In addition, the traditional prepaid plans were nonprofits. However, the Nixon administration encouraged the involvement of "banks, Wall Street investors," and other for-profit entities in the HMO business (Rothfeld, 1976, p. 354).

Congress enacted the HMO Act of 1973 to promote the development of HMOs (Kronenfeld and Whicker, 1984). The act overturned state laws restricting prepaid group practices, subsidized "HMO start-ups," and required businesses (with 25 or more workers) that provided coverage to their employees to offer an HMO option along with indemnity insurance (Robinson, 1999). The act also required federally assisted HMOs to offer comprehensive benefits, allow consumer input in governance, and charge no more than "traditional forms of health insurance" (Patel and Rushefsky, 1999, p. 173). The HMO Act was the opening volley in what Fuchs (1993) calls the "revolution in health care financing," a determined effort to root out inefficiency and waste in the health care system (Fuchs, 1993, p. 187).

Failed Efforts for National Health Insurance

The problem of health care inflation also renewed interest in national health insurance. In 1970, Senator Edward M. Kennedy (D-MA) and Representative Martha W. Griffiths (R-MI) introduced the Health Security plan, which resembled the Canadian system of socialized insurance. It included universal coverage and a national health care budget (also called a global budget) and promoted the development of prepaid group practices (Starr, 1982). The Kennedy–Griffiths bill enjoyed strong support from organized labor.

A year later, President Richard Nixon proposed legislation that allowed employers to contribute to the cost of insuring their workers and created a federal plan "to provide a less generous package of benefits for low-income families" (Starr, 1982, p. 397). Critics objected that Nixon's plan would reduce spending for Medicare and "still leave uninsured 20 to 40 million people who fell outside its two programs"

(Starr, 1982, p. 396). The AMA and other organizations also developed proposals to reform the health care system.

In 1974, Nixon introduced the Comprehensive Health Insurance Plan, which required employers to pay 65 percent of the cost of buying insurance for their workers (Kotelchuck, 1976). Individuals with low incomes and those without jobs would be eligible for subsidies from the government (Kotelchuck, 1976). The new proposal also offered a wider range of benefits than the earlier one. Critics argued that the new bill still burdened consumers with high copayments and deductibles, which discouraged "preventive care or early treatment," and would leave many older adults worse off than they were under Medicare (Kotelchuck, 1976, p. 461). In an effort to reach a compromise, Kennedy abandoned the Kennedy–Griffiths bill and, with Wilbur Mills, introduced a bill similar to Nixon's (Kotelchuck, 1976). Ultimately, these efforts all failed. With Nixon under fire for the Watergate scandal, liberals anticipated the election of a "veto-proof" Congress; they rejected Kennedy's compromise and a stalemate ensued (Starr, 1982).

National Health Insurance (NHI) surfaced again, a few years later, during the Carter administration. In September 1979, Senator Edward Kennedy (D-MA) and Representative Henry Waxman (D-CA) introduced the Health Care for All Americans Act, which relied on a variety of mechanisms to achieve universal coverage and control costs (Rolde, 1992). Carter supported less ambitious legislation, which provided catastrophic coverage with a high deductible to workers (Rolde, 1992). Senators Robert Dole (R-KS), John Danforth (R-MO), and Pete Domenici (R-NM) introduced a similar bill (Rolde, 1992). However, with Democrats fighting among themselves and conservatives strongly opposed to any legislation, these bills languished.

The election of Ronald Reagan in 1980 ended serious discussion of NHI. However, in 1988, Congress, with support from Reagan, enacted the Medicare Catastrophic Coverage Act, the "largest extension of health care benefits for Americans since Medicare and Medicaid" (Rolde, 1992, p. 40). The Catastrophic Coverage Act limited patients' responsibility for copayments under Medicare Part B (physician's coverage) and gradually introduced prescription drug coverage (Rice et al., 1990). To pay for the act, Congress set "a new precedent" by imposing a tax solely on older adults (Rice et al., 1990, p. 77). The burden of this tax fell on individuals with high incomes, many of whom already had coverage for benefits provided by the Act. This tax, along with the Act's failure to significantly expand long-term care coverage, provoked widespread criticism and led Congress to repeal it in 1989 (Rice et al., 1990).

The Rise of Health Maintenance Organizations

As mentioned earlier, health care inflation gave impetus to the development and spread of prepaid health care under President Nixon. In 1970, amid growing concern over health care inflation, officials of the Nixon administration began working with Paul Ellwood, Jr., a Minnesota physician and advocate of prepaid health care. They developed plans for a system of prepaid group practices, or "health maintenance organizations," as Ellwood called them (Starr, 1982, p. 395). The logic behind HMOs was simple. In exchange for a lump sum of money for each patient, physicians would assume responsibility for meeting the health care needs of these individuals. As the provider would "share the financial risk of ill health with the consumer . . . both would have an interest in maintaining health" (Ellwood et al., 1976, p. 351). It was expected that this would encourage providers to address prevention as well as treatment and lead to lower health care costs. HMOs thus seemed a foolproof, market-driven approach to reforming the health care system (Kotelchuck, 1976).

In February 1971, Nixon urged Congress to approve funding to create a network of HMOs, which would eventually cover most of the population (Starr, 1982). By now, HMOs had been discovered and endorsed by governors (including Ronald Reagan), business groups, labor unions, and the media (Starr, 1982). With federal assistance, the number of HMOs tripled between 1970 and 1973, and Congress, in an amendment to the Public Health Service Act, eventually enacted the Health Maintenance Act (P.L. 93–222) of 1973 (Patel and Rushefsky, 1999).

In addition to providing funds for the development of HMOs, the Act altered the definition of a prepaid group practice. Whereas the original prepaid group practices were nonprofit corporations, HMOs could be for-profit companies (Starr, 1982). Moreover, as Starr (1982) points out, the expression *HMO* "referred not only to prepaid group practice," but also to independent practice associations (IPAs), "which receive prepayments from subscribers and then reimburse independent physicians and hospitals on a fee basis" (Starr, 1982, p. 397). These changes were to have a dramatic impact on the development of the health care system (Mizrahi, 1995).

Regulatory Reform

The government also tried planning as a way of bringing costs under control. The assumption here was that there were too many "health care facilities and services—too many hospitals, too many hospital beds and too much medical equipment" (Patel and Rushefsky, 1999, p. 42). This surplus seemed to be fueling inflation. In 1966, Congress enacted the Comprehensive Health Planning Act to provide funds for communities and localities to create health-planning agencies (Patel and Rushefsky, 1999). Ultimately, these agencies failed to receive the support or funding they needed and the Act had little impact (Starr, 1982).

Six years later, Congress created the Professional Standards Review Organization (PSRO), which required local physicians to review the decisions and practice patterns of colleagues in hospitals and nursing homes: "If PSROs denied payment for inappropriate care, the hospitals would lose reimbursement, even though a doctor authorized the treatment" (Starr, 1982, p. 402). The Reagan administration reduced funding for PSROs and narrowed their scope (Patel and Rushefsky, 1999).

In 1974, Congress combined the Comprehensive Health Planning Act, Hill–Burton, and other programs, and enacted the National Health Planning and Resources Development Act (McKinney, 1995). This legislation required the states to enact certificate-of-need laws by 1980: "Certificate-of-need laws require hospitals to document 'community need' to obtain approval for major capital expenditures for expansion of physical plants, equipment, and services" (Patel and Rushefsky, 1999, p. 169). These efforts had minimal impact on health care inflation (Patel and Rushefsky, 1999).

During the late 1970s, regulation and planning fell into disrepute, and market-oriented solutions became the order of the day (McKinney, 1995). Under the Omnibus Budget Reconciliation Act of 1981 (PL 97-35), funding for planning was cut and states were allowed to dismantle health-planning agencies. Not surprisingly, the Reagan and Bush administrations made little effort to support health planning (McKinney, 1995).

DIAGNOSIS-RELATED GROUPS

Despite its opposition to regulation, the Reagan administration altered the means by which Medicare reimbursed hospitals by introducing a new Prospective Payment System (PPS) in the early 1980s. The U.S. Department of Health and Human Services divided medical conditions into 468 diagnosis-related groups (DRGs) and calculated a reimbursement rate for each (Patel and Rushefsky, 1999). As a result, hospitals knew in advance, that is prospectively, how much they would receive for specific admissions. If a hospital treated a patient for less than its DRG reimbursement, it could keep the extra money (Garrett, 2000). To ensure that standards were not lowered, Peer Review Organizations (the old PSROs) were placed in charge of "monitoring the quality and appropriateness of care for Medicare patients" (Patel and Rushefsky, 1999, p. 176).

The impact of the PPS has been mixed. The system seems to have slowed the rate of increase in hospital costs through fewer admissions, lower occupancy rates, and shorter lengths of stay (Patel and Rushefsky, 1999). However, hospitals in rural and inner-city areas and public hospitals have faced difficulties under the PPS (Garrett, 2000). Previously, these institutions were able to bill Medicare for the cost of treating poor and uninsured people. The PPS made this type of cost shifting impossible, and many hospitals curtailed uncompensated care or closed their doors. In contrast, "hospitals located in areas rife with wealthy Medicare patients . . . turned large profits and drove up the overall costs of medical care in America" (Garrett, 2000, p. 387). Reinhardt (1996) suggests that the DRGs and other practices that encourage the transfer of patients from hospitals to subacute facilities and home care may actually increase "total national health spending" (Reinhardt, 1996, p. 152).

FROM HMOS TO MANAGED CARE (1980–90)

Despite the HMO Act of 1973, HMOs grew slowly, and through the 1970s they were confined largely to the west coast and Minnesota (Dranove, 2000). Toward the end of the decade, Luft (1978) published data showing that traditional HMOs, such as Kaiser, were less expensive than FFS medicine. In a review of the literature, HMOs had premium and out-of-pocket costs that were 10–40 percent lower than other types of coverage. Much of this difference was due to hospitalization rates, which were about a third lower for individuals in HMOs (Luft, 1978). Although other studies confirmed Luft's findings, it remained unclear whether the HMOs' advantage was due to greater efficiency, reduced quality, or healthier populations (Dranove, 2000).

The same year in which Luft's study appeared, Alain Enthoven, a Stanford professor and an official in the Carter administration, proposed a new HMO strategy, the Consumer Choice Health Plan (CCHP) (Enthoven, 1978). The CCHP was based in part on the Federal Employees Health Benefits Program (FEHBP), which covers most federal employees (Enthoven, 1993). Under the FEHBP, workers choose from a menu of "competing health plans," and the government pays a "fixed" share of the premium cost (Robinson, 1999, p. 40). An individual who selects an inexpensive plan thus pays less than someone who selects a more expensive plan. Under the CCHP, employers paid a share of the premium cost. Enthoven assumed that, given a choice, workers would prefer low-cost HMOs to more expensive indemnity coverage (Robinson, 1999). Although versions of the CCHP were introduced in Congress, they were unsuccessful (Patel and Rushefsky, 1999).

The "competition revolution," and the move away from open-ended financing, accelerated during the 1980s, as health care costs continued to grow (Fuchs, 1993). In 1982, Congress enacted the Tax Equity and Fiscal Responsibility Act (TEFRA), which made changes in Medicare that resulted a year later in the introduction of the Medicare PPS (Patel and Rushefsky, 1999). The PPS created a fee schedule so that hospitals knew in advance precisely how much Medicare would reimburse them (Patel and Rushefsky, 1999). The TEFRA also allowed HMOs to enroll Medicare beneficiaries, although a great number of older adults continued to prefer the traditional, FFS Medicare.

It was also during the 1980s that preferred provider organizations (PPOs) developed (Dranove, 2000). PPOs consist of networks of providers who remain in private practice and receive payment on an FFS basis, though often at discounted rates (Dranove, 2000). A consumer obtaining care from providers within the network, that is from preferred providers, owes only a small copayment; a consumer who obtains care outside the network must pay a higher amount. As "preferred providers" are guaranteed a steady stream of patients, they have an incentive to reduce their fees (Dranove, 2000).

In the beginning, PPOs were hindered by state laws making it illegal for insurers to refuse to negotiate agreements with "any willing provider" (Dranove, 2000). If insurers were unable to discriminate among physicians, they would also be unable to "boost volumes" for preferred providers. Providers would then have no incentive to charge less or change their practice patterns. With California leading the way, the states began changing their laws "to permit selective contracting by insurers" (Dranove, 2000, p. 70). Large employers also began self-insuring, or creating their own health care plans, which under federal law are exempt from state regulation (Dranove, 2000).

By the mid-1980s, the concept of managed care had emerged to refer to a range of efforts to control costs. According to Dranove (2000) managed care, ultimately, relies on three techniques: Selective contracting, innovative incentives, and utilization review (UR). With selective contracting, insurers enter agreements with providers offering the lowest prices, forcing providers to compete among themselves, to the benefit of insurers and, in theory, consumers. By innovative incentives, Dranove (2000) means the new forms of reimbursement introduced by prepaid health care. In staff-model HMOs, providers receive a salary and have no incentive to overtreat patients. Under capitated systems, providers receive a flat sum (and no more) for each patient, and there is an incentive to undertreat patients. This is a far cry from the FFS system. Finally, UR refers to techniques aimed at reducing unwarranted care, such as "preadmission screening, to determine if the patient should enter the hospital or receive treatment elsewhere" and "surgical second opinion programs" (Dranove, 2000, p. 81).

FROM MANAGED CARE TO MANAGED COMPETITION (1990–95)

Despite the rise of managed care, health care inflation continued to accelerate. By 1990, national health expenditures equaled 12.1 percent of GDP, up from 8.9 percent in 1980 (Levit et al., 1996). At the same time, 33.4 million people had no coverage for the year, and tens of millions more had limited or inadequate coverage (Lee et al., 1994). These were clearly related. As health care costs grew, many employers stopped covering their workers or shifted the burden by increasing employees' share of the premium cost and copayments and deductibles (Roberts and Clyde, 1993). Rising health care costs also contributed to the stagnation of wages during the 1980s, as employers sought to make up ground by paying workers less (White House Domestic Policy Council, 1993). This made it even more difficult for workers to afford health care coverage.

During the early 1990s, Enthoven, Ellwood, and others began to advocate an influential plan they called "managed competition" (Iglehart, 1994). Managed competition would transform the health care system into an "array of managed care plans," which would compete for patients based on cost and quality (Enthoven and Kronick, 1994, p. 286). This new system would be regulated by "quasi-public" agencies, which would promote competition and certify plans offering a minimum benefit package (Enthoven and Kronick, 1994). Employers would contribute 80 percent of the cost of insuring their workers in an average plan, with employees contributing the other 20 percent, and the government would cover individuals without jobs.

In the final analysis, the success or failure of managed competition, as the new approach was called, hinged on whether managed care could actually control costs. Enthoven (1993) believed it could, citing studies showing that "Group Health Cooperative of Puget Sound cared for its randomly assigned patients for a cost 28 percent below that for comparable patients assigned to a fee-for-service plan" (Enthoven, 1993, p. 37).

The data was not clear cut, however. The Congressional Research Service (CRS) found that staff- and group-model HMOs were only about 15 percent cheaper than indemnity plans, and suggested that this difference was largely due to one-time savings from lower hospital costs (CRS Issue Brief, 1993). The CRS also reported that independent practice associations (IPAs), PPOs, and other forms of managed care achieved "much smaller savings" than traditional prepaid plans (CRS Issue Brief, 1993, p. 11).

Critics of managed competition argued that managed care organizations (MCOs) faced the same "cost pressures as other insurers" (CRS Issue Brief, 1993, p. 11). Newhouse (1993) contended that the public was less concerned with the "level" of health care spending than with its "rate of growth" (Newhouse, 1993, p. 155). Since the 1940s, "real health spending" has risen by "roughly 4 percent per year in each decade" except for the 1960s, when it rose by 6 percent per year (Newhouse, 1993, p. 155). Newhouse (1993) attributed "the bulk of the cost increase" to "technological advances," which explained why HMOs and FFS costs were "rising at a similar rate" despite lower *levels* of spending among staff- and group-model HMOs (Newhouse, 1993, p. 162).

These concerns were generally disregarded, however, and managed competition was widely heralded as the solution to the nation's health care problems (Iglehart, 1994). President George Bush "included elements" of managed competition in his proposal for health care reform, and the Conservative Democratic Forum developed a managed competition plan, which was introduced in Congress as the Cooper bill (H.R. 5936) (CRS Issue Brief, 1993). California's insurance commissioner, John Garamendi, also developed a managed competition proposal (CRS Issue Brief, 1993).

President Bill Clinton incorporated elements of managed competition in his Health Security Act (HSA). However, there were crucial differences between Clinton's approach and the Enthoven/Jackson Hole version of managed competition (Starr and Zelman, 1993). To control costs, Clinton proposed competition, managed care, and, as a "backstop," a limit on the rate of growth of insurance premiums (Zelman, 1994). Enthoven was highly critical of these premium caps and believed they would doom Clinton's plan to failure (Enthoven and Singer, 1994). He characterized the HSA as "a single-payer system in Jackson Hole clothing," which relied on "the heavy hand of government control," rather than the market, "to control costs" (Enthoven and Singer, 1994, p. 81).

By the mid-1990s, health care inflation seemed to have moderated (Huskamp and Newhouse, 1994): "Spending in the year 2000 will be approximately $300 billion below projections made by the Congressional Budget Office in 1993" (Dranove, 2000, p. 84). Many analysts believe that managed care played an essential role in this development (Dranove, 2000). The Congressional Budget Office (1997) concluded that the rise of managed care and the growth of competition had "caused premiums for all types of health plans, including fee-for-service ones, to increase more slowly" (CBO, 1997, p. 19). Cutler and Sheiner (1997) found that as HMO enrollment in an area increased, health care inflation decreased (largely because of reduced growth in health care costs); the growth of HMOs also tended to reduce spending on new technology.

Again, however, the evidence was mixed (Sullivan, 2000). Although managed care has reduced some waste and inefficiency, it cannot go beyond these "easy savings," in large part because managed care organizations (MCOs), as "private, often for-profit, entities," lack the "political legitimacy" to curtail "beneficial care"

(Aaron, 2002, p. W86). Chernew et al. (2004) conclude that, because the introduction of technology is primarily driven by physicians' desire to achieve "improved outcomes" for patients, managed care is unlikely to "stem the rising share of GDP devoted to health care" (Chernew et al., 2004, p. 122).

Even if MCOs do reduce costs, it is not clear why. Critics have long argued that MCOs can attract younger and healthier people than FFS medicine (Dranove, 2000). Altman et al. (2000) found that, compared with indemnity plans, HMOs' lower costs were due to healthier patients and their ability "to pay lower prices for the same treatment." Glied (1999), in a review of the literature, also concluded that MCOs tend to enroll healthier individuals than does "conventional insurance."

MANAGED-CARE BACKLASH (1995–2005) AND PATIENTS' RIGHTS

As scholars and politicians debated the merits of managed competition, managed care became the dominant force in the nation's health care system. By 1995, 73 percent of workers receiving coverage through an employer belonged to managed-care plans; 38 percent of these individuals belonged to HMOs, 34 percent to PPOs, and 27 percent to point-of-service plans (Jensen et al., 1997). Physicians' participation in managed care also increased. Between 1988 and 1997, the fraction of physicians in practices with managed-care contracts grew from 61 percent to 92 percent (Kaiser Family Foundation, 1998).

The nature of managed care also changed. Although the original MCOs were nonprofits, during the 1990s the fastest-growing MCOs were for-profit companies (Gabel, 1997). By 1997, 63 percent of HMO enrollees belonged to for-profit plans, up from 46 percent in 1989 (Kaiser Family Foundation, 1998). The Kaiser Family Foundation (1998, p. 68) noted that the "stock market" played "an increasing role in the health industry, and investors' goals to maximize shareholder value have an increased role in driving health care companies' decision-making."

As managed care spread, observers began to express concern about its impact on the quality of care (Eckholm, 1994; Kassirer, 1995). Kane et al. (1996), in case studies of IPAs and network-model HMOs in Boston, Los Angeles, and Philadelphia, found little connection between a plan's "market success" and the "quality of care" it "provided" (Kane et al., 1996, p. ii). Similarly, Gabel (1997), in a discussion of changes in HMOs during the 1990s, observed that the "market" did not seem to penalize plans that failed to "deliver above-average quality of care" (Gabel, 1997, p. 143). Feldman and Scharfstein (1998) also concluded that MCOs might offer poorer-quality care than FFS plans.

Miller and Luft (1997), in a survey of peer-reviewed studies of managed care published between 1993 and 1997, found that HMOs did not necessarily deliver worse care than FFS plans and in some instances provided better care. However, three studies found that HMOs deliver significantly worse care to "patients with chronic conditions or diseases who need care the most" (Miller and Luft, 1997, p. 14). In a sense, these findings were not surprising, because "plans and providers face strong financial disincentives to excel in care for the sickest and most expensive patients" (Miller and Luft, 1997, p. 20). This argument, of course, lends credence to those who argue that managed care primarily reduces costs by treating only the healthiest patients.

A 1999 survey of physicians and nurses provides additional insight into the question of quality (Kaiser Family Foundation, 1999). Eighty-seven percent of physicians had patients who were refused coverage of "some type" during the previous two years. In more than a third of these cases, according to the physicians, the denials had caused a "serious decline" in a patient's health. Forty-six percent of doctors said that, if a friend or relative were a patient, they would be "very worried" that an MCO would care more "about saving money" than providing the right treatment. Seventy-two percent of physicians and 78 percent of nurses felt managed care had lowered quality of care (Kaiser Family Foundation, 1999).

Consumers also expressed concern about managed care (Davis et al., 1996; Ginsburg, 1998). In a 1997 survey, Blendon et al. (1998) found that 45 percent of the population believed managed care had "decreased" quality of care and 52 percent supported government regulation of MCOs. This "backlash" was based not only on media coverage, but also on individuals' personal experiences with managed care (Blendon et al., 1998).

In response to these concerns, President Clinton appointed an Advisory Commission on Consumer Protection and Quality in the Health Care Industry in March 1997. After extensive hearings, the commission released a report identifying the rights and responsibilities of consumers. These included the right to an adequate choice of provider and to access to emergency care "when and where the need arises" (President's Advisory Commission on Consumer Protection and Quality in the Health Care Industry, 1997, p. 3 – see www.consumersresearchcncl. org/advisory.htm).

The report also asserted that patients had a right to "fully participate" in "decisions related to their health care" (President's Advisory Commission on Consumer Protection and Quality in the Health Care Industry, 1997, p. 39 – see www.consumers researchcncl.org/advisory.htm). This was aimed at financial and contractual arrangements that thwarted communication between physicians and patients. The most publicized of these arrangements were the "gag rules," which prevented physicians in HMOs from making patients aware of all treatment options.

The most controversial section of the report dealt with complaints and appeals. It stated that patients had a right to "a rigorous system of internal review and an independent system of external review" (President's Advisory Commission on Consumer Protection and Quality in the Health Care Industry, 1997, p. 57 – see www.consumersresearchcncl.org/advisory.htm). Although most health plans had internal review systems, independent, external review systems were relatively rare.

In response to Clinton's effort, Democrats and Republicans, at times on a bipartisan basis, introduced "patients' bill of rights legislation" (Patel and Rushefsky, 1999). The ultimate point of disagreement was over the right to sue, which Democrats generally supported and Republicans opposed. In 2001, the U.S. Senate enacted the Bipartisan Patient Protection Act of 2001, which allowed "patients to seek redress in court for any wrong that causes an injury" (National Association of Social Workers [NASW], 2001). The House of Representatives enacted a weaker bill, which many advocacy groups, including NASW, opposed. Negotiators failed to reconcile these differences and could not send a bill to the president for signature. In the spring of 2005, representative John Dingell (D-MI) introduced another patients' bill of rights, which gives individuals the right to hold HMOs accountable if negligent medical decisions result in injury or harm (U.S. House of Representatives, 2005a).

The states also passed legislation protecting consumers; however, as Families USA (1998) noted, these laws lacked uniformity and were enacted on a "hit or miss" basis. In any event, the states have only limited ability to control managed care organizations. In 1974, Congress enacted the Employee Retirement Income Security Act (ERISA), which prevents states from regulating self-insured health plans, in which an employer "assumes . . . financial risk for the care provided to its employees" (Families USA, 1998, p. 27). Due to ERISA, in 1998, a third of individuals with employer-based coverage were not protected by state regulations (Families USA, 1998). ERISA also prevents almost anyone with employer-based coverage from suing in state courts for "improper delays or denials of needed care" (Families USA, 1998, p. 27). Individuals can sue in federal court, but only to seek "provision of the denied service or the cost of the denied service," not for "compensatory or punitive damages" (Families USA, 1998, p. 28). In 2004, in a unanimous decision, the Supreme Court ruled that ERISA prevents individuals in employer-based plans from suing managed-care companies for punitive damages (*AETNA Health Care, FKA, AETNA US Healthcare Inc. et al. v. Davila*, 2003).

MANAGED BEHAVIORAL HEALTH CARE (1990–2010)

Managed care has also been used in behavioral health care and, under the ACA, mental health services have been a required part of health insurance coverage. Managed behavioral health care (MBHC) developed in response to the rapid growth of mental health and substance abuse services during the 1970s and 1980s (Freeman and Trabin, 1994; Boyle and Callahan, 1995). By 1999, almost four out of five (78 percent) individuals with health insurance, including those in public plans, belonged to an MBHC plan (Findlay, 1999). This industry became particularly concentrated during the 1990s. In 1999, 15 companies cumulatively controlled almost 89 percent of the market, and the top 2 companies had a cumulative share of almost 50 percent, which amounted to 86.3 million individuals (Findlay, 1999).

MBHC has taken several forms. Some plans included case management and utilization review services, in which MBHC companies monitored the use of services; some plans were employee assistance plans (EAPs) (Findlay, 1999). A smaller number of beneficiaries belonged to plans that "provide an integrated behavioral health and EAP benefit" (Findlay, 1999, p. 119). Many MBHC enrollees have belonged to what are referred to as "carve-out" plans (Findlay, 1999), which are "devoted exclusively to mental health and chemical dependency issues" (Freeman and Trabin, 1994, p. 3). In exchange for a negotiated payment, carve-outs oversee the behavioral health care and treatment of a defined population. The employer determines the specific benefit package. Findlay (1999) found that some carve-outs were "risk based", in which the plan assumed financial responsibility for treatment (Findlay, 1999). Others were "non-risk-based" (or administrative-services-only) plans, whereby employers contracted with MBHC companies but "retain[ed] full insurance risk" (Findlay, 1999, p. 118). In addition, millions belonged to "carve-in" plans, which offer a range of health care services, including behavioral health care (Findlay, 1999).

Carve-out plans rely on many of the same techniques as other MCOs to control costs, including utilization review, gatekeeping, and case management (NASW, 1994). Carve-outs can limit the availability of services, impose copayments, and determine payments to providers (Frank et al., 1995). Capitation is another powerful means of reducing costs (Freeman and Trabin, 1994, p. 27).

Carve-out plans have discretion over the type of providers and arrangements used for service delivery (Frank et al., 1995; Vandivort-Warren, 1998). Freeman and Trabin (1994) identified three types of delivery: One is the "network model," which consists of groups of individual practitioners from a range of disciplines, including psychiatrists, psychologists, social workers, and mental health counselors. As a condition of inclusion, providers agree to lower their prices, utilize "managed care procedures," and adhere to "cost-effective approaches to treatment" (Freeman and Trabin, 1994, p. 4). A second type is the traditional staff model, in which clinicians serve as salaried employees; this approach, of course, raises concerns about treatment (Freeman and Trabin, 1994). A third type is the "hybrid model," which combines "groups and clinics" with "networks of independent providers" (Freeman and Trabin, 1994, p. 4).

Carve-out plans have had to address the issue of access, a particular problem in the area of behavioral health. In the late 1990s, Surgeon General David Satcher noted that, although every year mental and behavioral disorders affect a fifth of the population, they still are "spoken of in whispers and shame" (U.S. Department of Health and Human Services, 1999, p. vi). Due to this negative connotation or stigma, many people are reluctant to seek help for behavioral health problems (Freeman and Trabin, 1994). Some individuals are also emotionally and psychologically unable to find assistance, and others may seek help from practitioners who are "unable to respond to their needs" (Freeman and Trabin, 1994, p. 26). To address these problems and facilitate access, carve-out plans have taken a number of steps, including offering free, 24-hour phone lines to link "prospective" patients with practitioners and reducing required copayments (Freeman and Trabin, 1994). They have also introduced "telephonic warm lines for counseling and consultation" and other "innovations" aimed at integrating the "delivery system" with the lives and everyday needs of patients (Freeman and Trabin, 1994, p. 26).

States also experimented with behavioral health carve-out plans for Medicaid beneficiaries. Massachusetts pioneered this approach by creating a mental health and substance abuse carve-out in 1992 (Callahan et al., 1995). By 1998, 15 states had adopted Medicaid MBHC carve-outs for mental health care (U.S. Department of Health and Human Services, 1999). In some states, the carve-outs have organized provider networks, provide payments, and engage in utilization review; in others, the state has assumed responsibility for utilization (U.S. Department of Health and Human Services, 1999). However, since about 2010, in an effort to integrate behavioral health, physical health, and pharmaceutical care, several states have ended their Medicaid behavioral health carve-out programs, and instead have identified ways to manage all services under one umbrella, typically an MCO (Mandros, 2015).

Parity

The spread of MBHC also sparked debate about mental health parity. In 1996, Congress enacted the first Mental Health Parity Act, preventing employers "from imposing annual or lifetime dollar limits on mental health coverage that are more restrictive than those imposed on medical and surgical coverage" (U.S. General Accounting Office, 2000, p. 3). However, this act expired in September 2001; Congress passed a temporary extension until December 31, 2002. Although President Bush's Commission on Mental Health endorsed parity in 2003, Congress did not act on this legislation until October 2008, and for the first time coverage for mental health services equal to benefits for physical health was mandated with the passage of the Mental Health Parity and Addiction Equity Act (MHPAEA) of 2008. However, MHPAEA applied to employer-based private insurance offered by firms with 50 or more employees only, and it has taken the federal government many years to take action on implementing regulations to govern this practice, which has created confusion over what employers must cover (Domenici and Smith, 2012).

Questions have been raised about the meaning of parity under managed care. Mechanic and McAlpine (1999) suggest that, under managed care, which in essence rations health care, parity may work against individuals with serious mental illness, who often require more intense care than patients with other conditions. Others contend that parity should be seen as a necessary step toward a broader goal of *equity* (Burnam and Escarce, 1999; Hennessy and Goldman, 2001). Equity occurs when an individual with "a mental health problem" has the same likelihood of receiving care as an individual with a nonbehavioral health problem (Burnam and Escarce, 1999). In response, Gitterman et al. (2001, p. 73) argue that efforts for equity may undermine real steps toward "full parity in benefits." They suggest that equity matters less to patients than to providers, who see it as a way to oppose carve-outs, which have made parity possible, while lowering psychiatrists' incomes (Gitterman et al., 2001).

Clinical Practice

MBHC has brought both challenges and opportunities to mental health providers. For example, Vandivort-Warren (1998) points out that before managed care was introduced clinical social workers were regularly excluded from FFS reimbursement mechanisms. Behavioral health MCOs, on the other hand, have included social workers as approved providers in their networks of independent providers. At the same time, reimbursement rates for social workers and other mental health providers have declined, and the demands for record keeping and billing have increased.

MBHC has brought other challenges as well. Some provider networks exclude social workers, and even those that include them reject many practitioners because they lack the requisite skills or training or the network has filled its social work positions (Jackson, 1994). MCOs have also found it more efficient to develop relationships with "group practices rather than solo practitioners" (Jackson, 1994. p. 4). In addition, because referrals no longer come through colleagues or clients, social workers must develop ties with primary care physicians, case managers, and other "gatekeepers" (Jackson, 1994).

MBHC has also "placed in question" the "long-held" belief that, as Siskind (1998, p. 182) puts it: *"[m]ore treatment is better than less treatment"* (emphasis in original). Managed care has shifted practitioners' focus toward "short-term therapies," which have more specific goals and require less time, and thus less expense, than "long-term therapy" (Dziegielewski et al., 1998, pp. 288–289). This is not necessarily negative. Numerous studies have demonstrated the efficacy of many types of short-term therapy. As a result, "[t]he use of time-limited treatment, mutually negotiated goals and objectives, empirically based treatment, and careful clinical assessments taken before and during treatment are becoming part of responsible mental health practice" (Dziegielewski et al., 1998, p. 302).

Managed behavioral care has also placed new demands on schools of social work and clinical social workers over the past two decades. The *NASW Code of Ethics* (NASW, 1996) states that, although social workers' "primary" obligation is to their clients, they are also bound by "commitments" made to their employer. This raises the question of "divided" loyalty (Reamer, 1998). What should practitioners do if they believe clients "require greater assistance than managed care will authorize" (Reamer, 1998, p. 295)? What if their employer requires them to expose "clients to possible privacy and confidentiality invasions" (Reamer, 1998, p. 295)? These and related dilemmas raise ethical questions that practitioners and schools of social work have had to address (Corcoran and Vandiver, 1996; Reamer, 1998).

THE ACA AND COST CONTROLS (2010–16)

The cost of health care has certainly been a central factor in the debate over health care reform in the U.S. Orszag and Emanuel (2010), administration officials who played key roles in the effort to enact the ACA, noted that the bill incorporated several widely discussed proposals to control the growth of health care inflation. These included a tax on overly generous health plans, the elimination of "unjustified subsidies to Medicare Advantage plans," and an expansion of electronic record keeping. The ACA also promoted "enhanced horizontal cooperation among providers" through the creation of medical homes and accountable health care organizations, and introduced mechanisms for supplying providers and patients with "new information regarding the effectiveness of various medical technologies and interventions." In essence, the ACA attempted to address almost every aspect of the country's inflationary health care system by controlling both consumer and industry costs, including cost-controlling measures that affect all consumers, hospitals, prescription drug manufacturers, medical device makers, public and private health insurance providers, and more.

Perhaps the critical "institutional change in the ACA" was the creation of an Independent Payment Advisory Board (IPAB), designed to advise Congress on ways of reducing the growth of Medicare's costs when they "exceed a certain threshold" (Orszag and Emanuel, 2010). The IPAB's proposals would become law unless "Congress enact[ed] alternative policies leading to equivalent savings." Referring to the IPAB as "Congress's 'Good Deed,'" Aaron (2011, p. 2378) noted that the ACA incorporated "a broad and potentially powerful portfolio of cost-control instruments". When it became clear which of these mechanisms work[ed] best and how best to implement them, the IPAB would use the "power" of Medicare, the nation's "largest health care buyer to effect system change."

The IPAB was scheduled to be operational in 2013, but President Obama did not fill the board's 15 seats. As Medicare spending rates have not risen much and have not needed to be reduced, there has been no trigger for the IPAB to need to take action (Capretta, 2016). (For 2013–17, the IPAB-targeted growth rate for Medicare was the average of the consumer price index for all products and services and the consumer price index for medical care. After 2017, the IPAB's targeted growth rate for Medicare was the aggregate GDP growth rate plus 1 percentage point. However, the IPAB is constrained in its recommendations for reaching its targets because whatever they recommend cannot increase beneficiary premiums or cost sharing, reduce benefits, or increase taxes.)

The CBO has consistently found that the ACA will reduce, rather than, as critics have alleged, expand, the nation's budget deficit. In a July 2012 letter to Speaker John Boehner, the CBO (2012) estimated that, between 2013 and 2022, a bill to repeal the ACA would *increase* the deficit by $109 billion. In 2013, MedPAC (Medicare Payment Advisory Commission, 2013), the independent commission appointed by Congress to advise it on Medicare payment policies, reported that due largely to the ACA, the growth "in Medicare spending over the next 10 years is projected to be much smaller than in the past 10 years," despite the increasing number of beneficiaries due to the aging of the baby boomers (MedPAC, 2013, p. xii).

More recent studies reach the same findings. The Restoring Americans' Healthcare Freedom Reconciliation Act of 2015 was introduced by Republicans in Congress to repeal portions of the ACA by first eliminating the law's mandate penalties and subsidies, but leaving the ACA's insurance market reforms in place. Two years after enactment, the bill would also eliminate the ACA's expansion of Medicaid eligibility and the government subsidies for those who purchase insurance through the health marketplace established by the ACA.

The CBO (2017) found that the number of uninsured would increase by 18 million in the first year of the new plan; after eliminating the Medicaid expansion eligibility and subsidies for insurance purchase, that number would increase to 27 million, and then to 32 million in 2026. Premiums for individual policies purchased through the marketplaces or directly from insurers would increase by 20–25 percent in the first year of the new plan, and reach an increase of approximately 50 percent once Medicaid expansion and the marketplace subsidies were eliminated; insurance premiums would about double by 2026. Once again, the CBO has made the case that the ACA has had a positive impact on reducing the nation's health care spending and budget deficit.

Despite this, it is unclear whether in the long run the ACA, if it remained intact, could truly bring health care costs under control (Marmor and Oberlander, 2012). Berenson et al. (2004) expressed concern about clout from the ACA to keep providers from driving up premiums and offseting other reforms put in place to lower premiums. On the other hand, Mahar (2010) points out that the new initiatives make it more difficult for insurance companies to pass along hospital overcharges to consumers, which could encourage them to pressure hospitals to keep costs down. These reforms could also encourage states to take a closer look at variations in hospital rates found in different regions of their states (Mahar, 2010). Berenson et al. (2004) argued that additional legislation may be needed to regulate private sector rates. Marmor and Oberlander (2012) argued that the U.S. would do well to look at strategies used in other countries, such as "global budgets, fee schedules, system wide payment rules, and concentrated purchasing" to reduce spending because they "have the advantage of working" (Marmor and Oberlander, 2012, p. 12).

THE ACA, COSTS, AND THE TRUMP ADMINISTRATION (2017)

The Secretary of Health and Human Services, Tom Price, who was appointed by the Trump administration and forced to resign in September 2017, was a major proponent of "repealing and replacing" the ACA, eliminating the ACA's expansion of Medicaid, and removing the mandate to purchase individual insurance. He was philosophically opposed to the shift to value-based methods of payment for providers and supports the old FFS model. As noted by Kilgore (2016):

> Until now there was not much question the "quality revolution" in health-care policy would continue no matter which party controlled Washington: Other than simple denial of care, getting more "bang for the buck" has made sense to Republicans as well as Democrats, regardless of their differences in the role they assign to markets or governments in promoting better-quality health care at lower costs.

Although the Trump administration and Republican-controlled Congress have failed to "repeal and replace" the ACA, the elimination of the penalty for the individual mandate, which was passed in the 2017 tax reform bill, will have an impact on spending and cost. The Rand Corporation (Saltzman and Eibner, 2015) found that the federal government would face higher costs without the penalty in place. Not only would it lose tax revenue from the mandate, it would also need to subsidize a more expensive population who are older and less healthy.

HIGHLIGHTS

- The U.S. has the most expensive health care system in the world. In 2013, per capita health care spending in the U.S. was $9086 compared with $4361 in France, the second highest-spending country (Squires and Anderson, 2015). The U.S. figure represents more than 17 percent of its gross domestic product (GDP), which is far higher than the percentage of GDP spent on health care in any of the other 33 countries in the Organisation for Economic Co-operation and Development (OECD), including the wealthiest nations, such as Norway. The primary cause is higher prices for pharmaceuticals, hospital stays, and physician services than those found in other countries.

- Although the U.S. spends far more per capita than other countries, this does not alleviate concerns about the overall quality of care in the system. Both overuse and underuse of services and errors in health care practice raise concerns about quality in the delivery of care.

- Health care inflation in the 1970s and 1980s exacerbated the problem of health insurance coverage and briefly renewed national interest in universal health insurance. However, none of these was really taken seriously by Congress. Instead, regulatory reforms, such as certificate-of-need laws and a Prospective Payment System for Medicare reimbursement to hospitals, were introduced. Health maintenance organizations (HMOs) also emerged, supported by the Health Maintenance Act of 1973. These reforms did little to reduce the nation's growing health care costs.

- By the mid-1980s, managed care became the primary method of controlling costs. Managed-care techniques focused on selective contracting, innovative incentives, and utilization review. With selective contracting, insurers enter into agreements with providers that offer the lowest prices, forcing providers to compete among themselves, to the benefit of insurers and, in theory, consumers. Innovative incentives refer to new forms of reimbursement introduced by prepaid health care, such as a flat payment for each patient, in an effort to reduce the overtreatment of patients. Utilization review techniques were introduced to help reduce unwarranted care. Despite these measures and the growth of managed care throughout the health care system, including behavioral health, health care inflation continued to accelerate. By 1990, national health expenditures equaled 12.1 percent of GDP, up from 8.9 percent in 1980 and led to a managed-care backlash in the 1990s.

- The next round of efforts to control costs includes bundled payments, value-based purchasing, patient-centered medical homes, and accountable care organizations (ACOs) organized through the Centers for Medicare and Medicaid Services (CMS). These strategies stem from the Affordable Care Act and recent private sector initiatives. The potential to reduce spending through these measures is unclear and unknown. In the end, it may not prove sufficient, just as managed care has done little to impact overall spending.

- Those who support more dramatic reforms suggest that the U.S. would do well to look at strategies used successfully in other countries to reduce spending while still maintaining equal or better population health outcomes.

REFERENCED LEGAL CASES

AETNA Health Care, FKA, AETNA US Healthcare Inc. et al. v. Davila. (2003, October Term). Supreme Court of the United States. Retrieved from www.supremecourtus.gov/opinions/03pdf/02-1845.pdf

REFERENCES

Aaron, H. J. (2002, January 8). The Unsurprising Surprise of Renewed Health Care Cost Inflation. *Health Affairs*. Retrieved from http://content.healthaffairs.org/content/early/2002/02/23/hlthaff.w2.85.citation

——. (2011, June 23). The Independent Payment Advisory Board—Congress's "Good Deed." *New England Journal of Medicine*, 364(25), 2377–2379.

Altman, D., Cutler, D. M., and Zeckhauser, R. (2000, August). Enrollee Mix, Treatment Intensity, and Cost in Competing Indemnity and HMO Plans. National Bureau of Economic Research (NBER) Working Paper No. W7832. Cambridge, MA: NBER. Retrieved from http://papers.nber.org/papers/W7832

American Hospital Association. (2011). *Report of the Task Force on Variation in Health Care Spending*. Retrieved from www.aha.org/content/11/11taskfcreport-variation.pdf

Berenson, R. A. (2004, December 15). Medicare Disadvantaged and the Search for the Elusive "Level Playing Field." *Health Affairs*. Retrieved from http://content.healthaffairs.org/content/early/2004/12/15/hlthaff.w4.572.citation

Blendon, R. J., Brodie, M., Benson, J. M., Altman, D. E., Levitt, L., Hoff, T., and Hugick, L. (1998, July–August). Understanding the Managed Care Backlash. *Health Affairs*, 17(4), 80–94.

Boyle, P. J. and Callahan, D. (1995). Managed Care in Mental Health: The Ethical Issues. *Health Affairs*, 14(3), 7–22.

Burnam, M. A. and Escarce, J. J. (1999). Equity in Managed Care for Mental Disorders. *Health Affairs*, 18(5), 22–31.

Callahan, J. J., Shepard, D. S., Beinecke, R. H., Larson, M. J., and Cavanaugh, D. (1995, Fall). Mental Health/Substance Abuse Treatment in Managed Care: The Massachusetts Medicaid Experience. *Health Affairs*, 14(3), 173–184.

Capretta, C. (2016). *The Independent Payment Advisory Board*. Mercatus Center, George Mason University. Retrieved from www.mercatus.org/publication/independent-payment-advisory-board

Centers for Medicare & Medicaid Services. (2017). *What Are the Value-based Programs?* Retrieved from www.cms.gov/Medicare/Quality-Initiatives-Patient-Assessment-Instruments/Value-Based-Programs/Value-Based-Programs.html

Chernew, M. E., Jacobson, P. D., Hofer, T. P., Aaronson, K. D., and Fendrick, A. M. (2004). Barriers To Constraining Health Care Cost Growth. *Health Affairs*, 23(6), 122–132.

Committee on Quality of Health Care in America, Institute of Medicine. (2001). *Crossing the Quality Chasm: A New Health System for the 21st Century*. Institute of Medicine. Retrieved from www.nap.edu/catalog.php?record_id=10027

Congressional Budget Office. (1997, April). *Trends in Health Care Spending by the Private Sector*. Washington, DC: CBO.

——. (2012, July 24). Letter to the Honorable John Boehner providing an estimate for H.R. 6079, the Repeal of Obamacare Act. Retrieved from www.cbo.gov/publication/43471

_____. (2017, January 17). How Repealing Portions of the Affordable Care Act Would Affect Health Insurance Coverage and Premiums. Retrieved from www.cbo.gov/publication/52371

Corcoran, K. and Vandiver, V. (1996). Maneuvering the Maze of Managed Care: Skills for Mental Health Practitioners. New York: Free Press.

CRS Issue Brief. (1993, June 4). *Health Care Reform: Managed Competition*. Washington, DC: Library of Congress.

Cutler, D. M. and Sheiner, L. (1997, August). Managed Care and the Growth of Medical Expenditures. NBER Working Paper No. W6140. Cambridge, MA: NBER. Retrieved from http://papers.nber.org/papers/w6140

Davis, K., Collins, K. S., and Morris, C. (1994). Managed Care: Promises and Concerns. *Health Affairs*, 13(4), 178–185.

Davis, K., Schoen, C., and Sandman, D. R. (1996, Summer). The Culture of Managed Care: Implications for Patients. *Bulletin of the New York Academy of Medicine*, 73(1), 173–183.

Dentzer, S. (2011, April). Still Crossing the Quality Chasm: Or Suspended over It? *Health Affairs*, 30(4), 554–555.

Domenici, P., and Smith, G. H. (2012, April 12). Americans are Waiting for Mental Health Parity. *Washington Post*. Retrieved from www.washingtonpost.com/opinions/americans-are-waiting-for-mental-health-parity/2012/04/12/gIQA-NhrnDT_story.html

Dranove, D. (2000). *The Economic Evolution of American Health Care*. Princeton, NJ: Princeton University Press.

Dziegielewski, S. F., Shields, J., and Thyer, B. (1998). Short term Treatment: Models, Methods, and Research. In J. Williams and K. Ell (Eds.), *Advances in Mental Health Research* (pp. 287–308). Washington, DC: National Association of Social Workers.

Eckholm, E. (1994, December 18). While Congress Remains Silent, Health Care Transforms Itself. *New York Times*, p. A1.

Ellwood, P. M. Jr., Anderson, N. N., Billings, J. E., Carlson, R. J., Hoagberg, E. J., and McClure, W. (1976). Health Maintenance Strategy. In D. Kotelchuck (Ed.), *Prognosis Negative: Crisis in the Health Care System* (pp. 348–351). New York: Vintage Books.

Enthoven, A. C. (1978, March 30). Consumer-choice Health Plan (second of two parts). A National-Health-Insurance Proposal Based on Regulated Competition in the Private Sector. *New England Journal of Medicine*, 298(13), 709–720.

——. (1993, Supplement). The History and Principles of Managed Competition. *Health Affairs*, 12, 24–48.

Enthoven, A. C. and Kronick, R. (1994). Universal Health Insurance through Incentives Reform. In P. R. Lee and C. L. Estes (Eds.), *The Nation's Health*, 4th edn. (pp. 284–291). Boston: Jones and Bartlett.

Enthoven, A. C. and Singer, S. J. (1994, Spring [I]). A Single-payer System in Jackson Hole Clothing. *Health Affairs*, 13(1), 81–95.

Families USA. (1998, July). *Hit and Miss: State Managed Care Laws*. Washington, DC: Families USA.

Feldman, S. and Scharfstein, D. (1998, April). Managed Care Provider Volume. NBER Working Paper No. W6523. Cambridge, MA: NBER. Retrieved from http://papers.nber.org/papers/W6523.

Findlay, S. (1999, September/October). Managed Behavioral Health Care in 1999: An Industry at a Crossroads. *Health Affairs*, 18(5), 116–225.

Frank, R. G., McGuire, T. G., and Newhouse, J. P. (1995, Fall). Risk Contracts in Managed Mental Health Care. *Health Affairs*, 14(3), 50–64.

Freeman, M. A. and Trabin, T. (1994, October 5). *Managed Behavioral Healthcare: History, Models, Key Issues, and Future Course*. Washington, DC: U.S. Department of Health and Human Services, Center for Mental Health Services.

Friedman, E. (1996, March 27). Capitation, Integration, and Managed Care: Lessons from Early Experiments. *Journal of the American Medical Association*, 275(12), 957–963.

Fuchs, V. (1993). *The Future of Health Policy*. Cambridge, MA: Harvard University Press.

Gabel, J. (1997). Ten Ways HMOs Have Changed During the 1990s. *Health Affairs*, 16(3), 134–145.

Galvin, R. (2005, January 12). Interview: "'A Deficiency of Will and Ambition:'" A Conversation with Donald Berwick. *Health Affairs*. Published online January 24, 2005. Retrieved from www.ihi.org/resources/Pages/Publications/Adeficiencyofwillandambition.aspx

Garber, A. M. and Skinner, J. (2008, Fall). Is American Health Care Uniquely Inefficient? *Journal of Economic Perspectives*, 22(4), 27–50.

Garrett, L. (2000). *Betrayal of Trust: The Collapse of Global Public Health*. New York: Hyperion.

Ginsburg, P. B. (1998, July–August). Health System Change in 1997. *Health Affairs*, 17(4), 165–169.

Gitterman, D. P., Sturm, R., and Scheffler, R. M. (2001, July–August). Toward Full Mental Health Parity and Beyond. *Health Affairs*, 20(4), 68–76.

Glied, S. (1999, July). Managed Care. NBER Working Paper No. W7205. Cambridge, MA: NBER. Retrieved from www.nber.org

Hennessy, K. D. and Goldman, H. H. (2001, July–August). Full Parity: Steps toward Treatment Equity for Mental and Addictive Disorders. *Health Affairs*, 20(4), 58–67.

Huskamp, H. A. and Newhouse, J. P. (1994). Is Health Spending Slowing Down? *Health Affairs*, 13(5), 32–38.

Iglehart, J. K. (1994). Managed Competition. In P. R. Lee and C. L. Estes (Eds.), *The Nation's Health*, 4th ed. (pp. 224–230). Boston: Jones & Bartlett.

Ikegami, N. and Anderson, G. F. (2012, May). In Japan, All-Payer Rate Setting Under Tight Government Control Has Proved to Be an Effective Approach to Containing Costs. *Health Affairs*, 31(5), 1049–1056.

Institute of Medicine. (2013). *Variation in Health Care Spending: Target Decision Making, Not Geography (Report)*. Washington, DC: National Academic Press. Retrieved from http://nap.edu/18393

Jackson, V. (1994). *A Brief Look at Managed Mental Health Care*. Washington, DC: National Association of Social Workers.

Jensen, G. A., Morrisey, M. A., Gaffney, S., and Liston, D. K. (1997). The New Dominance of Managed Care: Insurance Trends in the 1990s. *Health Affairs*, 16(1), 125–136.

Kaiser Family Foundation. (1998, August). *Trends and Indicators in the Changing Health Care Marketplace*. Washington, DC: The Foundation.

——. (1999, July). *Survey of Physicians and Nurses*. Washington, DC: The Foundation.

Kane, N. M., Turnbull, N. C., and Schoen, C. (1996, January). *Markets and Plan Performance: Summary Report on Case Studies of IPA and Network HMOs*. New York: Commonwealth Fund.

Kassirer, J. P. (1995). Managed Care and the Morality of the Market Place. *New England Journal of Medicine*, 333(1), 50–52.

Kilgore, E. (2016, November 29). Trump's Health Secretary Might Want to Undo a Key Reform Holding Down Medical Costs. *New York Magazine*. Retrieved from http://nymag.com/daily/intelligencer/2016/11/tom-price-at-hhs-a-bad-sign-for-value-based-health-care.html

Kohn, L. T., Corrigan, J. M., and Donaldson, M. S. (Eds.). (2000). *To Err is Human: Building a Safer Health System*. Committee on Quality of Health Care in America, Institute of Medicine. Retrieved from www.nap.edu/catalog.php?record_id=9728

Kotelchuck, D. (Ed.). (1976). *Prognosis Negative: Crisis in the Health Care System*. New York: Vintage Books.

Kronenfeld, J. J. and Whicker, M. L. (1984). *U.S. National Health Policy: An Analysis of the Federal Role*. New York: Praeger Special Studies.

Leape, L. (2000, January 25). Testimony Concerning Patient Safety and Medical Errors. U.S. Senate. Subcommittee on Labor, Health and Human Services, and Education. Retrieved from www.apa.org/ppo/issues/sleape.html

Lee, P. R., Soffel, D., and Luft, H. S. (1994). Costs and Coverage: Pressures toward Health Care Reform. In P. R. Lee and C. L. Estes (Eds.), *The Nation's Health*, 4th edn. (pp. 204–313). Boston: Jones & Bartlett.

Levit, K. R., Lazenby, H. C., and Sivarajan, L. (1996, Summer). Health Care Spending in 1994: Slowest in Decades. *Health Affairs*, 15(2), 130–144.

Luft, H. S. (1978, June 15). How Do Health-Maintenance Organizations Achieve Their "Savings"? *New England Journal of Medicine*, 298(24), 1336–1343.

McKinney, E. A. (1995). Health Planning. In R. L. Edwards (Ed.), *Encyclopedia of Social Work*, 19th edn. (pp. 1199–1205). Washington, DC: National Association of Social Workers.

Mahar, M. (2008, October 21). The Truth about Spiraling Health Care Prices in the U.S.: Medical Technology, Low Productivity and Paying More for Everything (Part 1 of 2). *Health Beat*. Retrieved from www.healthbeatblog.org/2008/10/thetruth-about.html

Mandros, A. (2015, September 2). The Landscape of Behavioral Health Carve-ins. *Open Minds*. Retrieved from www.openminds.com/market-intelligence/executive-briefings/are-you-prepared-for-the-behavioral-health-carve-in/

Marmor, T. and Oberlander, J. (2012, Spring). From HMOs to ACOs: The Quest for the Holy Grail in U.S. Health Policy. *Journal of Internal Medicine in Physicians for a Nation Health Program Newsletter*, 10–13.

Mechanic, D. and McAlpine, D. D. (1999). Mission Unfulfilled: Potholes on the Road to Mental Health Parity. *Health Affairs*, 18(5), 7–21.

Medicare Payment Advisory Commission. (2013, March). *Report to the Congress: Medicare Payment Policy*. Retrieved from www.medpac.gov/documents/Mar13_EntireReport.pdf

Miller, R. H. and Luft, H. S. (1997). Does Managed Care Lead to Better or Worse Quality of Care? *Health Affairs*, 16(5), 7–25.

Mizrahi, T. (1995). Health Care: Reform Initiatives. In R. L. Edwards (Ed.), *Encyclopedia of Social Work*, 19th edn. (pp. 1185–1198). Washington, DC: National Association of Social Workers.

Mullan, F. (2001, January/February). Interview: A Founder of Quality Assessment Encounters a Troubled System Firsthand. *Health Affairs*, 20(1), 137–141.

National Association of Social Workers. (1994, May). *A Brief Look at Managed Mental Health Care*. Washington, DC: National Association of Social Workers.

——. (1996). *NASW Code of Ethics*. Washington, DC: National Association of Social Workers.

——. (2001, August 20). *NASW Supports a Fair and Principled Patients Bill of Rights.* Retrieved from www.socialworkers.org/advocacy/updates/2001/082001.asp

Newhouse, J. P. (1993, Supplement). An Iconoclastic View of Health Cost Containment. *Health Affairs*, 12, 152–171.

Orszag, P. R. and Emanuel, E. J. (2010, August 12). Perspective: Health Care Reform and Cost Control. *New England Journal of Medicine*, 363, 601–603.

Patel, K. and Rushefsky, M. E. (1999). *Health Care Politics and Policy in America.* Armonk, NY: M. E. Sharpe.

Rachlis, M. and Kushner, C. (1989). *Second Opinion: What's Wrong with Canada's Health Care System and How to Fix It.* Toronto: Collins.

Reamer, F. G. (1998). Managed Care: Ethical Considerations. In G. Schamess and A. Lightburn (Eds.), *Humane Managed Care?* (pp. 293–298). Washington, DC: National Association of Social Workers.

Reinhardt, U.E. (1996, Summer). Spending more through "cost control:" our obsessive quest to gut the hospital. *Health Affairs*, 15(2), 145–154.

Rice, T., Desmond, K., and Gabel, J. (1990). The Medicare Catastrophic Coverage Act: A Post-Mortem. *Health Affairs*, 9(3), 75–87.

Roberts, M. J. and Clyde, A. (1993). *Your Money or Your Life: The Health Care Crisis Explained.* New York: Doubleday.

Robinson, J. C. (1999). *The Corporate Practice of Medicine: Competition and Innovation in Health Care.* Los Angeles, CA: University of California Press.

Rolde, N. (1992). *Your Money or Your Health.* New York: Paragon House.

Rothfeld, M. (1976). Sensible Surgery for Swelling Medical Costs. In D. Kotelchuck (Ed.), *Prognosis Negative: Crisis in the Health Care System* (pp. 352–363). New York: Vintage Books.

Saltzman, E. and Eibner, C. (2015, July 15). The Effect of Eliminating the Affordable Care Act's Tax Credits in Federally Facilitated Marketplaces. *Rand Health Quarterly*, 5(1), 7. Retrieved from www.ncbi.nlm.nih.gov/pmc/articles/PMC5158240/

Singer, S. J. (2000, July–August). What's Not to Like about HMOs. *Health Affairs*, 19(4), 206–209.

Siskind, A. B. (1998). Agency Mission, Social Work Practice, and Professional Training in a Managed Care Environment. In G. Schamess and A. Lightburn (Eds.), *Humane Managed Care?* (pp. 180–186). Washington, DC: National Association of Social Workers.

Squires, D. (2011). Explaining High Health Care Spending in the United States: An International Comparison of Supply, Utilization, Prices, and Quality. Commonwealth Fund. Retrieved from www.healthreformgps.org/wp-content/uploads/1595_Squires_explaining_high_hlt_care_spending_intl_brief.pdf

Squires, D. and Anderson, C. (2015, October). U.S. Health Care from a Global Perspective: Spending, Use of Services, Prices, and Health in 13 Countries. The Commonwealth Fund. Retrieved from www.commonwealthfund.org/publications/issue-briefs/2015/oct/us-health-care-from-a-global-perspective

Starr, P. (1982). The Social Transformation of American Medicine. New York: Basic Books.

——. (1986). Health Care for the Poor: The Past Twenty Years. In S. H. Danziger and D. H. Weinberg (Eds.), *Fighting Poverty: What Works and What Doesn't* (pp. 106–132). Cambridge, MA: Harvard University Press.

Starr, P. and Zelman, W. A. (1993, Supplement). Bridge to Compromise: Competition under a Budget. *Health Affairs*, 12, 7–23.

Sullivan, K. (2000, July–August). On the "Efficiency" of Managed Care Plans. *Health Affairs*, 19(4), 139–148.

U.S. Department of Health and Human Services. (1999, December). *Mental Health: A Report of the Surgeon General.* Rockville, MD: U.S. Department of Health and Human Services, Substance Abuse and Mental Health Services Administration, Center for Mental Health Services, National Institute of Mental Health.

U.S. General Accounting Office. (2000, May). *Mental Health Parity Act: Despite New Federal Standards, Mental Health Benefits Remain Limited.* Washington, DC: U.S. General Accounting Office.

U.S. House of Representatives. (2005a, April 26). Committee on Energy and Commerce. *Protect Patients, Not HMO Profits.* Cosponsor the Patients Bill of Rights of 2005. (Letter from John Dingell to colleagues) Retrieved from www.house.gov/commerce_democrats/Press_109/109dc4.pdf

_____. (2005b). Committee on Energy and Commerce. Designing a Twenty-First Century Medicare Prescription Drug Benefit: Hearing Before the Subcommittee on Health, House Committee on Energy and Commerce. Statement of Bruce C. Vladeck, pp. 28–34. Retrieved from http://energycommerce.house.gov/108/action/108-25.pdf

Vandivort-Warren, R. (1998). How Social Workers Can Manage Managed Care. In G. Schamess and A. Lightburn (Eds.), *Humane Managed Care?* (pp. 255–267). Washington, DC: National Association of Social Workers.

Wachter, R. M. (2004, November 30). End of the Beginning: Patient Safety Five Years after "To Err is Human." *Health Affairs*, pp. W4–534–W4–545. Available at: www.content.healthaffairs.org/cgi/content/abstract/hlthaff.w4.534

Wennberg, J., Brownlee, S., Fisher, E. S., Skinner, J. S., and Weinstein, J. N. (2008, December). *An Agenda for Change. Improving Quality and Curbing Health Care Spending: Opportunities for the Congress and the Obama Administration.* A Dartmouth Atlas White Paper. The Dartmouth Institute for Health Policy and Clinical Practice. Retrieved from www.dartmouthatlas.org/downloads/reports/agenda_for_change.pdf

White, C. (2008, May/June). Marketwatch: Why Did Medicare Spending Growth Slow Down? *Health Affairs*, 27(3), 793–802.

White House Domestic Policy Council (1993). *Health Security: The President's Report to the American People.* Washington, DC: U.S. Government Printing Office.

Zelman, W. A. (1994, Spring [1]). The Rationale Behind the Clinton Health Care Reform Plan. *Health Affairs*, 13(1), 9–29.

Structure and Funding of U.S. Health, Mental Health, and Behavioral Health Care System

INTRODUCTION

Part II provides an overview of the major components within the complex structure and funding of the U.S. health care system—although it is actually misleading to refer to it as a "system" because it is has so many fragmented parts (as demonstrated in Part I). Also, it is unique to health care systems in the world because it does not provide access to care for all of its citizens. The system includes many organizations and agencies, both private and public, including providers (preventive, primary, acute, emergency, rehabilitative, behavioral, continuing, end of life, and integrated care), insurers, payers, educational and research institutions, and medical and pharmaceutical suppliers. It has a complex combination of private (employment-based and direct purchase), public (Medicare, Medicaid, CHIP—Children's Health Insurance Plan), military (TRICARE and CHAMPVA—Civilian Health and Medical Program of the Uniformed Services), and federal employee (FEHB—Federal Employees Health Benefit) health insurance plans that provide variable access to care. Within the private sector, there are multiple insurance companies and plans. The complexity of billing, collection, and record keeping for providers for multiple payers creates enormous administrative inefficiencies and adds to the high cost of the U.S. health care system.

All health care systems have basic functional components, including financing, insurance, delivery of services, and payment. In the U.S., these components do not necessarily work together given the lack of central organization and planning that exists in most other industrialized nations (Figures II.1 and II.2). Medicare evolved as an employer-/employee-financed federal insurance for older retired and disabled workers. Medicaid evolved as a publicly financed insurance for low-income individuals who meet the government's standards for eligibility. Overall, however, the system is dominated by the private sector. The lack of supervision across the entire system creates duplication, overlap, inadequacies, inefficiencies, and waste, which contribute to the high cost of the U.S. system in comparison to others. Most developed countries have health care systems that provide universal coverage through: National health insurance (government financing/private delivery), such as in Canada; a national health care or single-payer system (government financing/government delivery), such as in England; or socialized health insurance (government-mandated private financing/private delivery), such as in Germany. In the U.S., both financing and delivery are primarily private; employment-based insurance dominates the system.

FIGURE II.1

Insurance Coverage by Type in U.S., 2016

PRIVATE INSURANCE	**67.5%**
Employer-based	55.7%
Private purchase	16.2%
PUBLIC INSURANCE	**37.3%**
Medicare	16.7%
Medicaid	19.4%
Military (Tricare & CHAMPVA)	4.6%
Uninsured	8.8%

Note: Some individuals have coverage from multiple types of insurance.
Source: Barnett, J. C. and Berchik, E.R. (2017, September). Current Population Reports, P60–260, *Health Insurance Coverage in the United States: 2016*, Washington, DC: U.S. Government Printing Office.

FINANCING	INSURANCE	DELIVERY	PAYMENTS
WHO PAYS FOR INSURANCE?	WHO PROVIDES A PACKAGE OF BENEFITS TO COVER THE FINANCIAL RISK OF COSTLY CARE WHEN IT IS NEEDED?	WHO PROVIDES CARE?	WHO PAYS THE BILLS?
Employers	Private companies	Physicians and other providers	Private insurance companies
Government	Employer self-insurance	Hospitals	Government (primarily through private insurance companies)
		Clinics	Contracted claims processors
Individual self-financing		Nursing homes	Individuals
		Assisted living facilities	
		Diagnostic centers	
		Community health centers	
		Community mental health centers	
		Vendors of pharmaceuticals and medical equipment	

FIGURE II.2

Functional Components of the U.S. Health Care System

CHAPTER 5

Private Insurance and the Role of Employers

EMPLOYMENT-BASED HEALTH INSURANCE IS THE MOST COMMON form of health insurance in the U.S. (see Figure II.1), but this coverage has been in serious decline for at least the past two decades. The Affordable Care Act (2010) had two significant aims: Constrain growing health care costs and expand access to care. The latter was a response not only to the growing number of Americans who lacked coverage and were uninsured, but also to growing concerns about the market structure of health care and the erosion of employment-based insurance. Without government reforms, the problem of access to care seemed destined to worsen over time as health care costs soared and employers played a declining role in coverage. This chapter provides a brief overview of declining employment-based coverage and examines changes that have occurred as a result of the passage of the ACA under the Obama administration, and reform efforts to overturn the ACA by the Trump administration.

DECLINING COVERAGE

The decline of employment-based insurance over the last two decades has had a dramatic effect on insurance coverage in the U.S. The primary cause of the decline has been the increased cost of private insurance, which has triggered reductions in employment-based coverage. Between 1987 and 1995, the segment of the nonelderly population insured by employers fell from 69.2 percent to 63.8 percent (Employee Benefit Research Institute, 1997). With rising costs, many employers seemed to feel that "their contribution … should be even less" than it had been in the past (Rovner, 1997, p. 56). Between 1998 and 1999, employment-based insurance expanded as the economy grew stronger and unemployment declined, but. with the economic downturn in 2001, employment-sponsored coverage continued to decline. The percentage of Americans with employment-based coverage fell from 61.3 percent to 60.4 percent between 2002 and 2003, and in 2010 reached a new low of 55.3 percent (Kaiser Family Foundation, 2004; U.S. Census Bureau, 2007; DeNavas-Walt et al., 2011). Even more disturbing, low-wage workers lost enormous ground. Schmitt (2012) found that only 25 percent of low-wage workers (defined as those in the bottom 20 percent of hourly wages) had insurance through their employers in 2010. Even with the ACA's mandate for large businesses to provide coverage, employer-sponsored coverage was 55.7 percent in 2016 (Barnett and Berchik, 2017).

The erosion of employment-based coverage has also adversely affected family dependents, especially young people under the age of 18. In 2007, only 64 percent of children had private insurance, compared with 73 percent in 1989 (U.S. General Accounting Office [GAO], 1995; U.S. Census Bureau, 2007). Fairbrother et al. (2010) found that children with private health insurance were 6.5 times more likely to lose coverage in the 3 months after a parent lost a job than children with employed parents.

As the percentage of young people with private coverage declined, the importance of Medicaid and the State Children's Health Insurance Plan (S-CHIP) program grew. Without Medicaid, at least 4 million additional pregnant women and children would have been uninsured during the late 1980s and early 1990s (Holahan, 1997). Without Medicaid and S-CHIP, the uninsured rate among low-income children would not have dropped from 23 percent in 1996 to 19 percent in 2002 (Kaiser Family Foundation, 2005), and, even more dramatically, to 11 percent in 2007 (U.S. Census Bureau, 2007). Dorn et al. (2008) showed a direct correlation between declining employment-based insurance and rising rates of coverage through Medicaid and S-CHIP. The study found that every one percentage point rise in unemployment led to a 1.1 million increase in the uninsured population and a one million increase in Medicaid and S-CHIP enrollment.

Rising Costs

Health costs in the U.S. are particularly problematic. Health care costs rose rapidly in the late 1980s and early 1990s, far outpacing wages, family incomes, and consumer prices. Between 1988 and 1996, the average premium for family coverage rose almost 10 percent (Kaiser Family Foundation, 1998). Businesses and employers, especially small businesses, began to shift these costs to their employees. In 1988, employees paid 11 percent of the cost of single coverage; in 1996, although premiums had finally stabilized, employees were paying 21 percent of the cost (Kaiser Family Foundation, 2000). From 1996 to 2000, premiums dropped, but double-digit inflation in premiums returned in 2001. In 2004, the average employee share of premiums was 16 percent (Kaiser Family Foundation, 2000), and premiums continued to rise at a rate higher than overall inflation and wage gains. From 2001 to 2008, premiums increased 79 per cent for family coverage (Kaiser Family Foundation, 2008), and by 2011 employees were responsible for 34 percent of the cost of family coverage (U.S. Bureau of Labor Statistics, 2011) (Figure 5.1). However, with the ACA mandate for large businesses to provide coverage and financial subsidies to individuals, the employer/employee share of the cost of premiums declined in 2016 (Figure 5.1).

Overall, over the last few decades, employers raised the premium share paid by *employees*, and health insurance became unaffordable for many families, particularly those employed in small businesses and low-wage jobs. In 2007, low-wage earners paid on average 34 percent of the premium for family coverage. In comparison, high-wage workers paid on average 27 percent (Kaiser Family Foundation, 2007).

YEAR	SINGLE COVERAGE		FAMILY COVERAGE		FIGURE 5.1
	Employer share (%)	Employee share (%)	Employer share (%)	Employee share (%)	*Percentage of Insurance Premium Paid by Employer and Employee in Private Sector, 2004–16*
2004	82	18	69	31	
2005	82	18	71	29	
2006	82	18	70	30	
2007	81	19	71	29	
2008	81	19	71	29	
2009	80	20	70	30	
2010	77	23	67	33	
2011	76	24	66	34	
2016	**79**	**21**	**68**	**32**	

Source: U.S. Bureau of Labor Statistics (2011, 2016a).

The financial burden of sharing the cost of health insurance proved to be too great for many families. An increasing number of employees were eligible for benefits, yet declined coverage because they could not afford to pay their premium share. In 2010, 16.4 percent of workers declined coverage; 67.5 percent were offered insurance, but only 56.6 percent had coverage (Fronstin, 2012). With the enactment of the ACA, large businesses were required to offer coverage that capped the amount individuals had to pay in out-of-pocket costs each year, which helped to decrease the cost of coverage for an individual or family. Workers were allowed to deny the employer-based coverage made available to them, but, if they did so, they would be ineligible for the marketplace plans (unless eligible for a waiver) and ineligible for individual subsidies. Both of these policies seemed to serve as an incentive to enroll in the employer-based coverage. According to the U.S. Bureau of Labor Statistics (2016b), in 2016, 78 percent of civilian workers, 75 percent of private industry workers, and 90 percent of government workers with access to a health plan participated in the plan.

Jobs Without Coverage

A separate but related problem in private sector health insurance coverage was the *decline in jobs that provided insurance coverage*. The service-sector job market, which is less likely to provide insurance benefits than manufacturing jobs, continued to grow. As discussed earlier, labor unions played a major role in the development of employer-based insurance, particularly in manufacturing, and today unionized workers are still far more likely to receive coverage (Fronstin, 2012). However, the number of workers in unionized jobs also decreased. In 2000, 69 percent of all firms offered health insurance coverage; by 2007, this declined to 60 percent. Of those firms that did not offer insurance, the majority were small firms with fewer than 50 employees (Kaiser Family Foundation, 2007), and nearly 40 percent of all employers worked in small businesses (National Coalition on Health Care, 2008).

Changes in Workforce

The *structure of the work force* also changed. The number of "contingent" or "alternative" jobs, including part-time, temporary, contractual, and self-employed positions, has increased, and these jobs are less likely to provide coverage. Thorpe (1999) estimated that employees in these categories made up 25 percent of the workforce. In 1997, according to Thorpe (1999), 53.3 percent of employees ineligible for coverage were either part-time or partial-year employees. Workers who did not receive employment-based insurance and did not purchase it on their own cited *cost* as the primary reason for lack of insurance.

IMPACT OF ACA ON EMPLOYERS AND EMPLOYEES

A central factor in the enactment of the ACA was the need to address declining coverage; the ACA was designed to impact employment-based health insurance plans. Some of the major changes were summarized in Chapter 1 and include the following:

Initial Insurance Reforms (effective 2010):

- lifetime and unreasonable annual limits on benefits eliminated;

- rescissions of health insurance policies prohibited;

- assistance for those who are uninsured because of a preexisting condition provided;

- preexisting condition exclusions for children banned;

- coverage for preventive services and immunizations required;

- dependent coverage up to age 26 extended;

- uniform coverage documents developed so consumers can compare policies;

- insurance company nonmedical, administrative expenditures capped;

- consumer access to effective appeals process and assistance with appeals and accessing coverage ensured;

- temporary reinsurance program created to support coverage for early retirees;

- internet portal established to assist with identifying coverage options;

- administrative simplification facilitated to help lower health system costs.

Insurance Reforms (effective 2014):

- "individual mandate" established, which requires nearly all individuals not already covered by an employer or public insurance to buy an approved private insurance policy or pay a penalty for noncompliance (as noted in Chapter 1, the tax reform bill passed in 2016 eliminates the penalty for noncompliance);

- employers with 50 or more full-time-equivalent employees must provide coverage or pay a penalty for noncompliance;

- subsidies provided to low-income individuals to help purchase the mandated coverage;

- preexisting condition exclusions for adults banned;

- access to mental health services expanded by increasing funding for community health centers.

Thus, the ACA employs multiple strategies to expand coverage in the private sector, including incentives, mandates, penalties for noncompliance, and required changes in benefits. The ACA also relies on new organizational models, such as health exchanges.

However, overall, as noted by Schmitt (2012), the "preferred path to coverage is [still] through existing employer-provided private insurance." The ACA establishes a "pay or play" system for employers with 50 or more full-time employees. If employers do not "play," they will "pay" a tax penalty. Employers with fewer than 50 employees will not face tax penalties, but many will be eligible for incentives to offer coverage through tax credits and will also be able to purchase insurance through newly created, state-level, health-insurance exchanges.

As a result of these reforms, the number of people covered through employment-based insurance was expected to decrease somewhat given the subsidies available for the purchase of insurance through the health insurance exchanges, and expanded eligibility for Medicaid and CHIP (Congressional Budget Office [CBO], 2012). The CBO (2012) estimated that three to five million fewer employees per year between 2019 and 2022 would receive employer coverage. The impact of the ACA on employers clearly varies, however, depending on the size of the employer (small, medium, and large employers). Critics of the ACA have raised concerns about the impact of the ACA on small companies (fewer than 50 employees), which historically have found it more difficult financially to compete with larger employers and offer coverage for their workers; however, the Urban Institute (McMorrow et al., 2011) found that the ACA should help the smallest employers (fewer than 25 employees) expand coverage and help employers with fewer than 50 employees save money on their coverage. Most importantly, coverage for employees in small companies is expected to increase significantly: "the uninsurance rate for individuals in families with at least one small-firm worker falls dramatically following reform from 24 to 11 percent" (McMorrow et al., 2011, p. 7).

Concerns were also raised about the future role of employment-based insurance under the ACA, even if the ACA "builds on, rather than eliminates" (Eibner et al., 2010) the employment-based system. Will its role diminish over time? Again, Eibner et al. (2010) found that the ACA would result in a large net increase in offers to employees for employer-sponsored insurance: "Many employers will find that offering coverage through the exchanges is an attractive option, owing to wider risk pooling, low administrative costs, and expanded choices" (Eibner et al., 2010, p. 1395).

HIGHLIGHTS

- In the U.S., both the financing and the delivery of health care are primarily private; employment-based insurance dominates the health care system. However, this coverage has been in serious decline for at least the last two decades due to rising costs in the health care system.

- In an effort to meet the rising cost of health insurance, employers have eliminated benefits, reduced coverage for family members, and increased the employee share of insurance premiums. The percentage of Americans with employment-based coverage fell from 61.3 percent to 60.4 percent between 2002 and 2003, and in 2010 reached a new low of 55.3 percent.

- These conditions have caused more and more people to lose access to health insurance. Those affected most are working adults with low and moderate incomes and their dependent family members, especially young people under the age of 18.

- The Affordable Care Act (ACA) employs multiple strategies to expand coverage in the private sector, including incentives, mandates, penalties for noncompliance, and required changes in benefits. The ACA also relies on new organizational models, accountable care organizations (ACOs), to motivate competition and control costs. ACOs create incentives for health care providers to work together to treat an individual patient across care settings.

- The ACA will help the smallest employers (fewer than 25 employees) expand coverage and help employers with fewer than 50 employees save money on their coverage. Most importantly, insurance rates for employees in small companies are expected to increase significantly.

REFERENCES

Barnett, J. C. and Berchik, E. R. (2017, September). Current Population Reports, P60–260, Health Insurance Coverage in the United States: 2016, Washington, DC: U.S. Government Printing Office.

Congressional Budget Office. (2012, March 15). *The Effects of the Affordable Care Act on Employment-Based Health Insurance.* Retrieved from www.cbo.gov/publication/43090

DeNavas-Walt, C., Proctor, B., and Smith, J. (2011, September). *Income, Poverty, and Health Insurance Coverage in the United States: 2010, Current Population Reports: Consumer Income.* U.S. Census Bureau. Retrieved from www.census.gov/prod/2011pubs/p60-239.pdf

Dorn, S., Garrett, B., Holahan, J., and Williams, A. (2008, April). *Medicaid, SCHIP and Economic Downturn: Policy Challenges and Policy Responses. A Report for the Kaiser Commission on the Uninsured and Medicaid.* Washington, DC: Kaiser Family Foundation.

Eibner, C., Hussey, P., and Girosi, F. (2010, October 7). The Effects of the Affordable Care Act on Workers' Health Insurance Coverage. *New England Journal of Medicine,* 363(22), 1393–1395.

Employee Benefit Research Institute. (1997, May). *Trends in Health Insurance Coverage (No. 185)*. Washington, DC: Employee Benefit Research Institute.

Fairbrother, G., Carle, A., Cassedy, A., and Newacheck, P. (2010, July). The Impact of Parental Job Loss on Children's Health Insurance Coverage. *Health Affairs*, 29(7), 1343–1349.

Fronstin, P. (2012, April). *Employment-Based Health Benefits: Trends in Access and Coverage, 1997–2010*. Employee Benefit Research Institute. Retrieved from www.ebri.org/pdf/briefspdf/EBRI_IB_04-2012_No370_HI-Trends.pdf

Holahan, J. (1997). *Expanding Insurance Coverage for Children*. Washington, DC: Urban Institute.

Kaiser Family Foundation. (1998, September). *How Well Does the Unemployment-Based Health Insurance System Work for Low-Income Families?* Washington, DC: Kaiser Family Foundation.

——. (2000, May). *The Uninsured and Their Access to Health Care*. Washington, DC: Kaiser Family Foundation.

——. (2004). *Employer Health Benefits*. Washington, DC: Kaiser Family Foundation.

——. (2005, March). *Enrolling Uninsured Low Income Children in Medicaid and SCHIP*. Washington, DC: Kaiser Family Foundation.

——. (2007). *Employer Health Benefits, 2007 Annual Survey*. Washington, DC: Kaiser Family Foundation.

——. (2008). *Fast Facts*. Retrieved from http://facts.kff.org

McMorrow, S., Blumberg, L., and Buettgens, M. (2011, June). *The Effects of Health Reform on Small Businesses and Their Workers*. Urban Institute. Retrieved from www.smallbusinessmajority.org/_docs/resources/Urban_Small_Biz_Report.pdf

National Coalition on Health Care. (2008). *Facts About Health Care*. Retrieved from www.nchc.org

Rovner, J. (1997, May). The Uninsured: An American Time Bomb. *Business and Health*, 15(5), 55–59.

Schmitt, J. (2012). *Health-insurance Coverage for Low-wage Workers, 1979–2010 and Beyond*. Center for Economic and Policy Research. Retrieved from www.cepr.net/documents/publications/health-low-wage-2012-02.pdf

Thorpe, K. (1999, March–April). Why Are Workers Uninsured? Employer-sponsored Health Insurance in 1997. *Health Affairs*, 18(2), 213–219.

U.S. Bureau of Labor Statistics. (2011, March). National Compensation Survey: Employee Benefits in the United States: Private Industry, table 9, "Health Care Benefits: Access, Participation, and Take-up Rates, Private Industry Workers." Retrieved from www.bls.gov/ncs/ebs/benefits/2011/ownership/private/table05a.pdf

——. (2016a, July 22). Employee Benefits in the U.S.—March 2016 News Release. Retrieved from www.bls.gov/news.release/pdf/ebs2.pdf

——. (2016b, July 28.) Employee Benefits in Private Industry—News Release. Retrieved from www.bls.gov/news.release/ebs2.toc.htm

U.S. Census Bureau. (2007). *March Demographic Profiles*. Current Population Surveys. Retrieved from www.census.gov/population/socdemo

U.S. General Accounting Office. (1995, July). *Health Insurance for Children—Many Remain Uninsured Despite Medicaid Expansion (GAO/HEHS-95-175)*. Washington, DC: U.S. Government Printing Office.

CHAPTER 6

Medicare

INTRODUCTION

THIS CHAPTER PROVIDES AN OVERVIEW OF MEDICARE and the impact of the 2010 health care reform legislation, including new programs to improve quality and care, and mechanisms to slow the growth of Medicare spending, which will be impacted by demographic trends. In the absence of a national health care system, Medicare and Medicaid are the two largest and most important health insurance programs in the U.S. According to the Kaiser Family Foundation, the Medicare program finances approximately 23 percent of all physician and clinical services in the U.S. (down from one-third in 2008) and 25 percent of all hospital services (down from 45 percent in 2008) (Kaiser Family Foundation, 2011b; Cubanski and Newman, 2017), while Medicaid is the primary payer for long-term care. Together, they form the bedrock of the health care "system" in the U.S.

MEDICARE'S LEGISLATIVE, POLITICAL, AND SOCIAL HISTORY

After decades of political reform efforts to achieve national health insurance, Congress enacted Medicare and Medicaid in 1965 as Titles XVIII and XIX of the Social Security Act. Medicare and Medicaid are both health insurance programs, but Medicare is a social insurance program (an entitlement for retired older adults), whereas Medicaid is a means-tested public assistance program (to be eligible, recipients must demonstrate need by meeting established income and asset eligibility criteria).

Robert Ball, one of the architects of Medicare and commissioner of Social Security under Presidents Kennedy, Johnson, and Nixon, argued that Medicare's original designers viewed it as a first step toward universal coverage (Ball, 1995). They reluctantly crafted a program that was politically viable by focusing on older adults and building on a Social Security pension system that already provided income support for adult retirees.

Before Medicare, half of the nation's older adults lacked health care coverage, and millions more had inadequate coverage. Private insurance rates for older adults were very expensive, and the idea of pooling risks for this population was appealing. The final element of the compromise was to establish a separate program for low-income families. With the spotlight on economically disadvantaged groups during President Johnson's War on Poverty, Congress enacted Medicaid to address the needs of this population.

Together, Medicare and Medicaid have enabled millions of adults and children to access health care and have contributed significantly to the social and economic welfare of individuals and the nation as a whole. Medicare has reduced poverty among older adults and people with disabilities measurably, and has also "forced hospitals to desegregate even before it began paying benefits" (Eichner and Vladeck, 2005, p. 368). After Medicare's enactment, over "1,000 hospitals integrated their medical staff's waiting rooms and hospital floors in a period of less than four months" (Eichner and Vladeck, 2005, p. 368). Medicare provided health care coverage to 47 million people in 2010 (Kaiser Family Foundation, 2010b), and Medicaid provided health and long-term care coverage to 60 million people (Kaiser Family Foundation, 2010a).

When the programs were first enacted, the federal government did not place any limits or restrictions on hospital and physician fees. Within just a few years, the nation's health care costs had skyrocketed. To address escalating costs (as discussed in Chapter 4), health maintenance organizations (HMOs) emerged during the 1970s; during the Reagan administration, despite its opposition to regulation, a prospective payment system for Medicare was established. In 1997, after bitter legislative struggles between the Republican-controlled Congress and the Clinton administration over the proposed Health Security Act, Congress passed the Balanced Budget Act of 1997, which established Part C Medicare (managed-care plans) and created the State Children's Health Insurance Program (S-CHIP). These were the most significant changes made to the Medicare and Medicaid programs since their enactment, that is until the Bush administration enacted the landmark Medicare Prescription Drug, Improvement and Modernization Act (MMA) of 2003, which finally added prescription drug coverage to Medicare.

Managed Care and Medicare

Managed care was first introduced into Medicare with the Tax Equity and Fiscal Responsibility Act (TEFRA) of 1982, which allowed approved HMOs to enroll Medicare beneficiaries on a capitated basis. In exchange for a monthly, per-patient payment, Medicare HMOs, or plans, agreed to provide enrollees with the same services guaranteed to traditional or fee-for-service (FFS) beneficiaries. If an HMO provided these services for less than the amount paid by Medicare, it had to provide additional benefits of equivalent value. These additional benefits often included prescription drug coverage.

Medicare-managed care grew slowly, however; by 1993, only 5 percent of the Medicare population had joined managed-care organizations (MCOs) (Kaiser Family Foundation, 1999). Over the next four years enrollment accelerated and, by 1997, 14 percent of the Medicare population belonged to MCOs (Kaiser Family Foundation, 1999). In 1997, in an effort to expand enrollment in Medicare-managed care, Congress, as part of the Balanced Budget Act (BBA), created Medicare Part C, the Medicare + Choice (M + C) program. This expanded the types of plans that could be offered under Medicare to include not only HMOs and other types of coordinated care plans, but also private FFS plans and medical savings accounts (Medicare Payment Advisory Commission – see www.medpac.gov/search-results/page/37?indexCatalogue=searchresultsindex&searchQuery=Report+to+Congress+1998&wordsMode=0).

Although the purpose of M + C was to allow beneficiaries a greater choice of plans, it was a constant source of controversy. The private FFS and medical savings options, in particular, generated concern (Patel and Rushefsky, 1999). Moon (2000) noted that "some" M + C plans "treated" beneficiaries poorly, "limiting access to new technology" and inappropriately denying care (Moon, 2001, p. 2). In an "interim" assessment of whether M + C had met its goals, such as expanding choice and improving measures of quality, Gold (2001) argued that at best the program deserved a grade of D. Although the number of individuals in M + C plans increased between 1997 and 1999, by 2004 the number had fallen below that for 1997 (Medicare Payment Advisory Commission, 2004). When the BBA was enacted, analysts believed that by 2005 one-third of Medicare beneficiaries would belong to M + C plans; this did not happen.

Despite difficulties with M + C, efforts to infuse managed care into Medicare moved forward during the late 1990s. As part of the BBA, Congress created a National Bipartisan Commission on the Future of Medicare (see http://medicare.commission.gov/medicare/index.html), chaired by Senator John Breaux (D-LA) and Representative Bill Thomas (R-CA), to examine Medicare and "strengthen" it in anticipation of the retirement of the baby-boom generation. This commission developed a "premium support" model, which was introduced in Congress by Senators John Breaux (D-LA) and Bill Frist (R-TN) (Reinhardt, 2003). Moon (2000, pp. 1–2) summarized this approach as follows:

> Medicare beneficiaries would choose from a range of insurance plans—in this case both private plans and traditional Medicare. The government would pay part of the premium with the contribution established as a share of the national average premium price. Individuals who choose more expensive plans would pay a substantially higher price than those choosing less expensive plans. The goal would be to give beneficiaries a financial incentive to opt for less expensive plans while offering them a choice among a variety of options.

Although the Breaux–Frist bills did not become law, they provided the basis for the Medicare Prescription Drug, Improvement, and Modernization Act (MMA) of 2003.

A central concern with the Breaux–Frist bills was their reliance on managed care, which "actually cost" Medicare more "money, rather than achieved savings" (Iglehart, 1997, p. 68). Historically, Medicare payments were based on a measure known as the adjusted average per capita cost (AAPCC), a "county-level estimate of the average cost Medicare incurs for each beneficiary in the fee-for-service program" (Medicare Payment Advisory Commission, 1999, p. xxxi). As Medicare HMOs tend to have healthier patients than FFS medicine, they received 95 percent of the AAPCC. However, studies during the 1990s found that Medicare HMOs could actually treat enrollees for 88–92 percent of the AAPCC (Iglehart, 1997). This enabled them to offer benefits such as prescription drug coverage and health club memberships, which further enhanced their ability to attract healthy enrollees (Hearing before the Subcommittee on Health, House Committee on Energy and Commerce, 2002; Iglehart, 1994).

The BBA tried to resolve this problem by reducing payments to Medicare MCOs, but between 1998 and 2001 many plans still received around "8.5 percent more . . . than . . . under . . . the pre-BBA payment method" (Berenson, 2004, p. 575). Although Medicare analysts sought to develop "risk adjusters," which would ensure that plans were reimbursed on the actual health status of their enrollees, Reinhardt (2003) noted that this effort remained at a relatively primitive stage. In 2004, Biles et al. observed that some plans were still seeking to design "benefit packages to attract fewer high-cost enrollees" (Biles et al., 2004, p. 589).

Medicare Prescription Drug, Improvement and Modernization Act of 2003

The MMA of 2003 brought two significant changes to Medicare: First, it added a new Part D prescription drug benefit; second, it changed Part C Medicare Choice + to Medicare Advantage (managed-care plans).

Prescription Drugs (Part D). At the time of Medicare's enactment in 1965, prescription drugs did not play a significant role in the care of older adults; between 1968 and 1978, the percentage of Medicare beneficiaries' incomes spent on prescription drugs actually fell (MedPAC, 1999). However, pharmaceuticals have played an increasingly important role in health care since then: "Older adults are far more likely to suffer from chronic conditions for which drug treatment [is] an important part of care, such as arthritis, diabetes, high blood pressure, heart disease, Parkinson's disease, and depression" (MedPAC, 1999, p. 4).

As the importance of prescription drugs has grown, so too has their cost to consumers. Between 1990 and 2002, spending for prescription drugs grew by a factor of four (Families USA, 2005b). From 2001 to 2004, the prices of the 30 leading brand-name drugs increased at 3.6 times the rate of inflation (Families USA, 2005b). During the 1990s, as costs grew, pressure developed for Congress to add prescription drug coverage to Medicare. In December 2003, after contentious debate, Congress enacted and President Bush signed into law the MMA of 2003, which created a Medicare Part D to provide drug coverage to Medicare recipients (effective 2006).

Critics raised several concerns about this legislation. First, although the act provided subsidies for low-income individuals, they warned that its "cost-sharing" provisions could create financial difficulty for "beneficiaries with multiple chronic conditions—the heaviest users of prescription drugs" (Anderson et al., 2004, p. W4-397). Second, beginning in 2010, the legislation created a demonstration project to "test competition" between MCOs and traditional Medicare; critics warned that this could be an effort to privatize Medicare (Gorin, 2003) (see also MMA of 2003), and, although the Affordable Care Act (ACA) was passed in 2010, those who opposed the bill are still promoting efforts to privatize Medicare. Third, the act did not include provisions for cost control, such as allowing Medicare to negotiate directly with drug companies (Anderson et al., 2004). This is something that the Obama administration tried unsuccessfully to have included in the ACA. However, the Obama administration had suggested the need to find savings in Medicare by purchasing generic brands and speeding up the introduction of generic brands of medicine into the market, which was included in the ACA.

Medicare Advantage (Part C). Although much attention has focused on the drug benefit created by the MMA (see www.cms.hhs.gov/medicarereform/MMAactFullText.pdf), the MMA introduced other changes that had profound implications for the future of Medicare (Berenson, 2004). The law changed the name of M + C to Medicare Advantage (MA) and created regional preferred provider organizations (PPOs) to "be added to existing county-based private plans participating in Medicare Advantage" (Kaiser Family Foundation, 2005, p. 2). To "encourage" plans to join the PPOs, the MMA established a $10 billion "stabilization fund" and a "'network adequacy fund' to assist regional plans in contracting with rural hospitals" (Berenson, 2004, p. W4-575).

In addition, the MMA increased payments to MCOs. In 2004 and 2005, plans received "on average . . . about 108 percent of what should have been spent for the same beneficiaries in traditional Medicare," as well as an additional 2.3–4 percent due to the unusual way Medicare "risk-adjusted" payments to the MCOs (Berenson, 2004, p. 572). (Gold [2005] placed the overpayment to MCOs at 115–116 percent.) The Medicare Payment Advisory Commission (MedPAC, 2004), which the BBA created to advise Congress on Medicare, expressed concern that these payment increases undermined the commission's goal of "payment equity" between Medicare FFS and "private plans" (MedPAC, 2004, p. 213).

The original House version of the MMA contained a provision to change Medicare into a premium support system and require traditional FFS Medicare to compete with HMOs and other private plans, beginning in 2010 (Gorin, 2003). The assumption was that competition would help fix our failing Medicare system and bring it into the twenty-first century. Yet, as Reinhardt (2003) pointed out, many of the traditional Medicare's alleged problems have had less to do with the structure of the program than with Congress, which prevented traditional Medicare from introducing "managed care techniques" and soliciting "competitive bids for the products and services it purchases on behalf of seniors" (Reinhardt, 2003, p. 8).

Critics also noted that private plans did not have a particularly good record in servicing Medicare beneficiaries. Between 2001 and 2003 HMOs in that state increased premiums and copayments and reduced the number of services they offered. As long as beneficiaries could switch from private plans back to traditional Medicare, this would not be an insurmountable difficulty. However, if costs in traditional Medicare were to rise dramatically or the rules changed to "lock" enrollees into a plan, it could become a serious problem, particularly for vulnerable beneficiaries (Biles et al., 2004; Laschober, 2005).

Traditional Medicare serves as the "insurer of last resort," providing coverage for those who cannot obtain it in the market (Reinhardt, 2003). If, under a premium support approach, Congress were to allow traditional Medicare to pull out of "unprofitable" markets, what would happen to beneficiaries in areas without private plans? On the other hand, if Congress were to prevent Medicare from withdrawing from these markets, how could the traditional program compete with private plans, which face no such restriction (Reinhardt, 2003)?

Medicare Improvements for Patients and Providers Act of 2008

In 2008, Congress passed the Medicare Improvements for Patients and Providers Act (MIPPA) and did so with sufficient support to override President Bush's plan to veto the bill. The legislation extended expiring provisions under the Medicare program, improved access to preventive and mental health services, improved low-income benefit programs, and helped maintain access to care in rural areas. The bill temporarily blocked a 10 percent cut in payments to physicians and a 1 percent increase in fees scheduled for 2009. This change was introduced to address growing concerns about providers who were threatening to leave the Medicare program due to inadequate payments for services.

At the same time, however, with Medicare Advantage and government incentives to move beneficiaries into HMO and PPO plans, private managed-care plans were paid more than traditional Medicare to cover the same beneficiaries; plans were paid, on average, 9–13 percent more, which resulted in higher Part B premiums for all beneficiaries in 2009, and cost the federal government an additional $14 billion more than it would have had Medicare Advantage plan enrollees remained in the traditional Medicare program. This bill reduced payments to Medicare Advantage plans and, in doing so, helped to move Medicare closer to its original purpose of providing public health coverage to older adults and to ensure their access to medical care. Efforts to implement competitive bidding for medical equipment (to reduce costs) that were required by the MMA of 2003 were, however, delayed.

Other important changes in the 2008 legislation addressed mental health and prevention. Starting in 2010, beneficiaries would no longer be expected to pay discriminatory coinsurance rates of 50 percent (Barry et al., 2010) and by 2014 would pay 20 percent of the cost, as has been the practice for most other provider services. Prevention was also targeted; the bill allowed coverage for new preventive services recommended by the program without waiting for approval from Congress (Barry, 2008; Barry et al., 2010).

Finally, new policies were also established with passage of the MIPPA to use Medicare to help reduce racial and ethnic health disparities. The legislation called for improved data collection for measuring and evaluating health disparities, outreach to previously uninsured individuals, and compliance with cultural competency standards (Families USA, 2008). Many of these and other issues targeted in MIPPA were addressed in the new ACA legislation, but on a broader scale and not limited to Medicare.

Medicare and the Affordable Care Act (2010)

Costs associated with the Medicare program continue to raise concern. In 2005, Congress passed the Deficit Reduction Act in an effort to slow the pace of spending growth in both Medicare and Medicaid by $11 billion between 2005 and 2010. In 2009, Medicare expenditures reached $524 billion and were projected to reach $949 billion by 2020 (Kaiser Family Foundation, 2010b).

The ACA brought significant changes to the Medicare program, many of which helped to reduce costs for beneficiaries and for the federal government. According to the Center for Medicare Advocacy, Inc. (2012), the ACA expanded Medicare coverage by eliminating cost-sharing for preventive services, adding a yearly wellness visit which includes a "Mini-Mental" and basic cognitive exam, limiting some cost-sharing in private Medicare plans, and closing the Part D "Donut Hole." The ACA was also projected to reduce spending by $428 million over 10 years (2010–20), even after increasing spending by over $100 million, and to extend the life of the Medicare trust fund by 10 years. The largest saving ($332 billion) would occur through a series of phased-in reductions in overpayments to private Medicare Advantage (MA) plans (Congressional Budget office, 2010).

Other savings included the adjustment of scheduled increases to providers based on productivity, and would therefore reduce expected annual FFS provider payment increases. Beginning in 2015, the new Independent Payment Advisory Board would recommend program changes, if program-spending growth exceeded specified savings targets of almost $16 billion for the years 2015–2019. However, as mentioned earlier in Chapter 1, Congress introduced bills to repeal it, dozens of medical associations including the American Medical Association (AMA) asked for its repeal, and President Obama never appointed any members to the panel. The ACA includes other provisions that both decrease and increase spending, such as coverage of the gap in Part D prescription coverage (Kaiser Family Foundation, 2011a).

The ACA also addressed the delivery of services in an effort to both improve quality of care and reduce spending. The reform legislation has provisions that encourage providers to improve the quality and coordination of care, such as a new Medicare Shared Savings program for accountable care organizations (ACOs) and bundling payments for a hospital stay. A new Center for Medicare and Medicaid Innovation was established to explore more efficient and innovative payment and service delivery models, particularly focused on Medicare and Medicaid dual eligible enrollees and other "high-need" populations (Kaiser Family Foundation, 2011b).

Overall, the ACA has had a significant impact on the Medicare program. As outlined by the Commonwealth Fund (2015), since the ACA was enacted it has been (Davis et al., 2015):

- closing the gap in preventive care (by providing free flu shots and screenings for cancer, diabetes, and other chronic diseases) and prescription drug coverage;

- strengthening chronic care management;

- encouraging health care providers to emphasize high-value care; and

- slowing the growth of spending as a result of discounts and the gradual elimination of the donut hole (8 million beneficiaries saved $11.5 billion between 2010 and 2015).

Medicare Access and CHIP Reauthorization Act of 2015

In 2015, Congress enacted the Medicare Access and CHIP Reauthorization Act (MACRA), which provided new federal funding for the Children's Health Insurance Program (CHIP) through 2017, and changed the Medicare payment system for physician services. Under the new law, physicians and other professionals affili-ated with certain alternative payment models (APMs) are eligible for automatic 5 percent bonuses on their Medicare payments, starting in 2019. This new payment approach rewards providers for delivering high-quality and cost-efficient care. According to the Centers for Medicare and Medicaid Services, in 2017, approximately 70,000 and 120,000 providers were affiliated with qualifying APMs (Kaiser Family Foundation, 2017a). Alternative payment models fall into three categories (Baseman et al., 2016):

1. **Medical homes**. These provide a team-based model of care that require pri-mary care providers and their care team to serve as the main source of delivery and coordination of care. In addition to FFS reimbursement for care, insur-ers provide monthly management fees or other payments for other activities related to patient care and coordination.

2. **ACOs.** These organizations are groups of doctors, hospitals, and other health care providers who collectively share accountability for the quality and cost of care delivered to the patients in their ACO. Insurers include financial incen-tives in their payments to ACOs (bonuses or penalties) for their performance on identified metrics of quality and cost.

3. **Bundled payments.** This model establishes an overall budget for services provided to a patient receiving care and treatment for a specific medical/clinical condition over a defined period of time. By "bundling payments," insurers provide incentives for providers to provide care at less cost for spe-cific episodes of care.

BENEFITS AND FINANCING

Medicare is one of a group of social insurance programs legislated by the Social Security Act referred to as OASDHI—Old Age (OA), Survivors (S), Disability (D), and Health Insurance (HI or Medicare). The original Social Security Act of 1935 provided old-age pensions for retired workers. In 1939, retirement benefits were extended to workers' dependents and survivors. Congress amended the act again in 1956 to add disability insurance for employed workers who were unable to continue working due to physical or mental impairments, and Medicare was added in 1965. Medicare has four components: Hospital Insurance (Part A), Medical Insurance (Part B), Medicare Advantage (Part C), and Medicare Prescription Drug (Part D). Medicare is administered by the federal government, which governs policies related to eligi-bility criteria, financing, benefits, payments to providers, and decisions about service delivery (e.g., FFS vs. managed care). Figures 6.1, 6.2, and 6.3 provide a full overview of the benefits and services provided by the Medicare program (see www.medicare.gov for updated information regarding premiums, deductibles, and copayments). The following sections provide basic information about the primary components—what is provided to beneficiaries and how the program is funded.

Financing for the Medicare program comes from several sources: A dedicated Medicare payroll tax (Part A is funded by a tax of 2.9 percent of earnings paid by

FIGURE 6.1

*Medicare:
Overview of
Benefits*

PART A (HOSPITAL INSURANCE) Mandatory

- Hospital stays: Covers first 60 days of hospitalization (semi-private rooms, meals, general nursing, drugs, supplies, and other services). Beneficiaries pay 1) an annual deductible, 2) a daily co-insurance for hospital stays over 60 days, and 3) 190 days lifetime inpatient psychiatric care.
- Skilled nursing facility care: Covers 20 days of care (semi-private room, meals, nursing and rehabilitative care, supplies, other services) subject to three-day prior hospitalization. Beneficiary pays a daily coinsurance for days 21–100, and for all care over 100 days.
- Home health care: Covers part-time skilled nursing, physical therapy, occupational therapy, speech–language therapy, home health aides, supplies, durable medical equipment, other services. Beneficiary pays copayment for medical equipment, but no costs for care.
- Hospice care: Provided for terminally ill patients (with 6 months or less life expectancy). Covers Medicare-approved medical and support services, drugs, short-term respite care, other services. Beneficiary pays copayment for prescription drugs and respite care, but no costs for hospice.
- Inpatient care in a religious nonmedical health care institution: these facilities prohibit both traditional and nontraditional medical care. Covers inpatient, nonreligious, nonmedical items and services, such as room and board.

PART B (SUPPLEMENTARY MEDICAL INSURANCE) Voluntary

- Medical and Other Services
    - Outpatient hospital and surgical services and supplies
    - Outpatient mental health care
    - Physician and other provider services
    - Lab services
    - Urgent Care, Emergency Room services, Federal Qualified Health Care Center services, Rural Health Clinic Services, Transitional Care Management services
    - Diagnostic tests including foot exams, hearing and balance exams, and Durable medical equipment including prosthetic and orthotic items
    - Transplants and immunosuppressive drugs
    - Kidney Dialysis
    - Covered preventive services: Initial routine physical examinations and yearly wellness exam. Cancer screening tests including mammograms, cervical and vaginal, colorectal, liver, and prostate. Additional screening tests including abdominal aortic aneurisms, alcohol misuse, bone density, cardiovascular, cholesterol and blood, depression, diabetes, glaucoma, HEP C, HIV, obesity, and sexually transmitted infection. Shots including flu, pneumococcal, and HEP B.Smoking and tobacco use cessation counseling.
    - Other services: Advance care planning, ambulatory services, services provided in an ambulatory surgical center, cardiovascular rehabilitation, chemotherapy, chiropractic services (medically necessary and limited), chronic care management services, clinical research studies, continuous positive airway pressure (CPAP) therapy for sleep apnea, eyeglasses after cataract surgery, nutrition therapy, second surgical opinions, surgical dressing services, and telehealth.
- Clinical laboratory Services (no cost)
    - Blood tests, urinalyses, and some screening tests (EKG or ECG)
- Home Health
    - Part-time or intermittent skilled care
    - Occupational therapy, Speech–language therapy
    - Hospice consultation and end-of-life counseling
- Services NOT COVERED
    - Most dental care
- Eye examinations related to prescribing glasses
- Dentures
- Cosmetic surgery
- Acupuncture
- Hearing aids and exams for fitting them
- Long-term care
- Concierge care (also called concierge medicine, retainer-based medicine, boutique medicine, platinum practice, or direct care).

PAYMENT

- For Part B, beneficiaries who have "Original Medicare" pay (1) a monthly premium, (2) an annual deductible, (3) 20% copayment for most health services. No cost for most preventive services. Physicians and other health care providers agreee to accept the Medicare-approved amount ("assignment") as full payment for covered services.
- There are 4 kinds of Medicare Savings Programs for those with limited incomes and resources:
    1. **Qualified Medicare Beneficiary (QMB) Program** which helps pay for Part A and/or Part B premiums. Not responsible for deductibles, coinsurance, and copayments, except outpatient prescription drugs.
    2. **Specified Low-Income Medicare Beneficiary (SLMB) Program** which helps pay Part B premiums only.
    3. **Qualifying Individual (QI) Program** which helps pay Part B premiums only. Beneficiary must apply each year for QI benefits; applications are granted on a first-come first-served basis.
    4. **Qualifed Disabled and Working Individuals (QDWI) Program** which helps pay Part A premiums only. Beneficiary may qualify if disabled and working.

PART C (MEDICARE ADVANTAGE) Optional (not Original Medicare): Managed care coverage provided through private companies approved by Medicare.

- Most plans offer extra coverage, like vision, hearing, dental, and other health and wellness programs. Most include Medicare prescription drug coverage (Part D).
- In addition to the Part B premium, there may be a monthly premium for the plan.

PART D (PRESCRIPTION DRUGS) Effective January 1, 2006: Drug plans (generic and brand name) provided through private companies approved by Medicare

- Beneficiary must have Part A and B, pay premiums, deductibles, and copayments, which vary by plan, and might be subject to a penalty if they didn't join when first eligible.
- Beneficiary must enroll in a stand-alone prescription drug plan (PDP) or Medicare Advantage prescription drug (MA-PD) plan.

Source: Centers for Medicare and Medicaid Services (2017).

PRIVATE MANAGED-CARE PLANS (HMOs AND PPOs) THAT PROVIDE PARTS A, B, AND D BENEFITS

Type of MA plans	Medicare health maintenance organizations (HMOs)
	Medicare preferred provider organizations (PPOs)
	Medicare private fee-for-service plans (PFFS)
	Medicare special needs plans (SNPs)
	HMO point-of-service (HMOPOS) plans
	Medicare medical saving accounts (MSAs)

Source: www.medicare.gov

FIGURE 6.2

Medicare Part C: Medicare Advantage (Optional)

BENEFICIARY PAYS

- Monthly premium (variable; in addition to Part B premium)

- Yearly deductible

- Copayments

- Coverage gap ("donut hole"): Begins after enrollee has spent certain amount for covered drugs. Then responsible for 35% of costs for brand name drugs and 44% of costs for generic drugs until reach end of coverage gap.

- Catastrophic coverage: Once out of "donut hole", pay reduced coinsurance or copayment rates for balance of year.

- Late enrollment penalty: Amount added to monthly premium if join Part D after the Initial Enrollment Period and not covered for 63 or more consecutive days.

Extra Help assists people with limited income and resources pay for Part D. Medicaid and SSI recipients automatically qualify for the Extra Help program. Those who qualify:

- Get help paying for the drug plan

- Have no coverage gap

- Have no late enrollment penalty

- Have the chance to switch plans at any time

Source: www.medicare.gov/Pubs/pdf/10050-Medicare-and-You.pdf

FIGURE 6.3

Medicare Part D: Prescription Drugs (New Program as of January 1, 2006)

employers and workers, at 1.45 percent each); general revenue, primarily from federal income taxes (Parts B and D); premiums paid by beneficiaries (Parts B and D); a tax on Social Security benefits; and, since 2006, payments from states for the Part D prescription drug benefit (which shifted some state Medicaid program expenditures to Medicare). A primary source of revenue is the payroll tax, which, in 2009, provided 85 percent of all the revenue contributed to the Medicare Trust Fund. The ACA increased the Medicare payroll tax for higher-income taxpayers; those earning more than $200,000/individual and $250,000/couple per year contribute an additional 0.9 percent as of 2013 (Kaiser Family Foundation, 2011a). Overall, primary funding for Medicare is provided by general revenues (45%), the payroll tax (36%), and beneficiary premiums (13%) (Cubanski and Newman, 2017).

Hospital Insurance (Part A). Part A covers inpatient hospital, skilled nursing facility, home health, and hospital care. Most nursing home care is custodial and is not covered by Medicare. Part A is funded primarily (87%) (Cubanski and Newman, 2017) by the dedicated payroll tax.

Medical Insurance (Part B). Part B covers physician and other providers, outpatient, and preventive services. With the MMA of 2003, Part B deductibles are indexed to the increase in the average cost of Part B services. General revenues (75%) and beneficiary premiums (23%) fund Part B (Cubanski and Newman, 2017).

Medicare Advantage (Part C). The Medicare Advantage program, formerly called Medicare + Choice, gives beneficiaries the option to join private managed-care plans that provide hospital and supplementary medical benefits (Parts A and B). Most of these plans are HMOs, though enrollees are encouraged to join regional PPOs. The Medicare Advantage program (Part C) is not separately financed.

Medicare Advantage plans essentially provide all Medicare-covered benefits, but are required to pass along savings to beneficiaries in the form of lower premiums and copayments, additional benefits, or contributions to a reserve fund. Enrollees are allowed to disenroll from these plans once a year during a three-month period.

However, the cost per enrollee of Medicare Advantage has actually exceeded traditional FFS plans. From 1999 to 2004, out-of-pocket expenses tripled for enrollees in Medicare managed-care plans (Kaiser Family Foundation, 2004), and then increased again in 2005 (Kaiser Family Foundation, 2008). In 2010, the cost per enrollee averaged 13 percent higher than the Medicare FFS program (Kaiser Family Foundation, 2011a).

The number of beneficiaries enrolled in Medicare Advantage has increased steadily from 5.3 million in 2003 to 11.4 million in 2010, or approximately 25 percent of all Medicare beneficiaries (Kaiser Family Foundation, 2010b) to 19 million in 2017 (Kaiser Family Foundation, 2017c) (see Figure 6.2 for an overview of Medicare Advantage).

Medicare Prescription Drug (Part D). Medicare Part D is a voluntary outpatient prescription drug benefit offered under contracted private plans through Medicare (effective January 1, 2006). Medicare reformers have wanted a prescription drug benefit for many years; however, according to Families USA (2005b),

there have been winners and losers with the structure of this relatively new benefit. Most Medicare beneficiaries have coverage that is limited to an approved drug
list and pay high premiums and deductibles that continue to rise each year. The
pharmaceutical companies, on the other hand, were able to defeat efforts to reduce
the cost of prescription drugs through governmental price negotiations and the
importation of prescription drugs from Canada and other countries. According to
Anderson et al. (2004), if the Medicare program were to pay comparable prices to
Canada, the U.K., and France, it would be possible to eliminate the "doughnut
hole" cost ($1780) to the beneficiary in its prescription drug benefit.

The Medicare Modernization Act established a new "Extra Help" program to
assist beneficiaries with limited income and assets with prescription drug costs.
Those who qualify for this program automatically include low-income Medicare
beneficiaries referred to as "dual eligibles" (eligible for both Medicare and Medicaid).
Those who are dually eligible no longer receive drug coverage through the Medicaid
program; instead, the MMA Prescription Drug program covers them. In 2017, about
nine million Medicare beneficiaries were subsidized by the Medicaid program (Kaiser
Family Foundation, 2017b). States contribute to the financing through a complex
formula that includes a provision known as the "clawback" payment, because it
creates an incentive for states to drop dually eligible beneficiaries from the Medicaid
program. As noted by Families USA (2005b), some states reduced or eliminated
Medicaid coverage for dual-eligible older and disabled poor adults, many of whom
lived at home or with their families. This state-level policy puts them at risk of losing
other important Medicaid-funded health services. Dual eligibles in state Medicaid
plans also face enormous difficulties because states may automatically enroll these
recipients in Medicare managed-care plans that may or may not cover needed drugs.

GAPS IN COVERAGE AND COST SHARING

A major concern with Medicare has always been its gaps in coverage. Legislation
enacted in 2003 added coverage for prescription drugs and initial routine examinations starting in 2006. However, Medicare still does not provide payment for
many services often needed by older adults, including routine dental and eye
examinations, hearing aids, regular physical examinations, and immunizations
(except annual flu shots and shots for pneumonia and hepatitis B, which are covered). Perhaps most importantly, Medicare does not cover long-term custodial care,
home health visits not covered by Part A, and other outpatient services (Centers for
Medicare and Medicaid Services, 2005).

Out-of-pocket costs and cost-sharing requirements are another concern. Most
physicians who treat Medicare patients accept the program's approved fees as full
payment for their services, but others exercise their right to charge beneficiaries an
additional restricted fee. The cost of physician fees, omissions in coverage, premiums, deductibles, and copayments add up to significant costs that must be paid
either out of pocket or with supplemental insurance. About 25 percent of beneficiaries purchase private Medigap, or Medicare Supplement Insurance, to provide coverage for the gaps in Medicare coverage, and about one-third receive supplemental
coverage through employee retirement benefits (Kaiser Family Foundation, 2016).

About 25 percent (Kaiser Family Foundation, 2013a) of beneficiaries (low-income and disabled "dual eligible" workers), who are eligible for Medicare but unable to afford the premiums, receive coverage through state Medicaid assistance programs referred to as Medicare buy-in programs. The Medicare buy-in program or "Medicare Savings Program" was originally introduced in the 1988 Medicare Catastrophic Coverage Act. Although the 1988 legislation was repealed, the provisions of the buy-in program were adopted and expanded through legislative reforms passed in 1990, 1993, 1995, and again in 1997 with a block grant program. The Medicare buy-in program allows Medicaid to cover premiums, deductibles, and coinsurance payments for beneficiaries whose incomes are below or near the federal poverty level (FPL) (Families USA, 2005a).

In 2006, Medicare covered only 48 percent of the total health care cost of services received by beneficiaries. Beneficiaries spent *one-quarter* of their incomes on health care services and insurance premiums combined (Kaiser Family Foundation, 2011). The Medicare buy-in program was established to prevent individual financial hardship, but there are often insufficient outreach efforts, difficulties with enrollment processes, and delays in activating eligibility (Kaiser Family Foundation, 1999). Mandatory Medicaid benefits are made available to low-income Medicare beneficiaries through four primary categories of eligibility: Qualified Beneficiaries ("quimbies"), Specified Low-income Beneficiaries ("slimbies"), Qualified Working Disabled Individuals, and Qualifying Individuals (in addition to Supplemental Security Income [SSI] beneficiaries) (see Figure 6.1).

BENEFICIARIES

In 2009, Medicare insured 47 million beneficiaries (39 million adults over the age of 65 and 8 million younger individuals with disabilities and end-stage kidney disease; Medicare was amended in 1972 to include the latter group) (Kaiser Family Foundation, 2010). In 2016, the number of beneficiaries rose to 59 million (Kaiser Family Foundation, 2017a). The Medicare program serves the medical needs of a diverse population with variations in age, race, ethnicity, gender, income, and health status. However, Medicare serves a greater number of older women than older men, and more disabled men than disabled women. In 2011, 9 percent of the Medicare population was African American, and 9 percent was Latinx (Kaiser Family Foundation, 2016). The majority of Medicare beneficiaries are very poor; 47 percent have incomes below 200 percent of the FPL (Kaiser Family Foundation, 2010). In 2014, median per person income for African American and Latino Medicare beneficiaries ($16,150 and $12,800, respectively) was considerably lower than for white Medicare beneficiaries ($27,450); savings disparities were even greater, with the amount of savings for white beneficiaries found to be seven times greater than for African American or Latino beneficiaries (Kaiser Family Foundation, 2016). These racial disparities are reflected in health disparities as discussed later in the book.

Older Adults. The overwhelming majority of Medicare beneficiaries are over the age of 65; about 17 percent are under age 65 (Kaiser Family Foundation, 2017a). Demographic projections for the U.S. suggest that its older population is likely to continue to grow as a percentage of the population. In the late 1990s, older adults made up 13 percent of the U.S. population; in 2016, the number of individuals over age 65 grew to 15.2 percent. By 2050, the number of older adults in the U.S. is expected to double and grow to 20 percent of the population. Moreover, within the older population, those over the age of 85 continue to live longer and are projected to represent 4.5 percent of the population (up from 2.5 percent in 2030). These demographic trends have implications for future growth in the number of Medicare beneficiaries. Older people tend to be sicker than younger people and to spend more on health care. Thus, the changing demographics of Medicare also fuels concern about financing the program (Fronstin and Copeland, 1997).

Adults with Disabilities. Medicare is available to certain nonelderly individuals aged under 65 with disabilities who are eligible for Social Security Disability Insurance (SSDI); in 2016, Medicare covered 9.1 million people aged under 65 with disabilities (16 percent of Medicare beneficiaries). A larger share of beneficiaries aged under 65 are male, have lower incomes, and represent communities of color compared with their counterparts aged over 65. In addition, in 2012, almost two-thirds of younger Medicare beneficiaries (65 percent) had a cognitive or mental impairment (compared with 29 percent of older beneficiaries). Younger Medicare beneficiaries report poorer health and more limitations in their activities of daily living compared with Medicare beneficiaries aged over 65.

As discussed in Chapter 7, the ACA gave people with disabilities greater access to health insurance through expansion of Medicaid or Marketplace plans, which could be especially helpful for SSDI recipients in the 24-month Medicare waiting period. Before the ACA, many people with disabilities in the waiting period for Medicare faced difficulties obtaining or affording health insurance in the private market (Cubanski et al., 2016).

Women. Women make up about 56 percent of Medicare's beneficiaries and two-thirds of all beneficiaries aged over 85 are women. Both Social Security and Medicare are important sources of support for women. Female beneficiaries aged over 65 have lower median per capita income than men, and significantly fewer financial assets and less retirement savings. In addition, older female beneficiaries spend more on health care (including premiums), long-term services and supports than older men, all of which creates a greater financial burden as they age, given their lower incomes and greater need for long-term services (Kaiser Family Foundation, 2013b).

Clearly, the Medicare program is vitally important to women. Women are more likely to live in poverty than men are and many outlive their husbands. As discussed later in this text, women have experienced economic inequity through occupational segregation, job discrimination, and pay inequity. Consequently, older women in particular have been more likely to depend on their spouses for financial support; widowhood or divorce compounds this problem.

Women are also more likely to live alone than men due to increased longevity, have had a tendency to marry slightly older men, and have been less likely to remarry as widows than men. As a result of their longevity, women are more susceptible to multiple chronic conditions, such as hypertension, arthritis, and osteoporosis, and have a greater need for long-term care (Health Care Financing Administration, 2000b). These concerns are addressed in greater depth later in the book.

MEDICARE SPENDING AND TRUST FUND

The ACA had an impact on Medicare spending soon after it was enacted. In fiscal year 2012, Medicare spending per beneficiary increased by only 0.4 percent while cutting no "benefits for beneficiaries" (Kronick and Po, 2013, p. 1). This was a "substantially" lower increase than "the 3.4% increase in per capita GDP" (Kronick and Po, 2013, p. 1). The CBO estimated that, between 2013 and 2022, Medicare spending per beneficiary would grow at a rate of between 0.3 percent and 0.8 percent under the rate of increase of GDP. In comparison, between 1970 and 2010, Medicare spending per beneficiary increased by around 2.7 percent *above* GDP. According to Kronick and Po (2013), the "slow growth in spending per beneficiary" was "unprecedented" and could improve the program's "ability to meet its commitments . . . to future generations" (Kronick and Po, 2013, p. 2). They credited the ACA with being "the primary" cause of projections for slower growth in the next ten years. MedPAC (2013), the independent commission appointed by Congress to provide advice on Medicare payment policies, reported that, as a result of the ACA, and despite the increasing number of beneficiaries due to the aging of the baby-boomers, the growth in Medicare spending during the next decade "is projected to be much smaller than in the past 10 years" (MedPAC, 2013. p. xii).

Despite this, the Medicare Hospital Insurance Trust Fund is projected to be depleted by 2029 (Cubanski and Newman, 2017); however, the economic prospects for Medicare may not be as dire as some observers have suggested (Cutler, 2005; Lubitz, 2005). More than a decade ago, Reinhardt (2003) pointed out that the aging of the population is not by itself responsible for the financial challenges facing Medicare. In fact, with some notable exceptions, Medicare has had a better record of controlling costs than private insurers (Reinhardt, 2012). The real issue is the high cost of health care in the U.S., not the aging of our population. As the history of Medicare and the recent experience of the ACA demonstrate, with political will costs can be brought under control (White, 2008).

Potential Threats to Medicare

In 2011 and 2012, Representative Paul Ryan (R-WI) introduced a bill that would end traditional Medicare by giving beneficiaries the option to purchase private health insurance with government premium supports, or vouchers. There are several problems with this approach (Gorin, 2012). Premium supports would likely be unable to keep up with the escalating cost of private insurance, which would not be controlled if the ACA were repealed. This problem would be compounded by the likelihood that higher-cost beneficiaries would remain enrolled in traditional Medicare as private insurance companies marketed their plans to healthier (lower-cost) beneficiaries; this could destabilize the Medicare program. Ultimately, the aim of the Ryan plan was to gradually shift the cost of coverage to beneficiaries and weaken the Medicare program. In 2013, Ryan introduced a similar failed version of his bill, which would have taken effect for new beneficiaries beginning in 2024 and pose a serious threat to future beneficiaries (Greenstein, 2013). In 2017, the House of Representatives led by House Speaker Paul Ryan have threatened to take up this effort to privatize Medicare once again.

MEDICARE MILESTONES

- Medicare was created in 1965 as Title XVIII of the Social Security Act.

- In 1967, Early and Periodic Screening, Diagnosis and treatment (EPSDT) was added for children under the age of 21.

- In 1972, Health Care Financing Administration (HCFA) was created.

- In 1980, home health services coverage expanded and Medicare supplemental insurance, Medigap, was brought under federal oversight.

- The Tax Equity and Fiscal Responsibility Act of 1982 provided incentives for HMOs to join the Medicare program and expand quality oversight efforts.

- In 1983, the inpatient acute hospital prospective payment system (PPS) was created (to replace cost-based payments).

- The Emergency Medical Treatment and Labor Act of 1985 required hospitals to provide appropriate emergency room medical screenings and stabilizing treatments.

- The Balanced Budget Act of 1997 established new managed-care and other private health plan choices for beneficiaries, designed to slow the rate of growth in spending and extend the life of the trust fund (Part C).

- In 1998, www.medicare.gov was launched to provide updated information.

- In 1999, a nationwide toll-free number (1-800-MEDICARE) was made available and the first annual *Medicare & You* handbook was distributed to beneficiary households.

- The Benefits Improvement and Protection Act (BIPA) of 2000 increased payment level to providers, and managed health care organizations, reduced certain copayments, and improved coverage of preventive services.

- In 2001, the HCFA was renamed Centers for Medicare and Medicaid Services.

- The Medicare Prescription Drug, Improvement, and Modernization Act (MMA) of 2003 established the most significant changes since enactment; it created a prescription drug discount card until 2006, allowed for competition among health plans to foster innovation and flexibility in coverage, covered new preventive benefits, and other changes.

- In 2006, new voluntary Part D outpatient prescription drug benefits were made available.

- Medicare Improvements for the Patients and Providers Act (MIPPA) of 2008 extended expiring provisions under the Medicare program, improved access to preventive and mental health services, improved low-income benefit programs, and helped maintain access to care in rural areas. This bill reduced payments to Medicare Advantage plans.

- The Affordable Care Act of 2010 expanded Medicare coverage by eliminating cost sharing for preventive services, adding a yearly wellness visit, limiting some cost sharing in private Medicare plans, and closing the Part D "donut hole."

HIGHLIGHTS

- Medicare, a social insurance program, provides health insurance to almost 47 million adult retirees, individuals with disabilities who have difficulty continuing their employment, and individuals with end-stage kidney disease.

- Medicare has four parts: (Part A) Hospital Insurance, (Part B) Medical Insurance, (Part C) Medicare Advantage, and (Part D) Medicare Prescription Drug (effective January 1, 2006). Parts C and D were created by the Medicare Prescription Drug, Improvement, and Modernization Act (MMA). Medicare is financed by a payroll tax on employers and employees; self-employed workers pay both taxes. Recipients incur substantial out-of-pocket expenses for additional physician fees, copayments, deductibles, and services not covered by Medicare. The most costly services not covered are prescription drugs, long-term care, and physician payments.

- About one-quarter of Medicare beneficiaries purchase Medigap insurance or have supplemental insurance through their employers that provides additional coverage; other beneficiaries have reduced some of their expenses by joining managed-care plans or participating in the Medicare buy-in program. However, many eligible enrollees do not participate in the buy-in program as dual-eligible beneficiaries.

- Medicare has undergone two significant reforms. First, managed care was introduced, starting in the early 1980s, and has expanded since the 1990s. Second, a prescription drug benefit was finally added, effective 2006.

- With the Affordable Care Act (2010) reform legislation, Medicare is likely to reach millions more beneficiaries and reduce costs for both individual beneficiaries and the federal government.

- Although Medicare has often had a better record of controlling costs than private insurers, the potential depletion of the Medicare Hospital Insurance Trust Fund in 2029 remains a cause for concern. With political will, this can be addressed.

WEBSITES TO OBTAIN UPDATED AND ADDITIONAL INFORMATION

U.S. Department of Health and Human Services:

www.hhs.gov/Medicare

Centers for Medicare and Medicaid Services:

www.hcfa.gov/Medicaid

Kaiser Family Foundation:

www.kff.org

REFERENCES

Anderson, G. F., Shea, D. G., Hussey, P. S., Kenhari, S., and Zephyrin, L. (2004). Market Watch: Doughnut Holes ND Price Controls. *Health Affairs*. Online. Retrieved from http://content.healthaffairs.org/content/early/2004/07/21/hlthaff.w4.396.full. pdf+html

Ball, R. (1995, Winter). Perspectives on Medicare: What Medicare's Architects Had in Mind. *Health Affairs*, 14(4), 62–100.

Baseman, S., Boccuti, C., Moon, M., Griffin, S., and Dutta, T. (2016, November 17). *Payment and Delivery System Reform in Medicare: A Primer on Medical Homes, Accountable Care Organizations, and Bundled Payments*. Washington, DC: Kaiser Family Foundation. Retrieved from www.kff.org/report-section/payment-and-delivery-system-reform-in-medicare-executive-summary/

Berenson, R. A. (2004, December 15). Medicare Disadvantaged and the Search for the Elusive "Level Playing Field." *Health Affairs*. Online. Retrieved from http://content. healthaffairs.org/content/early/2004/12/15/hlthaff.w4.572.citation

Biles, B., Dallek, G., and Nicholas, L. H. (2004, December 15). Medicare Advantage: Déjà Vu All Over Again? *Health Affairs* (online). Retrieved from http://content.healthaf fairs.org/content/early/2004/12/15/hlthaff.w4.586.citation

Center for Medicare Advocacy, Inc. (2012, July 5). *Health Care Reform Does Not Cut Medicare Benefits*. Retrieved from www.medicareadvocacy.org/good-news-for-medi care-supreme-court-upholds-affordable-care-act

Centers for Medicare and Medicaid Services. (2005). *Medicare & You, 2005*. Retrieved from www.medicare.gov

____. (2017). *Medicare & You, 2018*. Retrieved from www.medicare.gov/Pubs/pdf/10050-Medicare-and-You.pdf

Congressional Budget Office. (2010, June). *Long-Term Budget Outlook*. Available at www. cbo.gov/publication/21546

Cubanski, J. and Newman, T. (2017, July 18). *The Facts on Medicare Spending and Financing*. Washington, DC: Kaiser Family Foundation. Retrieved from www.kff.org/medicare/issue-brief/the-facts-on-medicare-spending-and-financing

Cubanski, J., Newman, T., and Damico, A. (2016, August 12). *Medicare's Role for People Under Age 65 with Disabilities*. Retrieved from www.kff.org/medicare/issue-brief/medicares-role-for-people-under-age-65-with-disabilities

Cutler, D. M. (2005, September 26). The Potential For Cost Savings in Medicare's Future. *Health Affairs*. Online. Retrieved from http://content.healthaffairs.org/content/early/2005/09/26/hlthaff.w5.r77.citation

Davis, K., Guterman, S. and Bandeali, F. (2015, June). *The Affordable Care Act and Medicare: How the Law is Challenging the Program and the Challenges that Remain.* The Commonwealth Fund. Retrieved from www.commonwealthfund.org/~/media/files/publications/fund-report/2015/jun/1821_davis_aca_and_medicare_v2.pdf?la=en

Eichner, J. and Vladeck, B. C. (2005). Medicare as a Catalyst for Reducing Health Disparities. *Health Affairs*, 24(2), 365–375.

Families USA. (2005a). *The 2006 Federal Medicaid Battle*. Retrieved from www.familiesusa.org

——. (2005b, July). *Trouble Brewing? New Medicare Drug Law Puts Low-Income People at Risk*. Washington, DC: Families USA.

——. (2008, October). Issue Brief – Congress Delivers Help to People with Medicare: An Overview of the Medicare Improvements for Patients and Providers Act of 2008. Retrieved from research.policyarchive.org/15455.pdf

Fronstin, P. and Copeland, C. (1997, September). *Medicare on Life Support: Will It Survive? Employee Benefits Research Institute Issue Brief, 189*. Washington, DC: Employee Benefits Research Institute.

Gold, M. (2001, July–August). Medicare + Choice: An Interim Report Card. *Health Affairs*, 20(4), 120–138.

——. (2005, September–October). Private Plans in Medicare: Another Look. *Health Affairs*, 24(5), 1302–1310.

Gorin, S. H. (2003, November). Medicare and Premium Support: A Social Work Perspective. *Health & Social Work*, 28(4), 316–321.

——. (2012, August). The Ryan Plan Redux. *Health & Social Work*, 37(3), 131–132.

Greenstein, R. (2013, March 12). Statement by Robert Greenstein, President, On Chairman Ryan's Budget Plan. Center on Budget and Policy Priorities. Retrieved from www.cbpp.org/cms/index.cfm?fa=view&id=3920

Health Care Financing Administration. (2000b, July). *Medicare 2000, 35 Years of Improving America's Health and Security*. Baltimore, MD: Healthcare Financing Administration.

Hearing before the Subcommittee on Health, House Committee on Energy and Commerce. (2002). *Designing a Twenty-First Century Medicare Prescription Drug Benefit*. Statement of Bruce C. Vladeck, pp. 28–34. Retrieved from http://energycommerce.house.gov/108/action/108-25.pdf

Iglehart, J. K. (1994). Managed Competition. In P. R. Lee and C. L. Estes (Eds.), *The Nation's Health*, 4th edn. (pp. 224–230). Boston: Jones & Bartlett.

——. (1997, May–June). Changing with the Times: The Views of Bruce C. Vladeck. *Health Affairs*, 16(3), 58–71.

Kaiser Family Foundation. (1999, May). *Medicare and Medicaid for the Elderly and Disabled Poor. Kaiser Commission on Medicaid and the Uninsured Key Facts*. Washington, DC: The Foundation.

——. (2004, March). *Medicare Advantage*. Washington, DC: The Foundation.

——. (2005, April). *Medicare Advantage Fact Sheet*. Available online at www.kff.org/medicare/upload/medicare-Advantage-April-2005-Fact-Sheet.pdf

——. (2008, November). *Medicare at a Glance. The Medicare Program, The Kaiser Medicare Policy Project*. Washington, DC: The Foundation.

——. (2010, June) *Medicaid Primer 2010*. Washington, DC: The Foundation.

——. (2011a, February) *Medicare Financing and Spending 2011*. Washington, DC: The Foundation.

——. (2011b, July). *Medicare Chart Book*. Washington, DC: The Foundation.

____. (2013a, March 13). *9 Million Dual Eligible Beneficiaries are Covered by Both Medicare and Medicaid*. Retrieved from www.kff.org/medicaid/slide/9-million-dual-eligible-beneficiaries-are-covered-by-both-medicare-and-medicaid

____. (2013b, May 16.) *Medicare's Role for Older Women*. Retrieved from www.kff.org/womens-health-policy/fact-sheet/medicares-role-for-older-women

____. (2016, March). *Profile of Medicare Beneficiaries by Race and Ethnicity: A Chartpack*. Retrieved from http://files.kff.org/attachment/chartpack-profile-of-medicare-beneficiaries-by-race-and-ethnicity-a-chartpack

____. (2017a, November 22). *An Overview of Medicare*. Retrieved from www.kff.org/medicare/issue-brief/an-overview-of-medicare

____. (2017b). *Dual Eligible*. Retrieved from www.kff.org/tag/dual-eligible

____. (2017c, October 10). *Medicare Advantage*. Retrieved from www.kff.org/medicare/fact-sheet/medicare-advantage

Kronick, R. and Po, R. (2013, January 7). *Growth in Medicare Spending per Beneficiary Continues to Hit Historic Lows*. ASPE Brief. Retrieved from http://aspe.hhs.gov/health/reports/2013/medicarespendinggrowth/ib.pdf

Laschober, M. (2005, Spring). Estimating Medicare Advantage Lock-in Provisions Impact on Vulnerable Medicare Beneficiaries. *Health Care Financing Review*, 26(3), 63.

Lubitz, J. (2005, September 26). Health, Technology, and Medicare Care Spending. *Health Affairs*. Online. Retrieved from http://content.healthaffairs.org/content/early/2005/09/26/hlthaff.w5.r81.citation

Medicare Payment Advisory Commission. (1999, March). Report to the Congress: *Medicare Payment Policy*. Retrieved from www.medpac.gov/docs/default-source/reports/Mar99_Entire_report.pdf?sfvrsn=0

——. (2004, December). *Benefit Design and Cost Sharing in Medicare Advantage Plans*. Retrieved from www.medpac.gov/docs/default-source/reports/Dec04_CostSharing.pdf?sfvrsn=0

MedPAC (2013, March). *Report to the Congress: Medicare Payment Policy*. Retrieved from www.medpac.gov/documents/Mar13_EntireReport.pdf

Moon, M. (2000, June). *An Assessment of the President's Proposal to Modernize and Strengthen Medicare*. Washington, DC: Urban Institute.

Patel, K. and Rushefsky, M. E. (1999). *Health Care Politics and Policy in America*. Armonk, NY: M. E. Sharpe.

Reinhardt, U. W. (2003, November/December). Does the Aging of the Population Really Drive the Demand for Health Care? *Health Affairs*, 22(6), 27–39.

——. (2012, December21). Medicare Spending Isn't Out of Control. *New York Times*. Retrieved from http://economix.blogs.nytimes.com/2012/12/21/medicare-spending-isnt-out-of-control

White, C. (2008, May). Why Did Medicare Spending Growth Slow Down? *Health Affairs*, 27(3), 793–802.

CHAPTER 7

Medicaid and CHIP

INTRODUCTION

THIS CHAPTER PROVIDES AN OVERVIEW OF MEDICAID, the children's health insurance plan (chip), and the impact of the Supreme Court's June 2012 decision on the Affordable Care Act (ACA) (2010) and Medicaid. Although the ACA included mandatory reforms to expand Medicaid programs across all states, the court's decision gave each state the right to choose whether or not to participate in these reforms. Clearly, this was a major and unexpected outcome of the legal challenges to the ACA brought by conservatives and many states in the country. Medicaid is one of the largest and most important health insurance programs in the U.S.; it provides coverage for individuals with disabilities and low income, and is the primary payer for long-term care.

Medicaid and CHIP combined provide health coverage to more than 70 million recipients, an increase of 10 million beneficiaries since 2012, including children, pregnant women, parents, very-low-income older adults, and individuals with disabilities (Centers for Medicare and Medicaid Services, 2012; Rudowitz and Garfield, 2018). According to the Kaiser Family Foundation, 75 percent of the program's nonelderly recipients, who make up 25 percent of the Medicaid population, are in working families. Children make up about half of the Medicaid population, and seniors and people with disabilities make up the remaining 25 percent (Rudowitz and Garfield, 2018).

As the country's largest government health care program, Medicaid's coverage is far reaching, as shown in Figure 7.1. According to the Kaiser Commission on Medicaid and the Uninsured (Sanger, 2017), Medicaid covers 20 percent of all Americans, 49 percent of all births, and 76 percent of all poor children.

LEGISLATION

Medicaid was enacted in 1965 along with Medicare as part of a political compromise reform effort to expand health insurance coverage in the U.S. Today, millions of low-income children, adults, older adults, and individuals with disabilities depend on Medicaid for access to health care. Medicaid is a jointly funded federal–state public assistance program administered by the states. It provides a broad range of basic health and long-term-care services. The federal government

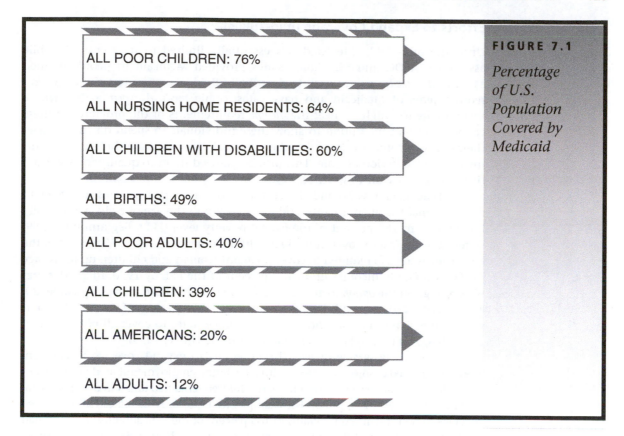

FIGURE 7.1

Percentage of U.S. Population Covered by Medicaid

establishes rules for state governance, but states have had increasingly wider discretion with determining eligibility, benefits, payments, and delivery of services since the program was enacted. The ACA intended to change this and bring broader requirements for coverage to the states, but, as mentioned, the Supreme Court found that it was unconstitutional to require states to participate in the reforms. The ACA, as discussed later in this section, has had an impact on state-administered Medicaid programs, however.

When Medicaid was first enacted, it was designed to provide insurance to dependent children and mothers (Aid to Families with Disabled Children [AFCD] recipients) and later in 1972 to poor older adults and disabled individuals (Supplemental Security Income [SSI] recipients). During the Clinton administration, significant reforms created the Children's Health Insurance Program (1997), which extended coverage to low-income children in families not eligible for AFDC, and also to some Medicare beneficiaries who would not have met earlier guidelines for Medicaid eligibility. Overall, more Medicaid money has been spent on nursing home care and long-term-care services than any other benefits, and Medicaid has become the nation's major source of financing for institutional and in-home care for both young and old people.

Efforts to Expand Coverage (mid-1980s)

Until the mid-1980s, Medicaid was essentially limited to recipients of public assistance (AFDC and SSI). Some states provided Medicaid to people defined as *medically needy*, a term used to describe individuals who meet the *categorical* requirements of Medicaid and have catastrophic *medical expenses*, but whose incomes are too high to meet the *income* requirements of the program. In these cases, states had the option to allow these individuals to spend down, or offset their excess income, by deducting their medical expenses from their income during a specified period of time. This process allowed them to qualify for Medicaid (U.S. General Accounting Office, 1995).

In 1986, Congress expanded access to Medicaid by giving states the *option* to cover pregnant women, infants, and children (up to the age of eight) with family incomes up to 185 percent of the federal poverty level (FPL). Beginning in 1989, states were *required* to cover individuals with incomes at or below 75 percent of the FPL. They were also required to cover pregnant women and children up to the age of six with family incomes up to 133 percent of the FPL by 1990. In 1990, states were also given the *option* to gradually phase in children born before September 30, 1983 (aged six to ten), with family incomes up to 100 percent of the FPL. The purpose of the phase-in expansion was to encourage states to cover all poor children through age 18 by 2002 (U.S. General Accounting Office, 1995).

After almost a decade of federal–state efforts to expand coverage to children, Medicaid "helped cushion the effect of [the] declining employment-based health insurance" discussed earlier in the text, but many children remained uninsured (U.S. General Accounting Office, 1995, p. 20). For example, in 1995, only 27 states had expanded coverage in their Medicaid programs to 185 percent of the FPL, and only 12 states had increased coverage to children to the upper age limit of 19 (U.S. General Accounting Office, 1995). By 1997, only two more states (Wisconsin and Arkansas) had expanded coverage to 185 percent of the FPL. A number of states increased the upper age limit from 12 to 14, 16, 17, or even 18, but no additional states had expanded coverage to age 19. Even among children eligible for Medicaid, more than one-third had not been enrolled (U.S. General Accounting Office, 1995; National Governors Association and National Conference of State Legislatures, 1998), and studies found that families seemed to be unaware of their children's eligibility or avoided enrollment because they perceived stigma attached to Medicaid (U.S. General Accounting Office, 1995).

Medicaid and Managed Care

As with Medicare, the escalating cost of health care in the U.S. has been an ongoing concern with the Medicaid program, particularly as this is a so-called "welfare" program financed with general revenues at both the federal and the state levels. Managed care was first introduced in the Medicaid program in the early 1980s. Medicaid managed care dates back to the Omnibus Budget Reconciliation Act of 1981, which allowed states to seek federal waivers from their obligation to provide Medicaid recipients fees-for-service (FFS) coverage. Between 1988 and 1992, largely as a way to control "program costs," states actively pursued managed care (Holahan et al., 1998).

Throughout the 1990s, the U.S. Department of Health and Human Services promoted the expansion of Medicaid managed care by using its authority to grant waivers and establish statewide demonstration programs (Kaiser Family Foundation, 1998). Consequently, the number of Medicaid beneficiaries enrolled in managed care grew from 750,000 (3 percent of all Medicaid beneficiaries) in 1983 to more than 17 million (47.8 percent) in 1997 (Kaiser Family Foundation, 1998). Initially, the demonstration programs were small scale and "carefully" limited to only the healthiest recipients—poor or low-income pregnant women, children, and families (Families USA, 2001). However, the potential for cost savings was less than it might have been for elderly or disabled Medicaid beneficiaries (Holahan et al., 1998).

During the mid-1990s, states experimented with managed-care plans for all Medicaid beneficiaries, including SSI recipients. By 2000, with the encouragement of the Balanced Budget Act (BBA) of 1997, the majority (57 percent) of all Medicaid recipients were enrolled in managed-care plans (Kaiser Family Foundation, 2001). The Government Accounting Office raised concerns about the impact of managed care on these (and other vulnerable) individuals and instructed the states to find ways of ensuring that managed-care plans provided appropriate, quality care (U.S. General Accounting Office, 1996).

Balanced Budget Act of 1997 and Managed Care

The BBA of 1997 significantly altered the Medicaid program. The act gave states the right to make managed care *mandatory* without federal waivers, except in the case of the Medicare–Medicaid (or dual-eligible) population, children with special needs, and Native Americans. Dual-eligible recipients presented a special challenge for managed care; in addition to being in very poor health, they are relatively few in number and economically disadvantaged. Approximately one-third of this population was also disabled (U.S. General Accounting Office, 1996). The BBA also provided protections for Medicaid recipients, though the states often failed to abide by them (Families USA, 2001).

Balanced Budget Act of 1997 and S-CHIP

In 1997, as part of the BBA, Congress enacted the State Children's Health Insurance Program (S-CHIP) as Title XXI of the Social Security Act. The purpose of S-CHIP, which became effective January 1, 1999, was to increase health insurance coverage to children in low-income working families. Matching funds were provided to states to expand coverage to children in families with incomes up to 200 percent of the FPL. States were given three broad options to increase coverage:

1. States could expand Medicaid by increasing the age of eligibility, the income level for eligibility, or both. The program had to be offered statewide.

2. States could establish new state programs or expand the state-run health insurance programs already available to children.

3. States could provide some combination of both options by changing the state Medicaid program, and establishing or expanding a state-run program (Edelman, 1999).

States that had already made provisions for families at 200 percent of the FPL were allowed to expand coverage to 300 percent. Medicaid, health maintenance organizations (HMOs), the state employees' plan, or the federal employees' Blue Cross Blue Shield plan could administer the benefit plans; in most states, the Medicaid plan was already the most comprehensive. Premiums or copayments could be charged only if the state decided to establish a new plan. Children eligible for traditional Medicaid coverage (family incomes less than 133 percent of poverty) would not be eligible for the new S-CHIP program (Edelman, 1999).

The primary targets of the S-CHIP program were children with parents who were unemployed, in transition between jobs, or employed in jobs that did not provide health insurance benefits. The states had to identify and reach families through outreach and provide flexible approaches to expand coverage to children in these families. Private insurance mechanisms, such as waiting periods for new employees, premiums, copayments, and deductibles, were known to be barriers to coverage for families with moderate incomes. The S-CHIP program allowed states to coordinate benefits coverage with private employers, subsidize employer-based insurance, pay for private insurance copayments and deductibles, and simplify the application, enrollment, and eligibility determination process. The stigma associated with Medicaid was also addressed by giving the states the option to give the programs their own names (Reschovsky and Cunningham, 1998).

Initially, states moved quickly to receive the program's matching federal funds. By September 1998, 50 states had submitted plans for their state programs. Four states raised eligibility to 300 percent of the FPL, and four others established eligibility requirements higher than 200 percent, but lower than 300 percent of the FPL. Nineteen more states determined eligibility as 200 percent of the FPL, but the remaining states were still at 185 percent or less (National Governors Association and National Conference of State Legislatures, 1998). By 1999, there was concern about the failure of states to reach out to uninsured children; in May 1999, less than 20 percent of available funds were being spent (Pear, 1999). In addition, a Families USA (1999d) study of the 12 states with the largest number of uninsured children (totaling two-thirds of all uninsured children in the U.S.) showed that from 1996 to 1999 almost one million children had lost Medicaid. Although the S-CHIP program had expanded coverage to children in low-income working families, AFDC reforms enacted in 1996 through the Personal Responsibility and Work Opportunity Reconciliation Act (discussed in the next section) had reduced the number of enrollees. The combined effect was a decline in coverage for children.

Personal Responsibility and Work Opportunity Reconciliation Act (1996)

The Personal Responsibility and Work Opportunity Reconciliation Act (PRWORA) of 1996 ended AFDC, the federal income assistance program that originated with the Social Security Act of 1935. The bill replaced AFDC with TANF, Temporary Assistance for Needy Families, a block grant program that provides state funds for income assistance for low-income families. PRWORA eliminated the federal entitlement to public assistance and gave each state a block grant to administer its own program.

Most important to our discussion here, the legislation delinked Medicaid and TANF. Before these reforms, most AFDC recipients were *automatically* eligible for Medicaid. This changed with the creation of TANF; eligibility for TANF and Medicaid became separate determinations. However, states were required under Section 1931 of the Social Security Act to provide coverage for families with dependent children who meet the income and resource eligibility criteria in effect before the repeal of AFDC on July 16, 1996 (Greenberg, 1998). However, income eligibility standards (percentage of FPL) for AFDC had been set so low by the states that many working parents were ineligible for coverage (Families USA, 2000). Congress gave states the option to use less restrictive guidelines and, as of August 1998, to provide coverage to two-parent low-income families (Health Care Financing Administration, 2000a). Thus, even if families were no longer eligible for TANF because of time limits, they were still likely to be eligible for Medicaid.

In 1997, as an "unintended consequence" of the new legislation, "an estimated 675,000 low-income people became uninsured . . . more than three out of five (62 percent) were children" (Families USA, 1999c, p. 2). A Families USA study (1999c) found that most of the children should not have lost coverage because they were still eligible for Medicaid. Coverage was lost in three primary ways. First, when recipients were terminated from income assistance, they were not informed of their eligibility for Medicaid. TANF recipients are terminated after two years if the recipient does not find employment or if he or she reaches the lifetime maximum of five years. As families reached these time limits, administrative errors led to loss of Medicaid.

Second, recipients lost coverage when they moved from "welfare to work," as prescribed by the PRWORA. Adult recipients typically found employment in jobs that did not offer health insurance benefits and were eligible for Medicaid only if they earned very little money (less than the FPL). Their children, on the other hand, were eligible at higher (family) income eligibility standards; yet they too were terminated at this point. Third, some states discouraged enrollment in the TANF program. They diverted families from the application process toward job-seeking activity, lump-sum cash payments, and other options. If families were unaware of their right to Medicaid independent of the TANF program, they were at risk of losing coverage.

Studies conducted by the Urban Institute (Ellwood, 1999; Garrett and Holahan, 2000) confirmed these findings. A follow-up study by Families USA (2000) showed that Medicaid enrollments declined from 1996 to 1999, not only for children, but also for low-income parents. In the 15 states with the highest enrollments of low-income adults, almost a million parents lost Medicaid coverage. In addition to the causes cited in the earlier study, this study found that few states had taken advantage of the options to expand coverage to low-income parents. A report prepared for the government suggested "an urgent need for welfare workers to be given assistance in understanding complex eligibility rules, and for automated eligibility systems to be brought up to date" (Dion and Pavetti, 2000, p. 32).

As of fiscal year 2000, 17 states had not reached the expanded income eligibility standard of 200 percent FPL, while 10 states exceeded the standard with the 200–300 percent FPL criterion. S-CHIP had reached and enrolled over three million children, but more than six million were eligible and still not enrolled (Children's Defense Fund, 2000; Health Care Financing Administration, 2000b).

Medicare, Medicaid, and S-CHIP Benefits Improvement and Protection Act (2000)

From the late 1990s to about 2012, states experienced significant declines in state revenues and major shortfalls in state budgets. In an effort to control spending, many states imposed restrictions on both Medicaid and S-CHIP. Between 2003 and 2004, 23 states introduced changes that made it more difficult for low-income families and children to be eligible for S-CHIP. These actions included freezing enrollments, increasing premiums, and adopting more complex enrollment procedures. For the first time since S-CHIP was introduced in 1997, enrollment actually fell in 2003 and most states eliminated outreach efforts (Kaiser Family Foundation, 2005a).

In 2007, the Bush administration issued a directive to prevent states from expanding S-CHIP coverage to children in families above 250 percent of FPL unless states could comply with a series of strict benchmarks. Although Congress considered bipartisan bills to reauthorize S-CHIP and expand coverage, the Bush administration vetoed these efforts. Meanwhile, enrollment remained stagnant.

In an effort to reach these children, Congress passed the Medicare, Medicaid, and S-CHIP Benefits Improvement and Protection Act in December 2000. This legislation adjusted the formula for reallocation of the unspent funds. The bill allowed states that had already spent their allocation to apply for up to 40 percent of the unspent funding, and states that had not used their full allocation to receive up to 60 percent. All states could use 10 percent of the funds for outreach activities (Children's Defense Fund, 2000). These incentives led to modest gains in the enrollment of low-income children through 2002.

However, as of 2008, only 43 states and the District of Columbia had reached the eligibility standard of 200 percent of the FPL (Kaiser Family Foundation, 2008b). As states struggled with decreased revenues, TANF families were also at risk of losing their Medicaid benefits due to policy changes that denied these benefits. For example, about one out of every four states imposed sanctions that denied cash assistance and Medicaid benefits to TANF recipients for violation of the state's work requirements. In Texas alone, the TANF population declined by almost one-third between 2003 (when the work violation sanction was introduced) and 2005, primarily due to this new sanction. Many of these recipients had difficulty complying with this requirement because they had physical and mental health problems, not because they were unwilling to seek and maintain employment (Dunkelberg, 2005; Hagert, 2005). Congress increased Medicaid matching funds and general grants to the states to assist with the increased demand for Medicaid created by the economic downturn in 2008–9.

State Medicaid Managed-care Plans

State Medicaid managed-care plans, largely targeting children and their parents, also continued to develop. From 1996 to 2004, Medicaid managed-care enrollment grew from about 40 percent to 60 percent of beneficiaries. One state, Tennessee, had 100 percent of its Medicaid population in managed care, whereas Georgia, Iowa, Kentucky, Michigan, and South Dakota had more than 90 percent enrolled (Centers for Medicare and Medicaid Services, 2005). Unlike Medicare, which, by comparison, had few beneficiaries in managed-care plans, managed care was quickly becoming the primary model for Medicaid.

Some studies found that managed care could reduce the rate of spending growth; however, there was concern that this came at the expense of quality (Holahan et al., 1998). The U.S. General Accounting Office (1996) noted the difficulty involved in developing satisfactory measures of quality and determining whether plans were living up to states' expectations. Holahan et al. (1998) reported "concerns" that Medicaid managed care could result in the elimination of "nonmedical services," such as case management, social services, and public health programs. Arguing the need for strong federal oversight of state plans, Families USA (2001, p. 2) noted that "advocates" had "documented an extensive record of harm to beneficiaries when the federal government did not aggressively monitor state activities."

Other studies presented a mixed portrait of the impact of Medicaid managed care. Hurley and Zuckerman (2002, p. 37) concluded that "in most instances" states had implemented managed care in a "responsible" manner and "generally . . . won over critics who doubted their motives . . . or questioned their capacity to select and contract with credible and creditable managed care vendors." Rowland et al. (2003) found that, although recipients' "experiences" had "varied," surveys "generally" found "improvements in access to regular providers, but problems in enrollees' satisfaction and access to needed services" (Rowland et al., 2003, p. 78). Coughlin et al. (2012) found that Medicaid recipients' access to care was similar to that of "the low-income privately insured," although "worse for dental services and prescription drugs" (Coughlin et al., 2012, p. 1073). On the other hand, as the authors noted, their comparison group was "the low-income privately insured population," who tend to have less than "comprehensive coverage" (Coughlin et al., 2012, p. 1082).

The initial growth of managed care in the Medicaid program was driven by state efforts to reduce rising costs. However, despite (1) doubts about the ability of managed care to adequately serve low-income recipients, older adults, and individuals with greater health needs than the rest of the population, (2) concerns about inadequate access to medical specialists and social services, and cost shifting rather than cost savings (Rowland et al., 1995; Holahan et al., 1998), and (3) inadequate consumer information about plans, interruptions in treatment, barriers to filing grievances, and insufficient assurance of quality of care (Families USA, 2001), the number of Medicaid managed-care plans grew by 16 percent between 2000 and 2003 (Kaiser Family Foundation, 2005c). By 2009, about two-thirds of all Medicaid beneficiaries were enrolled in managed-care plans (Kaiser Family Foundation, 2009a).

Efforts to Shift Responsibility to States (Bush Administration)

In 2001, the Health Insurance Flexibility and Accountability Initiative was passed to give states even more flexibility in the federal waiver process, but many criticized this as an invitation for states to scale back costs by reducing benefits and coverage. In 2004, the Bush administration proposed giving states even greater responsibility for Medicaid by providing block grants to states to fund the program; the federal government would no longer provide matching dollars to the states and federal funding for Medicaid, and the S-CHIP would be reduced by $500 billion over a ten-year period (Families USA, 2003).

Although the administration was unable to withdraw federal support to states, it enacted the Deficit Reduction Act (DRA) of 2005. The DRA impacted almost all aspects of the Medicaid program, including determination of eligibility (e.g., resource and asset rules, citizenship documentation, third-party liability), scope of benefits (prescription drug coverage, non-emergency transportation services, case management), and state purchasing of long-term-care insurance. It also introduced home- and community-based care options for children and adults with disabilities. States were given more flexibility by allowing them to make individuals ineligible for services or limiting the range of benefits provided. Although new strict requirements for citizenship documentation (such as original birth certificates and photo identification) did not apply to Medicare or SSI recipients, they were used for other categories of Medicaid recipients, including poor and low-income pregnant women, and children and S-CHIP.

The DRA also gave the states expanded authority to impose cost sharing on Medicaid beneficiaries, and in 2008 new federal Medicaid rules were written giving states the authority to charge premiums and higher copayments for doctors' services, hospital care, and prescription drugs provided to low-income people, and to deny care or coverage to Medicaid beneficiaries who do not pay their premiums or their share of the cost for service. This represented a significant change in the Medicaid program, one that reflects continuing concerns about cost and the Bush administration's desire to shift these costs to the states (National Health Law Program, 2007).

Children's Health Insurance Program Reauthorization Act (2009)

With the election of President Obama, S-CHIP was given support and approval and reauthorized by Congress in February 2009 as the Children's Health Insurance Program Reauthorization Act (CHIPRA). CHIPRA or "CHIP" (no longer S-CHIP) added $33 billion to the program for 2009–13 and was expected to provide health insurance to an additional 4.1 million children who otherwise would not have been covered (Kaiser Family Foundation, 2009b). Bush's directive to limit coverage to 250 percent of the poverty level was withdrawn by President Obama, and CHIP established a new upper income limit of 300 percent of the federal poverty guideline.

Other changes legislated by the reauthorization allowed states to cover certain low-income pregnant women through a state plan amendment, required states to cover dental services, and required parity of mental health services. Coverage for parents of enrolled children was phased out of the program, as was coverage for nonpregnant childless adults for the few states that had received federal permission to do so. CHIP removed the five-year waiting period for legal immigrant children and pregnant women to enroll, provided millions of dollars for outreach and enrollment activities, and gave states more options to offer premium assistance. A decade after S-CHIP first became effective, it finally received significant support from the federal government to sustain and expand its mission to cover uninsured children.

Medicaid and the ACA (2012)

Although the Supreme Court (June, 2012) upheld the ACA's public mandate that requires everyone to seek coverage, the court struck down the ACA's mandatory policy to expand the Medicaid program in 2014, which was expected to bring coverage to an additional 17 million people by 2022. The mandatory Medicaid expansion would have covered low-income adults without children who are *not* covered by almost all states; eligibility would have been expanded to 133 percent of the FPL (Center on Budget and Policy Priorities, 2012). The Center on Budget and Policy Priorities (2012) and others described the planned expansion as a "very good deal" for the states as the federal government expected to bear nearly 93 percent of the cost over the first *nine* years of the program. The Supreme Court, however, determined "that Congress had exceeded its constitutional authority by coercing states into participating in the expansion by threatening them with the loss of existing federal payments," giving states the *option* of participating in the expansion while receiving additional federal payments, or declining participation and retaining their existing payments (Liptak, 2012, p. A1).

As a result of the decision, the Congressional Budget Office (2012) predicted that three million fewer people would receive expanded Medicaid coverage than originally expected. Researchers found that this decision could have devastating health outcomes. Sommers et al. (2012b) compared states with expanded Medicaid coverage (New York, Arizona, and Maine) with states that had not expanded coverage to disabled adults or adults without children (Pennsylvania, New Mexico, Nevada, and New Hampshire), and found 1500 fewer deaths per year among people aged 20–64 in the states with expanded coverage (adjusted for population growth). In the states that had not expanded coverage, death rates increased. The study also found differences in delays in getting care between the two groups of states; expansion reduced cost-related delays in getting care.

The burden fell to individual states to consider the impact of their decision on whether or not to participate in the Medicaid expansion. One major complicating factor was the insurance premium tax credits created by the ACA to help people purchase insurance. The ACA planned for coverage of individuals below 100 percent of the FPL through the Medicaid expansion and did not include them in the income range for premium tax credits. Those with incomes between 100 percent and 400 percent of the FPL would be eligible for premium tax credits, whereas those with incomes *below* the FPL would not be eligible (Center on Budget and Policy Priorities, 2012). This inequity can be reversed only if the states opt *into* the Medicaid expansion.

As of January 2017, 32 states including the District of Columbia opted to expand Medicaid whereas 19 states did not. In the latter, 2.6 million adults fall into the category of incomes below 100 percent of the FPL, yet exceed their state's cutoff for Medicaid; they also have incomes too low to qualify for subsidies for private coverage in the ACA marketplaces. Overall, however, Medicaid and CHIP enrollment rose by nearly 17 million between 2013 and 2016, and Medicaid expansion has contributed to a decline in the uninsured rate among nonelderly individuals (which declined from 16.6 percent in 2013 to 10 percent in 2016) (Rudowitz and Garfield, 2018).

In addition to Republican efforts to "repeal and replace" the ACA, more recent threats to the Medicaid expansion option have surfaced. In 2017, several Republican plans to phase out federal matching funds for Medicaid expansion implemented under the ACA were debated. Under any of the proposals, if passed, millions fewer Americans would receive Medicaid coverage.

BENEFITS AND FINANCING

In 2017, the Medicaid program, the largest insurer in the U.S., provided health insurance coverage for more than 70 million people. Half of these beneficiaries are children, a quarter nonelderly adults, and the remaining quarter elderly adults and individuals with disabilities. The Kaiser Family Foundation (2010) estimated that, for every percentage point increase in unemployment, enrollment increases by one million recipients. Although the vast majority of recipients are children and adults living in poor families, spending is skewed toward the highest-cost recipients, i.e., it is skewed toward older adults and people with disabilities.

The federal–state Medicaid program has several mandatory and optional components, for both the benefits provided and recipients covered. This section provides basic information about the primary components—what is provided to beneficiaries and how the program is funded—and examines some of the strengths and weaknesses of the current program.

Mandatory Benefits

States participate in the Medicaid program on a voluntary basis; however, all states participate. They are free to determine the type, amount, duration, and scope of services offered within broad federal guidelines. To receive federal funding, states must provide coverage for the following "mandatory" services, but are free to offer "optional" services, as well (Centers for Medicare and Medicaid, 2012):

- inpatient hospital services;
- outpatient hospital care;
- physician services;
- certified pediatric and family nurse practitioner services;
- nurse midwife services (authorized by the state);

- Freestanding Birth Center services (licensed or otherwise recognized by the state);

- laboratory and X-ray services;

- nursing facility services;

- home health services;

- early and periodic screening, diagnosis, and treatment (EPSDT) for children and youth under age 21;

- family planning services;

- rural health clinic services;

- federally qualified health center services (FQHCs) and ambulatory services of an FQHC;

- transportation to medical care;

- tobacco cessation counseling for pregnant women.

Optional Benefits

States also have the option to provide the following benefits (Centers for Medicare and Medicaid, 2012):

- prescription drugs;

- clinic services;

- physical therapy;

- occupational therapy;

- speech, hearing, and language disorder services;

- respiratory care services;

- other diagnostic, screening, preventive, and rehabilitation services;

- podiatry services;

- optometry services;

- dental services;

- dentures;

- prosthetics;

- eyeglasses;

- chiropractic services;

- other practitioner services;

- private duty nursing services;

- personal care;

- hospice;

- case management;

- services for individuals age 65 or older in an institution for mental disease (IMD);

- services in an intermediate care facility for the intellectually disadvantaged;

- State Plan Home and Community Based Service (Section 1915i);

- Self-Directed Personal Assistance Services (Section 1915j);

- Community First Choice Option (Section 1915k);

- tuberculosis-related services;<AQ3>

- inpatient psychiatric services for individuals under age 21;

- other services approved by the Secretary.

Mandatory and Optional Eligibility

The federal Medicaid law identifies over 25 different eligibility categories which can be classified into five broad coverage groups: children; pregnant women; adults in families with dependent children; individuals with disabilities; and older adults. To participate in the Medicaid program, states must cover certain population groups (mandatory eligibility groups), but the federal government also gives states the flexibility to cover other population groups (optional eligibility groups). States must provide benefits to five specific categories of *poor or low-income individuals*: (1) pregnant women, (2) children, (3) older adult Medicare recipients (referred to as dual eligibles because they are eligible for both Medicare and Medicaid), (4) parents (under age 65) with dependent children (AFDC recipients until 1996; now TANF recipients), and (5) children and adults with disabilities (SSI recipients). However, millions of poor and low-income individuals do not meet the criteria for these defined categories, including adults without dependent children and those who are not disabled. Without federal support, states are not likely to extend coverage to these individuals, because they would bear the full cost of coverage. In addition, federal matching funds have been available for *some* individuals within an eligible category, but not available for others.

States must comply with five broad eligibility policies, two based on financial criteria (income limits and resource limits) and three on social status and residency criteria (categorical eligibility, immigration status, and residency). Many states have expanded coverage, particularly for children, above the federal minimums. For many eligibility groups, income status is based on a percentage of the FPL. For other groups, income standards vary. (The requirements for each can be found at www.medicaid.gov.) Although wide variation in Medicaid participation by the states leaves many without coverage, the ACA attempted to create a national Medicaid *minimum* eligibility level (133 percent of the FPL for almost all recipients under age 65). However, as noted above, due to the Supreme Court decision this may not take effect.

The ACA prohibits *undocumented* immigrants from receiving Medicaid and CHIP, but immigrants with family incomes under 138 percent of the FPL, and a minimum of five years of residency, are eligible for coverage with low or no premiums. Also, those in this income category who do not meet the residency requirement will be eligible for tax subsidies to purchase insurance through the state health exchanges (Clemans-Cope et al., 2012).

Financing

Both the federal government and the states finance Medicaid. The federal match rate is known as the Federal Medical Assistance Percentage, or FMAP, and varies by state. States receive between 50 and 75 percent of the cost of mandated services based on a formula that incorporates state per capita income (Kaiser Family Foundation, 2010, 2017). Under the ACA, the federal match rate for adults newly eligible for Medicaid due to the expansion is 95 percent in 2017, phasing down gradually to 90 percent starting in 2020 (Rudowitz and Garfield, 2018). States also receive funding for a wide range of optional services, such as dental, hearing, and eye care, and intermediate facility care for individuals with intellectual disadvantage, and also to extend services to optional populations. The majority of state funding for optional benefits is spent on long-term-care services; states also spent heavily on prescription drugs for older adults and disabled beneficiaries until the enactment of Medicare Part D Prescription coverage (Kaiser Family Foundation, 2010). Federal Medicaid matching funds are the largest source of federal revenue in state budgets (Rudowitz and Garfield, 2018).

TRENDS IN ENROLLMENT AND SPENDING

During the early 1990s, the number of Medicaid recipients increased significantly when the program expanded to include pregnant women, infants, and young children living at up to 133 percent of the FPL. States were given the option to expand coverage to pregnant women and infants up to 185 percent of the FPL. Court decisions also mandated coverage to children with learning disabilities. However, as discussed here, enrollments declined steadily after the 1995 state and federal reforms in the AFDC program which culminated in the Personal Responsibility and Work Opportunity Reconciliation Act of 1996 (Kaiser Family Foundation, 1999a). With the nation's economic downturn in 2008, enrollments increased steadily. A Center on Budget and Policy Priorities survey (Lav and McNichol, 2009) found that at least 47 states were expecting serious budget shortfalls, reduced state income taxes, and an increased demand for Medicaid.

Medicaid spending has continued to climb overall, but at variable rates of growth at different times for various reasons. In the early 1990s, Medicaid spending grew primarily due to increases in hospital payments for disproportionate share reimbursements. These are payments made to hospitals that serve a disproportionate share (DSH) of poor or low-income patients and are supplemental to the regular payments hospitals receive from Medicaid. However, between 1992 and 1995, growth in spending declined significantly to a rate of approximately 10 percent annually. This occurred for several reasons, including low rates of inflation and new federal limits on DSH payments (Kaiser Family Foundation, 1999b).

In the mid-1990s, growth in spending declined to an historic low (approximately 3 percent annually) because of the AFDC reforms discussed earlier and a reduction in DSH payments. With TANF and Medicaid delinked, one major unintended consequence of "welfare reform" was the decline in the number of Medicaid beneficiaries. In addition, payments to DSH hospitals declined overall during this period due to legislation passed in 1993 (Kaiser Family Foundation, 1999b). From 1997 to 1998, enrollments remained steady, but spending increased significantly due to the rising cost of prescription drugs, the increase in home and community-based care, and the increase in the size of the disabled population (Kaiser Family Foundation, 2001).

From 2000 to 2002, both spending and enrollment rose significantly; Medicaid spending increased $70 billion due to enrollment growth, particularly among working families, as adults lost employment-based health insurance due to the country's economic downturn. From 2003 to 2007, however, spending slowed due to state efforts to control costs, a decline in DHS spending, and reduced use of upper payment limits that allow states to receive extra federal funds (Kaiser Family Foundation, 2005b). There was also an administrative effort to promote the use of Section 1115 waivers to restructure state Medicaid programs through the Health Insurance Flexibility and Accountability Initiative, launched in 2001 by the Department of Health and Human Services. Some states, such as New York, used this initiative to expand coverage, but others, such as Oregon and Tennessee, made program changes that reduced or eliminated coverage for optional Medicaid categories. These waivers have also been used by states to shift federal CHIP funds to coverage for populations other than children. Seventeen states had waivers approved between 2001 and 2005 (Kaiser Family Foundation, 2005c).

Perhaps most significantly, in 2005, Congress threatened to reduce federal spending on Medicaid by as much as $10 billion, and President Bush created a commission to study proposals to achieve this goal. The National Governors Association boycotted the commission and instead offered its own proposals (July, 2005), such as changes in cost sharing, allowing states to offer different benefit packages to different groups of people, and expanding state flexibility to make changes without federal waivers (Families USA, 2005). In December 2007, the U.S. economy went into a recession and the states entered into a deeper period of difficulty with financing their budgets. New federal Medicaid rules enacted in 2008 gave states the option to require new or higher copayments from an estimated 13 million low-income recipients, allowing states to shift some of the burden of rising costs to recipients (Kaiser Family Foundation, 2008a). With the recession,

Medicaid enrollment grew 17.8 percent (over 3 million), and in 2010 exceeded 50 million recipients for the first time in its history. During this period, between 2007 and 2010, the unemployment rate in the nation doubled, which increased the demand for Medicaid in every state in the country (Kaiser Family Foundation, 2012).

The Obama Administration's national fiscal stimulus program helped provide support to the states and created Medicaid eligibility protections to help states address the growth in Medicaid enrollment. The 2009 American Recovery and Reinvestment Act included approximately $135–140 billion—or about 40 percent of projected state deficits—to help states maintain their Medicaid programs and reduce fiscal deficits. As reported by Lav and McNichol (2009), these funds would significantly reduce the depth of state budget cuts and moderate state tax and fee increases due to budget shortfalls, but were not likely to be sufficient to stem a reduction in services during the economic downturn.

The ACA extended the eligibility protections of the Recovery Act through 2014, when it was intended that Medicaid eligibility become mandatory for those previously ineligible for coverage. Enrollment and spending peaked in 2015. However, with discussion at the federal congressional level to "repeal and replace" the ACA, states have been left to make difficult decisions about their state budgets and Medicaid expansion. States have also been impacted by "other Medicaid budget issues related to the economy, health care costs, implementation of delivery system reforms, and addressing emerging public health issues like the opioid epidemic" (Rudowitz and Valentine, 2017).

RECIPIENT GROUPS: COVERAGE AND POLICY ISSUES

Poor and Low-income Pregnant Women, Children, and Families

Medicaid and the CHIP cover about 50 percent of all births in the U.S., 40 percent of all children, and 75 percent of poor children. States have more restrictive rules for covering adults, yet Medicaid still covers 40 percent of all poor nonelderly adults (Rudowitz and Garfield, 2018). CHIP benefits for children differ by state, but, in general, the state programs provide a wide range of services, including routine doctor visits, immunizations, dental and vision care, hospitalizations, and laboratory and X-ray services.

The federal government sets minimum guidelines (100 percent of the FPL) for Medicaid eligibility, but states can choose to expand coverage beyond the minimum threshold (most have done so). In addition, all states have expanded coverage to children from higher-income families through CHIP; upper-income eligibility varies by state.

All children from birth to age six with family incomes up to 133 percent of the FPL and children aged 6–18 with family incomes up to 100 percent are eligible for Medicaid (Medicaid.Gov, 2012). The ACA established a new eligibility methodology for Medicaid based on modified adjusted gross income (MAGI). MAGI is used to determine financial eligibility across programs including Medicaid, CHIP, and health insurance marketplace premium tax credits and cost-sharing reductions; the intent, using one set of rules and application process, was to make it easier for individuals to apply and enroll in the appropriate program (Centers for Medicare and Medicaid Services, 2017).

Poor and Low-income Children and Adults with Disabilities

Medicaid also covers about 48 percent of children and 45 percent of nonelderly adults with disabilities, including individuals with severe physical disabilities, developmental disabilities such as autism and traumatic brain injury, serious mental illness, Alzheimer's disease, and other chronic conditions (Rudowitz and Garfield, 2018). Most Medicaid recipients with disabilities qualify for the program because they are eligible for SSI. SSI was established under President Nixon in 1972 as a federal income-assistance program for poor older adults, and blind and disabled persons. Age is not a factor; SSI provides income assistance to children, youth, and adults. In 2016, SSI served 8.3 million individuals (U.S. Social Security Administration, 2017), about 85 percent of whom were adults. However, the number of children with disabilities served by SSI (1.2 million) has grown since the *Sullivan v. Zebley* case (discussed in the next section on children). SSI recipients are eligible for assistance due to a wide range of disabling conditions, including learning disabilities, mental illness, drug addiction and alcoholism, blindness, and diseases of the central nervous system. However, given the complexity of meeting disability criteria for eligibility, a number of legal challenges have been brought to the courts.

The Supreme Court ruling with the greatest potential for changes in long-term services in Medicaid is the case of *Olmstead v. L.C.* (1999). The *Olmstead* case found that unjustified institutional isolation of people with disabilities is a violation of the Americans with Disabilities Act of 1990. The case involved two women in Georgia with learning disabilities and other mental illnesses who had been institutionalized and denied community-based care for a number of years. Medicaid requires states to provide institutional services as a mandatory service, but classifies community-based care as an optional service. The court viewed this as a bias toward institutionalized care, particularly at a time when states and communities increasingly recognize the value of community-based services. The court's decision did not change Medicaid, but advocates of civil rights for people with disabilities see this ruling as one that has and will continue to help them combat barriers to community integration of people with disabilities (Kaiser Family Foundation, 2004). For example, the ACA has put more emphasis on community-based care and provides increased Medicaid funding to the states to offer more community-based long-term supports and services for people living with disabilities.

SSI and Children. Before 1983, SSI used a different definition of disability for adults than for children. For adults, disability was defined as physical or mental health problems that interfered with the ability to work. For children, specific medical criteria, such as learning disabilities or deafness, were used. In 1983, a class action suit, *Sullivan v. Zebley*, was brought against the federal government by the Legal Services office in Philadelphia on behalf of all children with disabilities who had been denied benefits. The Supreme Court ruled in favor of the children in 1990 and expanded the program's listing of eligible medical conditions to include learning disabilities, such as attention deficit disorder (ADD), and other functional impairments of activities of daily living, including speaking, walking, and bathing. In addition, because of the court's decision, two new standards for determination of eligibility were established: individualized functional assessments (IFAs) and functional equivalence. In essence, children who could not function at a level appropriate for their age became eligible for SSI (U.S. General Accounting Office, 1998).

As a result of these changes, between 1983 and 1990, the federal government reevaluated 288,000 denied cases at a cost of $3 billion in back payments (Pear, 1990). From 1989 to 1996, the number of children eligible for SSI tripled to almost one million because of the Supreme Court decisions (U.S. General Accounting Office, 1998). In 1995, as part of its focus on welfare reform, Congress considered elimination of the IFAs and revision of the medical listings. With the program's growth and the increase in the number of children eligible for SSI and Medicaid, the Republican-controlled Congress questioned the objectivity and consistency involved in determining need. It also believed that some families were guilty of fraud and abuse because of coaching their children to misbehave or fake disabilities (Pear, 1997b).

The PRWORA of 1996 changed the SSI eligibility criteria for children by eliminating the IFAs and restricting the medical listings, thus making it more difficult for children to qualify. Under the new law, effective July 1, 1997, children with medically proven physical or mental conditions that resulted in *marked* and *severe* functional limitations would be eligible, whereas children with more moderate, maladaptive conditions would not. The Social Security Administration projected that children with mood disorders would be affected most. However, they also found that children with pulmonary tuberculosis, learning disabilities, burns, intracranial injuries, schizophrenia, and arthritis would be denied benefits. The Congressional Budget Office estimated that 48,000 children would lose coverage between 1997 and 2003 and that 315,000 children who would have qualified under the previous law would be denied coverage (National Association of Social Workers, 1996).

In fact, in 1997 disability benefits were terminated for 95,180 children; most had mental health disorders (Pear, 1997a). However, in appeals and reviews of these cases, it was determined that benefits for many children were wrongly terminated, and the decisions were reversed (Pear, 1997b). More importantly, the BBA of 1997 *restored* Medicaid eligibility for children with disabilities who lost their SSI benefits due to the new restrictions (National Association of Social Workers, 1996). In 1998, the Social Security Administration issued a new plan for quality reviews of children's disabilities to improve the accuracy and consistency of determinations across the states (U.S. General Accounting Office, 1998). Nonetheless, the number of SSI awards for children with mental health disorders began increasing after 1997 and reached an all-time high in 2003 (U.S. Social Security Administration, 2008).

In 2010, controversy over SSI benefits for children with mental health disorders surfaced again with an investigative report published by the *Boston Globe* (Wen, 2011; see also Diament, 2011): "The youngsters who qualify based on behavioral, mental, or learning disorders grew by 7.2 percent [from 2009 to 2010], more than twice the overall rate, and represent 55 percent of all children's SSI cases" (Wen, 2011, first page of web link). The percentage of all SSI children with behavioral, mental, or learning disabilities has grown from 8.3 percent in 1990, to 24 percent in 1995, and to more than half of all children's cases (Wen, 2011). Questions about parents seeking and falsifying disability status for their children were once again under scrutiny. The Social Security Administration and Congress asked the U.S. Government Accounting Office (GAO) to conduct an investigation of these claims.

The report was released in June 2012; the GAO did indeed find that the number of cases of children with mental health disabilities had increased substantially between 2000 and 2011, even with more than half of the applicants in this category denied eligibility by the Social Security Administration. The rising number of children in poverty and the increase in certain mental health diagnoses "have likely contributed to this growth" (U.S. Government Accounting Office, 2012). The GAO study (U.S. Government Accounting Office, 2012) found that attention deficit hyperactivity disorder, speech and language delay, and autism (with claims growing steadily since 2000) were the most prevalent impairments among medically needy children in 2011.

SSI and Adults: Immigrants The PRWORA of 1996 also had a significant impact on adults with disabilities. Under the new policy, SSI benefits were denied to some *legal* immigrants (exceptions included veteran families, active-duty military families, permanent residents with 40 Social Security credited quarters, and others) until they became U.S. citizens, and Medicaid was denied to *legal* immigrants for a period of five years after entering the country. *Legal immigrants with disabilities* would be denied SSI and Medicaid until they could meet these new requirements (Families USA, 1999b).

However, the Balanced Budget Reconciliation Act of 1997 restored Medicaid benefits to some immigrants by giving states the option to provide coverage to legal immigrants who entered the country before August 22, 1996, if they became disabled after this date. These immigrants could receive emergency medical services only. S-CHIP was, however, made available to legal immigrant children who entered after August 22, 1996. In 1998, new regulations restored SSI–Medicaid-linked benefits to legal immigrants who were denied coverage based on the 1996 reforms, if they were receiving benefits on August 22, 1996.

Other changes in SSI have had a significant impact on the Medicaid program and coverage for adults with disabilities. In 1988, the U.S. Justice Department included acquired immune deficiency syndrome (AIDS) in the list of approved medical conditions. Today, Medicaid serves about 40 percent of all individuals living with AIDS (Kaiser Family Foundation, 2009a, 2016); most of these recipients are low-income, disabled SSI recipients. Medicaid is the single largest payer of *services* for people with AIDS (with the 2006 addition of Medicare Part D Prescription Drug coverage, Medicare is actually the largest public federal source of spending on HIV). Approximately 9.4 billion in federal and state Medicaid dollars was spent in the fiscal year 2016, providing coverage to about 242,000 people living with HIV/AIDS (Kaiser Family Foundation, 2016). Changes in the ACA and the option for states, starting in 2014, to expand coverage to low-income individuals created an enormous opportunity to expand coverage to the HIV/AIDS population. Before the ACA, most individuals living with HIV were not eligible for Medicaid unless they were very poor or permanently disabled due to an AIDS diagnosis.

SSI and Adults: Drug and Alcohol Addiction One of the most dramatic changes in the SSI program was the elimination of drug and alcohol addiction as the sole reason for eligibility for SSI and Medicaid. In 1994, Congress passed the Social Security Independence and Program Improvements Act, which restricted SSI benefits to 36 months and required recipients to be in treatment. SSI recipients dropped from SSI could continue to receive Medicaid, as long as they remained in treatment for 12 successive months. In 1999, *all* benefits (SSI and Medicaid) for *all* individuals solely disabled by alcohol or drug addiction were terminated from the program, effective January 1, 1997. Over 200,000 recipients were notified and, after reviewing their disability status, 50,000 were terminated. This group was given a second look in 1998, and a few hundred additional enrollees were terminated (Nibal, 2000). On the other hand, eligible Medicaid recipients who also have substance abuse problems "add much more to Medicaid costs than people think" (Clark et al., 2009, p. 16). A six-state study (Clark et al., 2009) of 150,000 recipients found that 29 percent of the Medicaid patients were diagnosed with substance abuse disorders; the six states in the study spent $104 million more for medical care and $105.5 million more for behavioral health care for recipients with substance abuse than for those patients who did not have an alcohol or drug abuse diagnosis. The increased costs were likely associated with "generally higher prevalence of physical illness among older people, the cumulative health impact of long-term substance abuse, greater reluctance among older adults to seek addiction treatment in specialty settings, and more severe chronic disease among older adults with addictions" (Clark et al., 2009, p. 39).

Under the ACA, Medicaid must cover all basic aspects of drug and alcohol dependency recovery. Medicaid covers substance abuse treatment for about 1.3 million beneficiaries (Zezima and Ingraham, 2017), but not all facilities accept Medicaid as a form of payment. In addition, at a time when the country has experienced an opioid epidemic, the Republican 2017 (failed) proposal to reform the ACA, which dropped coverage for essential services, would have eliminated the requirement for addiction services.

SSI and Adults: Employment. The most significant change for disabled individuals who want to work was the Ticket to Work and Work Incentives Improvement Act of 1999. Beginning on October 1, 2000, states had the option to expand Medicaid to (1) individuals with disabilities (ages 16–64) able to work by increasing the amount they can earn and (2) employed individuals with medically improved disabilities who lost their Medicaid coverage because they no longer met SSI's adult definition of disability. States could establish their own income and resource eligibility standards and impose premiums on a sliding scale basis (Health Care Financing Administration, 2000b) through the Medicaid buy-in program. According to the Centers for Medicare and Medicaid (2017), studies show that the program lowers annual costs for this population compared with other adult disabled Medicaid enrollees, and improves quality of life.

Medically Needy. Children and adults with disabilities can qualify for Medicaid if they are "medically needy" and "spend down" to the state's medically needy income limit (MNIL). The "medically needy" incur medical expenses in order to qualify for Medicaid and must repeatedly incur medical expenses to remain eligible. Although states have the option to set standards for individual and family income that can be protected from the high cost of incurred medical expenses, the original income limit set by the federal government was 133 percent of the state's 1996 AFDC payment level, and it was usually set well below SSI payment levels. Today, the federal minimum level remains below poverty in every state. However:

> Most states have expanded parent eligibility above this minimum through optional Medicaid authority or waiver or state-funded programs but often with more limited benefits and higher cost sharing than Medicaid. Parents can qualify for Medicaid medically needy coverage by having income below the state's MNIL or by incurring out-of-pocket health expenses that would reduce their income below the applicable MNIL.
>
> (Kaiser Family Foundation, 2012, p. 10)

In addition, from the beginning, there has been a significant disparity in access among the states based on medical need and income given the significant variation in 1996 AFDC state payment levels. For example, in 1999 in Vermont, elderly recipients had to spend down to a monthly income of $683, whereas elderly recipients in Louisiana were required to spend down to $100 monthly income. These guidelines also created inequities among older adults within states. For example, in Louisiana, an elderly SSI beneficiary with disabilities would receive full Medicaid coverage and $500 monthly income, whereas someone who is medically needy would receive only $100 monthly income. To make matters worse, nearly one-third of the states had no programs or coverage for the medically needy before 2000 (Families USA, 1999a). Today, there are about 16 states that still do not have medically needy Medicaid programs (U.S. Social Security Administration, 2016).

With states struggling to reduce spending during the recession in the 1990s, some states introduced Section 1115 waivers (available since 2001), which made it more difficult for medically needy children and adults to enroll in Medicaid. For example, Oregon reduced its enrollment by half in 2003, by increasing premiums for poor adults and eliminating their "medically needy" program, and about 325,000 of the poorest recipients in Tennessee were projected to lose coverage with the state's new definition of "medical necessity" (Kaiser Family Foundation, 2005a, 2005c).

In states that have chosen to expand Medicaid under the ACA to low-income, nonelderly adults (under age 65), this has made it easier for some of these individuals to qualify for "medically needy" assistance. However, the Medicaid expansion under the ACA does not apply to beneficiaries over age 65; therefore, state "medically needy" programs remain an important safety net for this population, especially those with high costs living in nursing homes. It is also important for children and adults with disabilities who are ineligible for categorically needy Medicaid because their incomes are too high. It is important for nondisabled children and adults, who may qualify based on having health care costs related to a serious accident or severe illness, such as cancer or inpatient health or behavioral health care.

Poor and Low-income Older Adults (Medicare and Medicaid Dual Eligibles). Without question, the largest health insurance program in the U.S. for older adults is Medicare. However, Medicaid is also a vital source of health insurance for the sickest and poorest recipients of either Medicare or Medicaid who are actually eligible for both Medicare and some level of support from Medicaid. These recipients are referred to as "dual eligibles". "Full" dual eligibles are entitled to the full range of Medicaid benefits and also receive assistance with their Medicare premiums and cost sharing. "Partial" dual eligibles do not receive Medicaid benefits directly; instead they receive "medical savings" through assistance with some or all of their Medicare premiums, deductibles, and other cost sharing. These "partial" dual-eligibles have not been eligible for other Medicaid services, such as hearing, vision, dental, and long-term care.

The Kaiser Commission on Medicaid and the Uninsured (2012a) reported 86 percent of dual-eligibles had annual incomes below 150 percent of the FPL in 2008 compared to 22 percent of nondual Medicare beneficiaries. Over 9.6 million Medicare beneficiaries were also eligible for Medicaid (full or partial dual-eligible) in 2010; over 60 percent were over age 65. Although dual eligibles are a relatively small part of Medicaid (14 percent), they account for about 36 percent of Medicaid spending and 33 percent of Medicare spending (Kaiser Commission on Medicaid and the Uninsured, 2012a). Although Social Security and Medicare play a major role in reducing poverty among older adults, many are still struggling to get by financially. Average out-of-pocket expenses and cost-sharing requirements are very high; for this population of poor and low-income recipients, these expenses can be financially devastating.

The Medicare–Medicaid dual-eligible population creates challenges for states in providing adequate services. As mentioned, they are poorer and sicker than other Medicare beneficiaries; they also tend to be over age 85, female, and persons of color. They have a higher prevalence of chronic conditions, including mental disorders and significant limitations of daily living, and are highly reliant on prescription medication. Much of Medicaid's spending on dual eligibles (65 percent in 2010) is on long-term care; states rely heavily on institutional care for these services (Kaiser Commission on Medicaid and the Uninsured, 2012a).

States have had the option to expand Medicaid coverage to poor and low-income Medicare beneficiaries through a number of program options, and with funds made available through block grants established by the BBA of 1997. Before 1997, states met the 20 percent cost-sharing requirement for dual eligibles who received full Medicaid benefits. However, because state Medicaid payments are often set lower than Medicare rates, states now pay cost sharing only up to the Medicaid rate. Also, physicians and other Medicare providers are prohibited from billing dual eligibles for copayments and deductibles not covered by the state.

The transition to Medicare Part D Prescription Drug coverage was particularly difficult for this population. During the transition to this coverage, many recipients were charged unnecessarily for their prescriptions or lost coverage; states provided assistance to maintain uninterrupted drug coverage for serious chronic conditions, including HIV/AIDS, but many still needed assistance with understanding this relatively new benefit. In addition, increases in monthly premiums by Medicare drug plans forced many recipients into lower-cost plans during the program's annual open enrollment period. A 2008 study conducted by the Lewin

Group on behalf of the Medicaid Health Plans of America (MHPA) and by the Association of Community Affiliated Plans (ACAP) found that enrolling all dual eligibles in managed-care plans over 5 years could save $50 billion of state and federal dollars and $300 billion over 15 years (Medicare Payment Advisory Commission [MedPAC], 2008).

As states struggle with decisions about the ACA and Medicaid expansion, the needs of this special population should also be considered given the heavy reliance of dual eligibles on institutional care. The ACA encourages states to explore community-based alternatives and to provide better coordination of care. Some states have already improved the integration of care for this population, including providing new ways to receive long-term care services while remaining in their community. The ACA created the Medicare–Medicaid Coordination Office and the Center for Medicare and Medicaid Innovation (CMMI) (within the Centers for Medicare and Medicaid Service), both of which focus on ways to improve care and reduce costs for dual eligibles (Kaiser Commission on Medicaid and the Uninsured, 2012a; Medicaid.Gov, 2012).

Nonelderly Adults without Children

As discussed earlier, state Medicaid programs will need to decide whether or not to participate in the ACA-funded expansion of coverage to all adults aged 19–64 with incomes below 133 percent of the FPL. This offers the promise of the most significant reform to Medicaid since it began in 1965 and the most significant expansion of access to health insurance. The Center on Budget and Policy Priorities referred to Medicaid as "the key to the future of U.S. health care" with 31 states and the District of Columbia, thus far, adopting the ACA's optional expansion to nonelderly adults without children in the home. These states have significantly decreased the number of uninsured in their states and saved money, in part through lower payments to hospitals for uncompensated care. These states have also been able to reduce unnecessary emergency room use, improve care for people with chronic conditions, and help people with mental illness by taking advantage of new flexibility in the Medicaid program (Center on Budget and Policy Priorities, 2016).

FUTURE OF MEDICAID

The downturn in the U.S. economy in 2008 demonstrates the importance of Medicaid as a safety net for those who would be without coverage if this program did not exist. Although the Obama administration responded to the economic crisis with the most unprecedented federal stimulus package since the Great Depression of the 1930s, and soon thereafter with plans to expand Medicaid in the states through enactment of the ACA, Medicaid participation rates among states still vary, as discussed earlier, and are likely to continue to vary without federal requirements and support for each state. A study of Medicaid participation rates (Sommers et al., 2012b) at the state level shows that "beyond the category of eligibility, no demographic factor played as large a role in predicting Medicaid enrollment as the state in which a person lived" (Sommers et al., 2012b, p. 913). Politically conservative states have significantly lower participation rates among eligible nonelderly adults than politically liberal states. The reasons are less generous benefits, lack of coverage for optional services, lower provider reimbursement rates, and higher cost sharing—all of these factors decrease the likelihood of enrollment.

On a more positive note, a comprehensive study of 153 studies that were published between January 2014—when the ACA provisions went into effect—and June 2017 of the impact of state Medicaid expansion, conducted by the Kaiser Family Foundation (Antonisse et al., 2017) clearly show the growth and impact of Medicaid expansion:

Coverage: State-level Medicaid expansion has significantly increased the rates of insured and decreased the rates of uninsured for low-income and vulnerable populations.

Access to care, utilization, affordability: State-level Medicaid expansion has positively affected access to care, utilization of services, affordability of care, and financial security among the low-income population.

Economic measures: State-level Medicaid expansion has positively affected multiple economic outcomes, has lowered uncompensated care costs for hospitals and clinics, and had positive or neutral effects on employment and the labor market.

To continue to expand access and coverage to low-income and vulnerable populations will require continued support for Medicaid expansion.

MEDICAID/CHIP MILESTONES

- Medicaid/CHIP were created in 1965 as Title XIX of the Social Security Act.

- In 1972, they were linked to a new Supplemental Security Income (SSI) program.

- Health Care Financing Administration (HCFA) was created in 1972.

- The Omnibus Budget Reconciliation Act (OBRA) of 1981 added payments to hospitals treating disproportionate shares of low-income patients and extended coverage to home and community-based long-term care.

- OBRA 1985 extended coverage to all who qualify for AFDC.

- OBRA 1986 expanded coverage for emergency care of illegal immigrants.

- OBRA 1986, 1988, and 1990 expanded coverage and benefits to additional pregnant women and children by changing income level requirements.

- OBRA 1990 created a prescription drug rebate program.

- The Personal Responsibility and Work Opportunity Rehabilitation Act (PRWORA) of 1996 ended AFDC and created TANF, delinking the income assistance program to Medicaid.

- The State Children's Health Insurance Program of 1997 (Title XXI of the Social Security Act) was enacted by Congress to increase health insurance coverage to children in low-income working families. It expanded coverage to children in families ineligible for Medicaid on January 1, 1999.

- The Ticket to Work and Work Incentives Improvement Act (TTWIA) of 1999 gave states the option to cover working adults with disabilities.

- The Balanced Budget Refinement Act of 1999 improved coverage of certain women's health services.

- The Deficit Reduction Act of 2005 created new eligibility restrictions and required strict citizenship documentation for poor and low-income women and children and S-CHIP.

- In 2008, new rules gave states the option to require new or higher copayments and disenroll beneficiaries who do not pay their premiums.

- Children's Health Insurance Program Reauthorization Act of 2009 (CHIPRA) reintroduced 300 percent of the poverty level as the eligibility ceiling and provided millions of dollars to expand coverage to uninsured children.

- The American Recovery and Reinvestment Act of 2009 provided much-needed support to states to address budget shortages and help maintain state Medicaid programs.

- The Affordable Care Act of 2010 required states to expand coverage to all with incomes under 138 percent of the federal poverty level.

- The Supreme Court *NFIB v. Sebilius* (2012) decision upheld the ACA overall, but ruled the Medicaid expansion unconstitutional, reasoning that states rely on Medicaid funds to balance their budgets and this gives them no option to decline participation. States were given the option of refusing to expand coverage *without* losing all federal Medicaid funds.

HIGHLIGHTS

- Medicaid and CHIP, means-tested programs, provide health insurance to more than 70 million individuals of all ages who are poor and low income, including: Children, families, and pregnant women; elderly adults; and people with disabilities. Although the vast majority of recipients are children and adults living in poor families, the vast majority of Medicaid spending is on older adults and people with disabilities.

- Medicaid, which is administered by each state, has mandatory and optional benefits. Mandatory benefits include hospital and health care provider services, and nursing facility and home health care. Optional benefits, which many states provide, include dental care, hearing devices, and intermediate care for individuals with intellectual disability. General revenues finance the program; the federal government provides matching funds to the states. States must comply with a number of eligibility policies that limit coverage to specific groups of poor and low-income persons who meet income and assets criteria, immigration status, and residency requirements.

- The first significant expansion of the Medicaid program occurred in 1997 with the creation of the State Children's Health Insurance Program (S-CHIP). Starting in 1999, states had the option to expand coverage to children in working families with incomes between 200 and 300 percent of the FPL. During the recession of the 1990s, many states imposed restrictions on both Medicaid and S-CHIP; in 2003, for the first time since S-CHIP was introduced in 1997, enrollment fell.

- In an effort to encourage states to make use of their S-CHIP allocations, Congress enacted legislation that allowed states that had exhausted their funding to apply for additional funds. However, with a decrease of about one million children eligible for Medicaid between 1996 and 1999 due to welfare reforms enacted in 1996, coverage for children declined further. Legislative efforts by Congress to expand eligibility were vetoed by President Bush.

- The introduction of managed care in the early 1980s and its expansion in the 1990s represents a dramatic change in the way services are delivered to this population. Many concerns have been raised about the inability of managed care to reduce costs for low-income families with few resources and disabled and poor elderly individuals with significant health and medical needs. Studies have shown that state Medicaid managed-care plans have had difficulty ensuring adequate access to specialists and raise doubts about cost saving with this population.

- The Children's Health Insurance Program Reauthorization Act of 2009 (CHIPRA) was enacted during the Obama administration (and renamed CHIP). CHIP removed the five-year waiting period for legal immigrant children and pregnant women to enroll, provided millions of dollars for outreach and enrollment activities, and gave the states more options to offer premium assistance. A decade after S-CHIP first became effective, CHIP finally received significant support from the federal government to sustain and expand its mission to cover uninsured children.

- The second significant expansion of Medicaid occurred with passage of the Affordable Care Act of 2010. The original legislation included a major mandatory expansion of Medicaid, which was projected to cover millions of ineligible beneficiaries. However, the June 2012 Supreme Court's decision about Medicaid expansion left it up to the states to decide whether or not to participate in the federal effort to expand coverage to all individuals under 138 percent of the FPL. As of 2016, 31 states and the District of Columbia have adopted the ACA's optional expansion to nonelderly adults without children in the home.

WEBSITES TO OBTAIN UPDATED AND ADDITIONAL INFORMATION

Centers for Medicare and Medicaid Services:

www.medicaid.gov

Kaiser Commission on Medicaid and the Uninsured; Kaiser Family Foundation:

www.kff.org

REFERENCED LEGAL CASES

Olmstead v. L.C. (1999) – see https://disabilityjustice.org/olmstead-v-lc
NFIB v. Sebilius (2012) – see www.casebriefs.com/blog/law/health-law/health-law-keyed-to-furrow/health-care-cost-and-access-the-policy-context/national-federal-of-independent-business-et-al-v-sebelius
Sullivan v. Zebley – see http://povertylaw.org/clearinghouse/articles/Zebley-Counsel-Look-Back

REFERENCES

Antonisse, L., Garfield, R., Rudowitz, R. and Artiga, S. (2017, September 25). The Effects of Medicaid Expansion under the ACA: Updated Findings from a Literature Review. *Kaiser Family Foundation*. Retrieved from www.kff.org/medicaid/issue-brief/the-effects-of-medicaid-expansion-under-the-aca-updated-findings-from-a-literature-review-september-2017/

Center on Budget and Policy Priorities. (2012, June 28). *Health Reform's Medicaid Expansion is a Very Good Deal for States*. Retrieved from www.offthechartsblog.org/health-reforms-medicaid-expansion-is-a-very-good-deal-for-states

——. (2016, July 19). *Medicaid Works: A Critical and Evolving Pillar of U.S. Health Care*. Retrieved from www.cbpp.org/blog/medicaid-works-a-critical-and-evolving-pillar-of-us-health-care

Centers for Medicare and Medicaid Services. (2005). *Managed Care Trends*. Washington, DC: Centers for Medicare and Medicaid Services.

——. (2012). *Medicaid.gov*. Retrieved from www.medicaid.gov/medicaid/eligibility/index.html

——. (2017). *Medicaid Employment Initiatives*. Retrieved from www.medicaid.gov/medicaid/ltss/employment/index.html

Children's Defense Fund. (2000, Spring). *Unspent Funds Mean Uninsured Children. Sign Them Up!* Washington, DC: The Fund.

Clark, R. E., Samnaliev, M., and McGovern, M. P. (2009, January). The Impact of Substance Use Disorders on Medical Expenditures for Medicaid Beneficiaries with Behavioral Health Disorders. *Psychiatric Services*, 60(1). Retrieved from http://ps.psychiatryonline.org/article.aspx?Volume=60&page=35&journalID=18

Clemans-Cope, L., Kenney, G. M., Buettgens, M., Carroll, C., and Blavin, F. (2012, May). The Affordable Care Act's Coverage Expansions will Reduce Differences in Uninsurance Rates by Race and Ethnicity. *Health Affairs*, 31(5), 920–930.

Congressional Budget Office. (2012, July 24). Estimates for the Insurance Coverage Provisions of the Affordable Care Act Updated for the Recent Supreme Court Decision. Retrieved from www.cbo.gov/publication/43472

Coughlin, T. A., Long, S. K., and Shen, Y. (2012, July). Assessing Access to Care under Medicaid: Evidence for the Nation and Thirteen States. *Health Affairs*, 24(4), 1073–1083.

Diament, M. (2011, July). As SSI Enrollment Surges, Lawmakers Call for Better Oversight. *Disability Scoop*. Retrieved from www.disabilityscoop.com/2011/07/11/as-ssi-surges-oversight/13507/

Dion, M. R. and Pavetti, L. (2000, March). *Access to and Participation in Medicaid and the Food Stamp Program*. Washington, DC: Mathematical Policy Research.

Dunkelberg, A. (2005, April). *Combined Impact of Medically Needy Cut and TANF Sanctions*. Austin, TX: Center for Public Policy Priorities.

Edelman, M. W. (1999). The State of America's Children, Children's Defense Fund Yearbook 1999. Boston, MA: Beacon Press.

Ellwood, M. (1999). *The Medicaid Eligibility Maze: Coverage Expands, but Enrollment Problems Persist: Findings from a Five-State Study*. Cambridge, MA: Mathematical Policy Research.

Families USA. (1999a). *Expanding Medicaid State Options*. Washington, DC: Families USA.

——. (1999b, September). *Medicaid Enrollment and Spending Trends*. Kaiser Commission on Medicaid and the Uninsured Medicaid Facts. Washington, DC: The Kaiser Family Foundation.

——. (1999c). *Immigrant Eligibility and Medicaid and CHIP Programs*. Washington, DC: Families USA.

——. (1999d). *Losing Health Insurance, the Unintended Consequences of Welfare Reform*. Washington, DC: Families USA.

——. (2000). *Go Directly to Work, Do Not Collect Health Insurance: Low-Income Parents Lose Medicaid*. Washington, DC: Families USA.

——. (2001, May). *Medicaid Managed Care Consumer Protection Regulations: No Patients' Rights for the Poor?* Special Report. Washington, DC: Families USA.

——. (2003, March). *Winners and Losers: Who Gets What under the Medicare Drug Benefit*. Washington, DC: Families USA.

——. (2005, March). *Enrolling Uninsured Low-income Children in Medicaid and S-CHIP*. Washington, DC: The Kaiser Family Foundation.

Garrett, B. and Holahan, J. (2000, March). *Welfare Leavers, Medicaid Coverage, and Private Health Insurance. Assessing the New Federalism*, Series B, No. B-13. Washington, DC: Urban Institute.

Greenberg, M. (1998, September). *Participation in Welfare and Medicaid Enrollment. Kaiser Commission on Medicaid and the Uninsured Issue Paper*. Washington, DC: Kaiser Family Foundation.

Hagert, C. (2005, March). *What's Happening with TANF Caseloads: Strict Rules Force Thousands off Rolls.* Austin, TX: Center for Public Policy Priorities.

Health Care Financing Administration. (2000a, September). *A Profile of Medicaid, Chartbook 2000*. Baltimore, MD: U.S. Department of Health and Human Services.

——. (2000b, July). *Medicare 2000. 35 Years of Improving America's Health and Security*. Baltimore, MD: U.S. Department of Health and Human Services.

Holahan, J., Zuckerman, S., Evans, A., and Rangarajan, S. (1998, May–June). Medicaid Managed Care in Thirteen States. *Health Affairs*, 17(3), 43–63.

Hurley, R. E. and Zuckerman, S. (2002). Medicaid Managed Care: State Flexibility in Action. Assessing the New Federalism Discussion Paper. Washington, DC: The Urban Institute.

Kaiser Commission on Medicaid and the Uninsured. (2012a, April). *Medicaid's Role for Dual Eligible Beneficiaries*. Retrieved from www.kff.org/medicaid/upload/7846-03.pdf

——. (2012b, July). *Program Integrity in Medicaid: A Primer*. Retrieved from www.kff.org/medicaid/upload/8337.pdf

Kaiser Family Foundation. (1998, October). *Medicaid and Managed Care. Kaiser Commission on Medicaid and the Uninsured Medicaid Facts*. Washington, DC: The Kaiser Family Foundation.

——. (1999a, July). *The Medicaid Program at a Glance*. Kaiser Commission on Medicaid and the Uninsured Key Facts. Washington, DC: The Kaiser Family Foundation.

——. (1999b, September). *Medicaid Enrollment and Spending Trends*. Kaiser Commission on Medicaid and the Uninsured Medicaid Facts. Washington, DC: The Kaiser Family Foundation.

——. (2001, February). *Medicaid Enrollment and Spending Trends*. Kaiser Commission on Medicaid and the Uninsured Medicaid Facts. Washington, DC: The Kaiser Family Foundation.

——. (2004, June). *Olmstead v. LC: The Interaction of the Americans with Disabilities Act and Medicaid*. Kaiser Commission on Medicaid and the Uninsured Medicaid Facts. Washington, DC: The Kaiser Family Foundation.

——. (2005a, March). *Enrolling Uninsured Low-Income Children in Medicaid and S-CHIP*. Washington, DC: The Kaiser Family Foundation.

——. (2005b, June). Medicaid Enrollment and Spending Trends. Kaiser Commission on Medicaid and the Uninsured Medicaid Facts. Washington, DC: The Kaiser Family Foundation.

——. (2005c). New Directions for Medicaid Section 1115 Waivers: Policy Implications. Washington, DC: The Kaiser Family Foundation.

——. (2008a, September). Headed for a Crunch: An Update on Medicaid Spending, Coverage and Policy Heading into an Economic Downturn. Kaiser Family Foundation. Retrieved from www.kff.org/medicaid/upload/7815ES.pdf

——. (2008b). Health Coverage of Children: The Role of Medicaid and SCHIP. The Kaiser Commission on Medicaid and the Uninsured Key Facts. Washington, DC: The Kaiser Family Foundation.

——. (2009a, January). *Medicaid: A Primer*. Retrieved from www.kff.org/medicaid/upload/7334_03.pdf

——. (2009b, February). *Children's Health Insurance Program Reauthorization Act of 2009 (CHIPRA)*. The Kaiser Commission on Medicaid and the Uninsured Medicaid Facts. Washington, DC: The Kaiser Family Foundation.

——. (2010, June). *Medicaid Primer 2010*. Washington, DC: The Kaiser Family Foundation.

____. (2012, December). *The Medicaid Medically Needy Program: Spending and Enrollment Update*. Retrieved from https://kaiserfamilyfoundation.files.wordpress.com/2013/01/4096.pdf

____. (2016, October 14). *Medicaid and HIV*. Retrieved from www.kff.org/hivaids/fact-sheet/medicaid-and-hiv/

Lav, I. and McNichol, E. (2009, March). *State Budget Troubles Worsen. Center for Budget and Policy Priorities*. Washington, DC: Center for Budget and Policy Priorities.

Liptak, A. (2012, June 28). Supreme Court Upholds Health Law, 5-4, in Victory for Obama. *New York Times*. Retrieved from www.nytimes.com/2012/06/29/us/supreme-court-lets-health-law-largely-stand.html?pagewanted=1&ref=policy

Medicaid.Gov. (2012). Medicaid and CHIP Program Information. Retrieved from www.medicaid.gov/Medicaid-CHIP-Program-Information/Medicaid-and-CHIP-Program-Information.html

Medicare Payment Advisory Commission (MedPAC). (2008 June). A *Data Book: Healthcare Spending and the Medicare Program*. Retrieved from www.medpac.gov/chapters/Jun08DataBookSec2.pdf

National Association of Social Workers. (1996, August 27). Personal Responsibility and Work Opportunity Reconciliation Act of 1996, Summary of Provisions. Government Relations Update. Washington, DC: NASW.

National Governors Association and National Conference of State Legislatures. (1998). *State Children's Health Insurance Program*. Washington, DC: National Governors Association and National Conference of State Legislatures.

National Health Law Program. (2007, April 16). Highlights of Recent Changes to the Medicaid Act. Retrieved from www.healthlaw.org/library/folder.103219-Deficit_Reduction_ Act_of_2005

Nibal, K. (2000, September 12). Testimony to the House Committee on the Budget, Task Force on Welfare on Implementation of the Drug and Alcohol Provisions of P.L. 104–121. Retrieved from www.ssa.gov/cgi-bin/cqcgi

Pear, R. (1990, November 19). Despite Order, U.S. Stalls Aid to Poor Children. *New York Times*, p. A1.

——. (1997a, August 15). After a Review, 95,180 Children will Lose Cash Disability Benefits. *New York Times*, p. A1.

——. (1997b, November 16). U.S. Mistakenly Cuts Benefits for Many Disabled Children. *New York Times*, p. A1.

——. (1999, May 9). Many States Slow to Use Children's Insurance Fund. *New York Times*, pp. A1, A16.

Reschovsky, J. D. and Cunningham, P. J. (1998, October). *Chipping away at the Problem of Uninsured Children*. Washington, DC: Center for Studying Health System Change.

Rowland, D., Rosenbaum, S., Simon, L., and Chait, E. (1995). *Medicaid and Managed Care: Lessons from the Literature. Kaiser Commission on Medicaid and the Uninsured Update*. Washington, DC: Kaiser Family Foundation.

Rowland, D., Garfield, R., and Elias, R. (2003). Accomplishments and Challenges in Medicaid Mental Health. *Health Affairs*, 22(5), 73–83.

Rudowitz, R. and Garfield, R. (2018, April 12). *10 Things to Know about Medicaid: Setting the Facts Straight*. Washington, DC: Kaiser Family Foundation. Retrieved from www.kff.org/medicaid/issue-brief/10-things-to-know-about-medicaid-setting-the-facts-straight

Rudowitz, R. and Valentine, A. (2017, October 19). *Medicaid Enrollment & Spending Growth: FY 2017 & 2018*. Retrieved from www.kff.org/medicaid/issue-brief/medicaid-enrollment-spending-growth-fy-2017-2018/

Sanger, K. (2017, June 22). How G.O.P. Health Plan Is Really a Rollback of Medicaid. *New York Times*, p. A15.

Sommers, B.D., Baicker, K., and Epstein, A.M. (2012a, July 25). Mortality and Access to Care among Adults after State Medicaid Expansions. *New England Journal of Medicine*. Retrieved from www.nejm.org/doi/full/10.1056/NEJMsa1202099#t=article

Sommers, B. D., Tomasi, M. R., Swartz, K., and Epstein, A. M. (2012b, May). Reasons for the Wide Variation in Medicaid Participation Rates among States Hold Lessons for Coverage Expansion in 2014. *Health Affairs*, 31(5), 909–919.

U.S. General Accounting Office. (1995). *Health Insurance for Children: Many Remain Uninsured Despite Medicaid Expansion* (GAO/HEHS-95-175). Washington, DC: U.S. Government Printing Office.

——. (1996). *Medicaid Managed Care: Serving the Disabled Challenges State Programs* (GAO/HEHS-96-136). Washington, DC: U.S. Government Printing Office.

——. (1998, May). *Supplemental Security Income: SSA Needs a Uniform Standard for Assessing Childhood Disability* (GAO/HEHS-98-123). Washington, DC: U.S. Government Printing Office.

U.S. Government Accounting Office. (2012, June 26). *Supplemental Security Income: Better Management Oversight Needed for Children's Benefits* (GAO-12-497). Retrieved from www.gao.gov/products/GAO-12-497

U.S. Social Security Administration. (2008). *Trends in the Social Security and Supplemental Security Income Disability Programs*. Retrieved from www.ssa.gov/policy/docs/chartbooks/disability_trends/index.html

——. (2016, August 2). *List of State Medicaid Programs for the Aged, Blind and Disabled*. Retrieved from https://secure.ssa.gov/poms.nsf/lnx/0501715020

——. (2017). *Facts and Figures about Social Security: SSI Program*. Retrieved from www.ssa.gov/policy/docs/chartbooks/fast_facts/2017/fast_facts17.html

Wen, P. (2011, July 11). *Disability Program, Concerns on Rise: SSI Youth Benefits Draw More Fire. Boston Globe*. Retrieved from www.boston.com/news/local/massachusetts/articles/2011/07/11/as_ssi_costs_rise_critics_step_up_call_for_tighter_controls/

Zezima, K. and Ingraham, C. (2017, March 9). GOP health-care bill would drop addiction treatment mandate covering 1.3 million Americans. *Washington Post*. Retrieved from www.washingtonpost.com/news/wonk/wp/2017/03/09/gop-health-care-bill-would-drop-mental-health-coverage-mandate-covering-1-3-million-americans/?utm_term=.528c57fcab0f

Policy Practice
Advancing Access to Health and Mental Health Care

CHAPTER 8

Social Workers and Policy Practice
Affecting Policy and Achieving Policy Action

INTRODUCTION

THIS CHAPTER PROVIDES A TRANSITION FROM PARTS I AND II, which provide an overview of the current health care system in the U.S., to Part III, which focuses on affecting policy and engaging in policy practice. In 2015, the Council on Social Work Education (CSWE) revised its Educational Policy and Accreditation Standards (EPAS) for professional social work competencies and practice behaviors for accredited social work education programs. CSWE's Competency 5: Engage in Policy Practice states that students and practitioners should be able to "1) identify social policy at the local, state, and federal level that impacts well-being, service delivery, and access to social services; 2) assess how social welfare and economic policies impact the delivery of and access to social services; and 3) apply critical thinking to analyze, formulate, and advocate for policies that advance human rights and social, economic, and environmental justice" (Council on Social Work Education, 2015, p. 8). The remaining chapters of this book examine issues of access, disparities in health and access to care, and advocate for more just policies in health care in this context.

WHAT IS POLICY PRACTICE?

Policy practice is not new. Social workers have engaged in the practice of using skills to change social policies to advance social and economic justice since their earliest days in the Settlement House and Charitable Society Organization movements (mid-to-late 1800s and early 1900s). As discussed in Part I, these efforts focused on helping to alleviate the severe poverty and poor working conditions that immigrants faced during the industrial revolution. Reformers worked to change policies in child labor, wages, working conditions, housing, and public health. Social workers were also instrumental in the creation of social welfare institutions during this period, such as the U.S. Children's Bureau, which played a central role in promoting maternal and child health. These practice behaviors have continued throughout social work's history, although some have argued that social work has "lost its way" from its original mission and needs a stronger emphasis on policy practice and social reform (Ehrenreich, 1985; Figueira-McDonough, 1993; Specht and Courtney, 1994; Reisch, 2002; Cummins et al., 2011).

However, with revised accreditation standards for schools of social work, CSWE has clearly identified policy practice as a central role and function in social work practice. This, in turn, has led to a renewal of emphasis on defining and understanding policy practice in social work, particularly in textbooks developed for use in the social work curriculum. The term "policy practice" emerged in the early 1990s and several authors in social work education have explored its meaning. In 1991, Wyers discussed "policy-practice" as "a recent development that attempts to integrate direct social work practice with social policy theory and advocacy for change" (Wyers, 1991, p. 241). Jansson (2012) defined policy practice in 1999 in the first edition of *Becoming an Effective Policy Advocate* as "efforts to change policies in legislative, agency, and community settings, whether by establishing new policies, improving existing ones, or defeating the policy initiatives of other people" (Jansson, 2012, p. 521). Barusch (2018) first discussed policy practice in 2002 in *Foundations of Social Policy* as something more than policy advocacy; she has focused on skill development for policy practitioners in several areas, including assessment and analysis, advocacy and empowerment. Cummins et al. (2011, p. 8) define policy practice as:

> using social work skills to propose and change policies in order to achieve the goal of social and economic justice. In doing policy practice, social workers apply generalist social work perspectives and skills to make changes in laws, rules, budgets, and policies and in the bodies that create these policies, whether they be local, state, or federal agencies or other decision-making bodies, in the pursuit of social work mission of social and economic justice. The goal . . . is to ensure . . . that all people, regardless of their socioeconomic status, race, ethnicity, religion, or sexual orientation, have opportunities to achieve success for themselves and their families . . . . This . . . has been part of the social work profession since its very beginning.

They also note that, although anecdotal evidence exists to show that more social workers are engaged in policy practice today, systematic research is needed to study the current role of policy practice in social work.

STAGES OF POLICY PRACTICE

For decades, many policy analysts have offered theoretical models for analyzing social welfare policies. These have included Gil's (1992) *Unraveling Social Policy* (5th edn.), Dolgoff and Feldstein's (2013) *Understanding Social Welfare* (9th edn.), Gilbert and Terrell's (2010) *Dimensions of Social Welfare Policy* (8th edn.), Dobelstein's (2003) *Social Welfare: Policy and Analysis* (3rd edn.), and Chambers' (2005) *Social Policy and Social Programs: A Method for the Practical Public Policy Analyst* (4th edn.). However, policy practice is more than policy analysis. In many ways, policy practice is a combination of multiple phases of the policy-making process, including policy formulation, analysis, implementation, and evaluation. Cummins et al. (2011) have identified eight stages of policy-making that integrate models of policy analysis (knowledge) with ways to engage with others to propose and change policies (action). Our own brief outline of the stages of policy practice (building on Cummins et al. [2011] and others) is as follows:

Stage 1: Identify the social problem

What is the social problem?

Who is affected?

What are the dimensions and boundaries of the problem?

Stage 2: Collect data and information about the problem

What evidence is there that a problem exists?

What is the extent of the problem?

How serious is the problem?

What is the perceived cause of the problem?

What explanations exist for the problem?

Stage 3: Identify relevant constituents and share information about problem

Who are the stakeholders?

How are they affected by the problem?

Would they be motivated to address the problem?

If so, why and in what ways?

What are the best means for sharing information about the problem (face-to-face meetings, calls, letters, news media, professional events, etc.)?

Stage 4: Develop policy goals and objectives

What should the policy achieve?

What are the options for achieving these goals?

How can the problem best be alleviated or ameliorated using evidence-based solutions? What is achievable?

What is the best fit with the target population?

What values guide the policy options?

What rights or benefits will be preserved or enhanced?

Are disparities in equality, equity, and adequacy addressed?

Stage 5: Identify and build support to engage in policy advocacy

Which stakeholders could play a role in advocating for change?

What roles could they play?

What resources could they bring to the effort?

Is it possible to develop a coalition?

Who would join?

Who could play a leadership role in the coalition?

What techniques are best to influence the targets for change (bargaining, compromise, and persuasion)?

Stage 6: Develop an action plan

What is the proposed policy (program and benefits) to address the social problem?

How will it be delivered? How will it be funded?

How will it be monitored and evaluated?

Stage 7: Implement and/or monitor the policy

Is there a role to oversee implementation of the policy and its programs and services?

Have sufficient resources been allocated for implementation?

Have mechanisms been established for coordination among segments of the delivery system?

Are there barriers to implementation?

Stage 8: Evaluate the policy

How successfully was the social problem addressed?

Was the target population served?

Were the goals of the policy met?

Were there sufficient resources?

What problems remain?

VALUES AND STANDARDS FOR ASSESSING POLICIES

Policy practice is also guided by professional values, ethics, and perspectives. Gilbert and Terrell (2013) provide a classic framework for judging the extent to which a policy achieves social justice by considering three core values: Equality, equity, and adequacy.

Equality "prescribes that benefits should be allocated so as to equalize the distribution of resources and opportunities" (Gilbert and Terrell, 2013, p. 76). Policies that remove barriers to basic needs and rights, such as access to health care, equalize the distribution of this essential resource. *Equity* "denotes a conventional sense of fair treatment" (Gilbert and Terrell, 2013, p. 76) with deservedness, related to contributions. However, this is tempered by one's abilities; not everyone has the same ability to contribute to society, yet everyone has the same basic needs. Again, policies that remove barriers to basic needs and rights, such as access to health care, regardless of one's ability to pay taxes, or purchase health insurance, or other forms of contribution, provide equity in access to health care. Finally, *adequacy* "refers to the desirability of providing a decent standard of material well-being" (Gilbert and Terrell, 2013, p. 78). "Decent" refers to the standard of need that is established by a community or nation. How little is acceptable? How much is supported? For example, is it acceptable for millions of adults and children to lack access to health care? Or, should universal coverage be a basic tenant of adequacy?

To consider principles of access to health care in policy practice, it is instructive to examine standards set forth in both social work and public health. According to the Association of State and Territorial Health Officials (2004), a national organization that represents state and territorial public health agencies, "All Americans should have access to appropriate, affordable and timely health services . . . that, at a minimum, cover basic, preventive and primary medical care." To achieve these goals, "the federal government must address access for all people." In addition, "health services should be appropriate. [They] . . . should be medically indicated, based on consumer needs, and where possible, evidence-based. . . . Vital preventive and emergency health services should be accessible to all persons" (Association of State and Territorial Health Officials, 2004, p. 1) (Figure 8.1).

For more than 60 years, the American Public Health Association (APHA, 1978 – see Association of State and Territorial Health Officials, 2004) has endorsed the "removal of economic and organizational barriers to health care for the American people" and supported "a universal system of financing health care for the entire population, including major changes in the organization and delivery of health services" (Association of State and Territorial Health Officials, p. 1). The association also believes that a universal system should "assure comprehensive and integrated preventive, therapeutic, and rehabilitative services" (Association of State and Territorial Health Officials, p. 1), do away with copayments and deductibles, include "effective measures to remedy deficiencies in rural and other underserved areas" (Association of State and Territorial Health Officials, p. 1), ensure patients' rights, and include provisions for cost containment (see Figure 8.1).

> The National Association of Social Workers (2003) supports the right to universal access to a continuum of health and mental health care to promote wellness, maintain optimal health, prevent illness and disability, treat health conditions, ameliorate the effects of unavoidable incapacities, and provide supportive long-term and end-of-life care.
>
> (Association of State and Territorial Health Officials, p. 172)

In the remaining chapters, as we examine the U.S. health care system in the context of policy practice, these values and standards offer guiding principles for understanding and assessing the current system.

HIGHLIGHTS

- CSWE's Competency 5: Engage in Policy Practice states that students and practitioners should be able to "1) identify social policy at the local, state, and federal level that impacts well-being, service delivery, and access to social services; 2) assess how social welfare and economic policies impact the delivery of and access to social services; and 3) apply critical thinking to analyze, formulate, and advocate for policies that advance human rights and social, economic, and environmental justice" (Council on Social Work Education, 2015, pp. 8).

FIGURE 8.1

Social Work and Public Health Principles: Access to Health Care

SOCIAL WORK[a]
Services should address access, choice, quality, and comprehensiveness of health and mental health care, including parity of mental health with health care.
Services should provide equal access to emerging technology and prescription drugs. Patient rights and protections should be guaranteed.
Government funding should be provided for education, training, and ongoing professional development for health and mental health providers.
Services should accommodate cultural and language differences and ensure adequate, appropriate care.

PUBLIC HEALTH[b]
Services should address geographic barriers, as well as social and cultural environments, accommodating different languages, practices, and customs.
Health care providers should be trained to address unique physical, mental, emotional, spiritual, cultural, and developmental needs.
Health care should be provided in community-based settings, close to family and community.
Evaluation of services should be based on a combination of achieving service delivery goals, cost-effectiveness, patient and provider satisfaction, and improved health outcomes.
Evaluation of services should also be based on an assessment of health needs and the outcomes of diverse populations, including racial and ethnic groups and individuals with disabilities.
Primary care clinicians should play a central role in linking people to needed personal health services and a contributing role in monitoring the health status of patients; primary care services should be integrated and accessible.
Disparities in health should be addressed for vulnerable populations who may have special health needs or experience persistent disparities in health based on race or ethnicity, age, sex, socioeconomic status, or disability; the federal government, through Healthy People 2010, calls for the elimination of racial and ethnic health disparities.

[a]National Association of Social Workers, Health Care Policy Statement, *Social Work Speaks* (2003).
[b]Association of State and Territorial Health Officials, *Access Policy Statement* (2004).

- The term "policy practice" emerged in the early 1990s; it refers to advocacy efforts to change policies in legislative, agency, and community settings. Policy practice is a combination of multiple phases of the policy-making process including policy formulation, policy analysis, policy implementation, and policy evaluation.

- Policy practice involves multiple stages of practice: (1) Identify the social problem, (2) collect data and information about the problem, (3) identify relevant constituents and share information about the problem, (4) develop policy goals and objectives, (5) identify and build support to engage in policy advocacy, (6) develop an action plan, (7) implement and/or monitor the policy, and (8) evaluate the policy.

- Policy practice is also guided by professional values, ethics, and perspectives. Gilbert and Terrell (2013) provide a classic framework for judging the extent to which a policy achieves social justice by considering three core values: Equality, equity, and adequacy.

REFERENCES

Association of State and Territorial Health Officials. (2004, September 29). Access to Health Care Services Policy Statement, 2004–2007. Retrieved from www.astho.org/policy_statements/Access%20Policy.pdf

Barusch, A. S. (2018). *Foundations of Social Policy: Social Justice in Human Perspective*, 6th edn. Boston, MA: Brooks/Cole.

Chambers, D. E. (2005). *Social Policy and Social Programs: A Method for the Practical Public Policy Analyst*, 4th edn. Boston, MA: Allyn & Bacon.

Council on Social Work Education (CSWE). (2015). *Educational Policy and Accreditation Standards (EPAS)*. Retrieved from www.cswe.org/getattachment/Accreditation/Accreditation-Process/2015-EPAS/2015EPAS_Web_FINAL.pdf.aspx

Cummins, L. K., Byers, K. V., and Pedrick, L. (2011). *Policy Practice for Social Workers: New Strategies for a New Era*. Boston, MA: Pearson Education.

Dobelstein, A. (2003). *Social Welfare: Policy and Analysis*, 3rd edn. Boston, MA: Allyn & Bacon.

Dolgoff, R. and Feldstein, D. (2013). *Understanding Social Welfare*, 9th edn. Boston, MA: Pearson.

Ehrenreich, J. (1985). *The Altruistic Imagination: A History of Social Work and Social Policy in the United States*. Ithaca, NY: Cornell University Press.

Figueira-McDonough, J. (1993, March). Policy Practice: The Neglected Side of Social Work Intervention. *Social Work*, 38(2), 179–188.

Gil, D. (1992). *Unraveling Social Policy*, 5th edn. Boston, MA: Schenkman.

Gilbert, N. and Terrell, P. (2013). *Dimensions of Social Welfare Policy*, 8th edn. Boston, MA: Pearson.

Jansson, B. (2012). *The Reluctant Welfare State: Engaging History to Advance Social Work Practice in Contemporary Society*, 7th edn. Belmont, CA: Brooks/Cole.

National Association of Social Workers. (2003). *Health Care Policy Statement. Social Work Speaks*. Washington, DC: NASW.

Reisch, M. (2002). *The Road Not Taken: A History of Radical Social Work in the U.S.* New York: Brunner-Routledge.

Specht, H. and Courtney, M. E. (1994). *Unfaithful Angels: How Social Work Has Abandoned Its Mission.* New York: Free Press.

Wyers, N. L. (1991, Fall). Policy-Practice in Social Work: Models and Issues. *Journal of Social Work Education*, 27(3), 241–250.

CHAPTER 9

Analyzing the Problem
Access to Care

INTRODUCTION

WHEN CONGRESS FAILED TO PASS THE HEALTH SECURITY ACT OF 1993, it ushered in a period of disillusionment and concern about the nation's willingness to reform the health care system and expand access to the uninsured. The Clinton administration's proposal provided a momentous opportunity to transform the system and achieve universal coverage. The failure to seize this moment was "most devastating" (Altman et al., 1998), and advocates of reform felt that the nation's "commitment . . . seemed to collapse . . . as if the problem of the uninsured had disappeared" (Altman et al., 1998, p. 1). In actuality, the number of people without insurance was growing and was projected to reach 60 million by 2007 (Health Insurance Association of America, 1999). The passage of the Affordable Care Act (ACA) 17 years later during the Obama administration renewed hope that the U.S. would pursue both expansion of access to health care and a significant reduction in the number of uninsured in the U.S. However, once again, with the Trump administration's efforts to "repeal and replace" the ACA, the nation's commitment to achieve universal coverage has been challenged.

This chapter addresses the basic policy practice questions raised in the early stages of analysis. The following outline puts the issues discussed in this chapter in this analytical context.

THE PROBLEM: THE NEED FOR ACCESS

The uninsured population in the U.S. has been a major public policy issue for the nation for decades. Unlike the rest of the industrialized world, the U.S. has failed to enact a universal system of access to health care. Instead, it has created a patchwork system of programs, including employment-based insurance, Medicare, Medicaid, CHIP, the Veterans Health Administration, the Indian Health Service, the Public Health Service, and Community Mental Health and Health Centers.

In 2013, the year before the major features of the ACA went into effect, more than 44 million nonelderly individuals were uninsured. With the expansion of Medicaid to adults with incomes below 138 percent of the federal poverty level (FPL), and tax credits for individuals with incomes up to 400 percent of FPL, the uninsured rate is at an historic low in the U.S. However, millions of individuals still lack access to health care coverage and services due to its high cost. Those at greatest risk are low-income individuals, adults, and people of color.

Almost half of the remaining uninsured are not covered by the ACA because they live in a state that has not joined in the Medicaid expansion program, they are subject to immigrant eligibility restrictions, or their income is too high for the tax credits. The other half are eligible for assistance for coverage but either find the cost too high or struggle with understanding and accessing their coverage options (Foutz et al., 2017).

WHAT IS ACCESS?

Most obviously, access is a measure of individual or population coverage for health care services through private or public health insurance. In 2016, 28.1 million people or 8.8 percent of the U.S. population had no medical insurance for the entire year (Barnett and Berchick, 2017). As discussed later, different measures have been used to count the *uninsured* population. However, there is an additional aspect of access. Many of those who have private or public health insurance have inadequate coverage, that is, their health plans will not cover all of their medical needs and expenses. Inadequate coverage, or *under-insurance*, is typically defined as out-of-pocket expenses, such as deductibles, copayments, and non-covered expenses that exceed 5 percent of an individual's personal low income and 10 percent of an individual's personal higher income. In 2016, according to researchers at the Commonwealth Fund (2017), 28 percent of insured working adults were *under*insured for access to care. This explosion in underinsurance primarily impacts low-income families, but increasingly puts families higher up on the income scale at risk; Schoen et al. (2011) found that 16 percent of adults with incomes between $40,000 and $60,000 were underinsured (19 percent were uninsured). The same study also showed that the ACA had the potential to reduce the number of uninsured by 70 percent by providing premium assistance and lowering out-of-pocket costs.

Outline of Analysis: Access

What is the social problem?	Access to care
Who is affected? What is the extent of the problem?	8.8% population uninsured in 2016 (Barnett and Berchick, 2017)
	28% of insured working adults *under*insured in 2016 (Commonwealth Fund, 2017)
What are the dimensions and boundaries of the problem?	Disparities in access and health status based on differences in socioeconomic status:

- Working/unemployed
- Age

- Race and ethnicity
- Gender
- Regional differences

What evidence is there that a problem exists?	National and regional data and studies on lack of coverage and its impact on health
How serious is the problem?	The uninsured and underinsured populations are not adequately protected from the medical or financial risks of illness and injury
What is the perceived cause of the problem?	The strain on both private and public sector insurance coverage to provide comprehensive, quality, and cost-effective care
What explanations exist for the problem?	The lack of universal health insurance coverage due to a patchwork system of health care policies and programs in the U.S. and the high cost of health care and insurance

Why is Access Important?

People who lack health insurance are more likely to lack a usual source or provider of care, to spend more on health services, and to experience more problems with treatment, quality of care, and continuity of care. Many people who lack health insurance forgo care until their condition worsens and becomes more expensive to treat. The uninsured population is not adequately protected from the medical or financial risks of illness and injury (Rhoades and Chu, 2000). According to Schoen et al. (2005), about half of the underinsured and uninsured had difficulty paying their bills. Many were forced to find ways to cover their costs by taking out loans and mortgages against their homes, or using credit cards and going into debt to pay their bills.

Communities are also affected by lack of insurance. High rates of noninsurance in a community tend to reduce hospital services, shift public resources away from disease prevention and surveillance, and reallocate federal and state tax dollars toward uncompensated medical care (Association of State and Territorial Health Officials, 2004). Overall, the magnitude of the uninsured population raises doubts about the efficiency of the current system and the adequacy of the current private–public sector arrangement in financing and managing access to care (Rhoades and Chu, 2000).

Trends in Coverage and Reasons for Concern

The fact that so many people (27.6 million nonelderly in 2016) lack coverage in the U.S. is troublesome for a society that is the richest nation in the world and prides itself on the quality of its medical care and research. The uninsured rate remained relatively unchanged from the late 1980s until 2010 when health care reform was legislated for with the passage of the ACA. The uninsured rate decreased dramatically from 2010 to 2016; there were 21.8 million fewer uninsured persons in 2016 than in 2010 (Figure 9.1). As discussed in this chapter, most health insurance coverage in the U.S. is employment based and therefore has been susceptible to changes in the economy and workforce (Mills, 1999; Kaiser Commission on Medicaid and the Uninsured, 2005). In general, as health care costs have increased, the number of uninsured has increased. Also, some jobs have provided coverage, whereas others have not and still do not, and, as the work force changes, coverage for some workers has improved, whereas coverage for others has worsened. However, the ACA has been a "game changer."

In 2015, employer-sponsored health insurance covered over half of the nonelderly population, half of whom received coverage as a dependent (Dawson et al., 2017). Under the ACA, employers with 50 or more full-time-equivalent employees must provide affordable coverage to their employees; if they do not they are assessed a fee up to $2000 per full-time employee (in excess of 30 employees). They must offer coverage that provides for at least 60 percent of covered health care expenses and they must ensure that the employee's share of the individual premium does not exceed 9.5 percent of the family income. Otherwise, employers

FIGURE 9.1

Uninsured Population in U.S., 1989–2016

YEAR	TOTAL (MILLION)	PERCENTAGE OF TOTAL POPULATION
2016	28.1	8.8
2010	49.9	16.3
2007	45.6	15.3
2005	45.8	15.7
2003	45.0	15.6
2001	41.2	14.6
1999	42.6	15.5
1997	43.4	16.1
1995	40.6	15.4
1993	39.7	15.3
1991	35.4	14.1

Source: U.S. Census Bureau (1990–2017).

are subject to penalties. The ACA also created the Small Business Health Options Program (SHOP) marketplace for employers with 50 or fewer full-time employees to help them purchase coverage, and employers with no more than 25 full-time employees and annual wages less than $52,000 to be eligible for tax credits (up to two years) (Foutz et al., 2017).

Until the ACA was enacted, as unemployment rose, the size of the uninsured population typically increased as well. Even a strong economy with a relatively low unemployment rate was no guarantee of improved rates of health insurance coverage. For example, during the boom years of the economy in the 1990s, the number of uninsured increased each year (except in 1999). This was followed by an economic recession in 2001, when job-based insurance decreased sharply and continued to decline. From 1999 to 2013, the percentage of companies, especially small companies, that offered health benefits to its employees declined from 66 percent to 57 percent, and the employee's share of the premium during this period nearly doubled. Thus, even with the ACA, small businesses, in particular, have struggled to finance insurance for its employees. During this period, health insurance premiums and the employee's share of those premiums nearly doubled (Foutz et al., 2017).

The composition of the uninsured population in the U.S. also raises concerns about equity and justice (equality) in the current system. The uninsured population is predominantly lower income, and people of color are disproportionately poor. As discussed in this chapter and Chapter 10, access to and quality of care for people of color are of major concern in the U.S. This chapter provides an overview of these trends in coverage. It also addresses broader public policy issues concerning access, coverage, and financing. The uninsured population as a whole and groups at greater risk of lack of coverage are examined. Finally, the role of insurance is discussed: Does health insurance really matter? How does it affect the utilization of health care services? What principles of access are important for the U.S.? How do we expand coverage?

HEALTH INSURANCE COVERAGE IN THE U.S.

In the early 1990s, during the debate on universal health insurance, about 35 million people (14 percent of the population) lacked health insurance coverage. According to the federal government's Current Population Survey (see Figure 9.1), the number of uninsured in the U.S. reached 49 million in 2010; however, these figures may not provide a true picture of the scope of the problem. Some analysts believe the Census Bureau data reflects an underestimate of the number of uninsured (Weinick and Drilea, 1998) because it does not include people who lose their insurance coverage for *part* of a year. The Census Bureau acknowledges this:

> Compared with other national surveys, the CPS ASEC's [Current Population Survey Annual Social and Economic Supplement] estimate of the number of people without health insurance more closely approximates the number of people

who were uninsured at a specific point in time during the year than the number of people uninsured for the entire year. There are several ongoing projects aimed at improving the quality of health coverage data from the CPS ASEC, including cognitive research and field testing to improve the wording of the CPS ASEC health coverage questions.

(U.S. Census Bureau, 2012, p. 21)

For example, other surveys have consistently shown higher estimates. The Medical Expenditure Panel Survey (MEPS), which is conducted by the Agency for Healthcare Research and Quality (AHRQ) at the U.S. Public Health Services (Rhoades and Cohen, 2008), showed a higher estimate for 2005 and 2006 than the CPS; it reported 83 million people (32 percent of the under-65 population) uninsured for at least one month during the full two-year period (calendar years 2005 and 2006). The Kaiser Family Foundation found 66.6 million uninsured for at least a month during a 28-month period as far back as the early 1990s (Kaiser Commission on Medicaid and the Uninsured, 1998b).

On the other hand, some analysts have argued that the Census Bureau exaggerates the scope of the problem (Institute of Medicine, 2001) because its data really does measure the number of people who lack coverage at a point in time, rather than those without coverage for an entire year (Congressional Budget Office [CBO], 2003). For example, according to CBO estimates, in 1998 between 21 million and 31 million people had no coverage for an entire year, whereas the Census Bureau estimated that 44.9 million people were uninsured. However one estimates it, the number of uninsured Americans is substantial.

In addition, as mentioned earlier, millions more have insurance that is *inadequate* to cover their medical needs and expenses. This kind of financial burden often results from a catastrophic illness or a serious accident or injury. Individuals who need expensive long-term care because of chronic illness or permanent disability are also at risk of *under*insurance. Studies have shown, for example, that Medicare recipients spend on average about 20 percent of their income on medical expenses. This is a disturbing finding. Elderly individuals actually spent, on average, less than this before Medicare was enacted (Himmelstein and Woolhandler, 1994).

THE UNINSURED POPULATION: DEMOGRAPHICS

Who are the uninsured? What are the demographics? Health insurance coverage in the U.S. varies not only by employment status and income level, but also by employer size and type of employment. Regional differences in employment patterns and state options to expand Medicaid under the ACA play a role in access to coverage. Age, race, and ethnicity play a considerable role in insurance patterns; Latinx and African Americans experience the highest uninsured rates, whereas young adults (age 26—the ACA cut-off age for coverage as dependents) are at greatest risk for lack of coverage.

WORKING ADULTS AND DEPENDENTS

Surveys show that most of the uninsured are working adults with low or moderate incomes and their dependent family members. In 2016, more than three-quarters (75 percent) of the uninsured came from working families (Kaiser Family Foundation, 2017). About a quarter (24 percent) were from households with incomes below the federal poverty level ($19,318 for a family of three), and a quarter (25 percent) were from households with incomes between $19,318 and $38,636. Among some households with higher incomes (three to four times the FPL), the uninsured rate was even higher (Figure 9.2).

Uninsured Workers

Employees in unionized and manufacturing jobs in the U.S. have been most likely to receive health insurance coverage. Unions have negotiated for coverage for their members, and large employers have been able to negotiate with insurance companies for group coverage for their workers. Small employers have had a much harder time providing coverage because they have too few employees to be able to negotiate group rates; they have often found themselves priced out of the insurance market. Some employers chose not to offer coverage at all and, thus, the creation of SHOP, mentioned earlier, by the ACA.

Although full-time employees were far more likely than temporary or part-time workers to have coverage, not all *full-time* workers have received health insurance benefits. In 2016, the percentage of full-time workers with no health insurance decreased to 9.9 percent and the gap between full-time and part-time employees with coverage narrowed (Figure 9.3). In the past, without subsidized insurance plans through the ACA, most of the uninsured population consisted of full-time workers and their dependents. In 2011, the Kaiser Commission on Medicaid and the Uninsured (2012) estimated that more than seven out of ten uninsured people had been full-time workers or their dependents.

PERCENTAGE OF TOTAL POPULATION (based on family size of 2 adults and 1 child)	
$19,318 or less (a)	24
$19,318 – 38,636	25
$38,636 – 57,954	31
$57,954 – 77,272 or more	20
(a) Federal poverty level (FPL) for a family of three was $19,318 in 2016.	

Source: U.S. Census Bureau (1990–2017).

FIGURE 9.2

Uninsured in U.S. Population by Family Income, 2016

FIGURE 9.3

Employment Status of Uninsured Workers (Ages 19–64), 2015

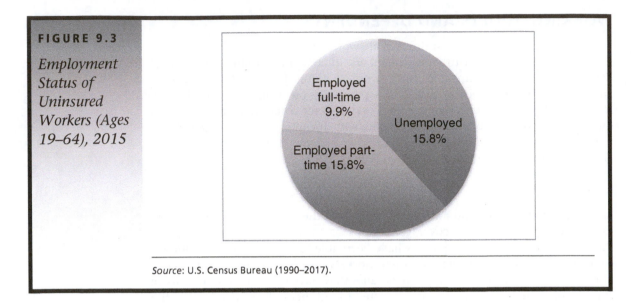

Source: U.S. Census Bureau (1990–2017).

Employers have also varied in their policies regarding coverage for family dependents. Some employee health plans have restricted dependents from preventive care or acute care, and provided protections for hospitalization and surgical services only. Other plans may have provided coverage for dependents only if they have no other options to access coverage. Another area of concern for dependent coverage was the definition of "eligible dependents." Historically, dependents have included spouses and children; however, family composition has changed dramatically since the 1960s. Increasingly, employers are faced with the need to decide whether to extend coverage to unmarried partners, gay partners, adopted or foster children, parents, or other family members residing in the employee's household.

One major change with the ACA is the requirement that all health insurance carriers in every state that offers coverage to both adults and their dependents must allow dependents to remain on their parents' or guardians' plans until the dependents are 26 years old. Employee group insurance plans must extend coverage to adult dependents through age 26.

Coverage by employers to same-sex partners has changed dramatically. In 2003, 14 percent of all employers (Kaiser Commission on Medicaid and the Uninsured, 2004) provided coverage to same-sex partners; this increased to 31 percent in 2010 and 52 percent in 2011, but still left about half without the offer of coverage. Coverage also varied widely by industry and region (Appleby, 2012). With the passage of the ACA, an insurance company that offers health coverage to opposite-sex spouses must do the same for same-sex spouses. In 2015, "nearly all" (about 84 percent) of employees who have access to health insurance also have access to opposite-sex spousal coverage. However, the provision of coverage still varies depending on employer size and some employers (about 11 percent) do not offer coverage (Dawson et al., 2017). Ironically, with the increase in states legalizing same-sex partnerships, growing numbers of employers have eliminated domestic partner health coverage and have required same-sex couples to be married before an employee's partner can receive health care benefits.

Historically, even fewer employers have offered coverage to unmarried opposite-sex partners. Some employers that offer domestic partner benefits have excluded coverage for unmarried opposite-sex couples on the grounds that they have a legal right to get married, which continues to be challenged in the courts. Employers are least likely to extend coverage to the parents of employees or to other relatives, yet many working, middle-aged adults find themselves caring for aging and elderly parents and for other relatives. As people in the U.S. continue to live longer, the financial and emotional burden of providing custodial, long-term care has fallen on their children. Some employers are beginning to provide employees with the opportunity to purchase long-term-care insurance but this is expensive coverage that remains out of reach financially for most families (Wiatrowski, 1995).

Occupation also plays an important role in accessing health insurance. Employees who work in private households in a variety of capacities are least likely to have access to health insurance, whereas executives, administrators, managers, and professionals are those most likely to have good coverage.

Regional and State Differences

Lack of health insurance is a problem in every state and region of the country, but varies by geographic location, and depends on differences in economic conditions and employment patterns, state Medicaid policies, availability of employer-based coverage, and demographics. As shown in Figure 9.4, in 2016 those who lacked coverage in the states ranged from a high of 14 percent or more in Texas, to a low of 7.9 percent or less in all of the New England states, the west coast (WA, OR, and CA), the Great Lakes region (MN, WI, IA, IL, MI, OH) and several other states (CO, ND, KY, MD, NJ, PA, and NY) in the country (U.S. Census Bureau, 2017a).

Historically, southern and western states have had more workers employed by small firms that have not provided coverage (Rowland, 1994). In addition, historically, many states in the South extended Medicaid coverage to *fewer* children; for example, between 1989 and 1993, the south had a higher number of poor, uninsured children than any other region in the country (U.S. General Accounting Office, 1995). Even in 2011 after enactment of the ACA, 9 of the 14 states in the south had uninsured rates that exceeded 20 percent (Gallup-Heathways Well-Being Index, 2012). In 2016, individuals living in the south and west are still the most likely to be uninsured; eight out of the twelve states with the highest uninsured rates in 2016 were in the south (see Figure 9.4).

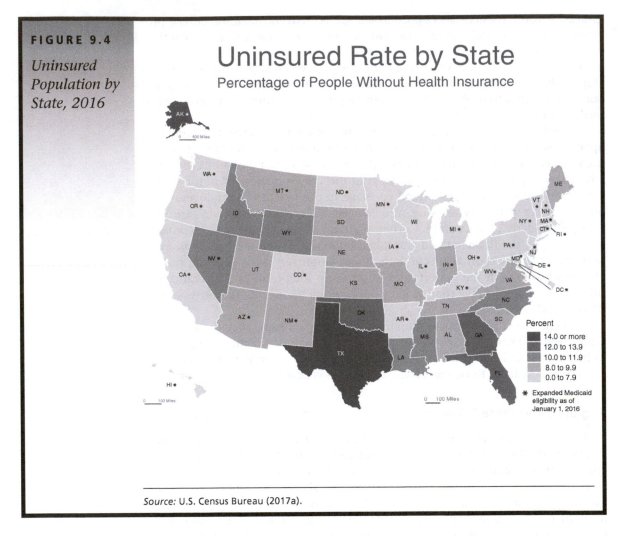

Source: U.S. Census Bureau (2017a).

Age

With the passage of the ACA, uninsured rates have declined across all age groups, especially among young adults aged 19–25. In 2015, the uninsured rate among young adults dropped to 14.5 percent. However, with the cut-off for coverage as dependents set at age 26, the uninsured rate among 26-year-olds is the highest of all ages at 19.5 percent. Similarly, the traditional Medicaid program or Children's Health Insurance Plan (CHIP) does not cover adults over the age of 18 unless they are parents with children or they are disabled and meet the original eligibility guidelines for income criteria. Thus, in 2015, the uninsured rate increases at age 19, particularly in states that have not expanded their Medicaid programs under the ACA guidelines (Collins, et al., 2016). As of January 2017, 31 states plus the District of Columbia had expanded Medicaid eligibility for adults under the ACA.

Millions of poor uninsured adults are ineligible for coverage because they earn too much to qualify for Medicaid and not enough to qualify for premium tax credits to purchase coverage in the marketplace.

On the other hand, the Medicaid program and CHIP are a true safety net for poor and low-income children under the age of 18. Without these programs, the number and proportion of uninsured children (aged 0–18) would be much higher. Medicaid expansions in the 1980s and 1990s played a significant role in increasing coverage for children. Between 1989 and 1993, changes made in the Medicaid program increased the number of insured children by 4.8 million. Although this increase did not offset the increase in the number of children who lost employment-based insurance during this same period, the number of children who lacked insurance would have been even greater without these reforms (U.S. General Accounting Office, 1995).

In 1997, S-CHIP (the state CHIP) allowed further expansions of the Medicaid program by extending coverage to more families who were unable to afford insurance. Unemployed parents, parents in transition between jobs, and employed parents without coverage were targeted. The Personal Responsibility and Work Opportunity Act of 1996 delinked Medicaid and the Temporary Assistance for Needy Families (TANF) program (which replaced Aid to Families with Dependent Children [AFDC]), however. Before this policy was enacted, families eligible for AFDC were automatically eligible for Medicaid; the Personal Responsibility Act changed this. As an "unintended consequence" of the new legislation, "in 1997, an estimated 675,000 low-income people became uninsured . . . [and] more than three out of five (62 percent) were children" (Families USA, 1999, p. 2). Moreover, this study found that most of these children should not have lost their coverage because they were still eligible for Medicaid.

Today the Medicaid and CHIP programs continue to play a vital role in health insurance coverage for children. In 2003, the four million children covered by these programs more than offset the decline of 2.5 million children in employment-based coverage (Holahan and Ghosh, 2004). In 2007, S-CHIP provided health coverage to more than seven million children (Families USA, 2008a), but, with many more children still in need of coverage, the Bush administration opposed Congressional efforts to expand eligibility for S-CHIP as part of its reauthorization (until 2012) in 2007. Instead, Congress was able to pass only a temporary 18-month extension at 2007 funding levels through March 2009 (Families USA, 2008b). With the election of the Obama administration, the CHIP program was reauthorized and extended until 2015 through the ACA, and the states were required to maintain (2009) income eligibility levels for Medicaid and CHIP through September 30, 2019. None the less, in 2011 there were still seven million children (9.3 percent) without insurance, and children in poverty were more likely to be uninsured (13.8 percent) (U.S. Census Bureau, 2012). As discussed in Chapter 1, Congress extended CHIP for two additional years to 2017, but the Republican-controlled Congress, under President Trump, failed to fully reauthorize CHIP when it was scheduled for renewal in September 2017. Instead they authorized a six-month extension until they could agree on funding for a program that covers nine million children. Finally, in January, 2018, Congress passed a six-year extension of CHIP funding to FY2023.

Race and Ethnicity

People of color (see Terminology Box and Figure 9.5) in the U.S. continue to experience significant inequality in their social and economic wellbeing. Compared with white people, a disproportionate number of people of color live in poverty and experience unemployment and inadequate education. These conditions are of concern in and of themselves. However, they also have a significant impact on health status, access to health care, and insurance coverage.

As a group, people of color made significant gains in health insurance coverage as a result of the health care reforms provided by the ACA. In 2011, people of color made up 35 percent of the nonelderly population, but represented a

TERMINOLOGY BOX   People of Color

The term "people of color" is used in this text in lieu of the term "minorities," which was used by sociologists for decades to describe the majority (dominant)–minority (subordinate) patterns of social relationships that have existed between whites (majority) and oppressed racial groups in the U.S. (Doob, 1996). However, it is important to note that "race" is a social construction. Sociologists have discredited the biological concept of race; they have shown that it is impossible to classify distinct groups of people based on physical characteristics or genes (Kottak, 1994). Most scientists today accept the finding that all humans are more similar than different (Jaret, 1995); we are essentially all the same.

None the less, four groups in the U.S. continue to be treated as distinct "racial" groups: Native Americans, African Americans, Hispanics or Latinx, and Asian Americans. Our cultural belief that race exists allows us to act as if it is real, even as our definitions and classifications of racial groups continue to evolve and change. For example, historically, individuals in the U.S. with "one drop" of black African blood in their heritage were legally and socially defined as African American. However, to be defined legally as Native American has required at least one-eighth Native American heritage. Until 1962, the U.S. Census defined only three races—White, Black/Negro, and Indian—when it added two new racial classifications, Spanish American and Oriental. In 1977, in an effort to include "Hispanic" groups, the U.S. Census Bureau established four racial categories—non-Hispanic White, non-Hispanic Black, Asian or Pacific Islander, and Native American—and two ethnic classifications, Hispanic and non-Hispanic. In 2000, the U.S. Census separated Asian and Pacific Islanders into two racial categories (Figure 9.5) and created a multiracial classification, "Two or More Races," which can result in 57 combinations of race (U.S. Census Bureau, 2000).

The U.S. Census defines Spanish-speaking people (Hispanic or Latino) as an ethnic group, not a racial group, because Spanish-speaking people can be of any race. In fact, for Census 2000, Hispanics were asked for the first time to identify their race (U.S. Census Bureau, 2000). These various and variable distinctions make the term "people of color" somewhat confusing. However, Latinx have been treated as a minority group in our society. For this reason, "people of color" has been used to include Latinx. In this text, we will continue this practice (recognizing that Hispanics can be of any race).

RACE (FIVE CATEGORIES)	ETHNICITY (TWO CATEGORIES)
American Indian or Alaska Native	Hispanic or Latino
Asian	Not Hispanic or Latino
Black or African American	
Native Hawaiian or other Pacific Islander	
White	

FIGURE 9.5

Classification of Federal Data on Race and Ethnicity

Source: U.S. Census Bureau (2000).

disproportionate 54 percent of the uninsured (U.S. Census Bureau, 2012). However, in 2016, 42 percent of the nation's nonelderly population were people of color, and represented 44 percent of the uninsured (Kaiser Family Foundation, 2017). As shown in Figure 9.6, Latinx (Hispanics) remain more likely than any other racial or ethnic group to be uninsured. People of color are particularly susceptible to the lack or loss of employment-based insurance described earlier. They have higher rates of unemployment than whites, and they are more likely to have low-wage jobs and "contingent" jobs.

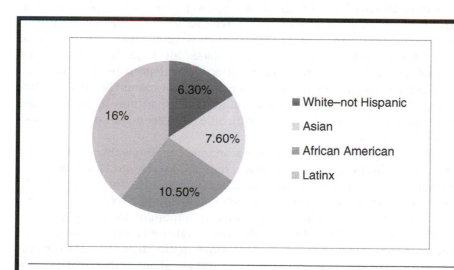

FIGURE 9.6

Nonelderly Uninsured Rates by Race and Ethnicity, 2016

Source: U.S. Census Bureau (1990–2017).

Income and socioeconomic status certainly play an important role in access to coverage. The fact that people of color are disproportionately employed in low-income jobs increases the likelihood that they will not have employment-based insurance. However, studies show that people of color in high-income jobs have also been at greater risk for lack of coverage than whites. For example, Hall et al. (1999) found that, in 1997, 70 percent of Latinx executives compared with 83 percent of white executives had employment-based coverage. The reasons for the disparity are not clear, but the fact that people of color have fewer family or reserve assets is a likely factor. They may be in a weaker financial position than whites to pay their share of the premiums and thus more likely to decline the coverage.

Latinx. The Hispanic or Latinx population in the U.S. has made the most significant gains in coverage for health insurance since 2010, but still struggles with other factors that impede progress. This population includes people with Mexican, Puerto Rican, Cuban, Central American, South American, and other Spanish-speaking origins; Latinx are the largest (17.6 percent) and fastest-growing minority population in the U.S. Although they have made the most gains in coverage, they are still the most uninsured minority population. In 2015, almost one in every five (19.5 percent) Latinx was uninsured (16% of nonelderly Latinos—see Figure 9.6). Within this group, Central Americans and Mexican Americans are affected most. In 2015, 21.5 percent of Mexican Americans, 8.5 percent of Puerto Rican Americans, 13.9 percent of Cuban Americans, and 28.2 percent of those from Central and South America lacked health insurance (U.S. Office of Minority Health, 2017b).

Latinx have consistently been less likely to have employment-based insurance than other people of color in the U.S. In 1996, only half of Latino (male) workers received coverage through their employers, compared with two-thirds of African American male workers and three-quarters of white male workers. Working Latinas (women) were at less risk than working Latinos, with over 60 percent of Latina workers receiving employer-based insurance (Kass et al., 1996). From 2000 to 2008, Latino workers in general experienced twice as large an increase in their uninsured rate compared with Latina workers (Economic Policy Institute, 2008). In 2017, Latinx remain more likely than non-Hispanic whites and other people of color to work in low-income jobs that do not provide health insurance (Leins, 2017).

All of these figures reflect larger socioeconomic conditions that contribute to this disparity in health insurance coverage. In 2015, Latinx and First Nation students had the highest high school dropout rates of any group in the U.S. (Figure 9.7). Education is a significant means of improving social and economic security; improving the quality of schools is particularly important for this population (Stone and Balderrama, 2008). In 1995, the poverty rate for Latinx exceeded that of African Americans for the first time and remained higher than African Americans until 1998. In 2016, the poverty rate for Latinx was about one in five (19.4%), compared with less than one in ten (8.8%) white non-Hispanics (Figure 9.8A and 9.8B) (U.S. Census Bureau, 2017b).

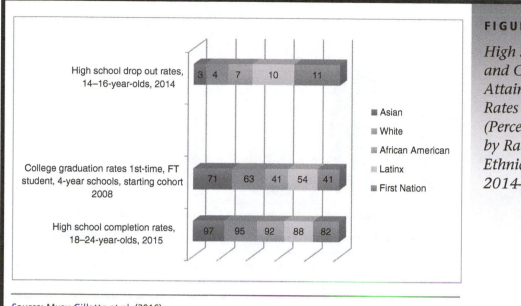

FIGURE 9.7

High School and College Attainment Rates (Percentage) by Race and Ethnicity, 2014–15

High school drop out rates, 14–16-year-olds, 2014: Asian 3, White 4, African American 7, Latinx 10, First Nation 11

College graduation rates 1st-time, FT student, 4-year schools, starting cohort 2008: Asian 71, White 63, African American 41, Latinx 54, First Nation 41

High school completion rates, 18–24-year-olds, 2015: Asian 97, White 95, African American 92, Latinx 88, First Nation 82

Legend: Asian, White, African American, Latinx, First Nation

Source: Musu-Gillette et al. (2016).

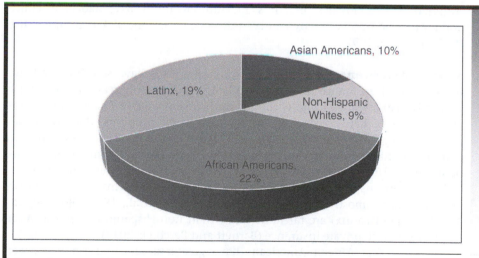

FIGURE 9.8 (A)

Poverty Rate for Racial and Ethnic Groups in the U.S., 2016

Asian Americans, 10%
Latinx, 19%
Non-Hispanic Whites, 9%
African Americans, 22%

Source: Semega et al. (2017).

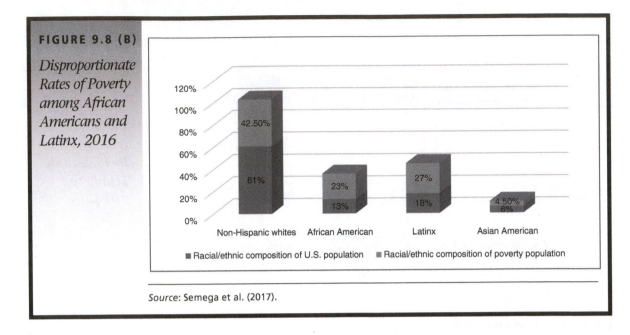

FIGURE 9.8 (B)

Disproportionate Rates of Poverty among African Americans and Latinx, 2016

■ Racial/ethnic composition of U.S. population   ■ Racial/ethnic composition of poverty population

Source: Semega et al. (2017).

Latinx workers, especially recent immigrants with little education and poor English-speaking skills, are more likely to work in low-skill, service-sector jobs, such as gardeners, nannies, and restaurant workers, or low-skill manufacturing jobs with no or few health benefits. Mexican American workers in California, for example, are concentrated in the clothing and furniture manufacturing industries (most Latinx live in Arizona, California, New Mexico, and Texas.) Many researchers blame discrimination in employment practices and culturally insensitive, inadequate education for the condition of many Latinx in the U.S. (U.S. General Accounting Office, 1992; Goldberg, 1997).

African Americans. In the U.S., African Americans have significantly better access to health insurance coverage than Latinx, but are still nearly twice as likely as non-Hispanic whites to go without health insurance (see Figure 9.6). African Americans have better access to employment-based insurance than Hispanics. However, they have less access than non-Hispanic whites, even though they are more likely than whites to work in large businesses. Rates of employment-based coverage for African American female and male workers are the same; however, African Americans are more likely than either whites or Latinx to have government insurance (mostly Medicaid or Medicare) (Kass et al., 1996). Both African Americans (and Latinx) are far more likely than non-Hispanic whites and Asian Americans to lack private insurance (Barnett and Berchick, 2017).

The fact that African Americans have greater access to insurance coverage than Latinx, yet are less likely to have private insurance than whites and other groups, may be a reflection of the widening economic gap among African Americans. The civil rights and affirmative action legislation of the 1960s provided unprecedented opportunities for African Americans and led to the development of an African American middle class. Since the 1960s, the number of affluent African Americans who are married and college educated, have annual incomes over $50,000, own homes, and live in the suburbs has grown substantially (O'Hare et al., 1991). At the same time, however, African Americans overall have lower rates of participation in the job market, higher rates of unemployment, and more single female-headed families. At the low end of the economic ladder, poor inner-city African Americans experience extreme economic hardship and in the 1980s were described as a permanent "underclass" (Wilson, 1987). Although African Americans who have achieved middle-class status have gained access to employment-based health insurance, a disproportionate number of poor women and their children (54 percent in 2016) are more likely to access coverage through the Medicaid program than non-Hispanic whites (Figure 9.9).

Asian Americans. African Americans and Latinx are the largest groups of people of color in the U.S.; together they make up about a third (31 percent) of the U.S. population. Asian Americans and Native Americans, on the other hand, comprise about 7.5 percent of the population (Semega et al., 2016). As a result, many studies of health and access to care by race or ethnicity have focused on whites, African Americans, and Latinx. Although this is changing, there has been less research on Asian Americans and Native Americans. As we approach the year 2055, however, this will likely change as the size of the Asian American population is projected to surpass the Latinx population by that year (Lopez et al., 2017).

Asian Americans have better access to health care than other groups of color; only 7.6 percent of Asian Americans are uninsured (see Figure 9.6). As a group, Asian

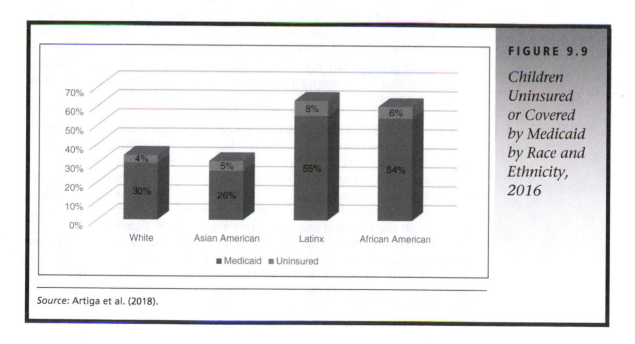

FIGURE 9.9

Children Uninsured or Covered by Medicaid by Race and Ethnicity, 2016

Source: Artiga et al. (2018).

Americans have achieved higher academic standing and socioeconomic status than African Americans, Latinx, and Native Americans. In 2015, about 97 percent of Asians/Pacific Islanders attained at least a high school education, which is higher than the rate for all whites in the same year (Musu-Gillette et al., 2016) (see Figure 9.7). The poverty rate in 2016 for Asian Americans (10 percent) is higher than non-Hispanic whites (9 percent), but significantly lower than that of other groups of color (see Figure 9.9) (Semega et al., 2016). However, this data can be misleading.

Asian Americans are part of an extremely diverse group that includes individuals with Chinese, Japanese, Filipino, Korean, Asian Indian (India, Pakistan, Bangladesh, Sri Lanka, Nepal, Bhutan, Burma), and south-east Asian (Vietnam, Cambodia, Thailand, Laos, Hmong tribe) origins. For decades, Asian Americans have been an "economically stratified group with a highly visible and successful layer of professionals—doctors, engineers, and scientists—a strong commercial middle class that includes grocers, nurses, and government workers, and a less visible group of immigrants" (Zaldivar, 1991, p. A1). Despite their academic achievements, the U.S. Census Bureau (2004) found that Asian Americans had a harder time than whites using their high levels of education to achieve high earnings.

Poverty rates also vary enormously among Asian American groups. For example, at the high end of the economic scale, Japanese Americans have a lower poverty rate than whites, whereas, at the low end, most Hmong immigrants, who began their emigration to the U.S. in 1973, had a poverty rate of 28.3 percent in 2016 (Lopez et al., 2017). Other Asian Americans from Vietnam, Cambodia, Thailand, Laos, Burma, and Bhutan have also lacked functional English-speaking skills, which has made it extremely difficult for them to compete in the job market and pursue training or education.

Jang and associates (1998), in a study of 1800 Chinese American residents of San Francisco, found a clear link between education and income, and health insurance coverage. People with higher levels of education and income were more likely to have health insurance. They also found a negative link between levels of acculturation and rates of insurance; the less acculturated (ranging from noncitizens to naturalized citizens to U.S.-born citizens) the residents were, the more likely they were to be uninsured.

Native Hawaiians and Pacific Islanders. In 2015, approximately 1.3 million (U.S. Office of Minority Health, 2018) Native Hawaiians and Pacific Islanders (alone or in combination with other racial groups) lived in the very rural state of Hawaii, on 104 other islands in the Pacific that are under U.S. jurisdiction, including Guam and American Samoa, or in mainland states, primarily California, Washington, Texas, Nevada, and Utah. Approximately 63 percent of the Hawaiian/Pacific Islander population lives on the islands (Figure 9.10) and most of these islanders (45 percent) live in Hawaii (U.S. Office of Minority Health, 2017a). Hawaii is a racially and ethnically diverse island; only 10 percent of the residents are Native Hawaiians (U.S. Office of Minority Health, 2018). Native Hawaiians are Polynesians; other Pacific Islanders are Polynesians, Micronesians, and Melanesians (Ross, 2000). Until 2000, federal officials and health policy analysts mostly overlooked the Hawaiian/Pacific

FLAG TERRITORIES, NATIONS ORIGINALLY UNDER U.S. JURISDICTION UNDER THE UNITED NATIONS TRUSTEESHIP OF 1947 (NOW INDEPENDENT NATIONS)	FREELY ASSOCIATED STATES
American Samoa	Federated States of Micronesia (Truk, Kosrae, Pohnpei, Yap)
Territory of Guam	Republic of Palau
Commonwealth of the Northern Mariana Islands	Republic of the Marshall Islands

FIGURE 9.10

The U.S. Associated Pacific

Source: National Institute of Medicine Pacific Partnerships for Health (1998).

Islander population. In an effort to gather more accurate data and address the specific health needs of this group, the U.S. Census Bureau created a new category (see Figure 9.5) in 2000 for Native Hawaiians and Pacific Islanders. Before this date, ethnic data were collected for Asians and Pacific Islanders as one category.

Jiang (2000) provides a realistic image of Hawaii (the "most remote land mass in the world," [Jiang, 2000, p. 4]—2500 miles from the California coast) and dispels some of the stereotyped images of the island created by the media and vacation travel advertising. Most visitors to Hawaii travel to Honolulu, Oahu, the most populated area and only urban center in the state, but the vast majority of Oahu (almost 90 percent) and all the other Hawaiian islands are extremely rural. The only means of transportation between the islands is by plane, which has made access to health care services challenging and expensive. For Pacific Islanders, who live in an area larger than the continental U.S., transportation and issues of isolation have been of even greater concern (Ross, 2000).

However, compared with other states, Hawaii has fewer uninsured people (only 3.5 percent in 2016) and was ranked the "healthiest state" in 2015 (Norris, 2018). This is because Hawaii is the only state that has an Employee Retirement Income Security Act (ERISA) waiver that mandates employer-based health insurance for employees who work at least 20 hours a week; in 1974, Hawaii implemented its Prepaid Health Care Act. As a result, Hawaii was the first to request and receive a waiver from state plans under the ACA because its state health plan requirements are greater than those required by the ACA. Nearly all nonelderly Hawaiians receive coverage through their employer, and very few need coverage through individual market plans. Hawaii did, however, expand Medicaid under the ACA and increased Medicaid coverage by 21 percent between 2013 and 2018 (Norris, 2018).

On the other hand, those at greatest risk for lack of coverage are Native Hawaiians who have "tend[ed] to be both unemployed and uninsured" (Aiu, 2000, p. 8) and experience higher rates of poverty (U.S. Office of Minority Health, 2017a). The uninsured rate is higher among Native Hawaiians (7.8 percent) than non-Hispanic white Hawaiians (6.3 percent) (U.S. Office of Minority Health, 2018).

Senator Daniel Inouye (D-HI) was instrumental in the passage of the Native Hawaiian Health Care Improvement Act, which was extended in 1988, reauthorized in 1992, and created an umbrella health care service organization, Papa Ola Lokahi (POC) and the Native Hawaiian Health Care Systems (NHHCS). POC is the research and administrative arm of the system, whereas NHHCS delivers services through five health centers (Ross, 2000); the health centers are funded by the U.S. Department of Health and Human Services to help serve populations with limited access to health care.

First Nations/Native Americans. In 2012, according to the U.S. Office of Minority Health (2017c), 22.6 percent of Native Americans lacked insurance. This is troubling given the unique social, political, and cultural position of Native Americans in the U.S. Since the 1800s, the federal government has had a special obligation to provide health care and improve the health status of Native American people. The Indian Health Service (IHS), an agency of the Public Health Service, U.S. Department of Health and Human Services, was established in 1955 and given responsibility for health care services for federally recognized Native American tribes (U.S. General Accounting Office, 1993).

Approximately 5.2 million Native Americans from 567 federally recognized tribes (about half in Alaska) make up about 2 percent of the U.S. population (U.S. Office of Minority Health, 2017c). To be *eligible* for direct care services, including hospitals and outpatient clinics operated directly by the IHS or indirectly by the tribal governments, tribal members must live on or near a reservation with designated services or be an eligible student, foster child, or transient person (U.S. General Accounting Office, 1993). Contract services, which are provided by a non-IHS facility or provider, are also provided in geographic areas called contract health service delivery areas (CHSDAs); eligibility requirements are stricter for these services. Of the roughly two million Native Americans served by the IHS system, about 600,000 are served by the few urban clinics that are available (Indian Health Service, 2012a; U.S. Office of Minority Health, 2017c). For most, however, access to IHS medical care, given the geographic size of many reservations, is still difficult. A Kaiser study in 2000 (Kaiser Commission on Medicaid and the Uninsured, 2000) found that only 20 percent of eligible residents reported access to services. In addition, as discussed later, the quality of services is of serious concern.

For most Native Americans (60 percent) who live in urban areas, access to IHS programs and services is especially problematic. To receive care, an individual must travel to the IHS located on or near the tribal reservation. Although the urban First Nation population has grown substantially since the inception of the IHS, few medical facilities have been established by the IHS in cities and urban areas where many Native Americans now reside. Since 1975, when Congress passed the Indian Health Improvement Act (IHIA), only a small portion of the IHS budget (1 percent) has been targeted toward urban areas. These services have been provided by nonprofit organizations administered by urban Native Americans with funds provided by the IHS. The programs have often used Medicare, Medicaid, and other private or public resources to supplement their budgets (Kaiser Commission on Medicaid and the Uninsured, 2001).

The IHIA expired in 2000, and its reauthorization was continuously delayed by Congress until 2010 when it was permanently extended by the ACA. Advocates for reauthorization, particularly First Nation tribal leaders, worked out "endless compromises," reached consensus with the federally recognized tribes on priority needs, and testified at many national hearings, yet no legislative action was taken during this ten-year period (Friends Committee on National Legislation, 2005). With the reauthorization of the IHS under the Obama administration, there was still much to tackle by way of addressing the health care needs of this population, but any efforts to "repeal and replace" the ACA and the unintended consequence of terminating the IHIA would be "catastrophic" (Collins, 2017).

Historically, Native Americans have been the most severely and consistently disadvantaged racial group in the nation. Poverty is a major concern (26 percent living in poverty in 2012); in 2012, more than one in three (38.1 percent) Native Americans relied on Medicaid as the primary source of insurance and almost a quarter (22.6 percent) had no coverage (U.S. Office on Minority Health, 2017c). In 2012, only 47.5 percent of Native Americans had private insurance, which, as discussed, is often tied to employment (U.S. Office on Minority Health, 2017c). Until the 1990s, when gaming and casinos were developed on some reservations, employment opportunities were scarce. For example, in 1995, the unemployment rate on the Pine Ridge Reservation in South Dakota was 75 percent (Brooke, 1995). In 2011, the unemployment rate among all Native Americans was about 15 percent; for Alaska Natives it was over 21 percent (Arrieta, 2011). The overall unemployment (4.9 percent) in 2017 shows a dramatic improvement in recent years. However, the same studies (Zeigler and Camarota, 2017) show that this figure obscures the long-term decline in the rate of labor force participation among working-age (18–65) natives without a college degree; almost one in every four adults in this age group was not in the labor force in 2017.

In 2010, "President Obama made efforts to work toward building a better relationship with native people, ordering his administration to seek the advice of native people on the best ways that federal programs and policies could serve them" (Arrieta, 2011). The Indian and Native American Program at the Department of Labor's Employment and Training Administration Indian awarded 178 grants to provide employment and training services for unemployed or underemployed and low-income Native American adults, and 78 tribes and tribal groups were awarded grants to provide summer employment and job skills training and placement assistance for Native American youth (Arrieta, 2011).

The ACA also played a significant role in this effort. It not only permanently reauthorized the IHCIA, but amended it to "expand programs that seek to augment the IHS health care workforce, increase the amount and type of services available at facilities funded by the IHS, and increase the number and type of programs that provide behavioral health and substance abuse treatment" (Heisler, 2011, p. 2). In addition to the general provisions of the ACA (see Chapter 1) that promise to impact all low-income, unemployed adults and their families, the ACA "authorizes new programs within the Indian Health Service to ensure the Service is more equipped to meet its mission to raise the health status of American Indians and Alaska Natives to the highest level" (Indian Health Service, 2012b, p. 2).

Overall Impact of the ACA on Disparities in Coverage for People of Color

According to the Kaiser Family Foundation analysis (Artiga et al., 2015) of changes in health insurance coverage under the ACA, President Obama's health reforms helped to reduce disparities in coverage for people of color. As shown in the previous sections and summarized in the foundation's report, the following challenges still remain:

1. All racial and ethnic groups had gains in coverage, which helped to narrow the gap in disparities in coverage.

2. Despite gains in coverage, gaps still exist, particularly for the Latinx population, which remains more likely to be uninsured than other groups.

3. The Medicaid expansion program under the ACA has increased the opportunity for people of color to be covered, but they remain less eligible than whites for this coverage. For African Americans, this is due to ineligibility as a result of states not opting into the Medicaid expansion program. For Asian Americans and Latinx, this is because of ineligibility due to noncitizen and immigrant status.

4. Repeal of the individual mandate and cuts in funding for outreach could disproportionately limit enrollment of eligible people of color.

Summary of At-risk Factors and Groups

Figure 9.11 provides a summary of the relative risk factors that influence access to health insurance in the U.S. These factors include income, employment status, occupation, locality, age, race and ethnicity, and gender.

BARRIERS TO ACCESS TO CARE: PROVIDERS, INSURERS, AND CONSUMERS

Disparities in access to care for at-risk groups in the U.S. is well documented. Researchers have demonstrated that many interrelated factors, including demographics, health insurance status, and the health care system itself, play a role in individual utilization of health care services. So far, we have examined the role of demographics (socioeconomic factors, race and ethnicity, gender, and disability) and health insurance status in access to care. In this section, we focus on the health care system itself—providers, insurers, and consumers—and examine its role in access to care.

Are the Uninsured Denied Access to Care?

Some have argued that uninsured "citizens are not denied care" (Stelzer, 1994). It is true that not every uninsured person goes without care; Donelan and colleagues (1996) found that 47 percent of uninsured adults had no trouble getting medical care.

Socioeconomic Factors	Higher Risk	Lower Risk
Income	Poor and near poor (100–300% FPL)	Nonpoor (>300% FPL)
Employment status	Unemployed	Employed
	Self-employed	Full-time employed
	Temporary, part-time employed	
Occupation	Non-unionized	Unionized
	Service Industry	Administrative
	Blue-collar manufacturing	Professional/technical white-collar
Locality	South	Northeast
	West	Midwest
		Hawaii
Age	Young adults (19–24)	Older adults (over 65)
	Middle age (25–54)	Infants, children, and adolescents
		Older adults (55–64)
Race and ethnicity	People of color	Whites
Gender*	Women	Men

* Gender risk factors are related to income, employment, and occupational status.

FIGURE 9.11

Summary of Socioeconomic Risk Factors for Lack of Health Insurance Coverage

Government-sponsored clinics and public hospitals offer reduced-cost or "free" care, and government programs sometimes offer care such as vaccinations and cancer screenings. Despite this, evidence suggests that many individuals without insurance have a difficult time obtaining the care they need. Medical facilities that offer reduced-cost or free care are not geographically accessible to all who need them, particularly those who live in rural areas. Hospital emergency rooms have become increasingly overcrowded, and many hospitals increasingly view "free" or "charity care" as an "unaffordable option" (Rosenthal, 1995; Preston, 1996). As Donelan and colleagues (1996) found, half of uninsured adults have trouble obtaining care, and for many these difficulties lead to serious consequences.

More recently, Hurley et al. (2005) found evidence of "a widening rift" in access and quality, based on economic disparities in the U.S. Individuals with employer-based coverage are benefiting from new advances in technology and medicine, including diagnostic and treatment techniques, and competitive developments in facility and hospital construction. Medicare beneficiaries are also benefiting because changes in this program parallel trends in the private market, including recent efforts to expand managed care in Medicare. However, for those who are uninsured or rely on Medicaid for coverage, access to care, particularly before the ACA's federally-supported Medicaid expansion program, was worsening, owing to cutbacks in services because of state budget problems, federal reductions in Medicaid and CHIP expansions, and inadequate state and federal spending for public mental health services (as discussed in Chapters 5 and 6). Kenney et al. (2012) found that access to care during the decade before enactment of the ACA (2000–10) brought a decline in access to care for nonelderly adults for essentially every insurance category (private, public, uninsured), but was most dramatic among the uninsured. Since the enactment of the ACA, access has most definitely improved, especially for those living in states that have opted to expand Medicaid coverage, and there is evidence of improvements in the quality of Medicaid care, particularly in the delivery of care in hospitals and health care centers. But research is limited and more is needed to examine services for this more vulnerable low-income population (Paradise and Garfield, 2013).

Is there a Free-care Safety Net for the Uninsured?

For most of the millions of people who are uninsured in the U.S., including those who live in states that have not opted to expand Medicaid coverage under the ACA, medical care is simply unaffordable. For them, the only available health care is hospital charity care. The existence of a free hospital-care safety net has been and continues to be a concern, however. Essentially, charity care is hospital care provided at no cost to patients who cannot afford to pay for the services rendered. Hospitals may provide reduced-cost services to patients who can afford partial payment; in general, however, hospitals do not expect to be reimbursed for the free or charity care they provide to the community.

Although laws and legal obligations require hospitals to provide free care (1985 Emergency Medical Treatment and Active Labor Act), there have been no standard rules, regulations, or laws that govern hospital practices across the country. For example, nonprofit hospitals are generally exempt from local, state, and federal taxes and, in return, are obliged to provide some form of service to the state or local community. Hospitals often meet this obligation by providing some degree of free or reduced-cost care. This does not, however, keep patients from incurring costs or experiencing severe economic consequences as a result of consuming non-emergency hospital services. For these services, hospitals often send bills to the consumer at full cost. One study (Dobkin et al., 2016) found that an individual without insurance who is hospitalized doubles his or her chances of filing for bankruptcy over the next four years.

States and communities have also expected community nonprofit insurers and health plans to provide benefits to the community. For example, when Blue Cross Blue Shield was originally structured as a nonprofit institution, it was an insurer "of last resort" and also provided community benefits. Some older health maintenance plans, such as Kaiser Permanente, were also originally organized as charitable nonprofit institutions and were expected to contribute to the community's health needs. For nonprofit health plans, community benefits take the form of subsidies for premiums, health screenings, and immunization programs or health education activities.

However, over time, changes in the delivery of health care reduced the level of community benefits. In the 1990s, contrary to common belief, 80 percent of uninsured people did not receive any reduced charge or free health services (Kaiser Commission on Medicaid and the Uninsured, 1998a) and the competitive market made it even more difficult for physicians and hospitals to finance uncompensated care. To compete for contracted services, health plans (which include doctors and hospitals) accepted lower payment rates. This, in turn, made it more difficult for doctors and hospitals to provide free care. For example, according to Cunningham and associates (1999), in 1996 and 1997, physicians in the Washington, DC, area who received 85 percent or more of their income from managed-care plans provided only 5.2 hours per month of charity care. In comparison, physicians who received no income from managed-care plans provided 10 hours per month of charity care to the community.

The managed-care market also affected hospitals. Many hospitals that were traditionally organized on a nonprofit or local government basis were purchased by private, for-profit organizations. For example, until the 1998 decision by Columbia/Hospital Corporation of America (HCA) to close many of its hospitals, Columbia/HCA owned 310 hospitals (Community Catalyst, 1998a). One study of such conversions conducted by Needleman et al. (1999) found that charity care declined substantially in Florida between 1981 and 1996. Public hospitals provided much less uncompensated care after their conversion to for-profit status. A study of seven hospitals in Nassau and Suffolk counties in Long Island, New York, found that none consistently made information available that the free care was available to low-income, uninsured people, and access to written policies was difficult to obtain (Giffords et al., 2005).

The complexity of hospital structures also contributed to the confusion surrounding free care. Hospitals are now made up of multiple subsidiaries, each with its own policies and procedures. Some services may be offered as free care, whereas others are not. For example, an individual patient may find that the hospital stay was free, yet was charged for diagnostic work or other medical services (Community Catalyst, 1998b).

None the less, "free" or "charity" care is an ongoing component of the delivery of care in the U.S. that impacts overall access, quality, and cost. Garthwaite et al. (2015) found that every uninsured person costs local hospitals an estimated $900 in uncompensated care costs each year. They also noted that hospitals average a 7 percent profit margin, whereas uncompensated care could cost hospitals more than 5 percent of their revenue. Before the passage of the ACA in 2010, these uncompensated costs were likely even greater because there is evidence that hospitals reduced their level of charity care with the expansion of access to care under the ACA (Bannow, 2018).

Nonprofit hospitals also feel in competition with an array of new walk-in clinics, urgent care centers, and other means of care that are less expensive than hospital emergency room care. They have major new competitors that have entered the fray, including major insurers and other businesses, like CVS which are purchasing medical groups, or merging to transform drugstores into "health care hubs." Major changes like these have made it more difficult for nonprofit hospitals to keep their doors open, and has led to "behemoth" nonprofit hospital mergers and acquisitions, some of which span dozens of states, with uncertain outcomes as to the benefit of these changes (Abelson, 2017).

Are there Differences in Utilization of Services by Insurance Status?

People who lack health insurance find it more difficult to access health care services and are therefore less likely to seek the care they need. This is especially true for early and preventive care. Studies have consistently shown that those who lack insurance regularly use physician services at lower rates than those who have insurance. In 1997, a survey conducted by the Kaiser Family Foundation (1997) found that only 58 percent of *uninsured* (nonelderly) adults, compared with 83 percent of *insured* (nonelderly) adults, received physician care. Similar results were found for children: 61 percent of *uninsured* children compared with 80 percent of *insured* children visited a physician. The differences found in the use of preventive services were especially disturbing. The Kaiser study (1997) found that uninsured persons were far less likely to receive mammograms, pap smears, prostate exams, or routine physical checkups. The more recent ten-year study (2000–10) conducted by Kenney et al. (2012) supports these findings. Their research shows that over this decade uninsured nonelderly adults became *more* likely to forgo or delay needed care, less likely to have a usual source of care, and less likely to have had an office visit with a physician or dentist.

The Kaiser survey (1997) also showed that uninsured people were more likely to postpone or avoid medical care because they could not afford to pay for the services. Thirty percent of those *uninsured* (compared with 7 percent of those *insured*) did not receive *necessary* medical care. Fifty-five percent of the *uninsured* in the study (compared with 14 percent of the *insured*) *postponed necessary* medical care, and 24 percent of those *uninsured* (compared with 6 percent of those *insured*) *did not fill a prescription*. In 1996, the U.S. Public Health Service (Krauss et al., 1999) obtained similar findings. Approximately 75 percent of those *with insurance* used ambulatory medical services, compared with only 50 percent of those who were *uninsured*; 43 percent of the uninsured population obtained prescribed medicine, compared with 65 percent of the insured population.

The Kaiser Family Foundation (Hoffman and Schwartz, 2008) conducted a follow-up study examining the years 1997–2006 and found that, by 2006, compared with 1997, more working-age adults had gone without or delayed needed medical care, delayed dental care, and gone without prescription drugs due to the cost of medical care and prescription drugs. The study found that, overall:

the number of working-age adults who reported costs as a barrier to needed care grew by about one million a year between 1997 and 2006, totaling 39 million in 2006. No gains in receiving preventive care and regular professional care were made over the ten year period

(Hoffman and Schwartz, 2008, p.1)

Kenney et al. (2012) found that a third of uninsured nonelderly adults had delayed needed care due to cost.

The most recent studies conducted by the Kaiser Family Foundation (2017) show little change in these patterns. In 2016, due to cost, uninsured nonelderly adults were more likely to postpone needed care (23 percent compared with 9 percent with public insurance and 6 percent with private insurance), less likely to have a usual source of care (49 percent compared with 12 percent with either public or private insurance), and less likely to receive needed care (20 percent compared with 8 percent with public insurance and 3 percent with private insurance). Uninsured nonelderly adults postponed or avoided getting a needed prescription medicine due to cost (18 percent compared with 14 percent with public insurance and 6 percent with private insurance).

The lack of preventive care and the tendency to delay treatment among the uninsured often leads to the onset of more serious conditions, which are also more difficult and expensive to treat once care is finally sought. As a consequence, people who are uninsured are also at greater risk for hospitalization for conditions that generally do not require hospital care (Kaiser Family Foundation, 2017). The same is true for people with low incomes (Billings et al., 1996). The uninsured population is more likely to be hospitalized for diabetes, hypertension, and other problems that are often treated with ambulatory care (Weissman et al., 1992).

Are There Differences in Utilization of Services by Race and Ethnicity?

For at least the past 20 years, surveys have shown differences in utilization patterns by race and ethnicity. The U.S. Public Health Service (Krauss et al., 1999) found that Latinx (60 percent) and African Americans (62 percent) were less likely to use ambulatory medical care than whites (75 percent). Latinx were less likely than African Americans or whites to have a usual source of hospital-based and office-based care. Given their socioeconomic status, Latinx were also less likely than other groups to be able to afford and therefore access health care services (Kass et al., 1996). In 1996 only 70 percent of Latinas in California received prenatal care in their first trimester of pregnancy. In comparison, 82 percent of white and Asian American women and 74 percent of African American women received prenatal care (Latino Coalition for a Healthy California, 1996).

Studies have also demonstrated that people of color have different utilization patterns for mental health services. The Surgeon General's 2001 report on mental health, culture, and race showed that people of color were disproportionately represented among a large population of individuals in the U.S. (two out of three) in need of mental health services, but failed to receive treatment. For Latinx, who still have the lowest rate of health insurance among people of color, language barriers further reduce access. For all people of color, the stigma of mental illness is a "further shame" (U.S. Department of Health and Human Services, 2001).

Skinner et al. (2005) suggested that people of color are also at risk for accessing "poorly performing hospitals" because they live in poor communities. For example, from 1997 to 2001, 70 percent of African American heart attack patients were treated by only 20 percent of medical centers in the U.S., and those who treated the most African Americans had higher death rates for all heart attack patients. Hospitals in poorer communities are working with fewer dollars and resources to provide care. Findings from the 2007 National Healthcare Disparities Report (Agency for Healthcare Research and Quality, 2008) showed that people of color, particularly Latinx and African Americans, continued to receive worse care than whites (the AHRQ released the first report in 2003). The Kaiser Family Foundation's 2007 report on race, ethnicity, and medical care suggested that more research was needed on patient preferences, site of medical care, and the impact of neighborhood of residence on patterns of care to understand the causes and consequences of health care disparities by race and ethnicity: "This research is needed to disentangle the many complex factors that account for these differentials" (Kaiser Family Foundation, 2007, p. 41).

More recently, with improved access to coverage under the ACA and Medicaid expansion, differences in access seem greatest for African Americans and Latinx with private insurance (Artiga et al., 2015). The Kaiser Family Foundation research shows that privately insured African American and Latinx adults do worse than privately insured white adults in access and use of care, and have greater concerns about their ability to afford medical costs. Privately insured African American and Latinx adults are less likely than whites to have a usual source of care or a regular provider, and to use medical or preventive services. Lower incomes seem to partially explain the differences in this utilization pattern, but other linguistic, cultural, and social and environmental causes beyond cost are likely substantial barriers to care.

HIGHLIGHTS

- The U.S. remains the only industrialized nation that does not have a system of health care with access to services for all of its citizens, regardless of race, ethnicity, gender, age, employment status, or income.

- In 2016, 8.8 percent of the population was uninsured. Historically, hospitals have provided some free care or charity care to people who lack insurance. However, in the age of rising costs, managed care, and stiff competition among for-profit and nonprofit providers for consumers of care, community benefits or "free care" has declined substantially.

- Under the current structure of the U.S. health care system, the primary reasons for lack of insurance are high costs and the failure of states to expand Medicaid to middle income families under the Affordable Care Act (ACA).

- In an effort to meet rising costs of health insurance, employers often eliminated benefits, reduced coverage for family members, or increased the employee share of insurance premiums. Under the ACA, employers are obligated to provide benefits on a more consistent basis.

- Before the ACA (2010), retired adults benefited from the Medicare program and poor adults and their children were eligible for Medicaid, leaving the near poor with incomes between 100 percent and 300 percent of the federal poverty level at greatest risk for lack of health insurance. The expansion of Medicaid under the ACA was designed to address this population.

- Health insurance coverage varies by employment status, income level, size of employment organization, and type of employment. Full-time workers are still more likely than temporary and part-time workers to have coverage.

- Age, race, and ethnicity still play a considerable role in access to coverage. Latinx and Native Americans lack health insurance more than other racial and ethnic groups.

- Lack of health insurance has an adverse effect on utilization of health care services, including preventive and usual care. Those without insurance seek care more infrequently, are more apt to postpone or avoid care, and, as a result, are more likely to be hospitalized for conditions that could have been treated with ambulatory care.

- The ACA has had a positive impact on access to care, particularly for middle-income families and people of color.

WEBSITES TO OBTAIN UPDATED AND ADDITIONAL INFORMATION

U.S. Census Bureau, Current Population Surveys:

www.census.gov/population

Kaiser Commission on Medicaid and the Uninsured, Kaiser Family Foundation:

www.kff.org

Agency for Healthcare Research and Quality U.S. Department of Health and Human Services, Medical Expenditure Panel Survey:

www.ahrq.gov

REFERENCES

Abelson, R. (2017, December 18). Hospital Giants Vie for Patients in Effort to Fend Off New Rivals. *New York Times*. Retrieved from www.nytimes.com/2017/12/18/health/hospitals-mergers-patients.html

Agency for Healthcare Research and Quality (2008). National Healthcare Disparities Report, 2007. Retrieved from www.ahrq.gov/qual/qrdr07.htm

Aiu, P. (2000, June–July). *Comparing Native Hawaiians to the Nation. Closing the Gap*. Washington, DC: U.S. Department of Health and Human Services.

Altman, S. H., Reinhardt, U. E., and Shields, A. E. (Eds.). (1998). *The Future U.S. Healthcare System: Who Will Care for the Poor and Uninsured?* Chicago, IL: Health Administration Press.

Appleby, J. (2012, May 14). Many Businesses Offer Health Benefits to Same-sex Couples ahead of Laws. *Kaiser Health News*. Retrieved from www.kaiserhealthnews.org/stories/2012/may/14/businesses-move-to-offer-health-benefits-to-same-sexcouples.aspx

Arrieta, R. M. (2011, January 3). The State of Native America: Very Unemployed and Mostly Ignored. *In These Times*. Retrieved from http://inthesetimes.com/working/entry/6801/the-state-of-native-america-very-unemployed-and-mostly-ignored/

Artiga, S. (2018, January 26). Health Coverage by Race and Ethnicity: Changes Under the ACA. *Health Affairs*. Retrieved from www.kff.org/report-section/health-coverage-by-race-and-ethnicity-changes-under-the-aca-issue-brief/

Artiga, S., Young, K., Garfield, R., and Majerol, M. (2015, August 6). *Racial and Ethnic Disparities in Access to and Utilization of Care among Insured Adults*. Washington, DC: Kaiser Family Foundation. Retrieved from www.kff.org/report-section/racial-and-ethnic-disparities-in-access-to-and-utilization-of-care-among-insured-adults-issue-brief

Association of State and Territorial Health Officials. (2004, September 29). Access to Health Care Services Policy Statement, 2004–2007. Retrieved from www.astho.org/policy-statements/Access%20Policy.pdf

Bannow, T. (2018, January 6). Charity Care Spending Flat among Top Hospitals. *Modern Healthcare*. Retrieved from www.modernhealthcare.com/article/20180106/NEWS/180109941

Barnett, J. C. and Berchick, E. R. (2017, September). *Health Insurance Coverage in the United States: 2016*. Current Population Reports. U.S. Census Bureau. Retrieved from www.census.gov/content/dam/Census/library/publications/2017/demo/p60-260.pdf

Billings, J., Anderson, G. M., and Newman, L. S. (1996). Recent Findings on Preventable Hospitalizations. *Health Affairs*, 13(3), 239–249.

Brooke, J. (1995, October 15). In the Budget Talk from Washington, Indians See the Cruelest Cuts of All. *New York Times*, p. 10.

Collins, E. (2017, January 24). Obamacare Repeal could put Native American Health Care at Risk. *USA Today*. Retrieved from www.usatoday.com/story/news/politics/2017/01/24/indian-healthcare-improvement-act-affordable-care-act/96987680/

Collins, S. R., Gunja, M. Z., and Beutel, S. (2016, September 13). *New U.S. Census Data Show the Number of Uninsured Americans Dropped by 4 Million, with Young Adults Making Big Gains*. Commonwealth Fund. Retrieved from www.commonwealthfund.org/publications/blog/2016/sep/2015-census-data-insurance

Commonwealth Fund. (2017). *Underinsured Rate Increased Sharply in 2016: More Than Two of Five Marketplace Enrollees and a Quarter of People with Employer Health Insurance Plans are Now Underinsured*. Retrieved from www.commonwealthfund.org/publications/press-releases/2017/oct/underinsured-press-release

Community Catalyst. (1998a, August). The Columbia/HCA Hospital Sales: An Opportunity to Re-Focus on Community Benefits. *States of Health*, 8(4), 1–8.

——. (1998b, September). Strengthening the Free Care Safety Net. *States of Health*, 8(5), 1–6.

Congressional Budget Office. (2003). *How Many People Lack Health Insurance and for How Long?* Retrieved from www.cbo.gov/showdoc.cfm?index=4210&sequence=2#pt2

Cunningham, P. J., Grossman, J. M., St. Peter, R. F., and Lesser, C. S. (1999). Managed Care and Physician's Provision to Charity. *Journal of the American Medical Association*, 281(12), 1087–1093.

Dawson, L., Kates, J., and Rae, M. (2017, September 25). *Access to Employer-sponsored Health Coverage for Same-sex Spouses*: 2017 Update. Washington, DC: Kaiser Family Foundation. Retrieved from www.kff.org/disparities-policy/issue-brief/access-to-employer-sponsored-health-coverage-for-same-sex-spouses-2017-update

Dobkin, C., Finkelstein, A., Kluender, R., and Notowidigdo, M. (2016, May). *The Economic Consequences of Hospital Admissions*. National Bureau of Economic Research. Retrieved from www.nber.org/papers/w22288.pdf

Donelan, K., Blendon, R. J., Hill, C. A., Hoffman, C., Rowland, D., Frankel, M., and Altman, D. (1996). Public Opinion and Health Care: Whatever Happened to the Health Insurance Crisis in the United States? Voices from a National Survey. *Journal of the American Medical Association*, 276(16), 1346–1350.

Doob, C. B. (1996). *Racism: An American Cauldron*. New York: HarperCollins.

Economic Policy Institute (2008, October 9). Briefing Paper #223. Retrieved from www.epi.org/briefingpapers/223/bp223.pdf

Families USA. (1999). *Losing Health Insurance: The Unintended Consequences of Welfare Reform*. Washington, DC: Families USA.

——. (July 2008a). *Detour on the Road to Kids Coverage: Administration Creates Roadblocks, So States Seek Alternate Routes*. Retrieved from www.familiesusa.org/assets/pdfs/detour-kids-coverage.pdf

——. (2008b). *About CHIP*. Retrieved from www.familiesusa.org/issues/childrens-health/about-chip/HealthCoverage in Communities of Color

Foutz, J., Damico, A., Squires, E., and Garfield, R. (2017, December 14). *The Uninsured: A Primer: Key Facts about Health Insurance and the Uninsured Under the Affordable Care Act*. Washington, DC: Kaiser Family Foundation. Retrieved from www.kff.org/uninsured/report/the-uninsured-a-primer-key-facts-about-health-insurance-and-the-uninsured-under-the-affordable-care-act

Friends Committee on National Legislation. (2005, July 20). *Imperative to Reauthorize Indian Health Care Improvement Act*. Retrieved from www.fcnl.org/issues

Gallup-Healthways Well-Being Index. (2012, March 2). *Texas Widens Gap Over Other States in Percentage Uninsured: No States Show Consistent Decline in Uninsured Since 2008*. Retrieved from www.gallup.com/poll/153053/texas-widens-gap-states-percentage-uninsured.aspx#1

Garthwaite, C., Gross, T., and Notowidigdo, M. (2015, June). *Hospitals as Insurers of Last Resort. National Bureau of Economic Research*. Retrieved from www.nber.org/papers/w21290

Giffords, E. D. Wenze, L., Weiss, D. M., Kass, D., and Guercia, R. (August 2005.) Increasing Access to Health Care: Examination of Hospital Community Benefits and Free Care Programs. *Health & Social Work*, 30(3), 213–218.

Goldberg, C. (1997, January 30). Hispanic Households Struggle as Poorest of the Poor in U.S. *New York Times*, p. A1.

Hall, A., Collins, K. S., and Glied, S. (1999). *Employee-Sponsored Health Insurance: Implications for Minority Workers*. New York: Commonwealth Fund.

Health Insurance Association of America. (1999). HIAA Study: *1 Out of 5 Non-Elderly Americans Will Lack Health Insurance in 2007*. Retrieved from www.hiaa.org

Heisler, E. J. (2011, December 14). *The Indian Health Care Improvement Act and Reauthorization and Extension as Enacted by the ACA: Detailed Summary and Timeline*. Congressional Research Service. Retrieved from www.ncsl.org/documents/health/IndHlthCareReauth.pdf

Himmelstein, D. U. and Woolhandler, S. (1994). *The National Health Program Book: A Source Guide for Advocates*. Monroe, ME: Common Courage.

Hoffman, C. and Schwartz, K. (October, 2008). *Trends in Access to Care Among Working-age Adults, 1997–2006*. Washington, DC: Kaiser Family Foundation.

Holahan, J. and Ghosh, A. (2004, September). *The Economic Downturn and Changes in Health Insurance Coverage*. Urban Institute for the Kaiser Commission on Medicaid and the Uninsured. Washington, DC: Kaiser Family Foundation.

Hurley, R. E., Pham, H. H., and Claxton, G. (2005, December 6). A Widening Rift in Access and Quality: Growing Evidence of Economic Disparities. *Health Affairs*. Retrieved from http://content.healthaffairs.org/content/early/2005/12/06/hlthaff.w5.566.long

Indian Health Service. (2012a). Frequently Asked Questions. Retrieved from www.ihs.gov/GeneralWeb/HelpCenter/CustomerServices/FAQ

——. (2012b). *Health Reform for American Indians and Alaska Natives*. Retrieved from www.ihs.gov/PublicAffairs/DirCorner/docs/Fact_Sheet.pdf

Institute of Medicine. (2001). *Coverage Matters: Insurance and Health Care*. Washington, DC: National Academic Press.

Jang, M., Lee, E., and Woo, K. (1998, May). Income, Language, and Citizenship Status: Factors Affecting the Health Care Access and Utilization of Chinese Americans. *Health & Social Work*, 23(2), 136–145.

Jaret, C. (1995). *Contemporary Racial and Ethnic Relations*. New York: HarperCollins.

Jiang, S. P. (2000, June–July). Correcting the Visions of Paradise. *Closing the Gap*. Washington, DC: U.S. Department of Health and Human Services.

Kaiser Commission on Medicaid and the Uninsured. (1998a). *Uninsured in America, Key Facts about Gaps in Health Insurance Coverage Today*. Washington, DC: Kaiser Family Foundation.

——. (1998b, July). *Uninsured Facts: The Uninsured and their Access to Health Care*. Washington, DC: Kaiser Family Foundation.

——. (2000, June). *Health Insurance Coverage and Access to Care among American Indians and Alaska Natives*. Washington, DC: Kaiser Family Foundation.

——. (2001, November). *Urban Indian Health*. Washington, DC: Kaiser Family Foundation.

——. (2004). *Employer Health Benefits*. Washington, DC: Kaiser Family Foundation.

——. (2005, February). *The Uninsured: A Primer—Update*. Washington, DC: Kaiser Family Foundation.

Kaiser Family Foundation. (1997, December). *Working Families at Risk: Coverage, Access, Costs, and Worries, Kaiser/Commonwealth National Survey of Health Insurance*. Washington, DC: Kaiser Family Foundation.

——. (2007, January). *Key Facts: Race, Ethnicity, and Medical Care*. Retrieved from www.kff.org/minorityhealth/upload/6069-02.pdf

——. (2017, November 29). *Key Facts about the Uninsured Population*. Retrieved from www.kff.org/uninsured/fact-sheet/key-facts-about-the-uninsured-population/

Kass, B. L., Weinick, R. M., and Monheit, A. C. (1996). *Racial and Ethnic Differences in Health. MEPS Chart Book No. 2* (AHCPR Pub. No. 99-0001). Rockville, MD: Agency for Health Care Policy and Research.

Kenney, G. M., McMorrow, S., Zuckerman, S., and Goin, D. E. (2012, May). A Decade of Health Care Access Declines for Adults Holds Implications for Changes in the Affordable Care Act. *Health Affairs*, 13(5), 899–907.

Kottak, C. (1994). *Cultural Anthropology*, 6th edn. New York: McGraw-Hill.

Krauss, N., Machlin, S., and Kass, B. (1999). *Use of Health Care Services, 1996. MEPS Research Findings No. 7* (AHCPR Pub. No. 99-0018). Rockville, MD: Agency for Health Care Policy and Research.

Latino Coalition for a Healthy California. (1996). *Latinos and Access to Health Care in California*. Retrieved from www.lchc.org

Leins, C. (2017, May 4). Latinos, Millennials Among Groups Least Likely to Have Health Insurance. *U.S. News*. Retrieved from www.usnews.com/news/best-states/articles/2017-05-04/latinos-millennials-among-groups-least-likely-to-have-health-insurance

Lopez, G., Ruiz, N. G., and Patten, E. (2017, September 9). *Key facts about Asian Americans, A Diverse and Growing Population*. Pew Research Center. Retrieved from www.pewresearch.org/fact-tank/2017/09/08/key-facts-about-asian-americans/

Mills, R. (1999). *Health Insurance Coverage. Current Population Reports*. U.S. Bureau of the Census. Retrieved from www.census.gov/population/socdemo/

Musu-Gillette, L., Robinson, J., McFarland, J., KewalRamani, A., Zhang, A., and Wilkinson-Flicker, S. (2016). *Status and Trends in the Education of Racial and Ethnic Groups 2016* (NCES 2016-007). Washington, DC: U.S. Department of Education, National Center for Education Statistics. Retrieved from http://nces.ed.gov/pubsearch

National Institute of Medicine Pacific Partnerships for Health. (1998). *Charting a Course for the 21st Century*. Washington, DC: National Academy Press.

Needleman, J., Lamphere, J., and Chollet, D. (1999, July–August). Uncompensated Care and Hospital Conversions in Florida. *Health Affairs*, 18(4), 125–133.

Norris, L. (2018, February 25). Hawaii and the ACA's Medicaid expansion. Retrieved from www.healthinsurance.org/hawaii-medicaid

O'Hare, W. P., Pollard, K. M., Mann, T. L., and Kent, M. M. (1991, July). African Americans in the 1990s. *Population Bulletin*, 46(1), 29–30.

Paradise, J. and Garfield, R. (2013, August 2). *What is Medicaid's Impact on Access to Care, Health Outcomes, and Quality of Care? Setting the Record Straight on the Evidence*. Washington, DC: Kaiser Family Foundation. Retrieved from www.kff.org/report-section/what-is-medicaids-impact-on-access-to-care-health-outcomes-and-quality-of-care-setting-the-record-straight-on-the-evidence-issue-brief

Preston, J. (1996, April 14). Hospitals Look on Charity Care as Unaffordable Option of Past. *New York Times*, p. A1.

Rhoades, J. A. and Chu, M. (2000, December). *Health Insurance Status of the Civilian Noninstitutionalized Population MEPS Research Design Findings No. 14* (AHRQ Pub. No. 01-0011). Rockville, MD: Agency for Healthcare Research and Quality.

Rhoades, J. A. and Cohen, S. B. (2008, August). *The Long-Term Uninsured in America, 2003–2006: Estimates for the U.S. Population under Age 65*. Statistical Brief No. 220. Rockville, MD: Agency for Healthcare Research and Quality.

Rosenthal, E. (1995, June 26). Two Hospitals Charging Poor for Medicine. *New York Times*, p. B1.

Ross, H. (2000, June–July). *New Federal Standards Recognize Native Hawaiians and Other Pacific Islanders as Distinct Group. Closing the Gap*. Washington, DC: U.S. Department of Health and Human Services.

Rowland, D. (1994, February 10). *Uninsured in America (Testimony before Committee on Finance, U.S. Senate Hearing on Health Coverage for the Uninsured)*. Washington, DC: Kaiser Family Foundation.

Schoen, C., Doty, M. M., Collins, S. R., and Holmgren, A. L. (2005, June 14). Insured but Not Protected: How Many Adults Are Underinsured? *Health Affairs*. Retrieved from http://content.healthaffairs.org/content/early/2005/06/14/hlthaff.w5.289.citation

Schoen, C., Doty, M., Robertson, R., and Collins, S. (2011, September). Affordable Care Act Reforms Could Reduce The Number Of Underinsured US Adults By 70 Percent. *Health Affairs*, 30(9), 1762–1771.

Semega, J. L., Fontenot, K. R., and Kollar, M. A. (2017, September). Income and Poverty in the United States: 2016. *Current Population Reports*. U.S. Census Bureau. Retrieved from www.census.gov/content/dam/Census/library/publications/2017/demo/P60-259.pdf

Skinner, J., Chandra, A., Staiger, D., Lee, J., and McClellan, M. (2005). Mortality after Acute Myocardial Infarction in Hospitals That Disproportionately Treat Black Patients. *Circulation*, 112, 2634–2641.

Stelzer, I. M. (1994, January 25). There Is No Health Care Crisis. *Wall Street Journal*, p. A12.

Stone, L.C. and Balderrama. (2008, February). Health Inequalities among Latinos: What Do We Know and What Can We Do? *Health & Social Work*, 23(1), 3–7.

U.S. Census Bureau. (1990–2017). March Demographic Profiles. *Current Population Surveys*. Retrieved from www.census.gov/population/socdemo

——. (2000). *Race and Ethnic Classifications Used in Census 2000 and Beyond*. Retrieved from www.census.gov/population/socdemo/race

——. (2004, December). *We the People: Asians in the U.S.* (2000 Census Special Report). Retrieved from www.census.gov/prod/2004pubs/censr-17.pdf

——. (2012). *Income, Poverty, and Health Insurance Coverage in the U.S.: 2011*. Retrieved from www.census.gov/prod/2011pubs/p60-239.pdf

——. (2017a, September 14.) *Uninsured Rate by State: Percentage of People Without Health Insurance*. Retrieved from www.census.gov/library/visualizations/2017/comm/uninsured-map.html

——. (2017b). *Income and Poverty in the United States: 2016*. Retrieved from www.census.gov/content/dam/Census/library/publications/2017/demo/P60-259.pdf

U.S. Department of Health and Human Services. (2001, August). *Mental Health: Culture, Race, and Ethnicity (Supplement to Surgeon General's Report on Mental Health)*.

Rockville, MD: U.S. Department of Health and Human Services, Substance Abuse and Mental Health Services Administration, Center for Mental Health Services, National Institute of Mental Health.

U.S. General Accounting Office. (1992, January). *Hispanic Access to Health Care: A Significant Gap Exists* (GAO/PEMD-92-6). Washington, DC: U.S. Government Printing Office.

——. (1993, April). *Indian Health Service: Basic Services Mostly Available. Substance Abuse Problems Need Attention* (GAO/HRD-93-48). Washington, DC: U.S. Government Printing Office.

——. (1995, July). *Health Insurance for Children—Many Remain Uninsured Despite Medicaid Expansion* (GAO/HEHS-95-175). Washington, DC: U.S. Government Printing Office.

U.S. Office of Minority Health. (2017a). *Asian American/Pacific Islander Profile*. Retrieved from https://minorityhealth.hhs.gov/omh/browse.aspx?lvl=3&lvlid=65

——. (2017b). *Hispanic/Latino Profile*. Retrieved from https://minorityhealth.hhs.gov/omh/browse.aspx?lvl=3&lvlid=64

——. (2017c). *Native American Profile*. Retrieved from https://minorityhealth.hhs.gov/omh/browse.aspx?lvl=3&lvlid=62

——. (2018, June 29). *Asian American/Pacific Islander Profile*. Retrieved from https://minorityhealth.hhs.gov/omh/browse.aspx?lvl=3&lvlid=65

Weinick, R. M. and Drilea, S. K. (1998). Usual Sources of Health Care and Barriers to Care. *Statistical Bulletin Metropolitan Insurance Companies*, 789(1), 11–17.

Weissman, J. S., Gatsonis, C., and Epstein, A. M. (1992). Rates of Avoidable Hospitalization by Insurance Status in Massachusetts and Maryland. *Journal of the American Medical Association*, 268, 2388–2394.

Wiatrowski, W. J. (1995, June). Who Really Has Access to Employer-provided Health Benefits? *Monthly Labor Review*, 118(6), 36–44.

Wilson, W. J. (1987). *The Truly Disadvantaged: The Inner City, the Underclass, and Public Policy*. Chicago, IL: University of Chicago Press.

Zaldivar, R. A. (1991, June 12). Immigration Brings New Diversity to Asian Population in the U.S. *New York Times*, pp. A1, A16. Retrieved from www.nytimes.com/1991/06/12/us/immigration-brings-new-diversity-to-asian-population-in-the-us.html

Zeigler, K. and Camarota, S. A. (2017, May 10). *The Employment Situation of Immigrants and Natives in the First Quarter of 2017*. Center for Immigration Studies. Retrieved from https://cis.org/Report/Employment-Situation-Immigrants-and-Natives-First-Quarter-2017

CHAPTER 10

Analyzing the Problem
Disparities in Health for People of Color

THIS CHAPTER APPLIES THE BASIC POLICY PRACTICE QUESTIONS that are raised in problem analysis to the issue of disparities in health for people of color in the U.S. The following outline places the issues discussed in this chapter in this context.

Outline of Analysis: Disparities in Health for People of Color

What is the social problem?	Disparities in health for people of color
Who is affected? What is the extent of the problem?	People of color (African Americans, Latinx, Asian Americans, Native Americans), particularly low income
What are the dimensions and boundaries of the problem?	Disparities in health status in life expectancy, mortality, and morbidity
What evidence is there that a problem exists?	National and regional data and studies on disparities in health insurance coverage, access to health care, and quality of care
How serious is the problem?	People of color are at greater risk for infant mortality, death, cancer, cardiovascular disease, diabetes, HIV/AIDS, infectious diseases, and other health risks
What is the perceived cause of the problem?	Systemic and financial barriers to care; and cultural attitudes and preferences in the delivery and utilization of care
What explanations exist for the problem?	Lack of universal health insurance coverage due to a patchwork system of health care policies and programs in the U.S.; the high cost of health care and insurance; disparities in the quality of care; discriminatory practices in the delivery of care

WHAT DOES IT MEAN TO BE AT RISK FOR POOR HEALTH?

Socioeconomic risk factors that have an impact on access to health insurance coverage were outlined in Chapter 9. Similarly, and perhaps of even greater concern, there are groups in the U.S. that are at greater risk of poor health than the population as a whole. Members of these groups are "vulnerable to, or likely to be harmed by, a specific medical, social, political, or environmental circumstance" (Barker, 1999, p. 34). Aday (1993, p. 5) provides the following definition of this type of risk:

> The concept of risk assumes that there is always a chance that an adverse health-related outcome will occur. Correspondingly, we are all potentially at risk of poor physical, psychological, and/or social health. People may, however, be more at risk of poor health at different times in their lives, *while some individuals and groups are apt to be more at risk than others at any given point in time.* [emphasis added]

The concept of "any given point in time" illustrates the difference in risk factors. Like everyone else, people of color, women, children, youth, and older adults are susceptible to poor health at "different times" in their individual lives. They experience a variety of health risks associated with biological and genetic factors, developmental stages of the life cycle, and the aging process itself. However, these groups are also "*more at risk* [emphasis added] than others at *any* [emphasis added] given point in time" (Aday, 1993, p. 5) due to political and socioeconomic conditions that put them in greater jeopardy than other members of our society.

Disproportionate risk leads to "health disparities," which Braveman (2006, p. 15) defined as:

> systematic, potentially avoidable differences in health—or in the major socially determined influences on health—between groups of people who have different relative positions in social hierarchies according to wealth, power, or prestige. Because these differences adversely affect the health or health risks (construed here as exposures and vulnerabilities increasing the likelihood of ill health or adverse social consequences of ill health) of groups already at a disadvantage by virtue of their underlying social positions, they are particularly unfair.

In other words, health disparities are:

> differences in health (or in important influences on health) that are systematically associated with being socially disadvantaged (e.g., being poor, a member of a disadvantaged racial/ethnic group, or female), putting those in disadvantaged groups at further disadvantage.
>
> (Braveman, 2006, p. 15)

As discussed earlier, people of color have disproportionately higher rates of poverty and higher rates of unemployment, and are at greater risk of lack or loss of employment-based insurance. However, people of color are also at greater risk of poor health. In fact, racial and ethnic disparities in health are so embedded in our social and political life that, unlike other countries, the U.S. documents health status based on race rather than social class (Navarro, 1990). The National Center for Health Statistics (U.S. Public Health Service) collects data annually for its national report, *Health, United States*, on mortality, disparities in mortality, birth rates, morbidity, and health behaviors (these terms are discussed next) and presents the statistical data primarily by race, not social class. Data for most public health databases in the U.S. are collected in this way. For example, state health departments do not normally collect socioeconomic data about health status (Krieger et al., 1997a, 1997b).

MEASURING HEALTH DISPARITIES

Public health scholars and officials rely on a body of concepts and methods that have been developed to measure the health of individuals and population groups. Before we explore frameworks for understanding disparities and examining health outcomes for racial and ethnic groups in the U.S., there are several basic demographic and epidemiological terms and measures used to describe health status and health disparities that should be examined. In particular, there are some terms, such as *mortality* and *morbidity,* that are used throughout this chapter and Chapter 11. It is interesting to note that the most commonly used measures of health status do not focus on health; instead, they are measures of disease or death. This is a separate issue that we will revisit in Chapter 12.

Demography

Demography is the study of population characteristics, especially population size, fertility, mortality, growth, age distribution, migration, and vital statistics. Primary vital statistics include births (fertility) and deaths (mortality) and population characteristics by age, race and ethnicity, gender, marital status, socioeconomic status, residence, and migration. Mandatory reporting laws provide demographers with birth data; mandatory death certificates provide mortality data. Other data are collected by government agencies through population registries, census data, and special household surveys.

Demography is also the study of population trends—changes in population characteristics over time. Demographic transitions occur when the age distribution of a population changes significantly; this occurs primarily as a result of significant changes in birth and death rates. Natural disasters, war, famine, migration, disease patterns, and political strife also lead to substantial changes in populations.

Morbidity. Morbidity is a public health term used to define poor health. It usually refers to the incidence or prevalence of a disease, although it can refer to severity or duration. Incidence refers to the number of *new* cases of a disease or condition in a population group during a given *period* of time; prevalence refers to the number of *new and old* cases of a disease or condition in a population group at a given *point* in time or during a *specified period* of time. Morbidity can be measured in a variety of ways, including the number of individuals who are ill, the length of an illness, or periods of an illness.

Mortality. Mortality (death) statistics are fundamental to the study of populations. Mortality statistics are based on mandatory reporting laws that rely on federal standards and classifications of death. U.S. death certificates provide a wide range of information, including age, gender, race, ethnicity, marital status, occupation, residence, and cause of death. Immediate cause of death, underlying cause, and other significant health conditions are reported. This information allows demographers to study patterns of mortality at a given point in time or over a period of time. For example, a cohort from 2000 can be compared with a cohort from 1950 at the time of birth, or over a period of time. (A cohort is usually a group of individuals born in a given year. It may, however, be any other defined group.)

Patterns of mortality include differences or changes in age-specific mortality rates, such as infant or maternal mortality, or cause-specific mortality rates. For example, in 1999, heart disease, cancer, and HIV/AIDS mortality declined, whereas mortality from Alzheimer's disease, a newly classified cause of death, increased significantly (National Center for Health Statistics, 2001). The National Center for Health Statistics reports mortality statistics annually for leading causes of death (Figures 10.1–10.3). Throughout 1975–2016, heart disease and cancer have persisted as the two leading causes of death. Heart disease and cancer are the leading causes of death for both women and men, but everything changes after that.

Life Expectancy. Life expectancy refers to the average number of years a person (at a given age) is expected to live given the current mortality rates of a population. Life expectancy is traditionally measured at birth, but can be measured from any age. In the U.S., life expectancy at birth has risen dramatically from 47.3 years in 1900 to 78.6 years in 2016; however, this is a decrease of 0.1 year since 2011 (National Center for Health Statistics, 2017a).

CAUSE OF DEATH	NUMBER OF DEATHS, ALL PERSONS
1. *Heart disease*	**633,842**
2. *Cancer*	**595,930**
3. Chronic lower respiratory diseases	155,041
4. Accidents (unintentional injuries)	146,571
5. Stroke (cerebrovascular diseases)	140,323
6. Alzheimer's disease	110,561
7. Diabetes	79,535
8. Pneumonia–influenza	57,062
9. Kidney disease	49,959
10. Suicide	44,193

FIGURE 10.1

Ten Leading Causes of Death in the United States, 2016

Source: National Center for Health Statistics (2017a).

FIGURE 10.2

Ten Leading Causes of Death by Gender, 2016

Women	Men
1. **Heart disease**	1. **Heart disease**
2. **Cancer**	2. **Cancer**
3. Chronic lower respiratory diseases	3. Accidents (unintentional injuries)
4. Stroke	4. Chronic lower respiratory diseases
5. Alzheimer's disease	5. Stroke
6. Accidents (unintentional injuries)	6. Diabetes
7. Diabetes	7. Suicide
8. Influenza and pneumonia	8. Alzheimer's disease
9. Kidney disease	9. Influenza and pneumonia
10. Septicemia **(blood infection)**	10. Chronic liver disease and cirrhosis

Source: Bezerow (2017a).

FIGURE 10.3

Leading Causes of Death by Race and Ethnic Group, 2014

RANK	WHITES	BLACKS	LATINX	ASIANS	NATIVE AMERICANS
Cause of death 1	Heart disease	Heart disease	**Cancer**	**Cancer**	Heart disease
2	Cancer	Cancer	**Heart disease**	**Heart disease**	Cancer
3	Accidents	Accidents	Accidents	**Stroke**	Accidents
4	Chronic lower respiratory disease	**Stroke**	**Diabetes**	**Accidents**	**Diabetes**
5	Stroke	**Homicide**	Stroke	**Diabetes**	**Chronic lower respiratory disease**

Note: **Bold** indicates variation in rank compared with whites.
Source: National Center for Health Statistics (2017a).

In addition, a study by the Harvard School of Public Health and the University of Washington found a disturbing downward trend in life expectancy in poor sectors of the country (the Deep South, the southern portion of the Midwest, parts of Texas and Appalachia), especially for women. For a small minority, life expectancy began to level off or even decline, starting in the 1980s; this was found for 4 percent of men and 19 percent of women. As reported by the lead researcher, Majid Ezzati, "It's very troubling that there are parts of the wealthiest country in the world, with the highest health spending in the world, where health is getting worse . . . [it is] unheard of in any other developed country" (Bakalar, 2008).

Epidemiology

Epidemiology is the study of the distribution and extent of disease (or risk factor) in a population, the causes of disease, and the identification of potential interventions to prevent, control, and treat disease. The biopsychosocial risk factors that most directly influence health outcomes are referred to as *determinants* of health. Epidemiologists study populations at risk and identify determinants of health in an effort to reduce or eliminate health problems. Although health policy is usually shaped by political factors, scientific epidemiological findings play an important role. Demographic trends have a significant impact on our health care system, and our knowledge of risk factors and causes of disease should inform policy decisions.

Health Targets. Although there has not been a history of national health insurance or universal access to health care in the U.S., there has been a strong history of public health initiatives. In the late 1970s, the U.S. Department of Health and Human Services initiated a new public health initiative when it developed specific health targets for the nation. In 1979, the Surgeon General's Report on Health Promotion and Disease Prevention launched *Healthy People*, which established five life-stage health targets (e.g., reduced mortality rates) and 226 specific health objectives to be achieved over a 10-year period (by 1990). This initiative created a precedent for establishing national objectives for health outcomes and monitoring their progress.

Healthy People 2000 added new health targets in three areas: (1) Increase healthy life-spans, (2) reduce disparities in health, and (3) achieve universal access to preventive health care. The program established 297 specific health objectives in 4 major areas: Health promotion, health protection, prevention, and surveillance systems. *Healthy People 2010* had two overarching health goals: (1) Increase the number of years of healthy life and (2) eliminate disparities in health among different segments of the population, including women, youth, older adults, people of low income and education, and people with disabilities. Twenty-eight priority areas were established, with targets set for each objective within each targeted group. The most recent overarching health goals established by *Healthy People 2020* focus on (1) attaining high quality, longer lives free of preventable disease, disability, injury, and premature death, (2) achieving health equity, eliminating disparities, and improving the health of all groups, (3) creating social and physical environments that promote good health for all, and (4) promoting quality of life, healthy development, and healthy behaviors across all life stages.

A second health promotion effort was launched by the U.S. Department of Health and Human Services. The first effort was the 1998 Initiative to Eliminate Racial and Ethnic Disparities in Health, which grew out of President Clinton's 1997 Initiative on Race (U.S. Department of Health and Human Services, 1998). This health-promotion initiative relied on epidemiological studies of people of color to target improved health outcomes in six major areas: Infant mortality, cancer, cardiovascular disease, diabetes, HIV/AIDS, and infectious diseases; mental health, particularly suicide, is also targeted as a condition that disproportionately affects racial and ethnic groups. Although many people in the U.S. are affected by these health problems (see Figure 10.1), leading causes of death vary for the racial and ethnic groups discussed in this chapter (see Figure 10.3), and the six target areas disproportionately affect racial and ethnic groups. These health risks are responsible for much of the morbidity and mortality in racial and ethnic communities in the U.S.

In April 2011, the Department of Health and Human Services (HHS) released its first federal strategic Action Plan to Reduce Racial and Ethnic Health Disparities, including efforts to achieve goals under the Affordable Care Act such as expansion of health insurance coverage, diversification of the health care workforce, and the improvement of population health. HHS also released a set of goals and objectives for public and private sector initiatives and partnerships to address racial and ethnic health disparities: the National Stakeholder Strategy for Achieving Health Equity (Koh et al., 2011).

EXPLAINING RACIAL AND ETHNIC DISPARITIES IN HEALTH

"The consistent and repeated finding that black Americans receive less health care than white Americans . . . is an indictment of American health care" (Bhopal, 1998, p. 4). For at least the past 20 years, studies have shown that differences exist in the treatment of African Americans and whites as patients. For example, a number of studies from the 1990s (Wenneker and Epstein, 1989; Goldberg et al., 1992; Whittle et al., 1993; Carlisle et al., 1997) showed that African American patients received less coronary surgery and fewer cardiac procedures than white patients. A Sloan–Kettering Cancer Center study (Bach et al., 1999) found that African Americans were 13 percent less likely to receive surgery for lung cancer than whites.

However, as noted by Bhopal (1998), these studies did not provide conclusive evidence about the differences in treatment. Although many suspected that racism explained the difference, other reasons—including inadequate health care; patients' preferences for treatment; financial, organizational, and cultural barriers to treatment; and physicians' differences in treatment—all seemed to play a role. The "first large-scale study" (Kamat, 1999) to show racial bias in physician decision-making, conducted by Schulman et al. (1999), found that physicians were more likely to recommend sophisticated cardiac tests for whites who complained of chest pain than for African Americans with the same symptoms. The study controlled for other explanatory factors, such as insurance and patient willingness to accept referrals. In doing so, the "study . . . exclusively investigate[d] the effect of race/gender bias on the resulting physician treatment recommendations" (Kamat, 1999, p. 6).

Although many studies showed disparities in health care based on race, most, unlike the study of Schulman et al. (1999), did not focus on the role of racism;

yet few social researchers have denied the importance of race. Disparities in socio-economic conditions between people of color and whites—including housing, food and nutrition, environment, and safety—are precursors for poor health and increase the risk of death for African Americans and other people of color. A study conducted by the British researcher George Davey Smith, with researchers from the U.S. (Smith et al., 1998), concluded that racism was the underlying factor in the difference in mortality rates between whites and African Americans, and needed further investigation. The study examined deaths related to heart and renal disease, stroke, lung and prostate cancer, and homicide during the 1970s, and showed that the greatest mortality risks were income and socioeconomic status; the researchers found that racism had a direct impact on both.

More recently, a growing body of research is starting to show the direct effect of bias on treatment. For example, studies have shown that African–American patients often receive less prescribed pain medication than white patients with the same complaints, and African–American patients with chest pain are referred less often than white patients for advanced cardiac care. In response, medical schools have started to teach students to avoid "unconscious" or "implicit" bias in their treatment of people of color (Dembosky, 2015).

In 1985, the U.S. Department of Health and Human Services first began to study the health status of people of color, their access to care, and their utilization of services in an effort to document continual disparities in health between whites and African Americans, Hispanics, Native Americans, some Asian Americans, and Pacific Islanders. The initial report of the Secretary's Task Force on Black and Minority Health (U.S. Department of Health and Human Services, 1986) focused on differences in health status by race and ethnicity. Since then more research has focused on access to care, patterns of utilization, and health outcomes for different racial and ethnic groups.

In 1999, the Kaiser Family Foundation published a synthesis of studies conducted between 1985 and 1998 on racial and ethnic differences in access to medical care (Mayberry et al., 1999). In 1999, Congress asked the Institute of Medicine (IOM) to examine the extent of racial and ethnic disparities in health care. In their 2002 report, *Unequal Treatment*, the IOM concluded that there was some evidence of bias, prejudice, and stereotyping on the part of health care providers that may contribute to differences in care. Congress also directed the Agency for Healthcare Research and Quality (AHRQ) to track disparities in the delivery of care related to racial and socioeconomic factors. Their first reports, *National Healthcare Disparities Report* (AHRQ, 2003) and *National Healthcare Quality Report* (AHRQ, 2004), addressed some of the challenges inherent in tracking and measuring disparities, such as the confounding effects of race, ethnicity, socioeconomic status, and other factors. These studies show that racial and ethnic disparities in access to care clearly exist, but the reasons still need clarification. Further study is necessary to demonstrate to what extent racial and ethnic disparities result from "systemic and financial barriers as opposed to cultural preferences and attitudes" (AHRQ, 2003, p. 3). Understanding health disparities in the U.S. remains "complex and driven by multiple factors" and will require "equally diverse" solutions including "patient and provider education; use of community health workers; cultural competence training; and policy-level interventions" (Weinick and Hasnain-Wynia, 2011, p. 1838). The sections that follow provide information on findings to date on disparities in federal health targets in the U.S., including infant health, heart disease, cancer, diabetes, and HIV/AIDS for people of color and Latinx.

AFRICAN AMERICANS

The death rate for African Americans is generally higher than for whites for heart diseases, stroke, cancer, asthma, influenza and pneumonia, diabetes, HIV/AIDS, and homicide.

Life Expectancy

From 1985 to about 1990, the gap in life expectancy between African Americans and whites actually widened, something relatively unheard of in terms of life expectancy in the U.S.; this period has been referred to as "a lost decade" for African American longevity marred by homicides, AIDS, and the crack cocaine epidemic (Tavernise, 2016). In 1988 and 1989, life expectancy for African Americans was 69.2 years, whereas life expectancy for whites rose from 75.6 years in 1988 to 76.0 years in 1989. The primary reason for this widening gap was the health risk of acquired immune deficiency syndrome (AIDS) and neighborhood violence, particularly among young African American males aged 25–34 (Associated Press, 1992). From 1993 to 1998, life expectancy for African American males increased to a high of 67.6 years, primarily because of the decline in mortality from HIV/AIDS and homicide.

From 1999 to 2009, the gap in longevity between whites and African Americans continued to narrow until the recession hit and unemployment among blacks reached 16.1 percent compared with 8 percent among whites. Researchers argued that stress related to unemployment might explain the halt in improvement in longevity for blacks in 2009, which remained at 74.3 years. Also of concern and potentially related to the impact of stress, in 2009, suicides among African Americans increased slightly but just sufficiently to move suicide into the top ten causes of death (Ross, 2011). By 2011, African American life expectancy had risen to 75.3 years, but still remained almost four years behind the longevity rate for whites. Much of this increase in longevity was due to reductions in the rates of death from the major causes of death, namely heart disease, cancer, stroke, and chronic lower respiratory diseases (National Center for Health Statistics, 2012) (Figure 10.4).

More recently, the gap in life expectancy between African Americans has declined again, in part due to the greater rate of drug (opioid) overdose deaths among whites, and in part due to the continued decline in deaths among African Americans due to homicides, cancer, and AIDS. In 2014, the gap in life expectancy between African Americans and whites reached an historic low of 3.4 years

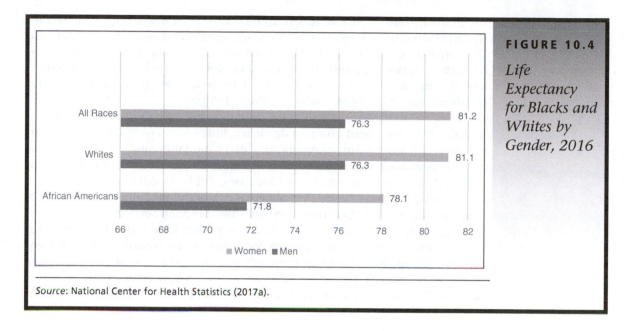

FIGURE 10.4

Life Expectancy for Blacks and Whites by Gender, 2016

Source: National Center for Health Statistics (2017a).

(75.6 years for African Americans and 79 years for whites) (National Center for Health Statistics, 2017a).

Life expectancy for poor African Americans who live in urban areas and inner cities is of even greater concern. A University of Michigan School of Public Health study found that premature death was "excessive" in all poverty-ridden areas, but reached alarming proportions in inner cities. For example, in the 1990s, *two-thirds* of young males living in Harlem were likely to die prematurely (Herbert, 1996). An often-cited study by McCord and Freeman (1990) found similar findings. This study compared living in Bangladesh, one of the world's poorest countries, to living in Harlem, and found that poor inner-city African Americans living in Harlem had less chance of surviving to age 65 than people living in Bangladesh. Little has changed since the 1990s; African American men have the shortest life expectancy (71.8 years in 2015; see Figure 10.4): "The black man's life expectancy, in fact, is closer to that of people living in West Africa than it is to the average white American" (Brown, 2006).

Infant Mortality

Since the early 1980s, infant mortality in the U.S. general population has declined substantially from about 11 to about 6 deaths per 1000 live births in 2015 (National Center for Health Statistics, 2017b). During this period, the infant mortality rate among African Americans also declined. However, the gap between infant mortality rates for African Americans and whites is wider than the gap for infant mortality rates for whites and any other racial or ethnic group; in fact, the mortality rate for African American infants in 2014 was 2.2 times the rate for white infants (Figure 10.5). In the 1990s, Schoendorf and associates (1992) found that premature births and low-birth-weight babies among women increased the risk for infant mortality. In addition, sudden infant death syndrome (SIDS) among African Americans was also about twice the rate found among whites (*Healthy People 2000*, 1998; Associated Press, 1999).

More recent data analysis from the Centers for Disease Control bears this out. In 2007, pre-term-related causes of death accounted for most of the higher infant mortality risk among African Americans. Infant mortality rates for SIDS, congenital malformations, and unintentional injuries were also substantially higher for African Americans (Macdorman and Mathews, 2011). In 2014, low birth weight was the leading cause of death, but maternal complications and SIDS also contributed significantly (U.S. Department of Health and Human Services, 2017a).

The disparity in infant mortality has been studied for decades. Initially, it was believed that this disparity affected only poor, low-income women, particularly teenage girls, who are indeed disproportionately affected, and who were viewed as more careless in their sexual behavior, uneducated, and lacking good health care. However, since 1987, Arline Geronimus has studied the link between stress and black infant

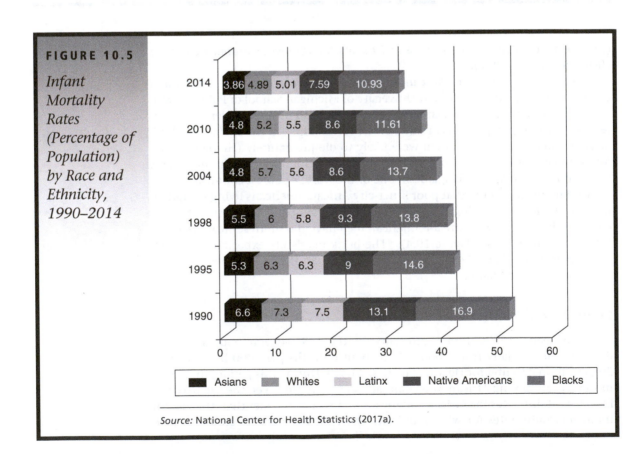

FIGURE 10.5

Infant Mortality Rates (Percentage of Population) by Race and Ethnicity, 1990–2014

2014: 3.86 | 4.89 | 5.01 | 7.59 | 10.93
2010: 4.8 | 5.2 | 5.5 | 8.6 | 11.61
2004: 4.8 | 5.7 | 5.6 | 8.6 | 13.7
1998: 5.5 | 6 | 5.8 | 9.3 | 13.8
1995: 5.3 | 6.3 | 6.3 | 9 | 14.6
1990: 6.6 | 7.3 | 7.5 | 13.1 | 16.9

Legend: Asians | Whites | Latinx | Native Americans | Blacks

Source: National Center for Health Statistics (2017a).

mortality rates and developed the theory of "weathering." Weathering refers to a toxic bodily stress that results from the repeated experience of discrimination. Her studies show that, even when controlling for income and education, persistent racial differences in health for African American women are likely due to the stress of discrimination and the double risk of gender and racial discrimination (Villarosa, 2018; Geronimus et al., 2006). Other researchers have disproved the theory that poverty on its own explains the disparity in infant mortality (David and Collins, 1997).

HIV/AIDS

The number of deaths from HIV/AIDS has declined dramatically in the U.S. as a result of new treatments and advances in AIDS research and medicine. However, African Americans still account for more AIDS-related deaths than any other racial or ethnic group in the U.S. and constitute a growing proportion of persons living with HIV. In the early 1990s, AIDS affected African Americans at more than twice the rate of whites. Cases of *heterosexual* AIDS were eight times higher, and African American women aged 16–21 were *15 times* as likely as white women to get HIV. As a result, African American infants were at a much higher risk for developing AIDS than white infants (Kaiser Family Foundation, 2000a).

AIDS remains a serious health crisis in the African American community. In 2001, HIV was the *leading* cause of death for African American women aged 24 to 34, and African Americans over the age of 13 were almost *ten 10 times* as likely as whites and *three 3 times* as likely as Latinx to have AIDS. In 2005, African Americans represented 13 percent of the nation's population, but accounted for *50 percent* of the new HIV/AIDS cases (Kaiser Family Foundation, 2000a; National Center for Health Statistics, 2008). Moreover, although the rate of HIV/AIDS cases for whites steadily declined from 1990 to 2005, the rate for African Americans steadily *increased*.

Today, African Americans still bear the largest health burden with HIV/AIDS. Although:

> African Americans represent 13 percent of the U.S. population, they account for 44 percent of HIV infection cases in 2016. African American males have 8.6 times the AIDS rate as white males. African American females have 18.6 times the AIDS rate as white females. African American men are almost 6 times as likely to die from HIV/AIDS as non-Hispanic white men. African American women are almost 18 times as likely to die from HIV/AIDS as non-Hispanic white women. In 2016, African Americans were 8.4 times more likely to be diagnosed with HIV infection, as compared to the white population.
>
> (U.S. Department of Health and Human Services, 2018a, p. 1)

Although AIDS is no longer ranked as one of the leading causes of death for African Americans or any racial or ethnic group in the U.S. (it was the ninth leading cause in 2010 for African Americans), the Centers for Disease Control and Prevention (CDC) still identifies AIDS as a "significant" cause of death among African Americans (Figures 10.6 and 10.7). Racial disparity in HIV/AIDS for African Americans is driven by several factors. The higher proportion of people living with HIV in many African

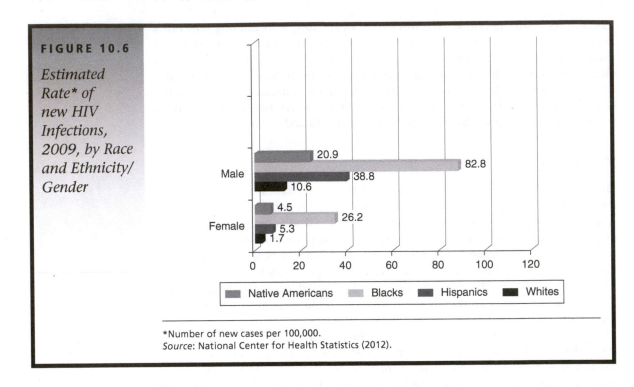

FIGURE 10.6

Estimated Rate* of new HIV Infections, 2009, by Race and Ethnicity/ Gender

*Number of new cases per 100,000.
Source: National Center for Health Statistics (2012).

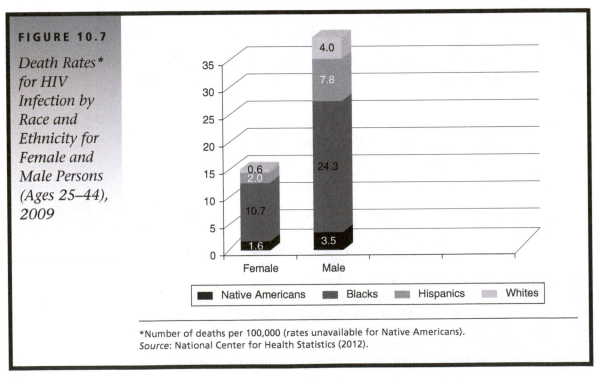

FIGURE 10.7

Death Rates* for HIV Infection by Race and Ethnicity for Female and Male Persons (Ages 25–44), 2009

*Number of deaths per 100,000 (rates unavailable for Native Americans).
Source: National Center for Health Statistics (2012).

American (and Latinx) communities increases the risk of infection with every sexual encounter. Stigma and homophobia prevent some individuals from seeking HIV prevention. Poverty and lack of insurance limit access to health care including testing and treatment. High rates of incarceration among African American men can lead to concurrent sexual relationships that fuel the spread of HIV (Centers for Disease Control and Prevention, 2016).

The CDC does cautiously report early signs of an encouraging decrease in new HIV infections among African American women (based on a 21 percent decrease between 2008 and 2010) (Centers for Disease Control and Prevention, 2016). AIDS among women is especially troubling because of the risk of neonatal transmission. Although the use of increased testing for HIV among pregnant women and of zidovudine (AZT) by infected pregnant women and their newborn infants has decreased the incidence of pediatric AIDS, the majority of perinatal infections still occur among African Americans (Centers for Disease Control and Prevention, 2018).

The Office of HIV/AIDS Policy at the U.S. Department of Health and Human Services identified several contributing risk factors. First, young people are more predisposed to engage in high-risk drug behavior, as discussed in the section that follows on children and adolescents, and African American youth are even more vulnerable to these risks. Second, HIV itself is more widespread in the African American and Hispanic populations, which increases the risk of exposure. Sexual contact is the main risk factor for both black women and men. Even though African Americans are tested more often than whites, they are less likely to know that they carry HIV. A 2005 study showed that 67 percent of those who tested positive were unaware of their infection (Centers for Disease Control and Prevention, 2005a). Third, the perceived stigma associated with the disease prevents some African Americans from seeking treatment (Brooks, 1999). The survival rate after diagnosis of AIDS is lower for African Americans than for other racial/ethnic groups (Centers for Disease Control and Prevention, 2008b).

African American men who have sex with men are more affected by HIV/AIDS than any other group (Centers for Disease Control and Prevention, 2018). They may be at greatest risk for lack of prevention. A study conducted by the CDC from 1998 through 2000, among young (aged 23–29) *gay* African American males living in six major cities, found that the rate of infection was *increasing*. The CDC described the findings as "alarming," because the number of new cases of AIDS had been declining during this period. The stigma attached to homosexuality and the reluctance of gay African American men to identify themselves as gay may keep test rates low (Altman, 2001). In 2009, black men who had sex with men represented about 73 percent of new infections among all black men. In response to this concern, the CDC funded a campaign in 2011 to provide effective HIV prevention services over five years to young men of color who have sex with men and young transgender persons of color and their partners, regardless of age, gender, and race/ethnicity (Centers for Disease Control and Prevention, 2012). The CDC has continued to add funding opportunities to help health departments reduce HIV infections and improve medical care for this population.

The lack of access to health care (discussed in Chapter 9) compounds the problem of HIV/AIDS. African Americans are less likely to obtain drug therapy and treatment, and many who need care for HIV have not gotten any care (Brooks, 1999). As a result, African Americans are increasingly more likely to be living with the disease of AIDS than other racial and ethnic groups. In 2014, 56 percent of all individuals living with HIV/AIDS in the U.S. were African American gay and bisexual men (Centers for Disease Control and Prevention, 2018).

Cancer and Cardiovascular Disease

Cardiovascular diseases and cancer are leading causes of death in the U.S. and all other industrialized nations. However, in the U.S. heart disease has declined significantly since 1950, and cancer rates have declined since the early 1990s (Eheman et al., 2012). Lung cancer is by far the leading death-related cancer and the most common worldwide. From a public health perspective, this is disturbing because lung cancer is directly linked to smoking, which is a social behavior that can be altered through health promotion and education. Smoking is also a risk factor for cardiovascular disease and many other diseases and health problems. Public health measures to control and reduce the incidence of cancer have been successful. The *Annual Report to the Nation of the Status of Cancer, 1975–2014* (Jemal et al., 2017) shows that death rates from all cancers continue to drop among women, men, and children. Declines in death rates are due to overall improvements in prevention, early detection, and treatment, as well as reduced tobacco use.

Cancer. African Americans are at greater risk of cancer than any other racial or ethnic group. Lung cancer is of particular concern among African American males, who have a mortality rate that is twice the rate for the general population, and overall rates of cancer that are 15 percent higher than those of white men (Eheman et al., 2012). Since 1990, the mortality rate for African Americans has declined significantly, and cigarette-smoking habits are about the same among African American adults as among white adults. However, smoking among African American *teens* has increased sharply in recent years and seems to have had a negative long-term effect on the rate of lung disease.

Breast and prostate cancer are two additional cancer risks for African Americans. African American males are 60 percent more likely to get prostate cancer than white males. More importantly, they are more than twice as likely to die from this disease as whites (U.S. Department of Health and Human Services, 2012a). Similarly, although the rate of newly diagnosed cases of breast cancer is lower than the rate for white women, African American women are still more likely to die from breast cancer than any other racial/ethnic group (Agency for Health Care Policy and Research, 1999; Meadows, 2000; U.S. Department of Health and Human Services, 2012a). In 2015, death rates from breast cancer were higher among African American women (29.5 per 100,000) than any other racial or ethnic group (Figure 10.8). In the past decade, death rates from breast cancer have declined both in the general population and among African American women. However, the decline has not been as significant as it has been for white women; in fact, the decline for white women since 1990 is far greater than the rate of decline experienced by African American women (Figure 10.8).

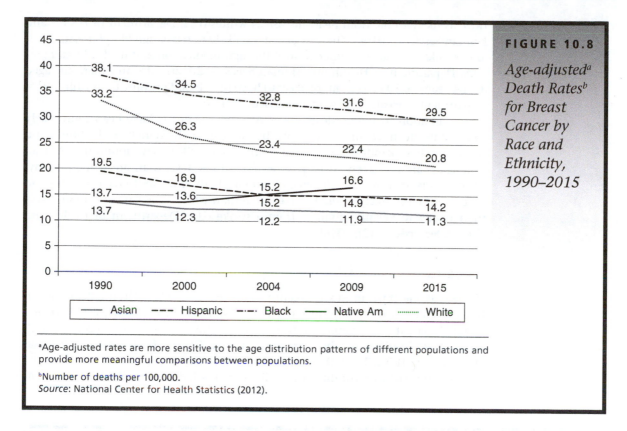

FIGURE 10.8

Age-adjusted[a] Death Rates[b] for Breast Cancer by Race and Ethnicity, 1990–2015

[a]Age-adjusted rates are more sensitive to the age distribution patterns of different populations and provide more meaningful comparisons between populations.

[b]Number of deaths per 100,000.

Source: National Center for Health Statistics (2012).

Before the mid-1990s, lower rates of breast cancer screening among African American women over the age of 50 played a significant role in this health disparity. Since then, however, women of all races have been equally likely to receive mammograms (Centers for Disease Control and Prevention, 2012). This dramatic change in preventive care could have a positive effect on future breast cancer rates for African American women. However, other risks, such as lack of access to care and lack of insurance, may impede progress in the decline of breast cancer rates and mortality related to this disease. More attention may be needed to help overcome barriers to mammogram screenings for African American women (Meadows, 2000).

Cardiovascular Disease. Cardiovascular disease refers to a group of heart-related diseases, including coronary heart disease (blocked arteries), cerebrovascular disease (stroke), and hypertension (high blood pressure). The mortality rate for cardiovascular disease has declined dramatically for both the general population and African Americans since 1950 (National Center for Health Statistics, 2000). As shown in Figure 10.9, all racial and ethnic groups in the U.S., particularly whites and African Americans, are still at significant risk of mortality due to heart disease. However, when age-adjusted rates are examined (2010), African Americans are 30 percent more likely than whites to die from heart disease (U.S. Department of Health and Human Services, 2012f). Of particular concern, African Americans aged 18–49 are *twice* as likely to die from heart disease as whites (U.S. Department of Health and Human Services, 2016a). They are also more likely to have high blood pressure, but are less likely to have it under control through medication and medical treatment (U.S. Department of Health and Human Services, 2012f). African Americans aged 35–64 years are 50 percent more likely to have high blood pressure than whites (U.S. Department of Health and Human Services, 2016a).

In addition to higher death rates, African Americans have been more likely than whites to have an initial stroke before age 65 (Broderick et al., 1998), and several studies (Schulman et al., 1999; Chen et al., 2001) have found that African Americans are less likely to be referred for cardiac tests than are whites. Today, African Americans remain 50 percent more likely than whites to have a stroke and 60 percent more likely to die from a stroke than whites; they are also more likely than whites to become disabled from a stroke (U.S. Department of Health and Human Services, 2012f, 2016b).

Diabetes

Diabetes is one of the most serious chronic diseases in the U.S. The incidence of diabetes has increased steadily since the 1950s (National Center for Health Statistics, 2000). Today, it remains the seventh leading cause of death and affects 30.3 million people, 7 million of whom are undiagnosed (Centers for Disease Control and Prevention, 2017b). The CDC also estimates that about one of every 3 adults (84 million adults) has a condition described as pre-diabetes in which blood sugar

FIGURE 10.9

Percentages of All Deaths Caused by Heart Disease by Racial and Ethnic Group, 2008

RACIAL OR ETHNIC GROUP	PERCENTAGE OF DEATHS
African Americans	24.5
American Indians or Alaska Natives	18.0
Asians or Pacific Islanders	23.2
Hispanics	20.8
Whites	25.1
All	25.0

Source: National Center for Health Statistics (2012).

levels are higher than normal, although not sufficiently high to be diagnosed as diabetes (a new diagnostic test was introduced in 2011, which dramatically increased the estimate from previous years); this condition raises a person's risk of type 2 diabetes, heart disease, and stroke.

Diabetes is a condition that results from the body's insufficient or impaired production of insulin, which leads to increased glucose (from digested food) in the bloodstream. If not carefully managed, high levels of blood glucose (sugar) can damage the body's vital organs. Diabetes is related to both genetic factors and diets that are high in fats. Type 1, or insulin-dependent diabetes mellitus, has been called juvenile diabetes because it usually affects children and adolescents. Type 2, or non-insulin-dependent diabetes, which is linked to obesity and physical inactivity, affects 90–95 percent of adults (usually over the age of 40) diagnosed with diabetes. However, type 2 is now being diagnosed with greater frequency among children (Centers for Disease Control and Prevention, 2001).

Diabetes is a major risk factor for heart disease and stroke, which can lead to many complications, including blindness, kidney disease (end-stage renal disease), and lower limb amputations. African Americans are almost twice as likely as whites to have diagnosed diabetes; diabetes is more prevalent among African American women and older adults. African Americans are at greater risk of death from diabetes-induced kidney disease than whites (Figure 10.10); complications from diabetes increase the

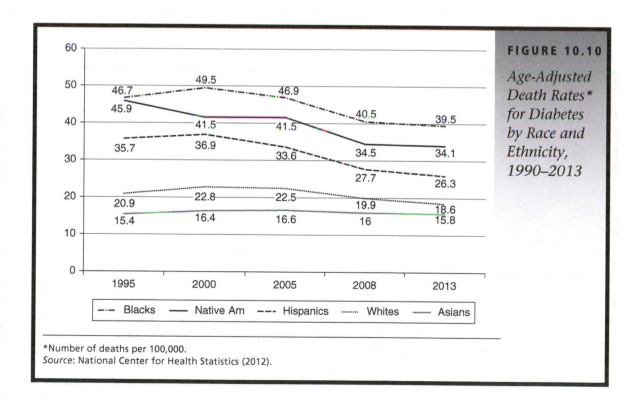

FIGURE 10.10

Age-Adjusted Death Rates* for Diabetes by Race and Ethnicity, 1990–2013

*Number of deaths per 100,000.
Source: National Center for Health Statistics (2012).

risk of other related health problems for this group, including end-stage renal disease. In 1999, with the rate of diabetes triple the number it was 30 years earlier, Surgeon General David Satcher first brought attention to this problem, calling it a devastating "epidemic" in the African American community (West, 1999).

Unintentional Injuries: Neighborhood Violence

For many years, African Americans, particularly young males, have been at greater risk of mortality and morbidity related to neighborhood violence (Figure 10.11) than any other racial or ethnic group. In the early 1990s:

> more teenage boys die[d] from gunshots than from all natural causes combined, and a black male teenager [was] 11 times more likely to be murdered with a gun than a white counterpart. . . . In 1988, a black male age 15 to 19 was nearly three times more likely to die from a bullet than a disease.
>
> (Taylor, 1991, p. A10)

In 1998, the homicide victimization rate for African American males aged 15–34 was *eight* times the rate for young white males and more than twice the rate for young Latinos. African American youth living in urban, low-income communities continue to be at greater risk for exposure to community violence than any other population in the U.S. (Stein et al., 2003; Garbarino et al., 2004; Aisenberg and Herrenkohl, 2008; Centers for Disease Control and Prevention, 2017c).

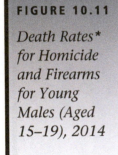

FIGURE 10.11

Death Rates* for Homicide and Firearms for Young Males (Aged 15–19), 2014

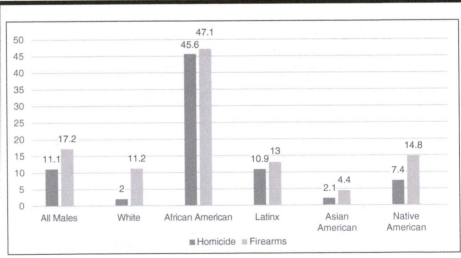

*Number of deaths per 100,000.
Source: Child Trends Databank (2015).

Although the rate of violent crime and victimization, including assault, rape, robbery, and homicide, among youth generally declined from the mid-1990s to 2002, the rate of drinking and drug use among adolescents and young adults increased during this period (National Center for Health Statistics, 2008). Drugs are often linked with gang violence and street homicide. As noted by Regulus (1995), gangs are more violent, in part due to increased drug use among gang members, and older adolescents remain connected to gangs as a source of "illicit employment in gang-controlled drug and organized criminal activities" (Regulus, 1995, p. 1045).

Promisingly, alcohol and drug use, including opioids, among all youth decreased between 2010 and 2017. However, homicide is the number one cause of death for African American youth (National Center for Health Statistics, 2017b). It seems that greater attention than ever has been given to the risk of violence for African American males, both adolescent and adult, particularly from gun violence, including discriminatory practices by law enforcement. The latter has been fueled by eyewitness reports through the use of social media (Facebook, Instagram, and others), which has increased awareness and put a spotlight on these acts of violence and excessive police force. In 2017, African Americans were disproportionately killed by police officers, and numerous concerns were raised about racial profiling (D'Onofrio, 2018). Overall, in 2015:

> Compared to the national average, the homicide rate was 54% lower for whites, 14% lower for Hispanics, and **267% higher for blacks**. Put another way, the homicide rate among African–Americans is nearly quadruple that of the national average.
>
> (Berezow, 2017a, p. 1)

LATINX (HISPANICS)

Life Expectancy and Infant Mortality

Life expectancy among Latinx in the U.S. has been something of a puzzle. Mortality rates for Hispanics and whites were estimated to be approximately the same until about the past 20 years, when Hispanic adults were found to have *lower* mortality rates than non-Hispanic whites. A 2010 study conducted by the Centers for Disease Control and Prevention found that Latinx lived on average two years longer than non-Hispanic whites and eight years longer than African Americans (Lamare, 2012). The so-called "Hispanic paradox" refers to the seemingly insignificant impact of socioeconomic factors (poverty, lowest educational attainment, greater lack of health insurance) on relative longevity.

There have been several explanations for this "paradox." A study funded by the National Institute on Aging (Palloni, 2004) found that the best explanation for this anomaly, given the socioeconomic status and related health risks of this group, might be return migration, especially among older male Mexican Americans. Older Mexican-born Latinx return to Mexico when ill, thus inflating the life expectancy rates for this population (Markides and Eschbach, 2005). Olshansky et al. (2013) also reported that, although some Hispanics return to their country of origin to die, others who emigrate from countries in Latin America tend to be healthier and more highly educated than those in their country of origin.

Causes of death also tend to be different for Latinx than for non-Hispanic whites (U.S. General Accounting Office, 1992; Sorlie et al., 1993; Vega and Amaro, 1994). Latinx have a lower rate of death from cardiovascular disease (see Figure 10.9) and breast cancer (see Figure 10.8) than non-Hispanic whites, but they have a higher rate of death from homicide (Figure 10.12), AIDS (see Figures 10.7 and 10.8), perinatal conditions, diabetes (see Figure 10.10), and cirrhosis and other liver diseases. The infant mortality rate is essentially the same as the white infant mortality rate (see Figure 10.5). However, variation exists within the Hispanic population. The highest rate is found among people of Puerto Rican descent; in 2014, the infant mortality rate was 6.68 deaths per 100,000 live births compared with 3.95 deaths among Cuban Americans (Figure 10.12).

More recent studies (Horvath et al., 2016) propose a completely different explanation; namely, that Latinx age at a slower rate than other groups. The UCLA School of Public Health study suggests that genetic or environmental factors that are linked to ethnicity may impact the aging process and longevity. The UCLA team used epigenetics—the study of changes in DNA molecules that impact genes—and developed an "epigenetic clock" to track an epigenetic shift in the genome that is

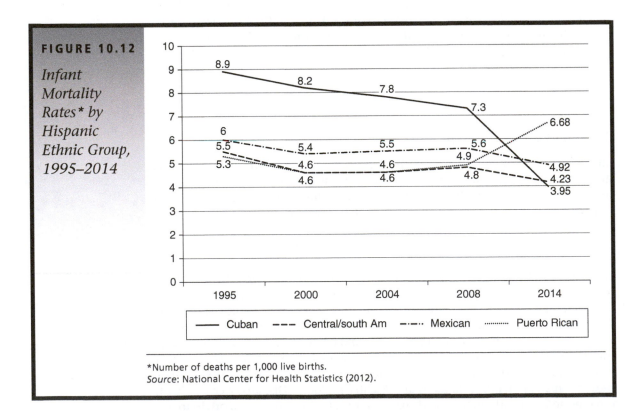

FIGURE 10.12

Infant Mortality Rates* by Hispanic Ethnic Group, 1995–2014

*Number of deaths per 1,000 live births.
Source: National Center for Health Statistics (2012).

linked to aging. The researchers argue that their findings may help us understand why lower than expected mortality rates exist among Hispanics, older African Americans, and women.

Other studies continue to argue that migration patterns explain the "paradox". Diaz et al. (2016) found that less healthy immigrants with limited access to health care in the U.S. were more likely to return voluntarily to Mexico than other immigrants. Rosmena et al. (2017) found that Mexican and Dominican immigrants living in the U.S. were less likely to smoke than their peers in their countries of origin, or non-Hispanic whites. Beltrán-Sánchez et al. (2016) found that Mexican-born immigrants in the U.S. were healthier than their nonmigrant peers and non-Hispanic whites on some biomarkers but not on others.

Diabetes

Almost 14 percent of all Mexican Americans and 12 percent of all Puerto Rican Americans have diabetes (Centers for Disease Control and Prevention, 2017b). The American Diabetes Association (2005) estimates that 52.5% of Latinas and 45.4% of Latinos will have type 1 or type 2 diabetes in their lifetimes (McQuillan, 2014). Overall, Latinx are 1.4 times as likely as non-Hispanic whites to die from diabetes (see Figure 10.10). However, the mortality rate for Latinx is not as high as the rate found among Native Americans and African Americans (Oxendine, 1999; West, 1999) (see Figure 10.10). Latinx are at greater risk for complications from diabetes than whites, and need information and education about the risks of diabetes and ways to help prevent its onset. The rate of early diagnosis needs improvement, and Latinx need assistance with disease management. In some cases, language barriers are an additional concern. The CDC and the American Diabetes Council have made a concerted effort to publish Spanish-language publications and resources, such as the National Diabetes Education Program Online Resource Center.

HIV/AIDS

As noted by the Kaiser Family Foundation (2012), "as the largest and fastest growing ethnic minority group in the U.S., addressing HIV/AIDS in the Latino community takes on increased importance in efforts to improve the nation's health." Although Latinx are not as at risk of contracting AIDS as African Americans, they are far more vulnerable to infection and the disease of AIDS than non-Hispanic whites (see Figures 10.7 and 10.8). Hispanic men are twice as likely as white men to die of AIDS; Latinas are three times more likely to die of AIDS than white women (U.S. Department of Health and Human Services, 2018b). In 2016, Hispanics represented almost 18 percent of the U.S. population, but they accounted for 26 percent of all new cases (Figure 10.13). Hispanic groups have different behavioral risk factors. Puerto Rican Americans have been at greater risk due to intravenous drug use, whereas Mexican Americans have been at greater risk as a result of sexual contact (Centers for Disease Control and Prevention, 2004, 2005b, 2011a).

FIGURE 10.13

New HIV Cases by Race/Ethnicity Compared with U.S. Population, 2016

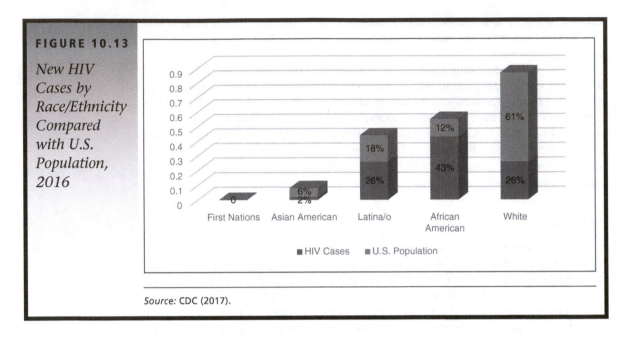

Source: CDC (2017).

The greatest disparity exists for Hispanic women. In 2016, Hispanic males over the age of 13 were *three times* as likely as non-Hispanic white males to have AIDS and more likely to have contracted the disease through intravenous drug use. Hispanic females, however, are even more vulnerable. In 2016, Latinas over the age of 13 were *four times* more likely than non-Hispanic white women to have AIDS (U.S. Department of Health and Human Services, 2018b). The CDC released *Revised Recommendations for HIV Testing of Adults, Adolescents, and Pregnant Women in Health-care Settings* in 2006. These advise routine HIV screening for adults, adolescents, and pregnant women in health care settings in the U.S.

Latinas, like African American women, are disproportionately poor and face discrimination based on both race and gender. All women of color are at greater risk than white women for poor health for socioeconomic reasons. However, studies suggest that Latinas may also be at risk of contracting AIDS for sociocultural and political reasons. Latinas, among both the less acculturated and more acculturated, particularly Puerto Ricans, are more likely than white women to be infected through heterosexual contact (Loue, 2006; Centers for Disease Control and Prevention, 2011b). One concern is that Latinas who hold traditional cultural values about gender roles and religious attitudes toward sexual practices may be at greater risk than other women. An early study conducted in 1993 by the Center for AIDS Prevention Studies at the University of California (Marin and Gomes, 1998) found that protection against infectious infections (by using condoms) occurred less frequently among those Latinx who held traditional views toward sexual intimacy. More recent studies (Suarez-el-Adam et al., 2000; Loue, 2006) show that Latinas may be hesitant to suggest condom use out of fear of abuse or loss of financial support.

In addition, the opposition of the Catholic Church to contraception seemed to function as a cultural reinforcement of these practices.

Another study of migrant workers, discussed by Horwitz (1998), found that the rate of AIDS among seasonal migrant workers was as much as ten times greater than the rate found in the general population. Migrant Latinas surveyed by the study said they overlooked their partners' sexual relationships because of the transient nature of their work. They were afraid to cause trouble for themselves or their spouses or partners, or risk losing their jobs, by complaining about their partners' and coworkers' behavior. A related concern is some Latinas "may avoid seeking testing, counseling, or treatment if infected out of fear of discrimination, stigmatization or immigration status" (Centers for Disease Control and Prevention, 2011a, p. 2).

Until more research is done it is difficult to discern the full significance of these studies. More studies are needed on disparities in health between women of color and white women, and even more on disparities in HIV/AIDS among women. It is a significant problem with serious health consequences for women, children, and families. Prevention strategies that are culturally appropriate for Latinx still need greater attention.

ASIAN AMERICANS AND PACIFIC ISLANDERS

Life Expectancy

Overall, Asian Americans are among the healthiest groups in the U.S. Life expectancy for Asian Americans (85.8 years in 2010) is greater than for any other racial or ethnic group. However, life expectancy varies significantly within this population. Japanese Americans have the highest life expectancy (82.8 years in 2000), whereas Native Hawaiians have the lowest life expectancy (74.3 years in 2000) (Braun et al., 2010; U.S. Department of Health and Human Services, 2012c). Fewer data is available for newer immigrant groups from south-east Asia, but other socioeconomic factors indicate that life expectancy may be lower (*Healthy People 2000*, 1997).

Cancer and Cardiovascular Disease

Asian Americans have lower rates of cancer and cardiovascular disease than whites but disparities exist within the population. Cancer and heart disease play a significant role in the lifespan of Native Hawaiians. According to Lin-Fu (1993), Native Hawaiians have the highest rates of cancer among Asian Americans and Pacific Islanders. Native Hawaiians also have higher rates of death from heart disease than any group in the U.S. (Chen, 1993). More recent data from the Office on Minority Health (U.S. Department of Health and Human Services, 2012d) indicates that Native Hawaiians/Pacific Islanders are 30 percent more likely than non-Hispanic whites to be diagnosed with cancer.

For other Asian–American groups, cancer is less of a concern overall than it is for non-Hispanic whites; yet, there is still greater concern for some groups within the Asian population for some types of cancer, such as stomach cancer. For example, Asian/Pacific Islander men are much less likely to have prostate cancer than white men, but are twice as likely to have stomach cancer and twice as likely to die as a result of it. Asian/Pacific Islander women are less likely to have breast cancer than white women, but are almost three times as likely to have stomach cancer and nearly three times as likely to die as a consequence of the disease (U.S. Department of Health and Human Services, 2012d). Cervical cancer among Asian American women has also been of concern (Chen, 1993; *Healthy People 2000*, 1997); in 2003, Asian American women over the age of 18 were least likely to have had a Pap test compared with women in other racial and ethnic groups (*Healthy People 2000*, 1997).

Diabetes

The Office of Minority Health (U.S. Department of Health and Human Services, 2016b) reports that Asian Americans are less likely to die from diabetes than whites, but that diabetes is 10 percent more likely to be diagnosed among Asian Americans than non-Hispanic whites. However, once again, disparities exist within the population. Native Hawaiians are more than three times as likely as whites to be diagnosed with diabetes (Koh, 2013); Native Hawaiians are nearly six times as likely as white Hawaiians to die from diabetes (U.S. Department of Health and Human Services, 2012e). Regional data and studies dating back to the 1990s (1988–95) indicate that Native Hawaiians are twice as likely as white Hawaiians to have diabetes (Oxendine, 1999). The Papa Ola Lokahi Native Hawaiian health care system has worked throughout the Pacific islands to help communities address diabetes (Oxendine, 2000). One ongoing concern has been nutrition and obesity and their impact on diabetes. More than a third of all U.S. citizens are obese; Native Hawaiians fit this profile and are the most obese of all ethnic groups in Hawaii (Pua'ala'okalani, 2000). In 2010, Native Hawaiians/Pacific Islanders were 70 percent more likely to be obese than non-Hispanic whites (U.S. Department of Health and Human Services, 2012h).

NATIVE AMERICANS

Chronic Diseases and Life Expectancy

> The Pine Ridge reservation with a population of about 250,000 spread over more than 3,100 square miles, is the United States' own third world. . . . The second largest reservation . . . has institutionalized squalor, with rampant alcoholism, diabetes, suicide and a male life expectancy rate of 56.5 years.
>
> (Kilborn, 1999, p. 1)

Conditions such as those found on the Pine Ridge reservation have often been cited to describe the extreme disparity in health experienced by Native Americans. An Indian Health Service (IHS, 1998) study of Native Americans in the IHS service area (or about 60 percent of the entire Native American population) found that age-adjusted death rates (between 1992 and 1994) were much higher than among the general population for a number of diseases and health problems. More recently, the IHS reported similar findings; Native Americans die from chronic diseases at significantly higher rates than the general population: Tuberculosis (600 percent higher), alcoholism (510 percent higher), and suicide (72 percent higher). Native Americans also experience the highest rates of youth suicide and type 2 diabetes (U.S. Senate, 2010).

Infant mortality statistics are also of concern but offer a somewhat more positive perspective. In each decade since 1950, infant mortality has declined dramatically (National Center for Health Statistics, 2000). In 2014, the infant mortality rate was significantly lower than the rate for African Americans; however, it was 1.6 times higher than the rate for non-Hispanic whites (see Figure 10.5). Native American babies are twice as likely to die from SIDS, 70 percent more likely to die from accidental deaths before the age of one year, and 2.5 times as likely to receive late or no prenatal care as white babies (U.S. Department of Health and Human Services, 2017b).

Alcoholism and Alcohol-related Health and Mental Health Problems

On March 21, 2005, at the high school on the Red Lake Indian reservation in Minnesota, a troubled American Indian teenager went on a shooting rampage, killing nine people before turning the gun on himself. Most of the news reports highlighted his past, including a history of depression and suicide attempts, and the daunting socioeconomic conditions in his reservation community. Reporters mentioned high rates of poverty, alcoholism, unemployment, and violence among young people as possible factors in the tragedy.

(Roubideaux, 2005, p. 1881)

Although cancer and heart disease are the leading causes of death (National Center for Health Statistics, 2012) among Native Americans, a government study conducted in the early 1990s (U.S. General Accounting Office, 1993) showed that alcohol and substance abuse was the leading cause of death among Native Americans aged 15–44. The mortality rate for this group was about 6.5 times higher than for the general population. In addition, other leading causes of death, including accidents (Figure 10.14), suicide (Figure 10.15), and homicide (see Figure 10.12), were often related to substance abuse. In 2012:

Native Americans of the Pine Ridge Indian Reservation . . . filed a $500-million lawsuit against beer manufacturers for the devastation that alcohol has wreaked on their community for decades. The Oglala Sioux Tribe said the extraordinary sum they are asking for would be used to pay for health care, social services and child rehabilitation. As in many other Native American communities in the U.S. and Canada, alcohol abuse has destroyed the lives of many in the reservation. For example, one-fourth of the tribe's children suffer from fetal disorders related to their parents' alcoholism.

(Ghosh, 2012, p. 1)

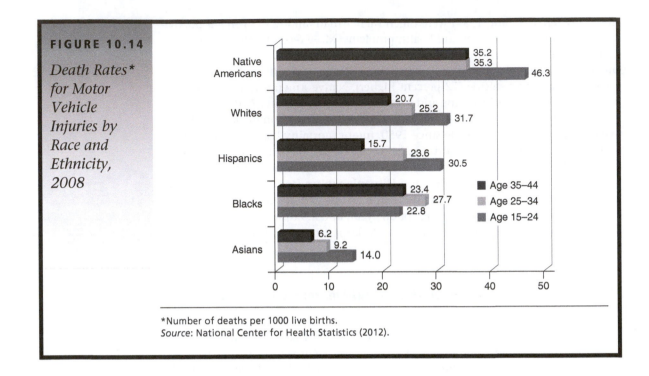

FIGURE 10.14

Death Rates* for Motor Vehicle Injuries by Race and Ethnicity, 2008

Native Americans: 35.2 (Age 35–44), 35.3 (Age 25–34), 46.3 (Age 15–24)
Whites: 20.7 (Age 35–44), 25.2 (Age 25–34), 31.7 (Age 15–24)
Hispanics: 15.7 (Age 35–44), 23.6 (Age 25–34), 30.5 (Age 15–24)
Blacks: 23.4 (Age 35–44), 27.7 (Age 25–34), 22.8 (Age 15–24)
Asians: 6.2 (Age 35–44), 9.2 (Age 25–34), 14.0 (Age 15–24)

Legend: ■ Age 35–44 ■ Age 25–34 ■ Age 15–24

*Number of deaths per 1000 live births.
Source: National Center for Health Statistics (2012).

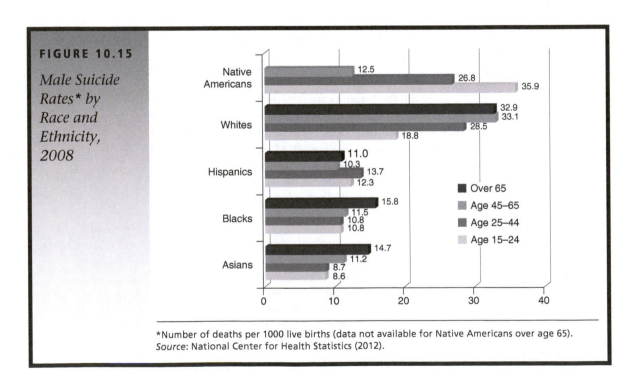

FIGURE 10.15

Male Suicide Rates* by Race and Ethnicity, 2008

Native Americans: 12.5 (Age 45–65), 26.8 (Age 25–44), 35.9 (Age 15–24)
Whites: 32.9 (Over 65), 33.1 (Age 45–65), 28.5 (Age 25–44), 18.8 (Age 15–24)
Hispanics: 11.0 (Over 65), 10.3 (Age 45–65), 13.7 (Age 25–44), 12.3 (Age 15–24)
Blacks: 15.8 (Over 65), 11.5 (Age 45–65), 10.8 (Age 25–44), 10.8 (Age 15–24)
Asians: 14.7 (Over 65), 11.2 (Age 45–65), 8.7 (Age 25–44), 8.6 (Age 15–24)

Legend: ■ Over 65 ■ Age 45–65 ■ Age 25–44 ■ Age 15–24

*Number of deaths per 1000 live births (data not available for Native Americans over age 65).
Source: National Center for Health Statistics (2012).

With alcohol illegal on the reservation, the nearby small town of Whiteclay, Nebraska, sells massive amounts of alcohol to the Oglala Sioux.

Early studies from the IHS found that 75 percent of accidents and 80 percent of suicides among young adults (aged 15–24) were alcohol related. Congress passed the Indian Alcohol and Substance Abuse Prevention and Treatment Act (PL 99–570) in 1986 to address the severity of this problem. In 1988, the National Center for Health Statistics reported that the suicide rate was 1.3 times higher among Native Americans than among the general population (U.S. General Accounting Office, 1993). Native American teenagers were four times as likely to commit suicide as white teenagers (Brasher, 1992), whereas an earlier study (Snipp, 1986) found that Native Americans were twice as likely to be murdered. A more recent CDC (2008a) study confirms that alcohol remains a major concern; nearly 12 percent of deaths among American Indians and Alaska Natives from 2001 to 2005 were alcohol related. In comparison, during the same time period, 3.3 percent of all deaths in the U.S. were related to alcohol.

Native Americans are also vulnerable to diabetes and cirrhosis of the liver. Although diabetes is related to a number of risk factors, including genetics and diet, both diseases are related to long-term patterns of heavy drinking that often begin at an early age. The mortality rate for Native Americans for diabetes in 2008 (34.5 per 100,000) was nearly 1.7 times the rate for whites (see Figure 10.10). Unlike other racial and ethnic groups, liver disease is one of the leading causes of death for Native Americans (Figure 10.16). The highest prevalence of diabetes in the world is found among the Pima Indians of Arizona (Kaiser Family Foundation, 2000b).

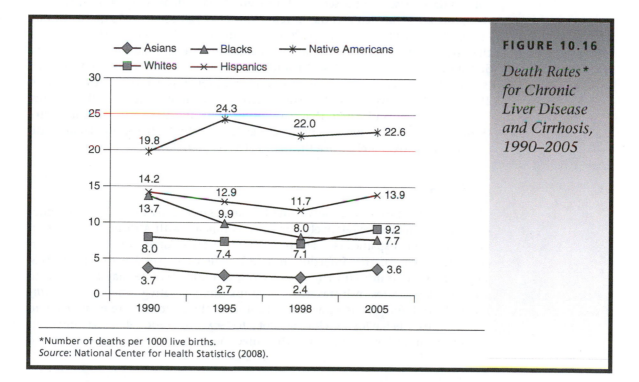

FIGURE 10.16

Death Rates* for Chronic Liver Disease and Cirrhosis, 1990–2005

*Number of deaths per 1000 live births.
Source: National Center for Health Statistics (2008).

The number of deaths from cirrhosis of the liver was also far greater (Figure 10.16); the rate for Native Americans was more than twice the rate for the general population (National Center for Health Statistics, 2008).

The relationship between alcohol use and domestic violence and physical abuse needs further study. Manson et al. (2005) found that both male and female Native American tribal members witness or experience physical attacks more often than their counterparts in the general population. However, they argue that it is unclear whether alcohol abuse increases the risk of aggressive behavior or whether traumatic life events lead to alcohol abuse.

A final word of caution is the need to avoid the stereotype of Native American alcoholism. Several studies have examined the myth of a predisposition to alcoholism and reasons for disproportionately high rates of alcohol-related deaths, which are rooted in sociocultural explanations rather than genetics (Dunbar-Ortiz and Gilio-Whitaker, 2016; Izadi, 2016).

Environmental Health Risks

Finally, Native Americans still suffer disproportionately from diseases such as tuberculosis, meningitis, and hepatitis, which are related to inadequate housing, poor sanitation, and lack of clean water. Rates of tuberculosis for the general population rose significantly between 1985 and 1992 due to the rise in HIV, which increases susceptibility to tuberculosis, and as a result of ineffective measures to control the disease in some sectors of the country. With federal public health initiatives, the rate of tuberculosis was lowered to 6.8 per 100,000 in 1998 (Kaiser Family Foundation, 2000b). However, in 2005, the rate was still 6.9 per 100,000, or more than five times the rate among non-Hispanic whites (National Center for Health Statistics, 2008). None the less, the problem of tuberculosis for Native Americans is related to extreme conditions of poverty and remains a problem today. From 1993 to 2002, Native Americans experienced the smallest decrease in the number of reported cases and a rate that was six times greater than the rate for whites (Schneider, 2005). Native Americans are at historically high risk for TB and still have rates approximately twice the national average (Iralu, 2016).

HIV/AIDS

The HIV death rates among Native American males recorded by the National Center for Health Statistics are relatively low when compared with African Americans, in particular, and Hispanics (see Figure 10.7), but Native Americans have a 30 percent higher rate of HIV infection and AIDS when compared with whites (U.S. Department of Health and Human Services, 2012g). This rate may be related to relatively lower rates of intravenous drug use among Native Americans (*Healthy People 2000*, 1995); at the same time, those who abuse alcohol are more likely to engage in risky behaviors, such as unprotected sex. The National Native American AIDS Prevention Center finds that HIV infection rates have been underestimated due to inadequate reporting and racial misclassification (Oropeza, 2001), and has worked on a national campaign to reduce the stigma of HIV/AIDS in Native American communities. However, little research has been done on drug use and HIV infection and some findings indicate that female Native Americans, in particular, may be engaging more in illicit drug behavior (Stevens et al., 2000). In 2016, Native American women were three times more likely to be diagnosed with AIDS than white women (U.S. Department of Health and Human Services, 2018c). Also, since 2005, the rate of HIV/AIDS among Native Americans has been consistently higher than the rate among non-Hispanic whites (National Center for Health Statistics, 2008, 2012).

High rates of sexually transmitted infections, which can increase the chance of contracting or spreading HIV, have been found among Native Americans. In 2005, Native Americans had the second highest rate of gonorrhea and *Chlamydia trachomatis* infection. Access to HIV testing is another concern. Native Americans may lack access to testing due to inadequate access to health care, particularly those who live in rural areas and rely on the IHS. They may also be less likely to seek testing because it is difficult to protect confidentiality in close-knit communities where members may encounter friends, relatives, or acquaintances as they seek testing (Centers for Disease Control and Prevention, 2008d).

Cancer

Native Americans generally have lower rates of cancer than the non-Hispanic white population (U.S. Department of Health and Human Services, 2012b). However, efforts to identify the rate of cancer among Native Americans may have underestimated the incidence due to misclassifications of race and underreporting on death certificates. Some evidence (Puukka et al., 2005) shows that cancer rates among Native Americans may be considerably higher than previously recognized. More research is necessary to improve our awareness and understanding of cancer in this population.

Evidence of disparities in certain types of cancer does exist, however. Native American men are twice as likely as non-Hispanic white men to have liver cancer, 1.6 times as likely to have stomach cancer, and over twice as likely to die from stomach cancer. Native American women are 2.8 times more likely to have and die from liver cancer than non-Hispanic white women; women are also 40 percent more likely to have kidney/renal pelvis cancer (U.S. Department of Health and Human Services, 2012b).

HIGHLIGHTS

- Public health scholars and officials rely on a body of concepts and methods that have been developed to measure the health of individuals and population groups, including: The study of population characteristics (morbidity, mortality, life expectancy); the distribution and extent of disease, or risk factors, in a population; the causes of disease, and the identification of potential interventions to prevent, control, and treat disease.

The biopsychosocial risk factors that most directly influence health outcomes are referred to as *determinants* of health.

- Disparities in socioeconomic conditions for people of color and non-Hispanic whites in the U.S.—including housing, food and nutrition, environment, and safety—are precursors to poor health and increase the risk of poor health outcomes for death for people of color. Disparities in health exist for African Americans, Latinx, Native Americans, Alaska Natives, and Native Hawaiians, in particular. Asian Americans are among the healthiest groups in the U.S., but are at greater risk of some health problems, such as stomach cancer. What we currently know about biological and genetic differences among people of color does not explain the health disparities experienced by these groups. These health disparities seem to be the result of a complex interaction of biopsychosocial factors.

- Studies show that racial and ethnic disparities in access to care clearly exist and play a role in health outcomes, but the reasons still need clarification. Further study is necessary to demonstrate to what extent racial and ethnic disparities result from structural barriers as opposed to cultural behaviors and attitudes. Understanding health disparities in the U.S. remains complex and driven by multiple factors, as discussed in this chapter.

- The chapter reviews findings to date on health disparities in federal health targets in the U.S., including infant health, heart disease, cancer, diabetes, and HIV/AIDS for people of color and Latinx.

WEBSITES TO OBTAIN UPDATED AND ADDITIONAL INFORMATION

Healthy People 2020:

www.healthypeople.gov/2020/about/default.aspx

U.S. Department of Health and Human Services, Office of Minority Health:

http://minorityhealth.hhs.gov

Kaiser Family Foundation:

www.kff.org/minorityhealth/index.cfm

REFERENCES

Aday, L. A. (1993). *At Risk in America: The Health and Health Care Needs of Vulnerable Populations in the United States*. San Francisco, CA: Jossey-Bass.

Agency for Health Care Policy and Research. (1999). *AHCPR Women's Health Highlights*, Fact Sheet, AHCPR Pub. No. 99-PO17. Retrieved from www.ahrq.gov/research/womenh1.htm

Agency for Health Care Research and Quality. (2003). *National Healthcare Disparities Report*, Pub. No. 04–0035. Retrieved from www.qualitytools.ahrq.gov/disparitiesreport/download_report.aspx

——. (2004). *National Healthcare Quality Report*, Pub. No. 05–0014. Rockville, MD: AHRQ.

Aisenberg, E. and Herrenkohl, T. (2008). Community Violence in Context: Risk and Resilience in Children and Families. *Journal of Interpersonal Violence*, 23(3), 296–315.

Altman, L. K. (2001, June 1). Swift Rise Seen in HIV Cases for Gay Blacks. *New York Times*, p. A1.

American Diabetes Association. (2005). *Diabetes Statistics for Latinos*. Retrieved from www.diabetes.org

Associated Press. (1992, January 8). Black–White Gap in U.S. Life Expectancies Widens, Decade-long Trend Continues. *Concord Monitor*, p. A7.

——. (1999, May 15). Report Details Racial Disparities in Health, Access to Care, Insurance. *Dallas Morning News*, p. A8.

Bach, P. B., Cramer, L. D., Warren, J. L., and Begg, C. B. (1999). Racial Difference in the Treatment of Early-stage Lung Cancer. *New England Journal of Medicine*, 341(16), 1198–1205.

Bakalar, N. (2008, April 22). Life Expectancy is Declining in Some Pockets of the Country. *New York Times Online*. Retrieved from www.nytimes.com/2008/04/22/health/research/22life.html

Barker, R. L. (Ed.) (1999). *The Social Work Dictionary*. Washington, DC: NASW Press.

Beltrán-Sánchez, H., Palloni, A., Rosmena, F., and Wong, R. (2016, October). SES Gradients Among Mexicans in the United States and in Mexico: A New Twist to the Hispanic Paradox? *Demography*. Retrieved from https://link.springer.com/article/10.1007/s13524-016-0508-4

Berezow, A. (2017a, August 10). African–American Homicide Rate Nearly Quadruple the National Average. American Council on Science and Health. Retrieved from www.acsh.org/news/2017/08/10/african-american-homicide-rate-nearly-quadruple-national-average-11680

Bhopal, R. (1998, June 27). Spectre of Racism in Health and Health Care: Lessons from History and the United States. *British Medical Journal*, 316(7149), 1970–1973.

Brasher, P. (1992, March 25). High Risk of Suicide Found in Native American Youths. *Austin American–Statesman*, p. A4.

Braun, K., Mokuau, N., and Browne, C. (2010). *Life Expectancy, Morbidity, and Health Practices of Native Hawaiian Elders: A Review of Hawaii's Surveillance Data*. Retrieved from http://manoa.hawaii.edu/hakupuna/downloads/HK-techreportFinal2011.pdf

Braveman, P. (2006). Health Disparities and Health Inequity: Concepts and Measurement. *Annual Review Public Health*, 27, 167–194. Available at: www.coloradotrust.org/attachments/0002/0250/BravemanConceptsandMeasurements.pdf

Broderick, J., Brott, T., Kothari, R., Miller, R., Khoury, J., Pancioli, J., et al. (1998, February). The Greater Cincinnati/Northern Kentucky Stroke Study: Preliminary First-ever and Total Incidence Rates of Stroke among Blacks. *Stroke: A Journal of the American Heart Association*, 29(2), 415–421.

——. (1999). *The Minority AIDS Crisis. Closing the Gap*. Washington, DC: Office of Minority Health, U.S. Department of Health and Human Services.

Brown, D. (2006, September 12). Wide Gaps Found in Mortality Rates among U.S. Groups. *Washington Post*. Retrieved from www.washingtonpost.com/wp-dyn/content/article/2006/09/11/AR2006091101297.html

Carlisle, D. M., Leake, B. D., and Shapiro, M. F. (1997). Racial and Ethnic Disparities in the Use of Cardiovascular Procedures: Associations with Type of Health Insurance. *American Journal of Public Health*, 87(2), 263–267.

Centers for Disease Control and Prevention. (2001). *Diabetes: A Serious Public Health Problem* (CDC Publication No. PDF-699K). Washington, DC: U.S. Government Printing Office.

——. (2004). *HIV/AIDS Surveillance Report*, Vol. 15. Washington, DC: Government Printing Office.

——. (2005a). *HIV/AIDS Surveillance Report*, Vol. 16. Washington, DC: Government Printing Office.

——. (2005b). HIV Prevalence, Unrecognized Infection, and HIV Testing among Men who Have Sex with Men: Five U.S. Cities, June 2004–April 2005. *Morbidity and Mortality Weekly Report*, 54(24), 597–601.

——. (2006, September 22). *Revised Recommendations for HIV Testing of Adults, Adolescents, and Pregnant Women in Health-care Settings*. Retrieved from www.cdc.gov/mmwr/preview/mmwrhtml/rr5514a1.htm

—— (2008a, August 29). Alcohol-attributable Deaths and Years of Potential Life Lost among American Indians and Alaska Natives: United States, 2001–2005. *Morbidity and Mortality Weekly Report*, 57(34), 938–941.

——. (2008b, August). *Fact Sheet: HIV/AIDS among African Americans*. Retrieved from www.cdc.gov/hiv/topics/aa/resources/factsheets/aa.htm

——. (2008c, May). *Rising Tide of Diabetes among Asian Americans*. Retrieved from www2a.cdc.gov/podcasts/media/pdf/RisingTideAsians.pdf

——. (2008d, August). *HIV/AIDS among American Indians and Alaska Natives*. Available at: www.cdc.gov/hiv/resources/factsheets/aian.htm

____. (2011a, November). *HIV/AIDS among Latinos*. Retrieved from www.cdc.gov/hiv/resources/factsheets/pdf/latino.pdf

——. (2011b, November 8). *HIV among Latinos*. Retrieved from www.cdc.gov/hiv/latinos/index.htm

——. (2012). *Estimates of New HIV Infections in the United States, 2006–2009*. Retrieved from www.cdc.gov/nchhstp/newsroom/docs/HIV-Infections-2006-2009.pdf

____. (2016). *Fact Sheet: New HIV Infections in the United States*. Retrieved from www.cdc.gov/nchhstp/newsroom/docs/factsheets/new-hiv-infections-508.pdf

——. (2017a, November). *HIV/AIDS Surveillance Report*, Vol. 28. Retrieved from www.cdc.gov/hiv/pdf/library/reports/surveillance/cdc-hiv-surveillance-report-2016-vol-28.pdf

____. (2017b). *National Diabetes Statistics Report, 2017*. Retrieved from www.diabetes.org/assets/pdfs/basics/cdc-statistics-report-2017.pdf

____. (2017c, September 15). *Violence and Homicide Among Youth*. Retrieved from www.cdc.gov/healthcommunication/toolstemplates/entertainmented/tips/ViolenceYouth.html

____. (2018). HIV *Among African American Gay and Bisexual Men*. Retrieved from www.cdc.gov/hiv/group/msm/bmsm.html

Chen, J., Rathore, S. S., Radford, M. J., Wang, Y., and Krumholz, H. M. (2001, May 10). Racial Differences in the Use of Cardiac Catheterization after Acute Myocardial Infarction. *New England Journal of Medicine*, 344(19), 1443–1449.

Chen, M. S. (1993). A 1993 Status Report on the Health Status of Asian Pacific Islander Americans: Comparisons with Healthy People 2000 Objectives. *Asian American Pacific Islander Journal of Health*, 1(1), 37–55.

Child Trends Databank. (2015). *Teen Homicide, Suicide and Firearm Deaths*. Retrieved from www.childtrends.org/?indicators=teen-homicide-suicide-and-firearm-deaths

David, R. and Collins, J. (1997). Differing Birth Weight among Infants of U.S.-born Blacks, African-born Blacks, and U.S.-born Whites. *New England Journal of Medicine*. Retrieved from www.nejm.org/doi/full/10.1056/NEJM199710233371706

Dembosky, A. (2015, August 20). Can Health Care Be Cured of Racial Bias? National Public Radio. Retrieved from www.npr.org/sections/health-shots/2015/08/20/432872330/can-health-care-be-cured-of-racial-bias

Diaz, T., Chu, S. Y., and Sorvillo, F. I. (1995). Differences in Participation in Experimental Drug Trials among Persons with AIDS. *Journal of Acquired Immune Deficiency Syndromes and Human Retrovirology*, 10, 562–8.

Diaz, C. J., Koning, S. M., and Martinez-Donate, A. P. (2016, December). Moving Beyond Salmon Bias: Mexican Return Migration and Health Selection. *Demography*. Retrieved from https://link.springer.com/article/10.1007/s13524-016-0526-2

D'Onofrio, K. (2018, January 3). *The Data is in: Police Disproportionately Killed Black People in 2017*. Retrieved from www.diversityinc.com/news/data-police-disproportionate-ly-killed-black-people-2017

Dunbar-Ortiz, R. and Gilio-Whitaker, D. (2016, October 10). *What's Behind the Myth of American Indian Alcoholism? Pacific Standard*. Retrieved from https://psmag.com/news/whats-behind-the-myth-of-native-american-alcoholism

Eheman, C., Henley, S. J., Ballard-Barbash, R., Jacobs, E. J., Schymura, M. J., Noone, A. M., et al. (2012, March 28) *Annual Report to the Nation on the Status of Cancer, 1975–2008*. Retrieved from www.cancer.gov/newscenter/newsfromnci/2012/ReportNationRelease2012

Garbarino, J., Hammond, R., Mercy, J., and Yung, B. R. (2004). Community Violence and Children: Preventing Exposure and Reducing Harm. In K. I. Maton, C. J. Schellenbach, B. J. Leadbeater, and A. L. Solarz (Eds.), *Investing in Children, Youth, Families, and Communities* (pp. 13–30). Washington, DC: American Psychological Association.

Geronimus, A. T., Hicken, M., Keene, D., and Bound, J. (2006, May). "Weathering" and Age Patterns of Allostatic Load Scores Among Blacks and Whites in the United States. *American Journal of Public Health*. Retrieved from www.ncbi.nlm.nih.gov/pmc/articles/PMC1470581

Ghosh, P. R. (2012, February 11). Native Americans: The Tragedy of Alcoholism. *International Business Times*. Retrieved from www.ibtimes.com/native-ameri cans-tragedy-alcoholism-214046

Goldberg, K. C., Hartz, A. J., Jacobsen, S. J., Krakauer, H., and Rimm, A. A. (1992). Racial and Community Factors Influencing Coronary Artery Bypass Graft Surgery Rates for All 1986 Medicare Patients. *Journal of American Medical Association*, 18(11), 1473–1477.

Healthy People 2000. (1995, February 15). *Progress Report for American Indians and Alaska Natives*. Washington, DC: Public Health Service, U.S. Department of Health and Human Services.

——. (1997, September 13). *Progress Review. Asian Americans and Pacific Islanders*. Washington, DC: Public Health Service, U.S. Department of Health and Human Services.

——. (1998, October 26). *Progress Review. Black Americans*. Washington, DC: Public Health Service, U.S. Department of Health and Human Services.

Herbert, B. (1996, December 2). Death at an Early Age. *New York Times*, p. A15.

Horvath, S., Gurven, M., Levine, M. E., Trumble, B. C., Kaplan, H., Allayee, H., et al. (2016, August). An epigenetic clock analysis of race/ethnicity, sex, and coronary heart disease. *Genome Biology*. Retrieved from https://genomebiology.biomedcen tral.com/articles/10.1186/s13059-016-1030-0#Bib1

Horwitz, S. R. (1998, June–July). *Impact of Domestic Abuse on HIV Prevention in Hispanic Women. Closing the Gap*. Washington, DC: Office of Minority Health, U.S. Department of Health and Human Services.

Indian Health Service, U.S. Department of Health and Human Services. (1998). *1997 Trends in Indian Health*. Washington, DC: Government Printing Office.

Institute of Medicine. (2002). *Unequal Treatment: Confronting Racial and Ethnic Disparities in Treatment*. Washington, DC: National Academy Press.

Iralu, J. V. (2016). *Tuberculosis Diagnosis and Treatment*. Indian Health Service. Retrieved from www.ihs.gov/telebehavioral/includes/themes/newihstheme/display_objects/ documents/slides/clinicalrounds/tb0416.pdf

Izadi, E. (2016, February 12). Your assumptions about Native Americans and alcohol are wrong. *Washington Post*. Retrieved from www.washingtonpost.com/news/ post-nation/wp/2016/02/12/your-assumptions-about-native-americans-and-alco hol-are-wrong/?utm_term=.6b0e342f7da6

Jemal, A., Ward, E. M., Johnson, C. J., Cronin, K. A., Ma, J., Ryerson, A. B., et al. (2017, September 1). Annual Report to the Nation on the Status of Cancer, 1975–2014, Featuring Survival. *Journal of the National Cancer Institute*, Volume 109, Issue 9. Retrieved from https://doi.org/10.1093/jnci/djx030

Kaiser Family Foundation. (2000a, January). *Key Facts on Medicaid and Uninsured: HIV/ AIDS and African–Americans*. Washington, DC: The Foundation.

——. (2000b, June). *Key Facts on Medicaid and Uninsured: Health Insurance Coverage and Access to Care among American Indians and Alaska Natives*. Washington, DC: The Foundation.

——. (2012, December). *Fact Sheet: Latinos and HIV/AIDS*. Retrieved from www.kff.org/ hivaids/6007.cfm

Kamat, M. (1999, May–June). *Blacks, Women Less Likely to Be Referred for High-Tech Cardiac Tests, According to Study. Closing the Gap*. Washington, DC: Office of Minority Health, U.S. Department of Health and Human Services.

Kilborn, P. T. (1999, July 8). Clinton, amid the Despair on a Reservation, Again Pledges Help. *New York Times*, p. A1.

Koh, H. K. (2013, November). *The Burden of Diabetes on the Native Hawaiian and Pacific Islander Community*. The White House. Retrieved from https://obamawhitehouse. archives.gov/blog/2013/11/20/burden-diabetes-native-hawaiian-and-pacific-is lander-community

Koh, H. K., Graham, G., and Glied, S. H. (2011). Reducing Racial and Ethnic Disparities: The Action Plan from the Department of Health and Human Services. *Health Affairs*, 30(10), 1822–1829.

Krieger, N., Chen, J. T., and Ebel, G. (1997a). Can We Monitor Socioeconomic Inequalities in Health? A Survey of U.S. Health Departments' Data Collection and Reporting Practices. *Public Health Reports*, 112(6), 481–491.

Krieger, N., Williams, D., and Moss, N. (1997b). Measuring Social Class in U.S. Public Health Research: Concepts, Methodologies, and Guidelines. *Annual Review Public Health*, 18(1), 341–378.

Lamare, J. (2012, December 2). Latino Life Expectancy: Exploring the Hispanic Paradox. *New America Media: Health*. Retrieved from http://newamericamedia.org/2012/12/latino-life-expectancy-exploring-the-hispanic-paradox.php

Lin-Fu, J. S. (1993). Asian and Pacific Islander Americans: An Overview of Demographic Characteristics and Health Care Issues. *Asian American Pacific Islander Journal of Health*, 1(1), 20–36.

Loue, S. (2006). Preventing HIV, eliminating disparities among Hispanics in the United States. *Journal of Immigrant Health*, 8, 313–318.

McCord, C. and Freeman, H. (1990). Excess Mortality in Harlem. *New England Journal of Medicine*, 322(3), 173–177.

Macdorman, M. F. and Mathews, T. J. (2011). *Understanding Racial and Ethnic Disparities in U.S. Infant Mortality Rates*. Centers for Disease Control and Prevention. Retrieved from www.cdc.gov/nchs/data/databriefs/db74.htm

McQuillan, L. (2014, January 28). *Latinos and Hispanics and Diabetes: The Need for Outreach*. Insulin Nation. Retrieved from http://insulinnation.com/living/latinos-and-diabetes-the-need-for-outreach

Manson, S. M., Beals, J., Klein, S., Croy, C., and AI/SUPERPFP Team. (2005, May). Social Epidemiology of Trauma among Two American Indian Reservation Populations. *American Journal of Public Health*, 95(5), 851–859.

Marin, B. V. and Gomes, C. A. (1998, November). *Latinos and HIV: Cultural Issues in AIDS Prevention. The AIDS Knowledge Database*. San Francisco, CA: University of California.

Markides, K. S., and Eschbach, K. (2005). Aging, Migration, and Mortality: Current Status of Research on the Hispanic Paradox. *Journals of Gerontology Series B: Psychological Sciences and Social Sciences*, 60(2), 68–75.

Mayberry, R. M., Mili, F., Isam, G. M., Samadi, A., Ofili, E., McNeal, M. S., et al. (1999, October). *Racial and Ethnic Differences in Access to Medical Care: A Synthesis of the Literature*. Washington, DC: Kaiser Family Foundation.

Meadows, M. (2000, August). *More Research Needed on Breast Cancer in Black Women. Closing the Gap*. Washington, DC: Office of Minority Health, U.S. Department of Health and Human Services.

National Center for Health Statistics. (2000). *Health United States, 2000*. Hyattsville, MD: U.S. Department of Health and Human Services.

——. (2001, June 26). *Mortality Declines for Several Leading Causes of Death in 1999*. Hyattsville, MD: U.S. Department of Health and Human Services.

——. (2008). *Health United States, 2007*. Hyattsville, MD: U.S. Department of Health and Human Services.

——. (2012). *Health, United States, 2011*. Hyattsville, MD: U.S. Department of Health and Human Services.

——. (2017a). *Health United States, 2016*. Hyattsville, MD: U.S. Department of Health and Human Services. Retrieved from www.cdc.gov/nchs/data/hus/hus16.pdf

——. (2017b, December). National Institute on Drug Abuse. Monitoring the Future Survey: *High School and Youth Trends*. Retrieved from www.drugabuse.gov/publications/drugfacts/monitoring-future-survey-high-school-youth-trends

Navarro, V. (1990). Race or Class versus Race and Class: Mortality Differentials in the United States. *The Lancet*, 336(8729), 1238–1240.

Olshansky, S. J., Antonucci, T., Berkman, L., Binstock, R. H., Boersch-Supan, A., Cacioppo, J. T., et al. (2013, January). Differences in Life Expectancy Due to Race and Educational Differences are Widening, and Many may not Catch Up. *Health Affairs*, 31(8), 1803–1813.

Oropeza, L. (2001, Spring). *Native Americans Strategize to Integrate HIV Prevention and Substance Abuse. HIV Impact*. Washington, DC: Office of Minority Health, U.S. Department of Health and Human Services.

Oxendine, J. (1999, February–March). *Who Has Diabetes? Closing the Gap*. Washington, DC: Office of Minority Health, U.S. Department of Health and Human Services.

——. (2000, June–July). *Diabetes Programs Have Local Style. Closing the Gap*. Washington, DC: Office of Minority Health, U.S. Department of Health and Human Services.

Palloni, A. (2004). *Paradox Lost: Explaining the Hispanic Adult Mortality Advantage.* Retrieved from www.prb.org/cpipr

Pua'ala'okalani, A. (2000, June–July). *Comparing Native Hawaiians' Health to the Nation. Closing the Gap*. Washington, DC: Office of Minority Health, U.S. Department of Health and Human Services.

Puukka, E. J., Stehr-Green, P., and Becker, T. M. (2005). Measuring the Health Status Gap for American Indians/Alaskan Natives: Getting Closer to the Truth. *American Journal of Public Health*, 95(5), 838–843.

Regulus, T. A. (1995). Gang Violence. In R. L. Edwards (Ed.-in-Chief), *Encyclopedia of Social Work*, 19th edn. (pp. 1045–1055). Washington, DC: National Association of Social Workers.

Rosmena, F., Kuhn, R., and Jochem, W. C. (2017, January). Explaining the Immigrant Health Advantage: Self-selection and Protection in Health-related Factors Among Five Major National-origin Immigrant Groups in the United States. *Demography*. Retrieved from https://link.springer.com/article/10.1007/s13524-016-0542-2

Ross, J. (2011, May 24). Black–White Life Expectancy Gap Expands, Recession may be to Blame. *Huff Post Business*. Retrieved from www.huffingtonpost.com/2011/05/24/black-white-life-expectan_n_865945.html

Roubideaux, Y. (2005, November 3). Beyond Red Lake: The Persistent Crisis in American Indian Health Care. *New England Journal of Medicine*, 353(18), 1881–1883.

Schoendorf, K. C., Hogue, C., Kleinman, J., and Rowley, D. (1992). Mortality among Infants of Black as Compared with White College-educated Parents. *New England Journal of Medicine*, 326(23), 1522–1526.

Schneider, E. (2005, May). Tuberculosis Among American Indians and Alaska Natives in the United States, 1993–2002. *American Journal of Public Health*, 95(5), 873–880.

Schulman, K. A., Berlin, J. A., Harless, W., Kerner, J. F., Sistrunk, S., Gersh, et al. (1999). The Effect of Race and Sex on Cardiac Catheterization. *New England Journal of Medicine*, 340(8), 618–626.

Smith, G. D., Neaton, J. D., Wentworth, D., Stamler, R., and Stamler, J., for the MRFIT Research Group. (1998, March 28). So Much to Do, So Little Time: Care for the Socially Disadvantaged and the 15-minute Visit. *Lancet*, 351, 9107.

Snipp, C. M. (1986, October). American Indians and Natural Resource Development: Indigenous Peoples' Land, Now Sought After, Has Produced New Indian–White Problems. *American Journal of Economics and Sociology*, 45(4), 457–473.

Sorlie, P. D., Backlund, E., Johnson, N. J., and Rogot, E. (1993). Mortality by Hispanics in the U.S. *Journal of the American Medical Association*, 270, 2464–2468.

Stein, B. D., Jaycox, L. H., Kataoka, S., Rhodes, H. J., and Vestal, K. D. (2003). Prevalence of Child and Adolescent Exposure to Violence. *Clinical Child and Family Psychology Review*, 6(4), 247–263.

Stevens, S., Estrada, A., and Estrada, B. (2000). *HIV Drug and Sex Risk Behaviors among American Indian and Alaskan Native Drug Users: Gender and Site Differences*. Retrieved from www.ucdenver.edu/academics/colleges/PublicHealth/research/centers/CAIANH/journal/Documents/Volume%209/9(1)_Stevens_HIV_Drug_33-46.pdf

Suarez-el-Adam, M., Rafaelli, M., and O'Leary, A. (2000). Influence of Abuse and Partner Hypermasculinity on the Sexual Behavior of Latinas. *AIDS Education and Prevention*, 12(3), 263–274.

Tavernise, S. (2016, May 8). Black Americans See Gains in Life Expectancy. *New York Times*. Retrieved from www.nytimes.com/2016/05/09/health/blacks-see-gains-in-life-expectancy.html

Taylor, P. (1991, March 14). Gunshot Leading Killer of Teenage Boys. *Concord Monitor*, p. A10.

U.S. Department of Health and Human Services. (1986). *Report of the Secretary's Task Force on Black and Minority Health*. Vol. I–VIII. Washington, DC: U.S. Government Printing Office.

——. (1998). *Racial and Ethnic Disparities in Health, Response to President's Initiative on Race*. Washington, DC.

——. (2012a, December 4). *Cancer and African Americans*. Office of Minority Health. Retrieved from http://minorityhealth.hhs.gov/templates/content.aspx?ID=2826

——. (2012b, June 13). *Cancer and American Indians/Alaska Natives*. Office of Minority Health. Retrieved from http://minorityhealth.hhs.gov/templates/content.aspx?ID=3023

——. (2012c, June 15). *Cancer and Asians/Pacific Islanders*. Office of Minority Health. Retrieved from http://minorityhealth.hhs.gov/templates/content.aspx?lvl=2&lvlID=53&ID=3055

——. (2012d, June 15). *Cancer and Native Hawaiians/Pacific Islanders*. Office of Minority Health. Retrieved from http://minorityhealth.hhs.gov/templates/content.aspx?lvl=3&lvlID=4&ID=8593

——. (2012e, August 28). *Diabetes and Asians/Pacific Islanders*. Office of Minority Health. Retrieved from http://minorityhealth.hhs.gov/templates/content.aspx?lvl=2&lvlID=53&ID=3057

——. (2012f, August 29). *Heart Disease and African Americans*. Office of Minority Health. Retrieved from http://minorityhealth.hhs.gov/templates/content.aspx?ID=3018

——. (2012g, November 29). *HIV/AIDS and American Indians/Alaska Natives*. Office of Minority Health. Retrieved from http://minorityhealth.hhs.gov/templates/content.aspx?lvl=2&lvlID=52&ID=3026

——. (2012h, June 4). *Obesity and Native Hawaiians/Pacific Islanders*. Office of Minority Health. Retrieved from http://minorityhealth.hhs.gov/templates/content.aspx?lvl=3&lvlID=537&ID=8736

——. (2016a, January 28). *Heart Disease and African Americans*. Office of Minority Health. Retrieved from www.minorityhealth.hhs.gov/omh/browse.aspx?lvl=4&lvlid=19

——. (2016b, December 27). *Diabetes and Asians/Pacific Islanders*. Office of Minority Health. Retrieved from https://minorityhealth.hhs.gov/omh/browse.aspx?lvl=4&lvlid=48

_____. (2017a, November 9). *Infant Health and Mortality and African Americans*. Office of Minority Health. Retrieved from www.minorityhealth.hhs.gov/omh/browse.aspx?lvl=4&lvlid=23

_____. (2017b, October 6). *Infant Mortality and American Indians/Native Alaskans*. Office of Minority Health. Retrieved from https://minorityhealth.hhs.gov/omh/browse.aspx?lvl=4&lvlID=38

_____. (2017c, November 9). *Profile: Black/African Americans*. Office of Minority Health. Retrieved from https://minorityhealth.hhs.gov/omh/browse.aspx?lvl=3&lvlid=61

_____. (2018a, January 17). *HIV/AIDS and African Americans*. Office of Minority Health. Retrieved from www.minorityhealth.hhs.gov/omh/browse.aspx?lvl=4&lvlid=21

_____. (2018b, January 17). *HIV/AIDS and Hispanics*. Office of Minority Health. Retrieved from https://minorityhealth.hhs.gov/omh/browse.aspx?lvl=4&lvlid=66

_____. (2018c, April 8). *HIV/AIDS and American Indians/Alaska Natives*. Office of Minority Health. Retrieved from https://minorityhealth.hhs.gov/omh/browse.aspx?lvl=4&lvlid=36

U.S. General Accounting Office. (1992, January). *Hispanic Access to Health Care: Significant Gaps Exist (GAO/PEMD-92-6)*. Washington, DC: U.S. Government Printing Office.

——. (1993, April). *Indian Health Service—Basic Services Mostly Available; Substance Abuse Problems Need Attention* (GAO/HRD-93-48). Washington, DC: U.S. Government Printing Office.

U. S. Senate. (2010). *Health Reform for Native Americans, Patient Protection and Affordable Care Act*. Retrieved from http://dpc.senate.gov/healthreformbill/healthbill86.pdf

Vega, W. A. and Amaro, H. (1994). Latino Outlook: Good Health, Uncertain Prognosis. *Annual Review of Public Health*, 15, 39–67.

Villarosa, L. (2018, April 15). The Hidden Toll. Why are Black Mothers and Babies in the U.S. Dying at More Than Double the Rate of White Mothers and Babies? The Answer has Everything to do with the Lived Experience of being a Black Woman in America. *New York Times*, 31–39, 47–48, 51.

Wenneker, M. and Epstein, A. (1989). Racial Inequalities in the Use of Procedures for Patients with Ischemic Heart Disease in Massachusetts. *Journal of the American Medical Association*, 261(2), 253–257.

Weinick, R. M. and Hasnain-Wynia, R. (2011, October). Quality Improvement Efforts under Health Reform: How to Ensure that they Help Reduce Disparities – Not Increase Them. *Health Affairs*, 30(10), 1837–1843.

West, J. (1999, February–March). *National Diabetes Education Program. Closing the Gap*. Washington, DC: Office of Minority Health, U.S. Department of Health and Human Services.

Whittle, J., Conigliaro, J., Good, C. B., and Lofgren, R. P. (1993, August 26). Racial Differences in the Use of Invasive Cardiovascular Procedures in the Department of Veterans Affairs. *New England Journal of Medicine*, 329(9), 621–627. Retrieved from www.ncbi.nlm.nih.gov/pubmed/8341338

CHAPTER 11

Analyzing the Problem

Disparities in Health for Women, Children, Older Adults, and the LGBTQ Community

INTRODUCTION

THIS CHAPTER APPLIES THE BASIC POLICY PRACTICE QUESTIONS that are raised in problem analysis to the issue of disparities in health for women, children, older adults, and the LGBTQ community in the U.S. As in the previous chapter, the following outline puts the issues discussed in this chapter on disparities in this context.

Outline of Analysis: Disparities in Health for Women, Children, and Older Adults

What is the social problem?	Disparities in health based on gender, age, and sexual identity
Who is affected? What is the extent of the problem?	Women Children Older adults LGBTQ community
What are the dimensions and boundaries of the problem?	Disparities in health status in life expectancy, mortality, and morbidity. Disparities in health and mental health
What evidence is there that a problem exists?	National and regional data and studies on disparities in health insurance coverage, access to health care, and quality of care
How serious is the problem?	Health disparities exist for women related to maternal health, family planning, HIV/AIDS, sexual and domestic abuse; health disparities exist for children related to infant mortality, chronic illnesses, abuse and neglect, risky behaviors; health disparities exist for older adults related to heart disease, cancer, dementia, elder abuse, long-term care; health disparities exist for LGBTQ community in cancer, suicide, mental health, exposure to violence, and HIV/AIDS
What is the perceived cause of the problem?	Systemic and financial barriers to care. Stigma, discrimination and minority stress
What explanations exist for the problem?	Lack of universal health insurance coverage due to a patchwork system of health care policies and programs in the U.S.; the high cost of health care and insurance; disparities in the quality of care; discriminatory practices in the delivery of care

EXPLAINING GENDER AND AGE-BASED DISPARITIES IN HEALTH

Women

As discussed in Chapter 10, health disparities are differences in health (or in important influences on health) that are systematically associated with being socially disadvantaged. Women, children and youths, and, to some extent, older adults, all fall into this social status of social disadvantage. Research in gender inequalities in health dates back to the 1960s with a focus on Britain, Europe, and North America and was in part influenced by sociopolitical interests in the effects of patriarchy on women's health. A much-simplified summary of the findings dating back to the 1970s shows that men die earlier, but women get sicker (Annadale and Hunt, 2000). Generally, as noted by the World Health Organization (2012), although women may live longer, they tend to experience more long-term and chronic illness, which impacts the quality of their lives. Also, the gap in male and female life expectancy "narrows and even disappears" among less privileged groups. In the U.S., although overall mortality fell between 1992 and 2006 in most counties, female mortality actually increased in 42.8 percent of counties; during the same period, rates of mortality among males grew in only 3.4 percent of counties (Kindig and Cheng, 2013).

As noted by Ostlin et al. (2006, p. 25):

> there is overwhelming evidence from all fields of health research that women and men are different as regards their biology (sex differences), their access to and control over resources and their decision-making power in the family and community, as well as the roles and responsibilities that society assigns to them (gender differences). Together gender and sex, often in interaction with socioeconomic circumstances, influence exposure to health risks, access to health information and services, health outcomes and the social and economic consequences of ill-health. Recognizing the root causes of gender inequities in health is crucial therefore when designing health system responses. Health promotion as well as disease prevention needs to address these differences between women and men, boys and girls in an equitable manner in order to be effective.

Thus, as with racial and ethnic disparities in health, gender disparities in health are complex and require further research to understand the extent to which disparities result from biology (sex differences) and social status (gender differences) and, in the U.S., other compounding social factors, such as race and ethnicity. Gender differences in health also have implications for health policy. For example, family planning services and prenatal care are critical to maternal, prenatal, and child health. Women are also vulnerable to the risk of mortality and injury that stems from domestic and sexual violence. Many of these health-related risks were addressed

Bans Preexisting Condition Exclusions

The private insurance market has routinely denied coverage for "preexisting conditions" for conditions that exclusively or primarily affect women, such as previously having given birth by Caesarean section, being pregnant at the time they seek coverage, having medical treatment related to domestic violence, or receiving medical treatment after sexual assault.

The ACA prohibits this practice and requires insurers to sell insurance to anyone who wants to buy coverage (known as "guaranteed issue").

Bans Gender Rating

The private insurance market has routinely charged women higher premiums than men of the same age, regularly including female and male nonsmokers.

The ACA prohibits this practice.

Prohibits Sex Discrimination

For the first time, the ACA prohibits sex discrimination in federal health programs, health programs receiving federal dollars, and other programs, including the health insurance exchanges. Insurers receiving federal funds are covered by this provision.

Makes Comprehensive Health Insurance More Available and Affordable

The ACA subsidizes health insurance to those who lack affordable employer health insurance, which will particularly help women, who on average have lower incomes than men.

Expands Medicaid Eligibility

The ACA has the potential to cover up to 10.3 million new low-income women through Medicaid by 2014. *NOTE:* The Supreme Court ruled (June 2012) that states could not be *required* to expand eligibility, but could instead *opt* to expand coverage.

Guarantees Maternity Coverage for All

The majority of private insurance plans do not cover maternity care.

The ACA requires coverage for maternity care as an "essential health benefit."

Ensures New Plans Cover Recommended Preventive Care, Including Contraception, Domestic Violence Screenings, Pap Tests, and Mammograms, without Copayments

The ACA will provide access to these life-saving screenings. **Protects Nursing Mothers**

The ACA requires employers with more than 50 employees to provide breaks during work hours as well as a private place for mothers who are nursing to be able to express breast milk.

FIGURE 11.1

2010 Affordable Care Act and Women's Health

in reforms mandated by the 2010 Affordable Care Act (ACA) (Figure 11.1). However, as mentioned earlier in the text, there have been several attempts by conservative Republicans and the Trump administration to "repeal and replace" the ACA.

Children, Youth, and Older Adults

Individuals also confront age-based health risks with complex root causes, some of which are based on biology (during more vulnerable stages of the lifespan) and others that are rooted in socioeconomic status and issues similar to those for people of color and women. As noted by the National Institute for Health Care Management (2007, p. 2):

> Low-income and children of color continue to have poorer health status than their more affluent and White peers. Efforts to reduce, if not eliminate, health disparities among children are a vital means of improving the current status of children's health and securing their continued health into adulthood . . . . The association between socioeconomic status and health and persistent racial and ethnic disparities in health is well documented among children in the U.S.

Child health is inexorably linked to women's health through the childbearing role, and infants' and children's dependence on parents and guardians, who must protect them from disease and illness. Adolescents experiment with tobacco, alcohol, and other substances as they seek approval from their peers and independence from their parents or guardians. Older adults confront chronic illness and impairments, including impaired mobility or lack of transportation that limit their ability to function independently. In addition, many older retired adults have fixed and limited incomes, which make it difficult to cover health care expenses. These age-related risks are exacerbated by sociopolitical factors, including socioeconomic status and discrimination. In general, poor children, adolescents, and older adults are at greater risk for ill health.

LGBTQ Community

Lesbian, gay, bisexual, transgender, and questioning (LGBTQ) people are also vulnerable to disparities in health. As noted by the federal government's *Healthy People 2020* (2018) initiative, sexual orientation, and gender identity questions are not included in most national or state surveys, which makes it difficult to know the number of LGBTQ individuals with health needs. However, research suggests that LGBTQ individuals, like other groups who have faced negative treatment, face health disparities linked to societal stigma, discrimination, and denial of their civil and human rights. *Healthy People 2020* (2018) identifies several conditions linked to discrimination against LGBTQ persons, including high rates of psychiatric disorders, substance abuse, and suicide. In addition, frequent experiences of violence and victimization have long-lasting effects both on the individual and on the community.

The focus of *Healthy People 2020* (2018) is the elimination of health disparities and the pursuit of efforts to improve LGBTQ health. In addition to the behavioral and mental health issues mentioned above, concerns focus on reductions in disease transmission and progression, reduced health care costs, and collecting sexual orientation and gender identity (SOGI) data in health-related surveys and health records.

Today, more attention is being given to the LGBTQ community and efforts to collect data as a separate group through various surveys and reports by government and private agencies. In 2011, the Institute of Medicine (IOM, 2011) reported on the health status of (LGBTQ) individuals in *The Health of Lesbian, Gay, Bisexual, and Transgender People: Building a Foundation for Better Understanding*. The report found that policies, laws, and other daily challenges have led to health disparities. Other researchers have confirmed the findings of the IOM report. For example, Krehely (2009) found that LGBTQ individuals have worse health outcomes than heterosexuals. He reported greater risk for cancer, increased use of tobacco, drugs, and alcohol, and greater stress among adults.

Increased attention to the health needs of the LGBTQ has occurred in other ways, as well. The American Association of Medical Colleges published a guide to integrating the curriculum on LGBTQ health in medical schools. The National Institutes of Health created a Sexual and Gender Minority Research Office in 2015. The U.S. Department of Health and Human Services provides funding to the National LGBT Health Education Center, which trains staff at health centers and other institutions to recognize and address the unique health challenges of the LGBTQ community (Cahill, 2017).

GENDER, AGE-BASED, AND LGBTQ DISPARITIES IN HEALTH

Similar to Chapter 10, this chapter highlights major health areas, including infant mortality, cardiovascular disease, HIV/AIDS, and infectious diseases targeted by the U.S. Public Health Service (PHS). The primary focus, however, is gender, age-based and LGBTQ disparities in health that stem from particular differences in biopsychosocial experiences for women, adolescents and youth, older adults, and the LGBTQ community. Unlike Chapter 10, this chapter incorporates information about federal policies, programs, and services that address these health-related environmental issues and problems.

WOMEN AND INFANTS

The health status of women is inseparable from the status of women in society, and women are still not equal to men in their access to power, prestige, or wealth. Although women's stature may have improved, they still face inequities and discrimination in many aspects of social life. Disparities are found in occupational segregation, job discrimination, pay inequity, gender-specific education, sexual harassment, domestic violence, and representation in political structures (National

Association of Social Workers, 2000e). (To help address pay inequity, President Obama signed the Lilly Ledbetter Fair Pay Act of 2009, which restored the protection against pay discrimination that was denied by the Supreme Court's decision in *Ledbetter v. Goodyear Tire & Rubber Co.*)

In the area of health, gender roles and behaviors have certainly had an impact on health outcomes. Traditional male behaviors and risk factors, including smoking, alcohol consumption, risk-taking behavior, occupational hazards, and violent sports, have contributed to lower rates of life expectancy for men. In 2016, average life expectancy for women was 81.1 years, whereas average life expectancy for men was almost 5 years shorter, or 76.1 years (Kochanek et al., 2017). However, women bear disproportionate health consequences from living in poverty and having lower socioeconomic status. The poverty gap between women and men begins to widen during adolescence, continues throughout adult life, and is almost double during old age; the gap never closes.

Poverty statistics from the U.S. Census Bureau show that "women were hit hardest" in 2010, yet they seemed "invisible" in reports in the media on rising poverty in the U.S. (Bennetts, 2011). The poverty rate among women rose to 14.5 percent, the highest rate since 1993. (According to the U.S. Census Bureau [Semega et al., 2017] the poverty rate in 2016 was still 14 percent.) The "extreme poverty rate"—income below half of the federal poverty level (FPL)—among women rose to 6.3 percent, which was the highest ever recorded, and twice as many older women (over age 65) as men were living in poverty. Single mothers were twice as likely as single fathers to be poor; single mothers of color had the highest poverty rate. Across all racial and ethnic groups, women were more likely than men to be living in poverty (Bennetts, 2011).

Women who live in poverty have higher rates of illness, injury, disability, and death. Although women may have longer life expectancies than men, they are more likely to experience chronic illness during their lifetimes, as well as mental illness, such as depression. They also make use of health care facilities and prescription drugs more frequently and, during old age, are more dependent on long-term care due to multiple chronic conditions (Agency for Health Care Policy and Research [AHCPR], 1999; Lambrew, 2001).

The government first recognized disparities in health for women in the late 1980s and enacted the Women's Health Equity Act of 1990, introduced by Representative (D) Patricia Schroeder; the Office of Women's Health was established in 1991. The broad purpose of the bill was to improve women's health care and to address the ongoing exclusion of women from medical research. Studies from the late 1980s conducted by the U.S. PHS and the National Institutes of Health (NIH) indicated that so little data was available on women's health that it was difficult to understand women's health care needs (Shumaker and Smith, 1999). *Making the Grade on Women's Health: A National and State-by-State Report Card* (National Women's Law Center, 2007) found that the nation was not making progress on the agenda set forth for women in *Healthy People 2010*. The findings demonstrated that women were falling further behind on most heath indicators and that significant improvements were needed to achieve the goals established to improve women's health. A more recent interim report from the Office of Women's Health

(U.S. Department of Health and Human Services, 2010) on progress made toward 18 *Healthy People 2010* objectives showed mixed outcomes—some progress, some declines, and some areas with little or no change: "Differences between females and males continued to persist across all pertinent topics," and "disparities within and between genders were found by race and ethnicity, age, socioeconomic status (education and income), and urban/rural location" (U.S. Department of Health and Human Services, 2010, p. 31).

The most recent focus on women's health issues for the CDC's *Healthy People 2020* effort includes initiatives in the following areas, among 16 of the CDC's 42 topic areas:

- arthritis, osteoporosis, and chronic back conditions;
- cancer (breast, uterine, cervical);
- unintended pregnancy;
- family planning;
- HIV/AIDS;
- sexual violence and rape;
- maternal, infant, and child health.

Cancer and Cardiovascular Disease

Heart disease and cancer are the primary causes of death for both women and men (Kochanek et al., 2017). Heart disease is the leading cause of death for all women, and those over age 75 are at greatest risk (AHCPR, 2005). However, myths still seem to persist about heart disease being a mostly male health problem. For example, both female and male physicians are far less likely to refer women for cardiac catheterization, the most definitive test for heart disease (Schulman et al., 1999). Women are also less likely to be treated with therapy (clot busting) or to undergo surgery (coronary bypass) or surgical procedures (angiography or angioplasty) after hospital admissions, and thus are 20 percent more likely than men to die of a heart attack while still in the hospital; women are two to three times as likely to die following heart bypass surgery (Iezzoni et al., 1997; Canto et al., 2000; Women's Heart Foundation, 2007). They are also less likely than men to be treated for heart disease with lifesaving drugs such as aspirin, beta blockers, or statins (Canto et al., 2000; Women's Heart Foundation, 2007) or to have their cholesterol measured as often (Hoffer and Kerr, 2003). Advances have been made in understanding the difference in symptoms of heart disease for women and men, but research is just beginning to identify the biological, medical, and social underpinnings of these differences (Harvard Health, 2017).

Cancer is the second leading cause of death for all women. Younger women, aged 35–44, are far more likely to die from cancer than heart disease, but here, too, misconceptions about the dangers of different cancers seem to persist. Although breast cancer is the most common form of cancer (Centers for Disease Control and Prevention, 2012a) that women experience, since 1987 lung cancer has caused more deaths than breast cancer (*Healthy People 2000*, 1998b; Centers for Disease Control and Prevention, 2012a). However, low-income women are more likely to die from breast cancer than other women because diagnosis tends to occur at a more advanced stage of the disease (AHCPR, 1999). According to the American Cancer Society, death rates today are about 40 percent higher among African American women than among white women (Williams, 2012).

> Poverty and racial inequities are the primary factors driving the disparity, according to a study released . . . by the Avon Foundation. The study, which compared mortality rates between black and white women in the nation's 25 largest cities, states that "nearly five black women die needlessly per day from breast cancer" because they don't have information about the importance of breast screening and they don't have access to high quality care. The authors of the study, conducted by Sinai Urban Health Institute and published in *Cancer Epidemiology*, said genetics play only a small role in the disparity.
>
> (Williams, 2012)

At one time, cervical cancer was the leading cause of cancer death for women in the U.S. However, in the past 40 years, cervical cancer has decreased significantly due to the increase of regular testing for the disease (Pap tests) (Centers for Disease Control and Prevention, 2012a). However, older, low-income, and rural women are at special risk because they are less likely to obtain regular screenings (Office on Women's Health, 2001). In 2009, Latinas had the highest rate of cervical cancer, followed by African American women and Native American women (Centers for Disease Control and Prevention, 2012a).

HIV/AIDS

Although the majority of adult acquired immune deficiency syndrome (AIDS) cases are men (75 percent in 2018), HIV and the disease of AIDS are of serious concern for women, particularly African American women and Latinas. HIV/AIDS has been growing at a faster rate for heterosexual women than heterosexual men since the disease was first recognized in 1981. The number of newly diagnosed women with AIDS increased from 7 percent of new cases in 1985 to 24 percent in 2016. Women are more susceptible to the virus because it is more easily transmitted from male to female. Women of color are at especially high risk and, in 2016, represented 61 percent of the newly diagnosed cases of AIDS. This represents a 16 percent decline from 2011 to 2015 (Centers for Disease Control and Prevention, 2018a; Kaiser Family Foundation, 2012).

Young women aged 15–39 are especially vulnerable because transmission of the virus occurs most often during women's reproductive years. In 2009, more than 60 percent of the new HIV infections among African American women and Latinas were among younger women aged 13–39; more than a third were among even younger women, aged 13–29 (Kaiser Family Foundation, 2012). On a more positive note, advances have been made in reducing the number of babies infected with AIDS by their mothers during pregnancy. This is the result of prenatal treatments with the drug AZT (zidovudine). Between 1992 and 1997, the number of babies with AIDS declined by two-thirds to a total of fewer than 300 babies (Coleman, 1999).

HIV/AIDS also generates other health-related problems for women. For poor women, poverty is a compounding factor that makes dealing with this disease that much more difficult. For all women with HIV/AIDS, the need for psychological support has received less attention than it has for gay men, and few support groups exist. Many women are the primary caregivers in their households and continue to struggle with this role while caring for their own health. HIV/AIDS can also be traumatic for children who experience the loss of a parent to the disease (Hackl et al., 1997).

The Ryan White Comprehensive AIDS Resources Emergency (CARE) Act (PL 101-381) was enacted in 1990, reauthorized by Congress (1996, 2000, 2006), and reauthorized as the Ryan White HIV/AIDS Treatment Extension Act of 2009 (Public Law 111-87). Its original purpose was to provide funds to state, localities, schools, and organizations for prevention programs, medical treatment, and support services, including housing and case management. CARE has consistently served about half a million people living with AIDS and continued to do so in 2016 (U.S. Department of Health and Human Services, 2018a). The U.S. General Accounting Office (2000c, p. 11) reported that women and people of color "generally receive[d] less appropriate care for their disease" and were assisted by the CARE Act at rates disproportionate to their representation in the AIDS population.

As a result of ongoing efforts by the Congressional Black and Latino Congressional Caucuses, CARE was finally reauthorized in 2006 with much greater emphasis given to the needs of people of color. The amended Ryan White HIV/AIDS Treatment Modernization Act of 2006 made changes in the use of funding and shifted priorities to life-saving and life-extending services for people living with HIV/AIDS. Most of the funding focused on direct services for care, and the establishment of the Minority AIDS Initiative shifted the use of resources to address the needs of this population. In 2016, 47 percent of Ryan White clients were African American and 23 percent were Latinx (U.S. Department of Health and Human Services, 2018a).

President Obama signed the reauthorization of the 2010 CARE Act, noting that CARE:

> has evolved from an emergency response into a comprehensive national program for the care and support of Americans living with HIV/AIDS. It helps communities that are most severely affected by this epidemic and often least served by our health care system, including minority communities, the LGBT community, rural communities, and the homeless. It's often the only option for the uninsured and the underinsured. And it provides life-saving medical services to more than half a million Americans every year, in every corner of the country.
>
> (White House, 2009)

Maternal and Infant/Child Mortality

Despite billions of dollars spent annually on hospitalizations for pregnancy and childbirth, the U.S. fared worse than 49 nations in its maternal mortality rate and had the worst maternal mortality rate of any industrialized nation (Amnesty International, 2010). Maternal deaths in the U.S. increased significantly from 1990 to 2015, whereas maternal deaths globally decreased by 44 percent during the same time period (Harvard Maternal Health Task Force, 2018). Maternal mortality rates declined steadily from 1950 to 1990 (Agency for Healthcare Research and Quality [AHRQ], 2000), but have increased steadily since 2000. The mortality rate has gone from a national low (of 6.6 deaths per 100,000) in 1987 in the U.S. to a high (of 26 deaths per 100,000) in 2015 (Harvard Maternal Health Task Force, 2018). In 2010, African American women were more than three times as likely as white women to die from pregnancy and childbirth (U.S. Department of Health and Human Services, 2011).

Between 1990 and 2002, all women experienced increased access to prenatal care during the first trimester of pregnancy, which is of vital importance to the health of pregnant women and their babies (*Healthy People 2000*, 1998b). However, between 2002 and 2008 access to prenatal care did not improve (National Center for Health Statistics, 2008); even with passage of the ACA, about 25 percent of all women do not receive the recommended number of prenatal visits (Harvard Maternal Health Task Force, 2018). Women who lack prenatal care are more likely to have low-birth-weight babies, who in turn are at significant risk for neurological, congenital, and respiratory problems and disabilities (Balsanek, 1997). Low birth weight is responsible for almost 70 percent of infant mortality (AHRQ, 2000).

In an effort to address these disparities, the Maternal Health Accountability Act of 2011 was introduced but failed enactment. The intent of the bill was to amend Title V of the Social Security Act, Maternal and Child Health Services, to establish state-level maternal mortality review committees to gather information about pregnancy-related deaths, and to eliminate disparities in maternal health outcomes.

Infant mortality has declined steadily since the 1980s, but, as with maternal mortality, the U.S. lags far behind other industrialized countries. In 2010, the U.S. ranked twentieth in child mortality rates among 20 countries of the Organisation for Economic Co-operation and Development (OECD); infant mortality was 75 percent higher from 2001 to 2010 (Thakrar et al., 2018). Infant mortality rates for women of color, particularly African American women, are disproportionately high (over twice the rate for white women in 2015) (Centers for Disease Control and Prevention, 2018b). In addition, low-income women are at greater risk for poor birth outcomes. Inadequate prenatal care during the first trimester of pregnancy (*Healthy People 2000*, 1997), poor nutrition, and inadequate psychosocial supports are contributing factors (Homan and Korenbrot, 1998): "Mothers are less likely to obtain adequate . . . prenatal care if they are young, poor, unmarried, relatively uneducated, uninsured, or living in inner cities or rural areas" (Balsanek, 1997, p. 63).

Another concern is tobacco smoking. Overall, the use of tobacco during pregnancy has decreased since 1990 (*Healthy People 2000*, 1999b), but 1 in 14 women still smoked during pregnancy in 2015 (Howard, 2018). Pregnant low-income women and women of color are at greater risk for the stress-related use of drugs, alcohol, and cigarettes (Zambrana and Scrimshaw, 1997), and the rate of smoking among teenage girls has been increasing. Statistical reporting shows that both alcohol use and smoking during pregnancy are significantly higher among American Indian women. Smoking during pregnancy may explain the high rate of sudden infant death syndrome (SIDS), and alcohol use is related to the high rate of fetal alcohol syndrome found in this population (U.S. Department of Health and Human Services, 2008; Howard, 2018). Smoking is the leading cause of premature deaths and increases the risk of many health problems, including learning disabilities and low birth weight (Office on Women's Health, 2001). The Affordable Care Act requires that Medicaid cover smoking cessation services for pregnant women.

Maternal, Prenatal, and Child Health Services

A number of federal policies affect the availability and delivery of maternal, prenatal, and child health services. Title V of the Social Security Act of 1935 established

---

- Provide mothers and children with access to quality services

- Reduce infant mortality

- Reduce preventable diseases and handicapping conditions among children

- Reduce need for inpatient and long-term-care services

- Increase child immunization

- Increase number of low-income children receiving health assessments and follow-up diagnoses and treatment services

- Promote health of mothers and infants by providing prenatal, delivery, postpartum care for low-income, at-risk pregnant mothers

- Promote health of children by providing preventive and primary care services for low-income children

- Provide rehabilitative services for eligible blind or disabled children under age 16

- Provide and promote family-centered, community-based, coordinated care for children with special needs

FIGURE 11.2

Maternal and Child Health Program Goals, 2005

Source: Maternal and Child Health Bureau (2005).

FIGURE 11.3

Morbidity and Mortality

- Reduce the rate of fetal and infant deaths

- Reduce the rate of child deaths

- Reduce the rate of adolescent and young adult deaths

- Reduce the rate of maternal mortality

- Reduce maternal illness and complications due to pregnancy

- Reduce cesarean births among low-risk women

- Reduce low birth weight (LBVV) and very low birth weight (VLBVV)

- Reduce preterm births

Pregnancy Health and Behaviors

- Increase the proportion of pregnant women who receive early and adequate prenatal care

- Increase abstinence from alcohol, cigarettes, and illicit drugs among pregnant women

- Increase the proportion of pregnant women who attend a series of prepared childbirth classes

- Increase the proportion of mothers who achieve a recommended weight gain during pregnancy

Preconception Health and Behaviors

- Increase the proportion of women of childbearing potential with intake of at least 400 µg of folic acid from fortified foods or dietary supplements

- Reduce the proportion of women of childbearing potential who have low red blood cell folate concentrations

- Increase the proportion of women delivering a live birth who received preconception care services and practiced key recommended preconception health behaviors

- Reduce the proportion of persons aged 18 to 44 years who have impaired fecundity (i.e., a physical barrier preventing pregnancy or carrying a pregnancy to term)

Postpartum Health and Behavior

- Reduce postpartum relapse of smoking among women who quit smoking during pregnancy

- Increase the proportion of women giving birth who attend a postpartum care visit with a health worker

Source: U.S. Department of Health and Human Services (2018b).

the Maternal and Child Health Services (MCHS) program, as well as Crippled Children's Services (CCS) and Child Welfare Services (CWS), when it was originally enacted. Title V has undergone many legislative changes, however. Funding to the states for maternal and child health services for low-income children is now administered through the Maternal and Child Health Block Grant, which was established in 1981.

The Maternal and Child Health Bureau, Health Resources and Services Administration (HRSA), in the U.S. Department of Health and Human Services (HHS) provides leadership for the development of all Title V-funded maternal and child health services and administers the program. These services must be consistent with the nation's public health goals and objectives embodied in *Healthy People 2020* (2018) (see Figures 11.2 and 11.3, for 2005 and 2012 objectives, respectively). Two primary goals of the original block grant are to reduce infant mortality and increase women's access to prenatal care. *Healthy Start* is a special initiative that began in 1991 and focuses on at-risk or underserved areas with high infant mortality rates (Jaros and Evans, 1995). *Healthy Start*-funded projects address "the significant disparities in the health of mothers and babies experienced by racial and ethnic minorities in communities that face many challenges, including inadequate access to care and limited funding" (U.S. Department of Health and Human Services, 2012a). A comparison of Figures 11.2 and 11.3 shows how the nation's maternal and child health objectives have matured, which now include baselines, targets, and target setting methods.

The Special Supplemental Food Program for Women, Infants, and Children (WIC) (PL 92-433) (originally enacted in 1972) helps low-income women and their children attain adequate nutrition. The federal WIC program provides grants to states for supplemental foods, health care referrals, and nutrition education for women, infants, and children up to age five at nutritional risk. At the point recession in the U.S., 14.5 million women and children were eligible for WIC assistance during an average month in 2010—approximately 2.5 million infants or about 64 percent of all infants in the U.S., 9.2 million children age 1–4 or more than half of all young children, 1.3 million pregnant women, and 1.5 million postpartum women. The WIC program reached 9.1 eligible recipients in 2010 (U.S. Department of Agriculture, 2010). However, the number of WIC recipients has decreased and returned to pre-recession statistics (about 7.3 million in an average month) (U.S. Department of Agriculture, 2018). For many years, the Children's Defense Fund has encouraged expansion of the program because its funding ceiling does not allow it to reach everyone who is eligible (Edelman, 1999).

Community health centers, which were established by the Health Centers Consolidation Act of 1996 (PL 104-299) as an amendment to the Public Health Service Act, and signed into law by President Clinton, play a significant role in the provision of services to vulnerable and underserved women of childbearing age. The 1996 bill both reauthorized and consolidated four federal health programs: Community health centers, migrant health centers, health care for the homeless, and health care for residents of public housing programs. The centers were originally created to increase access to health care for low-income people, primarily in underserved inner cities and rural areas of the country. The bill also created a federal loan guarantee program to facilitate the movement of community health centers into managed care. As discussed in Chapter 3, federal support for community health centers doubled in 2000 under President Bush and, with enactment of the Affordable Care Act, the Obama administration reemphasized the importance and role of community health centers in expanding access to care for disadvantaged populations. In 2015, about 1375 non-profit, community-based, health centers provided services in more than 9750 communities to more than 24.3 million poor and low-income people in rural and urban medically underserved areas (Paradise et al., 2017). In some, the centers are the only source of primary care for this population. Most are young women and children, many of whom are eligible for Medicaid or are uninsured. The centers play a vital role in the provision of prenatal, maternal, and infant care (U.S. General Accounting Office, 2000a; U.S. Health Resources and Services Administration, 2007).

Family Planning Services

Family planning services and safe, legal abortions are essential services in the delivery of women's health care. Family planning prevents unwanted pregnancies and, in doing so, helps to reduce the incidence of abortion. Women who use family planning services are more likely to have prenatal care; thus, they are also more likely to have healthy babies and less likely to give birth to low-birth-weight babies or to lose their children during childbirth. Family planning also improves maternal health for women and decreases maternal mortality. However, access to family planning remains a significant problem in the U.S. and in recent years has worsened, as abortion, in particular, has become the focus of political debate and controversy. In 2011, more states passed abortion laws restricting access than in any other previous year, with more than half of all women of reproductive age (15–44) living in a state "hostile to abortion rights" (Guttmacher Institute, 2013). In 2018, *States Are Competing to Pass the Country's Worst Anti-Abortion Laws* (Osberg, 2018).

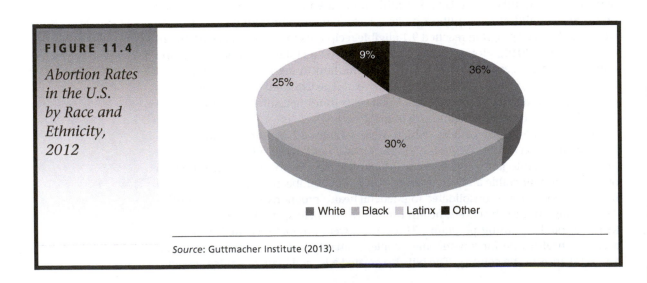

FIGURE 11.4

Abortion Rates in the U.S. by Race and Ethnicity, 2012

■ White ■ Black ■ Latinx ■ Other

Source: Guttmacher Institute (2013).

Despite efforts to provide family planning services, about half of all pregnancies in the U.S. are still unintended; by age 45 more than half of all women will have experienced an unintended pregnancy, and about one-third of unintended pregnancies will end with an abortion (*Healthy People 2000*, 1999a; National Women's Law Center, 2007; Guttmacher Institute, 2013). Those overrepresented among these women are young, poor or near-poor, African American, Latina, unmarried, or women who already have one child. According to the Guttmacher Institute (2009), the federal family planning program successfully eliminated racial and ethnic disparities in contraceptive use by 1995; however, by 2002, "ground had been lost" and these disparities rose precipitously. These trends in contraceptive use are reflected in the rates of unwanted pregnancies and the rates of abortion (Figure 11.4).

Medicaid has become the major source of public funding for family planning services (Figure 11.5). Medicaid expenditures for family planning increased dramatically from $100 million in 1980 to $2.1 billion in 2015. This increase parallels the overall growth in Medicaid spending, with 75 percent of the funding provided by Medicaid (Alan Guttmacher Institute, 2017). The Affordable Care Act has the potential to expand family planning services through the Medicaid program. The ACA simplifies the process for a state seeking to expand Medicaid eligibility for family planning and broadens access to coverage to a larger population.

However, inflation-adjusted appropriations for Title X, Family Planning and Population Research, of the Public Health Service Act (1970), which provides services for millions of women (and men) through a network of 4500 clinics across the country, declined by more than 70 percent between 1980 and 2012 (Sonfeld and Gold, 2012). This is concerning, because about 89 percent of family planning clinic users have low incomes, and about one-third are adolescents (*Healthy People 2000*, 1999a). In addition, appropriations since 2012 have declined, and for the first time the House voted in 2011 to defund family planning. Political struggles

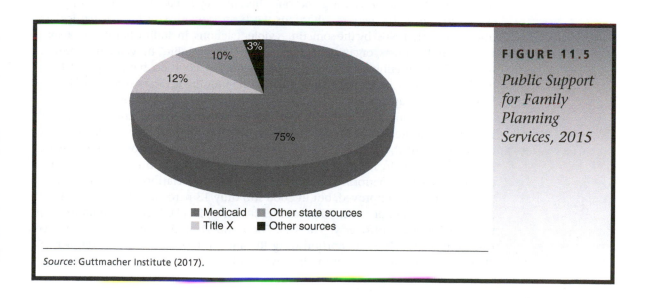

FIGURE 11.5

Public Support for Family Planning Services, 2015

Legend: Medicaid — Other state sources — Title X — Other sources

Source: Guttmacher Institute (2017).

to reduce funding and efforts to defund the program have continued under the Trump administration.

Congress has not taken action to reauthorize Title X since 1985 due to political pressures from the influential, right-wing antichoice movement, even though it does not represent a majority in the U.S. who support a woman's right to reproductive choice (National Association of Social Workers, 2000c). The Reagan administration issued a "gag rule" in 1987 that prohibited use of Title X funds to provide abortions or abortion-related counseling, referrals, or advocacy. This policy was challenged in the courts but was eventually upheld by the Supreme Court in 1991. President Clinton rescinded the policy in 1993, but the new guidelines still require Title X activities to be "separate and distinguishable" from abortion-related services (Cohen, 2007).

Congress has continued to appropriate funds for Title X, but, as mentioned earlier, with declining support. The Title X Family Planning program is important for several reasons. First, it subsidizes services for those ineligible for Medicaid and, second, Title X funds are used for far broader preventive services than Medicaid, which is limited to providing services to specific patients. Also, as noted by Cohen (2007), Title X sets standards for the public provision of voluntary, confidential, and affordable family planning services.

The primary method for the prevention of unwanted pregnancy is contraception, and even legally prescribed birth control has become an issue. Starting in 2005, "moral pharmacists" in a number of states refused to fill birth control prescriptions; some states upheld these practices. In response, the Support the Access to Legal Pharmaceuticals Act was introduced to protect women's rights to legal contraception, but contraceptives are not fail-proof. In such cases, women need access to safe, legal abortions. Since 1976, the right to an abortion for low-income women on Medicaid has been weakened. The Hyde amendment of 1976 prevents the use of federal funds for abortion except in the case of rape or incest, or when the woman's life is in danger; some state Medicaid programs go beyond this coverage. In addition, access to physicians and clinics that perform abortions has been jeopardized (this was particularly true in the early 1990s) by the sometimes violent actions, including bombings, arsons, assaults, and murders, organized by segments of the "pro-life" movement to prevent women from entering these facilities. Opponents of abortion have opposed funding for the Title X program because much of its funding is directed toward Planned Parenthood affiliates, which remain the primary providers of abortion services.

In 1994, Congress passed the Freedom of Access to Clinic Entrances Act (PL 103-259) to protect women, physicians, and other medical staff from these acts of violence, but the number of physicians and clinics that perform abortions has declined steadily. In 1999, only 4 percent of the counties in the U.S. had a health care provider who performed abortions (National Association of Social Workers, 2000c); access has improved, but in 2008 still only 13 percent of U.S. counties had a medical abortion provider (Guttmacher Institute, 2011). Medication abortion is the most recent controversy. The U.S. Food and Drug Administration approved the controversial French abortion drug RU-486 (mifepristone) on September 28, 2000 under President Clinton; however, this medication, which provides an

All states have received Title V State Abstinence Education Grant Program (AEGP) funding to teach the following educational goals. The focus of these grants is on those groups most likely to bear children out of wedlock (youth, ages 10–19, children who are homeless, in foster care, live in rural areas or geographic areas with high teen birth rates, or come from racial or ethnic minority groups).

- The sociological, psychological, and health gains to be realized by abstinence

- Abstinence from sexual activity outside marriage as the expected standard for school-age children

- Abstinence as the only certain way to avoid pregnancy, sexually transmitted diseases, and other health problems

- Mutually faithful monogamous relationships through marriage as the expected standard of human sexual activity

- Sexual activity outside marriage as likely to have harmful psychological and physical effects

- Bearing children out of wedlock is likely to have harmful consequences for the child, the child's parents, and society

- How to reject sexual advances

- How alcohol and drug use increases vulnerability to sexual advances and how alcohol and drug use increases vulnerability to sexual advances

- The importance of attaining self-sufficiency before engaging in sexual activity

FIGURE 11.6

Abstinence Education Grant Program (Title V) Goals, Personal Responsibility and Work Opportunity Act of 1996: Affordable Care Act of 2010 Authorized and Appropriated Funding, 2010–2017

Source: U.S. Department of Health and Human Services (2017b).

alternative to surgical abortions for women in the early stage of pregnancy, came under the scrutiny of the Bush administration. Although it is not a substitute for most women and is not covered by Medicaid in most states, early medication abortion is now an integral part of abortion services (Guttmacher Institute, 2011). Overall, the right to safe and legal abortions, first granted by the U.S. Supreme Court decision *Roe v. Wade* in 1973, still needs support and protection.

Finally, with the creation of the Abstinence Education program (under Title V) as part of the Personal Responsibility and Work Opportunity Reconciliation Act (PRWORA) of 1996, states have been promoting abstinence from sexual activity as the preferred method of avoiding unwanted pregnancies for school-age children (Figure 11.6), even in the absence of evidence to show that abstinence-only education delays sexual activity or reduces teen pregnancy (Alan Guttmacher Institute, 2005). Abstinence-only education may actually increase the risk of unintended teen pregnancy (Kirby, 2001), whereas comprehensive education programs have been shown to be the most effective (Sexuality Information and Education Council of the United States [SIECUS], 2005). President Obama supported comprehensive education for teen pregnancy prevention (2010 proposed budget), but the Trump administration fully supports abstinence-only programs by favoring funding for programs with this approach.

Violence against Women

In the U.S., about 7 million women are victims of rape, physical abuse, or stalking by an intimate partner; the U.S. has the highest rate of domestic violence among industrialized nations (Thomas, 2017). Twenty percent of all women report having been raped in their lifetime; a third of all women report being physically assaulted by an intimate partner (National Coalition Against Domestic Violence [NCADV], 2015). A recent study (Stop Street Harassment, 2018) found that 81 percent of all women experienced some form of sexual harassment or sexual assault in their lifetime. According to the Centers for Disease Control and Prevention, about a quarter of all women in the U.S. will experience an abusive relationship (Finley, 2013). In the U.S., both men and women are subject to societal violence. However, women are more likely to be victims of sex crimes, whereas men are more likely to experience physical violence (warfare, assault, homicide, suicide, injury, disability) (Gilligan, 1996). These differences are rooted in "the cultural construction of masculinity and femininity" (Gilligan, 1996, p. 229) and the gender roles into which men and women are socialized. For example, in *Real Boys' Voices*, Pollack (2000) describes our tolerance for "dangerous bullying" among boys as a "national disgrace" and the increasing fear among boys of "being victimized by the rage and violence of other boys" (Pollack, 2000, p. 199).

Gender-based socialization, coupled with women's traditional economic dependence on men, provides a social context for understanding domestic violence, which generally refers to violence between intimate partners. Legal definitions of domestic abuse typically refer to acts or threats of physical abuse, including rape or sexual assault, whereas clinical definitions are likely to additionally include patterns of psychological or economic coercion (Fantuzzo and Mohr, 1999).

Although men and women can experience domestic violence, men have historically inflicted physical abuse against women, and women have had little recourse against it. Wife beating was actually sanctioned by English common law, was not prohibited in the U.S. until 1883, and was not even taken seriously as deviant or criminal behavior until the 1970s. Before the 1970s, domestic violence was viewed as a private, family matter, not a legal issue, and police departments, until the 1980s, discouraged arrests in cases of domestic violence.

Today, with the changes in social roles that have occurred, even if men and women are more likely to engage equally in physical abuse toward their partners or spouses (Brush, 1990), women are still more likely to suffer physical injury due to the fact that men are usually physically stronger. In fact, studies (Browne, 1987; Schwartz, 1987) show that the vast majority (95 percent) of abuse victims are women. Women are also more likely to remain in abusive relationships because of their greater economic dependence on men, and poor and low-income women are at even greater risk for spousal abuse (Dibble and Straus, 1990; Gelles and Cornell, 1990). Native American women seem to be at particular risk, because statistics show that over 84 percent experience violence during their lifetimes, over half report having experienced sexual assault, and over half report intimate partner physical abuse. According to Amnesty International (2008), the federal government has created a complex interrelationship for federal, state, and tribal jurisdictions which undermines tribal authority and often allows perpetrators to evade justice. Tribal governments are hampered by a complex set of laws and regulations created by the federal government that make it difficult, if not impossible, to respond to sexual assault in an effective manner.

From a health perspective, violence against women is a major concern. Each year, more than ten million women suffer physical abuse; one-third of all women experience intimate partner physical abuse (NCADV, 2015). In 2009, "the proportion of violent crimes committed against females in which the offender was known by the victim was highest for rape and sexual assault (79.4 percent), followed by simple and aggravated assault (70.2 and 64.5 percent, respectively)" (U.S. Department of Health and Human Services, 2011). Violence in the form of rape increased from 1986 to 1994, although there has been a more positive downward trend since then with passage of the Violence Against Women Act in 1994 (*Healthy People 2000*, 1998b; U.S. Department of Health and Human Services, 2011). Also, since 1994, intimate partner physical abuse has declined 67 percent (NCADV, 2015). However, 72 percent of all murder suicides involve an intimate partner and 94 percent of these victims are female. Emergency departments report that 14 percent of women treated in emergency rooms have been injured due to domestic violence (Thomas, 2017). Pregnancy can be a particularly dangerous time for women in abusive relationships, putting them at risk for miscarriages and stillbirths, and creating a greater likelihood of bearing a low-birth-weight baby. Domestic violence also puts women at greater risk for mental health problems, including depression and suicide. Women who have experienced sexual or physical assault often experience posttraumatic stress disorder (PTSD) (Browne, 1993).

A meta-analysis of research on the chronic health consequences of partner violence on women (Macy et al., 2009) found that these women were more likely to have disabling physical conditions such as chronic pain, migraines, sexually transmitted infections, and gastrointestinal disorders. They also experienced more disabling mental health conditions, including depression, anxiety, PTSD, and substance abuse disorders, and were more likely to attempt/commit suicide. More recent experiences of partner violence, chronic or severe partner violence, and multiple forms of abuse—for example, child abuse—over a lifetime, also increase the risk of health problems.

Violence Against Women's Services

For many years, the widespread problem of violence against women in the U.S. received little attention, but in the past 40 years a number of legal and social reforms have occurred. In the early to mid-1970s, grassroots efforts by women's groups to help "battered" women led to the development of shelters or safe houses across the country. Divorce laws also changed during this period, making it easier for women to leave their husbands. The National Institute of Mental Health (NIMH) sponsored research on sexual assault during the 1970s and, between 1979 and 1981, the federal government established and administered the Office of Domestic Violence.

In 1984, the first federal effort to address domestic violence, the Family Violence Prevention and Services Act, was enacted to give states funds to raise awareness about domestic violence and to establish temporary shelters for abused women. It also provided funds for training and family violence services. In 1984, the Victims of Crime Act was also enacted to give women compensation for crime-related costs.

With growing awareness and concern for victims of domestic violence, Congress enacted the Violence Against Women Act (VAWA) of 1994 (as part of the Violent Crime Control and Law Enforcement Act, PL 103-3222), spearheaded then by Senator, and later by Vice-President, Joe Biden. This bill placed more emphasis on prevention and expanded federal funding for state-supported domestic violence prevention and training programs. It also classified sex crimes as hate crimes, increased penalties against offenders, and improved legal protections for victims of abuse, including the protection of abused immigrant women from deportation (Mathews, 1999). Abused immigrant women who depend on the legal citizenship or permanent resident status of their spouses for their own immigration status have been afraid to leave their spouses.

In 1996, a National Domestic Violence Hotline was created under VAWA, and by 1999 over 2000 agencies existed across the country, providing services to abused women and their children, including emergency hotlines, crisis counseling, support groups for women and men, vocational counseling, and assistance with housing, legal services, and health and mental health care. These agencies also offered training and education programs to improve public awareness and understanding of the problem and improve collaboration among law enforcement agencies, child protective services, and health care services (Saathoff and Stoffel, 1999). Congress has significantly increased support for VAWA resources each year since its inception and reauthorized the bill in 2000 and 2005.

VAWA 2000 strengthened protections for battered immigrants, survivors of sexual assault, and victims of dating violence. It also established new programs to address elder abuse, violence against individuals with disabilities, and the need for safe visitation and exchange of children in cases of domestic violence, child abuse, sexual assault or stalking, and legal assistance for victims. VAWA 2005 improved and expanded grant programs addressing domestic violence, dating violence, sexual assault, and stalking, and established a number of new programs with an increased emphasis on violence against Native American women, sexual assault, and youth victims (U.S. Department of Justice, 2006).

When VAWA came up for reauthorization in 2012, the House blocked its passage; conservatives opposed the bill's expansion of visas for undocumented victims of domestic violence, the extension of tribal authority over nontribe members who abuse Native American partners, and the establishment of protection for gay and lesbian victims of domestic violence. A new version of the bill was introduced in 2013 which removed the expansion of visas in the hopes of garnering support for reauthorization of this important legislation. According to the U.S. Department of Justice, VAWA has made a difference in violence against women; rates of intimate partner violence decreased 64 percent between 1994 and 2010 (Finley, 2013). The new bill was enacted in early 2013. Among those opposed to the reauthorization was the then Senator Jeff Sessions who four years later became Attorney General in the Trump administration. This has raised concerns among advocates of VAWA because it is up for reauthorization in 2018 and conservative groups like the Heritage Foundation have called for eliminating all VAWA grants.

Depression

According to the landmark report, *Mental Health: A Report of the Surgeon General* (U.S. Department of Health and Human Services, 1999, p. xiv):

> Socioeconomic factors affect individuals' vulnerability to mental illness and mental health problems. Certain demographic and economic groups are more likely than others to experience mental health problems and some disorders. Vulnerability alone may not be sufficient to cause a mental disorder; rather, the causes of most mental disorders lie in some combination of genetic and environmental factors, which may be biological or psychosocial.

The social roles of women in the U.S. have changed considerably since the 1960s, and patterns of gender-based inequity are improving. However, women today still experience adverse socioeconomic conditions, including occupational segregation, disparities in earnings, and disproportionate rates of poverty, as well as harmful psychosocial risks, such as sexual harassment at work or school, or domestic violence. Women at all socioeconomic levels often bear the double burden and stress of caring for children and working outside the home. Older women are more likely to experience the stress of a spouse's death, because women have a longer life expectancy than men. In addition to socioeconomic factors, some medical experts attribute the increased risk of depression to hormonal changes that occur throughout a woman's life, including puberty, pregnancy, menopause, and after giving birth or experiencing a miscarriage.

Men and women have about the same rates of mental illness, but women are twice as likely as men to develop clinical depression (WebMd, 2018). National studies from the 1980s (the NIMH, Epidemiologic Catchment Area studies), the 1990s (the National Comorbidity Survey), and more recent studies from the National Institutes of Health show that women are at greater risk than men for affective disorders (Glied and Kofman, 1995; Proctor and Stiffman, 1998). Low-income women aged 25–44 are particularly vulnerable (National Academy on an Aging Society, 2000; Kaiser Family Foundation, 2005).

The reasons for these differences between women and men are as yet unclear (NIMH, 2005; Harvard Medical School, 2011). Certainly, the socioeconomic and psychosocial factors that affect women's lives play a role in their mental health, but why are women at particular risk of depression? It may be that, because men tend to see depression as a weakness, they are more likely to exhibit depressive symptoms through alcohol and substance abuse. Research has had "limited success" in identifying biological factors that explain the disparity (Harvard Medical School, 2011).

WOMEN IN MEDICAL RESEARCH

A different, but related, kind of disparity for women is found in the nation's health research agenda. In the 1980s, the National Institutes of Health (NIH) agreed that women were excluded from research studies (many included only men), and few studies were designed to research women's health issues. The NIH is the federal agency with primary responsibility for medical research. It has a multibillion-dollar budget to conduct research through 25 institutes and centers, each of which focuses on a major disease or health concern, such as cancer. In 1990, the NIH established the Office of Research on Women's Health and started a Women's Health Initiative (WHI) in 1991 to study: (1) The prevention of cardiovascular disease, breast cancer, and osteoporosis through hormone replacement therapy and other preventive measures; (2) the relationship between lifestyle and specific disease outcomes; and (3) the role of community prevention efforts to promote healthy lifestyles, particularly among women of color.

However, as a result of concerns about implementation of the new NIH guidelines to include women in medical research, Congress enacted Women and Minorities as Subjects in Clinical Research as part of the NIH Revitalization Act of 1993 (PL 103-43). This legislation mandated the inclusion of women and men in all NIH clinical research studies. In 2000, the U.S. General Accounting Office (2000b) concluded that significant progress had been made. It was expected that the results of such studies would provide new information about (1) health conditions unique to women or more prevalent among women, (2) differences between women and men in medical risks, and (3) health conditions with insufficient clinical data based on research using women as subjects (U.S. General Accounting Office, 2000b). In 2001, the NIH guidelines for inclusion were updated to include racial and ethnic and sex/gender differences in intervention effects. In 2014, new policies were introduced to strengthen the requirement to include women and men in research designs and preclinical and clinical interventions (Office of Research on Women's Health, 2018).

CHILDREN AND ADOLESCENTS

Children and adolescents also have special health concerns and needs; the U.S. federal government recognizes disparities in health for children and youth. In 1999, the U.S. Agency for Health Care Policy and Research was reauthorized by Congress and renamed the U.S. Agency for Healthcare Research and Quality (AHRQ) under PL 106-129. AHRQ, which is responsible for research efforts to improve health care services and their access, identified children as one of its priorities and recognized children's health needs as different from those of adults (AHRQ, 2000). For example, *Healthy People 2010*, the nation's blueprint for improving the health of Americans, identified eight health indicators for adolescents and young adults, six of which targeted morbidity and mortality. These indicators were: (1) Deaths caused by motor vehicle crashes, (2) homicides, (3) the proportion of youth engaging in binge drinking of alcoholic beverages, (4) past-month use of illicit substances, (5) tobacco use, and (6) the proportion of youth who are overweight or obese. *Healthy People 2020* refined the health targets established for adolescents and young adults; as with the health targets for maternal women, infants, and children, the new health targets are much more specific and data driven and focus on both reducing poor health outcomes and improving good health outcomes. The 11 new health targets focus primarily on social determinants of health: Wellness check-ups, after-school activities, adolescent–adult connections, transition to self-sufficiency from foster care, educational achievement, school breakfast program, illegal drugs on school property, student safety at school, student harassment related to sexual orientation and gender identity, serious violent incidents in public schools, and youth perpetration of, and victimization by, crimes (U.S. Department of Health and Human Services, 2012a).

According to AHRQ (2000), children (under the age of 19) have the lowest mortality rates, but the highest rates of *acute* illness and, therefore, the need for frequent medical care. The rates of *chronic* illness for children and adults are about the same, but children experience different chronic illnesses, including asthma and attention deficit disorder. As children grow and change from infancy to adolescence, they are constantly vulnerable to new and changing environmental hazards, such as infectious diseases, as well as behavioral risks, such as alcohol and drug abuse, teenage pregnancy, and suicide. Finally, and most importantly, children depend on adults for their health and wellbeing.

Over 40 years ago, medical researchers at Harvard (Newberger et al., 1976) raised serious questions and concerns about the inability of the U.S. health care system to "reach and treat the children most in need of them" and the impact of "environmental forces" (Newberger et al., 1976, p. 249) on child health, particularly among poor and "non-white" children. They were concerned with the impact of accidents, lead poisoning, physical abuse, and other "causal" environmental factors that are readily viewed as risks to child health. However, they also raised broader concerns about the "relationship between adult dysfunction and childhood illness" (Newberger et al., 1976, p. 271) and the wider context of child health. Children clearly depend on adult care, and parents who are unable to provide fully for their children, because of their own socio-economic status, place their children at risk for ill-health, no matter how unintentional this may be. In other words, poverty "appears to cause—directly or indirectly—a great amount of morbidity and mortality in children" (Newberger et al., 1976, p. 272).

Today, the "state of America's children" (Edelman, 1999) and its potential impact on child health have not improved; surprisingly, they have worsened. In 1975, the "absolute" child poverty rate was 16 percent (U.S. Census Bureau, 1976); in 2018, the "absolute" poverty rate was 19 percent (National Center for Children in Poverty, 2018). Child poverty gradually increased from 2000 to 2012, has declined somewhat since then, but is still disturbingly high (U.S. Census Bureau, 2012; National Center for Children in Poverty, 2018). The "relative" poverty rate is even more alarming when compared with other industrialized nations. A 2012 UNICEF report, which defines "relative child poverty" as living in a household where disposable income is less than half of the national median income, shows that relative child poverty in the U.S. was the second highest among 35 of the world's richest countries (UNICEF, 2012). According to the National Center for Children in Poverty (2018), 41 percent or 29.8 million of America's children were living on the brink of poverty in 2016.

Poor children are at greater risk for ill-health. For example, poor children are more vulnerable to iron deficiency, which causes anemia and can affect children's attention, concentration, and motor coordination. Poor children are more likely to live in cold, damp, moldy housing that exacerbates asthma and other respiratory diseases. Cockroach infestations are found in damp housing conditions which stem from lack of heat, uneven heat, or leaky pipes, and cause allergies and asthma for poor children. Children living in such surroundings are more likely to be exposed to rats and mice, which can lead to respiratory problems; lead paint, which causes poisoning and can lead to brain damage (Epstein, 2013), and overcrowding, which contributes to stress, infection, injuries, and accidents. Homeless children are at greater risk of exposure to infectious diseases in shelters and have higher rates of asthma and inadequate immunizations (Sherman, 1994). Poor children are more likely to be exposed to secondhand smoke (20 or more cigarettes per day), which puts them at greater risk for asthma and chronic bronchitis (Williams, 1990; Gergen et al., 1998).

Infectious Diseases

Immunization is one of the most successful, cost-effective means of preventing disease. All 50 states require immunization of students for school entry (with exemptions for medical, philosophical, or religious reasons). To address the need for all children to be immunized from infectious diseases, Congress supported President Clinton's initiative for a federal vaccine program in 1993. Before this legislation, children's access to vaccination depended on their access to providers and health insurance coverage. Children enrolled in the Medicaid program were particularly vulnerable, because physicians found it costly to purchase the vaccines and then wait for reimbursement from Medicaid. Instead, physicians made referrals to public health clinics and, in the process, poor children often became infected before they had a chance to be immunized.

The 1993 Vaccines for Children Act (VFC) (PL 103-66) was enacted to address this problem; through this legislation the federal government can purchase vaccines and distribute them at no cost to physicians to administer. Free vaccines are available to children under the age of 18 who are eligible for Medicaid, have no health insurance, or are Native American or Alaska Native. The program has made an enormous difference in the rates of vaccination against diphtheria, tetanus, pertussis, measles, mumps, rubella, and polio. For example, from 1992 to 1997, the number of two-year-olds fully immunized against these contagious diseases increased by 33 percent (Edelman, 1999). However, coverage among children living below the poverty level still lags behind for newer vaccines and vaccines that require multiple doses (Centers for Disease Control and Prevention, 2012b).

As the list of recommended vaccines continues to grow and become more costly, public support for vaccination is becoming increasingly essential to public health. From infancy through age 18, vaccines alone cost roughly $1600 or more; from 2000 to 2007 the cost of recommended vaccines tripled. A survey published in *Pediatrics* (Freed et al., 2008) found wide disparities in payments to physicians by insurance companies for immunizations, sometimes at a financial loss. If this trend leads to decreases in the provision of immunization services by pediatricians and family practice physicians, public health clinics might not be equipped to meet growing demand, which, in turn, could lead to new outbreaks of childhood diseases such as measles, mumps, and rubella. As it is, there has been a trend among some parents, in recent years, to avoid vaccines for measles due to a fear that it may cause autism in children.

Public health clinics already play an important role in immunization, particularly in rural areas, where access to medical care is more limited (Slifkin et al., 1997). Senator Kennedy (D-MA) proposed a Childhood Vaccines Access Act 2008, which would include all public clinics in the distribution of pediatric vaccines under the Medicaid program, but Congress did not take action on this bill. This amendment would have supported and strengthened the VFC program, which is the primary source of childhood vaccinations in the U.S. (Figure 11.7). However, the 2010

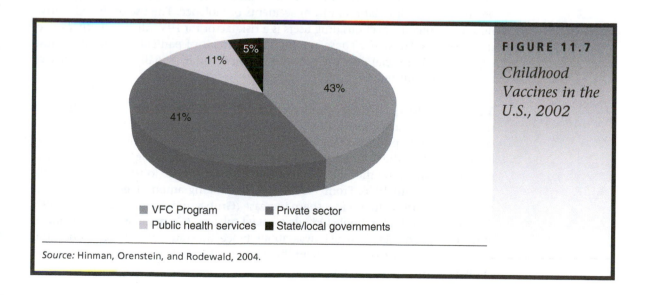

FIGURE 11.7

Childhood Vaccines in the U.S., 2002

- ■ VFC Program
- ■ Private sector
- ▨ Public health services
- ■ State/local governments

43%
11%
5%
41%

Source: Hinman, Orenstein, and Rodewald, 2004.

Affordable Care Act now requires health plans to cover recommended immuniza-tions to all its enrollees at no cost (when administered by an in-network provider) (Centers for Disease Control and Prevention, 2012b). Also, increased access to immu-nization for millions of children and adults is also expected through community health centers. The most basic public health investment we can make as a nation, next to clean water and sanitation, is vaccination against the most common illnesses.

Risky Behaviors: Substance Abuse

Substance abuse refers to the use of alcohol, tobacco, illicit drugs (marijuana, cocaine, heroin, hallucinogens), nonprescription and prescription drugs (depres-sants, such as sleeping pills or Valium; stimulants, such as amphetamines), and common household products often used as inhalants (glues, solvents, butane, gas-oline, and aerosols) in a way that results in health consequences or in impair-ment of social, psychological, and occupational functioning (National Association of Social Workers [NASW] 2000a). The profession of social work is increasingly concerned with the prevalence of substance use in our society and its widespread impact on social work practice, and more social workers are needed to help with patients being treated for substance abuse (NASW, 2013).

Millions of people in the U.S. use drugs every day. Some do so responsibly without incident; others are at risk for habitual, chronic use that results in per-sonal, familial, or legal problems. Substance abuse is difficult to assess because it is not only linked to other physical, psychological, and social problems, but also influenced by cultural norms. Substance abuse can be the cause of physical or psy-chological problems, or it can be the result of individual efforts to cope with other preexisting conditions or diseases.

Substance abuse is associated with a wide range of physical illnesses, includ-ing: Cancer, heart disease, liver and pancreatic disease, and respiratory arrest; men-tal illness, including psychosis, depression, and anxiety disorders; and drug-related deaths and injuries that result from accidents or violence. The use of shared "dirty" needles among intravenous drug users is a risk factor for HIV/AIDS and other infec-tious diseases. Substance abuse among adolescents is of particular concern because experimental or social drug use can lead to abuse and eventually to dependence or addiction in adulthood.

Youth Smoking. In 1995, the Maternal and Child Health Bureau established a new Office of Adolescent Health (OAH) in an effort to make the health of adoles-cents a national priority. OAH is concerned with several disturbing health trends among youth in the U.S. One area of concern is teenage smoking, which, according to studies funded by the National Institute of Drug Abuse (Johnston et al., 2000), reached a peak in 1976. From 1977 to 1992, smoking among teens declined, but from 1992 to 1997 there was a sharp increase (Gruber and Zinman, 2000). In 1997, 36.4 percent of high school students smoked tobacco (Centers for Disease Control and Prevention, 2004), which was about twice the rate for adults. Gruber and Zinman (2000) raise concerns about the relationship between teenage smoking and adult smoking, and estimate that 25–50 percent of adolescent smokers continue this habit as adults. Tobacco use among teens has declined dramatically since 2000, however. In 2007, it reached a low of about 26.5 percent of high school students (Centers for Disease Control and Prevention, 2008), and in 2012, according to the National Institute on Drug Abuse, youth smoking reached an all-time low of 10.6 percent of eighth, tenth, and twelfth graders. The decline was likely due mostly to a sharp increase in the federal tobacco tax (Dooren, 2012). Further reductions in adolescent smoking have occurred since—9.7 percent of twelfth graders, 5.0 percent of tenth graders, and 1.9 percent of eighth graders in 2017 (Miech et al., 2017), but the need for tobacco use prevention programs remains vital to adolescent health. The newest concern is e-smoke. The 2016 Surgeon General's report identified electronic cigarette (e-cigarette) use among adolescents and young adults as a major public health concern; e-smoking is associated with future tobacco product use.

Smoking is widespread and not confined to poor and low-income youth; in fact, white or suburban youth smoke even more than African American or urban youth. However, Gruber and Zinman (2000) estimated that 25 percent of the increase in teen smoking during the 1990s (until 1998) was due to the decline in cigarette prices and the advertising efforts of cigarette companies to target youth. Low-income communities and communities of color were specific targets of these campaigns; billboards advertising tobacco were four to five times more likely to be placed in African American or Latino communities (American Heart Association, 2003). Studies show that boys and girls choose to smoke for similar reasons—to relieve stress, because others around them smoke, to experiment, and to have "fun." Girls of color are less likely to smoke than boys across all racial lines, and Hispanic boys are more likely to smoke than white, African American, or Asian American boys.

In addition to socioeconomic status, family and childhood experiences play a role in teen smoking behavior. Parental attitudes about smoking, parental supervision, parent–child communication, and family stress, such as divorce, are factors in adolescent smoking. Abused boys and girls are at greater risk for smoking as a means of relieving stress (Schoen et al., 1998). As a result of a Master Settlement Agreement between 46 states and the tobacco industry, billions of dollars were made available to the states for a 25-year period (1998–2023) to advocate against the use of tobacco. One such campaign, the American Legacy Foundation's "truth" campaign, has shown positive shifts in teen attitudes toward smoking (Sly et al., 2001; Farrelly et al., 2002).

Youth Drinking. Although much attention has been paid to the use of illegal drugs by youth, alcohol is by far the most widely used and abused drug of teenagers (Centers for Disease Control and Prevention, 2012c; Substance Abuse and Mental Health Services Administration [SAMSHA], 2017). As reported by the National Center on Addiction and Substance Abuse (NCASA) at Columbia University (2002): "America has an epidemic of underage drinking that germinates in elementary and middle schools with 9- to 13-year-olds and erupts on campuses where 44 percent of the students binge drink and alcohol is the number one substance of abuse" (NCASA, 2002). For some youth, the consumption of alcohol becomes a major problem in itself, especially if it involves binge drinking, whereas for others alcohol abuse is but one of many high-risk behaviors that reflect other psychosocial difficulties. The National Household Survey on Drug Abuse and the National Survey of High School Seniors conducted by the SAMHSA defines heavy, episodic, or binge drinking as five or more successive drinks per occasion on five or more days a month. Under-age (under 21) binge and heavy alcohol use declined from 2002 to 2014, but, in 2014, more than 5 million youth between the ages of 12 and 20 reported being binge drinkers, and 1.3 million reported being heavy drinkers (SAMHSA, 2017).

The legal minimum drinking age in the U.S. is 21, but many teenagers not only consume alcohol, but also are at increasingly high risk of starting to drink at a young age, often between the ages of 13 and 15 (Johnson et al., 1995) and even between 9 and 13. Children and adolescents under age 21 consume about 11 percent of the nation's alcohol (Centers for Disease Control and Prevention, 2012c). In 2011, 33 percent of eighth graders and 70 percent of twelfth graders consumed alcohol during the month before being surveyed (Centers for Disease Control and Prevention, 2012c).

Teen drinking has potentially devastating health consequences. The leading causes of death among youth are motor vehicle accidents, other unintentional accidents, homicides, and suicides (*Healthy People 2000*, 1998a; Centers for Disease Control and Prevention, 2013). Alcohol is the primary cause of fatal automobile and motorcycle accidents that involve adolescent drivers (Long et al., 1993) and is also associated with homicide and suicide (Holinger et al., 1994). Studies of suicide and drinking do not clearly show a causal relationship between these two factors, but they do show a correlation (Kinkel et al., 1989; Felts et al., 1992; Garrison et al., 1993).

In addition to fatalities, alcohol abuse is linked to risky sexual behavior, as well as to mental illness among youth. For example, one study of teenagers in Massachusetts found that adolescents who had consumed alcohol were more likely to engage in sexual intercourse and less likely to use contraceptives (condoms) (Strunin and Hingson, 1992). Studies (Kushner and Sher, 1993) of college students show that youth with anxiety disorders or depression are more likely to abuse or depend on alcohol. However, it is unclear whether mental illness leads to alcohol abuse or vice versa; some studies show that depression is more likely to precede alcohol abuse (Deykin et al., 1987, 1992).

Youth Drug Abuse. Adolescents are at risk for drug use for many of the same reasons that they abuse alcohol. In addition to psychiatric disorders and other troubling childhood behaviors, such as impulsiveness or aggressiveness, adolescents confront many psychosocial risk factors, including the attitudes and behaviors of parents and peer pressure. The impact of parental attitudes and behaviors on adolescent substance abuse is unclear. Some studies, as reported by de Anda (1995), show that the attitude and behavior of parents toward drugs have both "direct and indirect effects," whereas others show "no significant relationship." The role of peers seems to be far more significant, however. Studies show that peer pressure to use substances may be the greatest risk factor for use and abuse of drugs by adolescents (de Anda, 1995).

Like alcohol abuse, the problem of substance abuse among teenagers is widespread. *Monitoring the Future*, an annual survey of thousands of adolescents and college students conducted by the University of Michigan's Institute for Social

Research (starting in 1975) with funding from the National Institute on Drug Abuse, is one of the best sources of data on substance abuse. In 1975, more than half (55 percent) of all adolescents had experimented with illegal drugs by the time they graduated from high school; the percentage increased to 66 percent by 1981. The survey shows a general decline in the use of illegal drugs from 1981 to 1992, a steady increase from 1992 to 1996 (a recent peak year), and a steady decline from 2001 to 2007 (Johnston et al., 2008). According to the 2000 survey, between 1975 and 2000, either by historical comparisons in this country or by international comparisons with other countries, young Americans achieved extraordinary levels of illicit drug use (Johnston et al., 2000).

Trends in drug use show that marijuana is the most widely used substance; its use, as well as that of many other drugs, was gradually declining until the mid-2000s, when marijuana use began to increase again. Of new concern in recent years was the increased use of inhalants and OxyContin (a narcotic drug) among teens. Evidence shows that young teens in particular are most likely to abuse these substances and to do so because they are inexpensive and legal (Johnston et al., 2005). The 2008 survey raised new concerns about the abuse of prescription medications.

The 2011 survey focused on the importance of "perceived risk" and its impact on use. Researchers have found that the more likelihood of harm that adolescents associate with a substance, the less likely they are to use it. Given this, the findings on perceived risk are concerning; between 2002 and 2010, the perception of "great risk" from using heroin, cocaine, LSD, and marijuana among adolescents decreased, whereas the perceived risk from marijuana use has increased since the mid-2000s. The 2011 survey also showed significant racial and ethnic differences in use rates. African American students had substantially lower rates of use of illicit drugs, alcohol, and tobacco than whites in all grade levels (eighth through twelfth). For Hispanic youth, the picture was more complex, however. Older Hispanic youth (twelfth graders) had a rate closer to white youth, but younger Latino youth (eighth graders) had the highest reported rates of use of the three groups studied (white, African American, Hispanic youth) on nearly all classes of drugs (Johnston et al., 2011).

The most recent 2017 survey found historic lows for drug use among adolescents, including heroin, prescription opioids, MDMA (Ecstasy or Molly), methamphetamine, amphetamines, and sedatives. Five-year declines were also shown for synthetic marijuana, hallucinogens other than LSD, and over-the-counter cough and cold medications, but the study found an increase in LSD use among high school seniors. "Perceived risk" was an issue once again. Students in different age groups were less concerned about trying varying substances, including synthetic marijuana and over-the-counter cough/cold medications (eighth graders), inhalants, powder cocaine, over-the-counter cough/cold medications (tenth graders), and cocaine, heroin, steroids, and LSD (twelfth graders). Marijuana use declined among tenth graders and remained unchanged among eighth and twelfth graders compared with five years ago (National Institute on Drug Abuse, 2017).

Child Abuse and Neglect

Some childhood illnesses "represent symptoms of severe distress in . . . families" (Newberger et al., 1976, p. 277). Although child abuse receives more attention, the neglect of children is far more widespread and, therefore, a more damaging risk to children. Child abuse refers to an act of intent to harm, or the "recurrent infliction of physical or emotional injury on a dependent minor, through intentional beatings, uncontrolled corporal punishment, persistent ridicule and degradation, or sexual abuse" (National Association of Social Workers, 1999, p. 70). Child neglect refers to an act of omission due to limited resources or abilities, or "the failure of those responsible for the care of a minor to provide the resources needed for healthy physical, emotional, and social development. Examples include inadequate nutrition, improper supervision, or [insufficient] . . . provisions for educational or health care requirements" (National Association of Social Workers, 1999, p. 72).

In 2016, there were an estimated 676,000 cases of child abuse and neglect in the U.S., which represents a 3 percent increase since 2012; about 75 percent were cases of neglect (a significant increase since 2006), more than 18 percent were cases of physical abuse, and 8.5 percent were sexual abuse cases. The age group at greatest risk of fatality was, by far, children under the age of three (70 percent). About 78 percent of the perpetrators involved at least one parent (U.S. Department of Health and Human Services, 2017a).

State-level child abuse and neglect-reporting laws to protect children from harm have been in place since the early 1960s. Federal child abuse and neglect prevention efforts began in the mid-1970s with the enactment of the 1974 Child Abuse Prevention and Treatment Act (CAPTA) (PL 93-247). CAPTA established the National Clearinghouse on Child Abuse and Neglect (NCCAN), which developed model reporting requirements and procedures, and required the states to establish protective legislation. However, each state relies on its own definition of child abuse and neglect.

The 1980 Adoption Assistance and Child Welfare Act (PL 96-272) was a response to the increasing problem of ineffective foster care services for abused and neglected children. Hundreds of thousands of children—particularly those from vulnerable populations, including children of color, older children, children with disabilities, children with AIDS/HIV, and medically needy children—were languishing in foster homes for years. This legislation emphasized permanency planning and reunification with families. States must make reasonable efforts to keep families together.

In 1988, CAPTA was amended (PL 100-294) to create the U.S. Advisory Board on Child Abuse and Neglect, to allow for an evaluation of CAPTA's efforts and impact. In 1990, the Advisory Board found that child abuse and neglect were a "national emergency"; in 1995, it reported that abuse and neglect were leading causes of death for very young children (under the age of four) (National Association of Social Workers, 2000b). In 1993, Congress enacted the Family Preservation and Family Support Services Act (PL 103-66) to continue emphasizing family unification, but also to give states resources to shift their attention toward prevention and crisis intervention. The "family preservation" model encouraged by the policy relies on intensive, short-term, community-based case management services for high-risk families to help them avoid and cope with crises.

By 1997, Congress was concerned that neither bill had significantly improved the problems of foster care. The Adoption and Safe Families Act of 1997 (PL 105-89) was passed to place renewed emphasis on permanency in planning for children's care, and to deal once again with the thousands of children placed for far too long in "temporary" foster care. The new policy required quicker action on the child's first permanency hearing (within 12 months rather than 18 months), encouraged termination of parental rights for children in foster care for more than a year, and amended the Family Preservation and Family Support Services Act, renaming it the Promoting Safe and Stable Families program to encourage permanency planning efforts as soon as children entered the system. The policy recognized the psychological and emotional trauma of being left in limbo for long periods of time that was being imposed on children. The Keeping Children and Families Safe Act of 2003 reauthorized and amended the Child Abuse Prevention and Treatment Act through fiscal year 2008, and was amended and reauthorized again in 2010 as the CAPTA Reauthorization Act of 2010 (PL 111-320) with various amendments to Titles I and II.

Exposure to Violence

The impact of violence in the lives of children in the U. S., as discussed in the section on unintentional injuries in Chapter 10, is especially troubling. Homicide rates in 2010 in the U.S. were seven times higher than the rates found in other high-income industrialized countries; homicide rates driven by a gun were 25 times higher. For 15–24 year olds, the gun homicide rate was 49 times higher (Grinshteyn and Hemenway, 2016). In 2010, homicide was the second leading cause of death among young people between the ages of 15 and 24 in the U.S. Homicide rates for African American youth exceeded those for white and Latino youth; in fact, homicide is the *leading* cause of death for African Americans aged 10–24 (Centers for Disease Control and Prevention, 2012d). However, exposure to violence—both real and simulated through various forms of media—creates additional health risks for children that are not fully understood and still in need of research.

Children of color who live in poor inner-city communities are particularly vulnerable to neighborhood violence. They witness shootings and beatings, often drug and/or gang related, and far too often fall victim to these behaviors (Powell, 1999). This kind of frequent exposure to guns and other weapons, drugs, and neighborhood violence is sometimes referred to as chronic community violence (Osofsky, 1999). In 1985, Surgeon General C. Everett Koop held a Conference on Violence as a Health Problem to recommend a public health solution to the problem of violence. Rather than reacting to harmful environmental influences, Koop's public health approach suggested the need for changes in the environments of children through education and public information campaigns (Prothrow-Stith and Quaday, 1995).

Studies show that poverty exacerbates individual and family problems and increases the risk of domestic violence and violence among peers. Violent influences in the home or in the community lead children and adolescents to resolve conflicts with violence, particularly if there are no mediating positive forces in their lives (Prothrow-Stith and Quaday, 1995; Powell, 1999). However, communities and schools from all socioeconomic sectors of the country are concerned with violent behavior and the problem of weapons in schools. All children are exposed to violence—in their communities, in their own families, or through the media. According to a study conducted by the American Psychiatric Association (APA, 1998) in the late 1990s, by age 18, the typical child in the U.S. has seen 16,000 simulated murders and 200,000 acts of violence through television, movies, video games, and the internet (APA, 1998). In 2014, over two-thirds of young children (under age 17) were exposed to violence (assaults, sexual victimization, child maltreatment by an adult) either directly (as victims) or indirectly (as witnesses) (Finkelhor et al., 2015).

The public health approach to the prevention of violence involves *primary* efforts to "create alternative problem-solving strategies, reward nonviolent problem-solving" through "mass media messages, classroom education, peer leadership and mediation, and community-based training programs" (Prothrow-Stith and Quaday, 1995, p. 4). Starting in the mid-1980s, communities across the country began to establish violence prevention programs with private and public funds. For example, one model program, the Boston Violence Prevention Program, taught anger management and conflict resolution to youth and used mass media to create a different attitude toward violent behavior. In 2008, the U.S. Conference of Mayors adopted a resolution calling youth violence a public health crisis and urged the government at all levels (federal, state, and city) to treat youth violence as a public health epidemic and pursue a multi-faceted approach focused on prevention.

The public health approach to the prevention of violence also involves *secondary* efforts to reach children and adolescents who are at greater risk of violence or who have already been exposed to or engaged in acts of violence. These are efforts to stop harmful behaviors through "mentoring/nurturing programs, individual and group counseling, 'in-school' suspension, first-offender programs, and special efforts for hospitalized children who were shot or stabbed" (Prothrow-Stith and Quaday, 1995 p. 3). Programs for children exposed to domestic violence have received attention only recently. Although domestic violence has been accepted as a serious threat to women's health, until recently little attention has been paid to the impact of exposure to domestic violence on children.

The number of empirical studies conducted in the past 20 years to examine the impact of exposure to violence is still limited, but growing. For example, a Canadian study (Fitzpatrick et al., 2012) examines the impact of violent television programming on mental health outcomes for second graders. The findings "empirically support the notion that access to early childhood violent television represents a threat to population health and should be discouraged by adult caregivers" (Fitzpatrick et al., 2012, p. 1). There are indications from these studies that children exposed to domestic violence are at risk of developing a wide range of physical, emotional, cognitive, behavioral, and social problems. The data available about the number of children exposed to domestic violence is also improving.

Studies show that children who witness violence have difficulty knowing whom to trust. They develop defensive behaviors against their fears, regressive behaviors and anxieties in response to trauma, and feelings of guilt for the violence around them. Children who witness a single act of abuse or violence often feel helpless or out of control, whereas children exposed to repeated abuse or violence often engage in denial of their experiences. These emotional and behavioral responses can be detrimental to a child's growth and development and can affect his or her personal relationships through adolescence and adulthood. Extreme inner-city conditions of recurrent violence can cause symptoms similar to PTSD, including nightmares, excessive clinging to parents, and dulled affect. For example, Graham-Bermann and Seng (2005) studied 160 low-income preschoolers from Michigan and found that three out of four were exposed to violence. These children suffered PTSD-like symptoms, including nightmares and bed-wetting, and had a higher rate of allergies, asthma, gastrointestinal ailments, headaches, and flu than their peers. Studies of resilience in children exposed to violence point to similar contributing factors—caring parent(s) (protection, support), community supports (schools, churches, synagogues, and community centers), and individual resources (intelligence, interpersonal skills, self-esteem, contact with positive role models, opportunities to access community resources, socioeconomic status) (Prothrow-Stith and Quaday, 1995).

In response to these concerns, the Office of Juvenile Justice and Delinquency Prevention (OJJDP) established a groundbreaking, multidisciplinary demonstration project in 2001 called the Safe Start Initiative (Kracke, 2001). The goal was to bring together service providers in selected communities to improve services to children exposed to violence or at high risk of exposure. In 2002, ten federal agencies and institutes joined forces to establish a national research agenda on exposure to violence and to fund research projects (National Institute of Child Health and Human Development, 2002). Between 2000 and 2006, 11 demonstration sites (communities across the country) were funded to engage in creating a continuum of care. In 2005 the focus shifted to quasi-experimental evaluations of the 15 most innovative programs in an effort to develop evidence-based, developmentally appropriate services for children exposed to violence; this phase continued through 2009 (Kracke and Cohen, 2008). Phase II began in 2010 with "Eight Promising Approaches II sites." The Safe Start Initiative Center hopes to promote evidence-based strategies for reducing the impact of children's exposure to violence.

In recent years, the nation has experienced some of its greatest challenges to child exposure to gun violence with the increase in mass shootings in schools; between 2012 and 2018, over 400 students were shot in more than 200 school shootings (Patel, 2018). The deadliest mass shooting in schools occurred in 2018 at the Marjory Stoneman Douglas High School in Parkland, Florida where 17 children were killed by a 19-year-old former student.

OLDER ADULTS

Older adults in the U.S. also experience discrimination and disparities in social status and, like women, their health is often associated with their social status. In the 1960s, one of three older adults in the U.S. lived in poverty, and the vast majority depended on Social Security as their only source of income. Congress enacted the Older Americans Act (OAA) (PL 89-73) in 1965 and established the Administration on Aging as part of President Johnson's War on Poverty, in an effort to ensure the health and wellbeing of older adults. With the passage of Medicare in 1965, and the introduction of cost-of-living adjustments to Social Security pensions in 1972, the official rate of poverty among older adults (over age 65) has fallen dramatically; it was 8.7 percent in 2011 (U.S. Census Bureau, 2012).

However, in 2010, for the first time in over 50 years, the U.S. Census Bureau developed an alternative supplemental formula to measure poverty. The new formula used reduced estimates for the cost of food, and higher estimates for the increased costs of health care (out-of-pocket costs for deductibles, co-pays, and prescriptions), childcare, housing and transportation; it included non-cash government supports, such as food stamps, and took into account differences in cost of living in different parts of the country. With this new formula, the supplemental poverty rate for older adults showed a significant increase from about 9 percent to 15.9 percent in 2010, which was essentially no different from the supplemental poverty rate among the general population. The new measure also indicated that the difference in poverty in 2010 among children (18.2 percent) and older adults (15.9 percent) was much closer than the statistics provided by the old measure (Fletcher, 2011; Fremstad, 2012). In 2016, the poverty rate among older adults was about 14 percent (Edwards et al., 2017).

Under either poverty measure, older women, people of color, and older seniors (over age 75 and over age 85) are at even greater risk of poverty. Although there has been a significant increase in the financial assets and net worth of older adults since the 1980s, older adults of color have not fared as well (Ozawa and Tseng, 2000). This population has a history of lower employment earnings, fewer financial assets, and smaller retirement pensions. Indeed, the 2010 official ("old") poverty rate among older African Americans (19.2 percent), Latinx (16.8 percent), Native Americans (15.4 percent), and even Asian Americans (10.8 percent) was substantially higher than for older non-Hispanic whites (8.9 percent) (U.S. Census Bureau, 2012).

Older adults, aged over 85, also experience higher rates of poverty (14.6 percent in 2009), primarily because older adults deplete their savings as they age, and most older adults are women (Employee Benefit Research Institute, 2012). Women make up about 70 percent of the over-85 population; they are more likely to live alone and less likely to be married than their male counterparts. These conditions compound an already weak financial position that older women face because of their limited lifetime employment earnings. For example, older men are almost twice as likely as older women to be college graduates (Federal Interagency Forum on Aging-Related Statistics, 2004). Ozawa et al. (1999) found that the net worth of individuals with at least some college education is significantly higher than the net worth of those who did not attend college. Poverty rates for all older women were nearly double those for older men in almost all years between 2001 and 2009 (Employee Benefit Research Institute, 2012).

To protect older workers from the economic impact of employment discrimination, Congress passed the Age Discrimination and Employment Act in 1978. This law prevents employers from age-based discrimination in hiring, firing, promotion, and other discriminatory treatments. However, employers have found ways to get around this law by using demotions, changes in work schedules, or additional work without additional pay to force older employees out of the workforce. Such actions exacerbate the problems of older workers, who often find it difficult to obtain comparable employment. With the "aging" or "graying" of society, assumptions about age norms have certainly changed, but in the area of employment the demand for productivity still places older people at risk of discrimination.

In the area of health, life expectancy has increased dramatically and people in the U.S. are living longer than ever. However, old age increases the risk of disease and functional disability, and many older people suffer from serious chronic health conditions, such as high blood pressure and arthritis. The oldest age group (aged over 85) experience multiple chronic conditions, debilitating disabilities, and frailty (Federal Interagency Forum on Aging-Related Statistics, 2004).

Healthy People 2010, the government's initiative to eliminate disparities in health, identified chronic disease, long-term care, and cancer and cardiovascular disease as major health risks and concerns for older people (Office of Minority Health, 2000). Since 1980, death rates from heart disease for people aged over 65 have declined substantially, but cardiovascular disease is still the leading cause of death. On the other hand, death rates from cancer, the second leading cause of death, increased slightly during the same period (Federal Interagency Forum on Aging-Related Statistics, 2004).

The goal of *Healthy People 2020* is to improve the health, function, and quality of life of older adults as people older than 65 are at risk of chronic conditions, including diabetes, arthritis, congestive heart failure, and dementia, including Alzheimer's disease. They are also vulnerable to hospitalizations, nursing home admissions, and loss of independent living (U.S. Department of Health and Human Services, 2012b). In 2000, approximately 16 million people, or one-third of all people with disabilities living in the community, were aged over 65 (*Healthy People 2000*, 1997); a typical recipient of caregiving was a 77-year-old woman with a chronic illness who was living alone (Oxendine, 2000, p. 4). A smaller population of disabled seniors (approximately two million) received care in nursing homes, mental hospitals, and other institutional settings (*Healthy People 2000*, 1997). With the aging of the population, however, these numbers have grown. In 2010, more than a third of all older adults reported some type of disability (U.S. Department of Health and Human Services, 2012b). In 1999, the need for long-term care among older adults was estimated to double by 2030 (Congressional Budget Office [CBO], 1999).

Long-term Care

Long-term care is a "marked departure from the traditional acute care model of health services and insurance." Traditional medicine focuses on the treatment and cure of disease; the purpose of long-term care is to "minimize, rehabilitate, or compensate for chronic illness or functional limitations" (National Association of Social Workers, 2000d, p. 209). Long-term care refers to the delivery of services to people with functional disabilities over a prolonged period of time. These individuals need assistance with everyday activities of daily living (ADL), such as eating and dressing, and instrumental activities of daily living (IADL), such as preparing meals and shopping. Skilled and therapeutic care for individuals with chronic conditions is also provided (Feder et al., 2000). Given the aging of the population, the need for long-term care services is enormous. By 2030 the number of Americans aged 65 years and older is projected to exceed 70 million, representing 20 percent of the population (Spetz et al., 2015). According to Chernof (2013), 70 percent of all older adults will need some degree of daily support for 3 years, on average. Today, 9 million older adults need long-term care supports and services; this need will increase dramatically to approximately 12 million by 2020 and 27 million by 2050.

The highly fragmented public and private health insurance system in the U.S. offers little protection against the high cost of long-term care. Private health insurance plans and long-term-care insurance, which are still fairly new to the industry, are a very small market and finance only about 7 percent of the nation's long-term care expenditures for nursing facility and home care (Feder et al., 2000). More people are purchasing long-term-care insurance, but it is very expensive and unaffordable for most middle-aged and senior adults. It is also difficult for people with chronic illnesses, disabilities, or serious preexisting conditions to buy long-term-care insurance. In addition, the private long-term-care insurance market is "shrinking" as private insurance carriers such as Prudential and Metlife pull out of the market, citing that this type of insurance is too "risky," meaning that it is too difficult to estimate the scale and cost of care, especially for conditions such as dementia (Beeson, 2012).

Medicare, the largest insurance program for older adults, does not cover custodial or unskilled care. As a result, it finances only about 20 percent of the nation's long-term care costs (Feder et al., 2000). To receive home health care, recipients must need intermittent skilled nursing care, such as intravenous feeding or physical therapy, and be confined to their residence. Medicare provides 21 days of daily care and intermittent care thereafter, with no limits on the number of days of service. To receive nursing facility care, recipients must be hospitalized for at least three consecutive days and need daily rehabilitative skilled nursing care. Medicare provides up to 100 days of care and requires a significant copayment after the first 20 days.

Individuals bear a significant portion of the nation's cost of long-term care. They are responsible for up to 80 days of Medicare coinsurance payments for skilled nursing care and pay out of pocket for home and nursing facility services not covered by insurance. As a result, older adults finance about 25 percent of the nation's cost of long-term care (Feder et al., 2000). However, given the high cost of long-term care, most older adults rely on informal (unpaid) care. One estimate, using 1994 data, found that it would cost $257 billion per year to replace informal (unpaid) care with formal (paid) care (National Alliance for Caregiving and AARP, 2004).

The National Alliance for Caregiving and AARP (2004) estimates that there are more than 44 million informal caregivers in the U.S. Most of the caregivers in the 2004 survey provided eight hours or less of care per week for an average of more than four years. Although it is still true that "the typical caregiver is a 46-year-old woman who is employed and also spends around eighteen to twenty hours per week caring for her mother who lives nearby" (Oxendine, 2000, p. 4), this picture is changing. Almost four out of ten caregivers are male. The study also shows that people of color are more likely than non-Hispanic whites to take on the caregiver role.

The physical and emotional stress that often accompany caregiving, the demands of juggling work and caregiving, the changing role of women, and the complex changes in the structure of families have all played a role in the need to address caregiving as a problem in itself. They have also increased the need to find ways to support formal caregiving. When Congress reauthorized the OAA in 2000, it legislated President Clinton's initiative for a National Family Caregiver Support Program. This new provision provided funds for respite care, adult day care, training, counseling, support for caregivers, and other caregiver support services. In 2006, Congress reauthorized all programs of the OAA through 2011. The new bill requires that state and area agencies on aging focus on programs and services for older adults at risk of institutional care and those with limited English proficiency, and on the promotion of home and community-based long-term care services to prevent or delay the need for institutional care. The new law also added responsibility to develop and implement systems for elder justice and to conduct an elder abuse national incidence study, to conduct new research and demonstration programs, including model projects to assist older people to "age in place," and to develop systems for mental health screening and treatment. However, the OAA has not kept pace with the rate of inflation or the growing needs of the aging population.

The OAA was reauthorized again in 2016–2019 under the Obama administration. The primary changes focus on: Improvements in promoting independent living, and home- and community-based services; best practices for working with cases of elder abuse; stronger ombudsman protection in long-term care facilities; and improvements to transportation. The reauthorized policy also includes behavioral health so as to recognize suicide prevention and substance abuse within mental health treatment for older adults (Yao, 2016).

Medicaid, which supports about *two-thirds* of all nursing facility residents, is the primary insurer of long-term services and supports (Rau, 2017). Medicaid provides coverage for long-term-care services for poor individuals or those who become impoverished as a result of "spending down" their personal incomes and assets to state eligibility levels. In 2013, Medicaid financed just over half (51 percent) of the nation's cost of long-term care; most of these dollars were spent on nursing facilities. Historically, most states have used Medicaid dollars to finance institutional care due, primarily, to fears that home health care will become an added expense, rather than a substitute for institutional care. However, more recently there has been a substantial shift in Medicaid spending toward home- and community-based care, accounting for almost half (46 percent) of Medicaid funding for long-term-care services in 2013 (Reaves and Musumeci, 2015). Long-term-care services for an individual in a nursing facility cost about $91,500 *annually* (Bernstein, 2012), and Medicaid is a publicly financed program.

Medicaid long-term-care benefits also vary widely from state to state. Home health services must be provided, but states are not required to offer personal care. States control the number of nursing facility beds available and set the rates for reimbursement to nursing facilities for Medicaid residents. For example, in 2015, the state share of Medicaid financing for nursing home residents varied significantly from less than 30 percent (11 states) to more than 50 percent (6 states)

(Kaiser Family Foundation, 2017). Optional services, including "case management, psychosocial rehabilitation, clinical services entailing outpatient therapy, partial hospitalization, and home-based personal care by non-physician providers" also vary from state to state (National Association of Social Workers, 2000d).

Overall, the inadequacy of insurance for the potentially catastrophic cost of long-term care led to the inclusion of the Community Living Assistance Services and Support (CLASS) provision in the 2010 ACA. This would have created a new, national, voluntary, long-term care insurance product. However, Congress repealed CLASS after the administration announced that it would be unable to implement it because of concerns over financing. Instead, Congress created a new Commission to establish a plan to finance and deliver a comprehensive and coordinated system of long-term services to meet current needs and propose solutions for future needs. This is a serious task. Older adults who need care often go without support because services are too expensive, unavailable, or too difficult to find. Older adults often find that they need to impoverish themselves before services can be made available, which, as Feder and colleagues (2000) indicate, "seems excessively harsh." Reform efforts to expand long-term-care coverage failed with the demise of the Health Security Act of 1993. The Obama administration recognized the need to add long-term care to the ACA, but the enactment of a national long-term-care policy still remains unsettled and in greater jeopardy than ever with reductions in Medicaid spending under review by the Trump administration.

Elder Abuse

> Elder mistreatment is unrecognized, hidden, and underreported. Studies show that health professionals . . . are largely unaware of the various forms of elder mistreatment that take place and of the proper course of action to pursue when mistreatment is suspected. . . . An estimated 700,000 to 1.2 million elders in the United States annually suffer mistreatment at the hands of others or self; 450,000 new cases are identified each year. Despite these alarming figures, our awareness of elder mistreatment is sparse.
>
> (Falk et al., 2012)

During the 1960s and 1970s, state and national efforts to address the problem of child abuse and family violence created a growing awareness of the problem of elder abuse and laid the basis for legislation to protect older adults. In 1981, Congress passed the Prevention, Identification, and Treatment of Elder Abuse Act, which was modeled on federal child abuse prevention legislation. The House Select Committee on Aging investigated and published a major report on the "hidden problem" of elder abuse (Tatara, 1995a), which unfortunately to this day still remains hidden.

Although the problem of child abuse helped to raise awareness of elder abuse, concerns were raised about the appropriateness of the child abuse model for adult protection. Advocates feared that mandatory reporting laws, similar to the child abuse reporting system, would stereotype older adults as dependents and ignore the problem of elderly spouse abuse, and could potentially violate civil rights. Therefore, in 1987, Congress authorized a federal elder abuse prevention program as part of the OAA and authorized funds for the program in 1990. For the first time, federal funds were made available to the states for prevention and treatment programs. The Administration on Aging established two national resource centers on elder abuse: The National Center on Elder Abuse (1988) and the National Eldercare Institute on Elder Abuse and State Long-Term Care Ombudsman Services (1991). In virtually all states, Adult Protective Services agencies serve as the primary vehicle for reporting and investigating suspected elder abuse. These agencies were initially established during the mid-1970s as a result of amendments to the Social Security Act that established state-mandated reporting systems for all adults aged over 18 (Tatara, 1995a; Wolf, 2000).

The Elder Justice Act was first introduced in 2003 in an effort to broaden protections for older adults. However, this historic legislation was not enacted until 2010 as part of the Affordable Care Act. Although elder abuse prevention and justice efforts still occur at the state and local level, this new legislation: Establishes a federal coordinating council; creates new forensic centers; provides funding for the collection, development, and dissemination of research and best practices on elder abuse prevention; provides funding to enhance state ombudsman programs; and provides protection for older adults in long-term-care facilities (Falk et al., 2012).

Elder abuse covers a wide range of abuses. The term "elder abuse" refers to: Physical, sexual, emotional, or psychological abuse; neglect; financial or material exploitation; and self-abuse and neglect. Acts of elder abuse and neglect are similar to child abuse only in that they include intentional acts of abuse, as well as acts of omission, or neglect. A primary difference, however, is the variation in the types of abusers and the complexity of these adult relationships. Abusers include family members (spouses, siblings, adult children, adult grandchildren, other relatives), informal (unpaid) or formal (paid) caregivers, staff of residential or institutional settings, other service providers, neighbors, friends, and other adults. The OAA specifically includes deprivation by a caretaker of essential goods or services in its definition of abuse.

Exploitation and *self-abuse/neglect* are types of mistreatment that are specific to older adults. The OAA defines exploitation as the illegal or improper use of an older person's resources for monetary or personal gain. Self-abuse or neglect is defined as the failure to provide for one's own essential needs, particularly if it threatens the person's life or safety. In doing so, it recognizes the need to protect elders whose disabilities or limitations may prevent them from taking proper care of themselves.

The Older Americans Act of 2006 required that the Administration on Aging conduct an elder abuse national incidence study. However, in the absence of a nationwide tracking system, our understanding of the incidence of elder abuse is based on studies that have been undertaken in the last 15–20 years (Pillemer and Finkelhor, 1988; Tatara, 1995b; Tatara et al., 1997; National Center on Elder Abuse, 1998, 2003; Bonnie and Wallace, 2002; Jogerst et al., 2003; Lachs and Pillemer, 2004). Estimates range from 2 percent to 10 percent of older adults; however, researchers and service providers believe this rate of abuse is grossly underestimated. Elder abuse is more difficult to identify than child abuse or domestic violence. Many seniors live alone;

they also have limited contact with members of the community, and often their only contact is with family members. Adult protective services (APS) agencies are more likely to receive reports about the most obvious and visible incidents of abuse than reports of neglect or forms of abuse that are less obvious. In addition, no incidence data on elder abuse in nursing facilities is available, but various reports and surveys of personnel indicate that a significant problem exists. A 2001 congressional review of state inspection records showed that elder abuse occurred in almost one of every three nursing homes between January 1999 and January 2001; these facilities were cited for 9000 abuse violations (McQueen, 2001).

The seminal National Center on Elder Abuse (1998) incidence study commissioned by Congress still provides the best data on the prevalence of elder abuse and represents the first attempt to estimate the incidence of *unidentified* and *unreported* cases. This study found that, in 1996, unidentified and unreported incidents of elder abuse were at least five times greater than the number of cases reported to APS agencies. The study also found a 150 percent increase in the number of reported cases from 1986 to 1996, even though the size of the elderly population aged over 60 increased only 10 percent during this same period. Ninety percent of the abusers were family members, primarily adult children. Most of the victims were women and over the age of 80, and women were found to be especially vulnerable to financial and psychological abuse. African American elders were more likely to be self-neglectors. The findings raise important questions for further study and highlight the important role of health and mental health practitioners and financial institutions (banks) in the identification of abuse and neglect. The 2003 Survey of State Adult Protective Services (National Center on Elder Abuse, 2004) conducted by the National Center on Elder Abuse showed a significant increase since 2000 in reports of abuse and neglect; it also found that self-neglect represented more than one-third of reported maltreatment.

Older Adults in Medical Research

Like women, older adults have been underrepresented in clinical research. Most clinical studies of major health risks, such as heart disease and cancer, have been carried out with nonelderly participants. Mitka (2003) found that older adults represent 63 percent of cancer patients, but only 25 percent of participants in clinical trials. Although there may be challenges to the inclusion of older adults in these studies, until this occurs with greater regularity, clinical findings from these studies may be limited for this population (American Geriatrics Society, 2001). More recent reports (American Geriatrics Society, 2008; Span, 2011) show that clinical trials continue to "neglect the elderly" despite recent improvements.

LGBTQ COMMUNITY

According to the American Psychological Association (see www.apa.org/pi/lgbt/resources/aging.aspx), LGBTQ refers to lesbian, gay, bisexual, transgender, and queer or questioning. Lesbian, gay, bisexual (LGB) refer to sexual orientation. Transgender (T) refers to people who identify with a gender different from the sex they were born with. The term includes people who are in transition between sexes or transsexuals. Queer (Q) is an umbrella term that refers to sexual and gender minorities that are not heterosexual; it was originally used as a derogative term, but its use was claimed by scholars and activists starting in the 1980s. (Q) can also refer to Questioning for those who are exploring and unsure of their identity, or do not want to apply a label to themselves.

Since the 1980s, there has been an increase in social acceptance and a reduction in social stigma toward the LGBTQ community. There has also been an increase in the number of adults who identify as LGBTQ, particularly among women and people of color (Gates, 2013, 2017). Public support for marriage equality and adoption for same sex couples has increased dramatically since the early 2000s, and for job protection against discrimination in the workplace (Flores, 2014). None the less, societal stigma, discrimination, and oppression still impact the health of this group, particularly in the area of behavioral and mental health. Other factors impact physical health including cancer and HIV/AIDS. Due to low rates of health insurance coverage, high rates of stress related to systematic harassment and discrimination, and a lack of cultural competency in the health care system, LGBTQ people are at a higher risk for cancer, mental illnesses, and other diseases, and are more likely to smoke, drink alcohol, use drugs, and engage in other risky behaviors. According to the Center for American Progress (Krehely, 2009), LGBTQ adults are less likely to have health insurance, more likely to delay or seek health care treatment, more likely to delay or avoid getting a prescription, and more likely to seek emergency care treatment.

Like other at-risk populations, the ACA was designed to improve access to health insurance for the LGBTQ community by including anti-discrimination and LGBTQ-inclusive protections. Insurance marketplaces were required to provide education, services and outreach that were culturally competent for LGBTQ communities. Companies that offered coverage for families and spouses must include married same-sex couples. The ACA required insurers to cover preventive care at no additional cost, prevent discrimination based on preexisting health conditions, and eliminate lifetime limits on coverage for individuals with chronic diseases. For the LGBTQ community, this provides access for those with HIV/AIDS.

Cancer

National cancer registries and surveys of cancer incidence in the U.S. do not collect data about sexual orientation or gender identity. This presents a problem with understanding cancer incidence among members of the LGBTQ community and developing prevention and treatment programs targeted at the disparities faced by this group. There is, however, research that has identified a set of risk factors due to the stress of living as a sexual/gender minority that point to a greater incidence of cancer and later-stage diagnosis, namely, a disproportionate burden of disease. Cancer treatment and survivorship are impacted by the discrimination and stress that LGBTQ patients may experience both within the healthcare system and in society at large.

The first National Summit on Cancer and the LGBTQ Communities was held in 2014 with experts in LGBTQ cancer research, clinical care, health care policy, and survivorship and included LGBTQ cancer survivors and advocates for health equity (Burkhalter et al., 2016). In 2015, the first comprehensive examination of cancer and the LGBTQ community was published (Boehmer and Elk, 2015) that summarized the knowledge base to date, with most of the information focusing on breast and prostate cancer survivorship. The limited research to date shows that rates of breast, lung, and colorectal cancers appear to differ for lesbians compared with heterosexual women. The potential reasons for the increased risk for lesbians are differences in parity, smoking status, cancer screening, and access to care (Boehmer et al., 2014), as well as higher rates of never having given birth and obesity (Quinn et al., 2015). The LGBTQ community has higher rates of smoking (Blosnich et al., 2010; Boehmer et al., 2012); 32.8 percent of LGBTQ adults smoke, a rate that is 68% higher than other adults (Fallin et al., 2016). This may increase the risk for 12 cancers caused by tobacco use (U.S. Department of Health and Human Services, 2015). Concerns have also been raised about disparities in cancer screening in the LGBTQ community (Austin et al., 2013)

HIV/AIDS

HIV/AIDS presents a dramatically greater health risk for gay and bisexual men than any other group in the U.S. In 2014, according to the CDC (2018c), gay and bisexual men accounted for 70 percent of the newly diagnosed HIV cases in the U.S. In 2015, the newly diagnosed rate declined a bit, but gay and bisexual men accounted for 82 percent of the newly diagnosed infections among all men. The risk is even higher among gay and bisexual youth and young adults under age 24; this group accounted for 92 percent of new diagnoses in their age group in 2015. Disparities also exist for people of color with African American gay and bisexual men at greatest risk.

In 2017, the *New York Times* published an in-depth, alarming feature story titled "America's Hidden H.I.V. Epidemic: Why do America's black gay and bisexual men have a higher H.I.V. rate than any country in the world?" (Villarosa, 2017). According to the CDC (2016), at the current rate of infection, one in two African American gay and bisexual men will be infected with HIV in their lifetime which calls for significant action and prevention strategies now to ensure that this does not occur. However, health experts have grown increasingly concerned about the Trump administration's commitment to fighting HIV/AIDS. The web page of the Office of National AIDS Policy, the architect of the National HIV/AIDS Strategy, was disabled on the White House website almost immediately after President Trump's inauguration. The administration's first proposed budget included a $186 million cut in the CDC's funding for HIV/AIDS prevention, testing, and support services. And, as mentioned earlier, efforts to "repeal and replace" the ACA have raised concerns about coverage, particularly for much-needed medications (Villarosa, 2017).

The CDC is concerned with several challenges in addressing the health needs of this population. A disproportionate number of gay and bisexual men are living with HIV compared with other groups in the U.S. and have a greater chance of having an HIV-positive partner. An estimated one in six gay and bisexual men living with HIV is not aware of his infection and therefore remains untreated and puts others at risk for transmission of the disease. The CDC has several initiatives to increase HIV prevention awareness that are targeted to several high-risk groups within the LGBTQ community (youth, Latino, African American) and provides direct funding for community-based projects (CDC, 2018c).

Alcohol and Substance Abuse

Members of the LGBTQ community face chronically high levels of social and psychological stress. This can include discriminatory laws and practices in employment, housing, personal relationships, and health care, as well as stigma and challenges with family and friends. Ongoing stress has the potential to lead to higher levels of anxiety, fear, isolation, depression, anger, and mistrust; these experiences, in turn, have the potential to increase the risk of self-medicating with alcohol and drugs, among other behavioral health issues. According to the CDC (2016), based on research conducted to date, gay and bisexual men, lesbian, and transgender individuals are more likely to use alcohol and drugs, have higher rates of substance abuse, and continue heavy drinking into later life. According to Medley et al. (2016), the National Survey on Drug Use and Health showed that lesbian, gay, or bisexual adults in 2015 were more than twice as likely as heterosexual adults to have used any illicit drug in the past year. A 2013 Census Bureau survey (Ward et al., 2014) showed a higher rate of binge drinking among lesbian, gay, and bisexual adults, and higher rates of substance use among lesbian, gay, and bisexual adolescents.

Services for alcohol and drug treatment tend not to be specialized for the LGBTQ community, and LGBTQ individuals may be reluctant to seek treatment or disclose their sexual identity. Yet, findings show that addiction treatment programs offering specialized groups for gay and bisexual individuals have better outcomes compared with nonspecialized programs (Seinreich, 2010). There is some evidence to suggest that treatment should address relevant factors such as homophobia/transphobia, family problems, violence, and social isolation (Gonzales and Henning-Smith, 2017). Effective treatment modalities for substance abuse disorder may include motivational interviewing, social support therapy, contingency management, and cognitive–behavioral therapy (CBT) (Green and Feinstein, 2012).

Exposure to Violence

Chronically high levels of social and psychological stress among members of the LGBTQ community are also related to exposure to violence and hate crimes as a social determinant of health. LGBTQ populations are significantly more likely to be the victims of hate crimes motivated by a single cause or issue. A 2014 FBI report shows that one of five reported hate crimes was due to sexual identity; this occurred in an environment where most crimes of this nature are not reported due to fear of being revictimized by the criminal justice system, feeling shame for being targeted for hate, or lacking knowledge of victims' rights and services. An alarming report of an epidemic of violence against transgendered people, "A Time to Act: Fatal Violence Against Transgender People in America in 2017," demonstrates the recent surge in hate-based violence and harassment. Since 2013, the Human Rights Campaign has documented at least 102 transgender people who were victims of fatal violence; at least 87 were transgender people of color (Trans People of Color Coalition, Human Rights Campaign, 2017).

Hate crimes are defined as a "criminal offense against a person or property motivated in whole or in part by an offender's bias against a race, religion, disability, sexual orientation, ethnicity, gender, or gender identity" (FBI, 2017). Hate and discrimination can become internalized and a source of chronic stress. This can lead to depression and other mental health issues, including alcohol and substance abuse, and suicide. Studies show that stress caused by discrimination is linked to poorer health outcomes, which creates health disparities between populations that experience discrimination and those that do not. Specifically, victims of bias-motivated crimes are more likely to experience posttraumatic stress, concerns about safety, depression, anxiety, and anger than victims of nonbias-motivated crimes (Gerstenfeld, 2011). A 2014 study by Duncan and Hatzenbuehler found a greater likelihood of suicide among LGBTQ public school students who lived in Boston neighborhoods with a higher prevalence of hate crimes targeting those in the LGBTQ community.

Witnessing or exposure to hate crimes can also have an impact on emotional health. One hate crime project at the University of Sussex, England (Paterson et al., 2018) investigated the wider impacts of hate crime on the LGBTQ and Muslim communities, examining the consequences of simply knowing a victim or hearing about an incident. Common responses were anger, anxiety, and feelings of vulnerability. The deadly mass shooting that occurred in 2016 in a gay nightclub in Orlando, Florida is one extreme example of the potential impact of exposure to hate crime: 49 people were killed and another 50 injured; almost all of those killed were LGBTQ people of color.

Mental Health Disorders

Using a meta-analysis, Meyer (2003) found that LGBTQ persons have a higher incidence of mental health disorders than heterosexuals or cisgender persons. His "minority stress theory," as already discussed, postulates that stress associated with discrimination and oppression creates unique stressors that may predispose an individual to mental health disorders. Meyer breaks down stress indicators into external factors (discrimination and victimization) and internal factors (concealing sexual identity and internalizing homophobia), the latter of which are unique to the LGBTQ community. Data collected through the 2009 California Health Interview Study, UCLA Center for Health Policy Research, one of the few comprehensive, ongoing state-level health surveys on sexual orientation, found the following (Krehely, 2009):

- LGB adults were more than twice as likely as heterosexual adults to experience psychological distress;
- LGB adults were more than twice as likely as heterosexual adults to need medication for emotional health issues;
- Transgender adults were 25 times more likely to have suicide ideation than heterosexuals and ten times more likely than LGB adults; and
- LGB youth were almost four times as likely as heterosexual youth to attempt suicide.

Although these statistics cannot be generalized to the national LGBTQ population, this data is helpful because California has the largest LGBTQ population in the U.S.

Collecting data on mental health disparities among the LGBTQ community and examining, improving, and expanding targeted mental health services are both essential to improving health for this population. Mental health services may be underutilized due to embarrassment, fear of being stereotyped, or fear of rejection, particularly among youth in school settings (Huggins et al., 2016). There is some evidence that LGBTQ people feel discrimination or disrespect when seeking care for health or mental health problems and may avoid treatment (Holley et al., 2016). The history of mental health treatment in the LGBTQ community is troublesome. In the 1950s and 1960s, the psychiatric profession treated homosexuality and bisexuality as a mental illness. Gay men and lesbians were often forced into aversion therapy, electroshock therapy, and hospitalization for treatment. The American Psychiatric Association removed homosexuality from the *Diagnostic and Statistical Manual of Mental Disorders* (DSM) in 1973. Clearly, significant strides in attitude, understanding, and treatment have occurred, but there are still disparities and unequal treatment among LGBTQ groups seeking care. The effectiveness of mental health care may be hampered by stigma, lack of cultural sensitivity, and unconscious and conscious reluctance to address sexuality (Sabin et al., 2015).

HIGHLIGHTS

- Women experience disparities in health for a variety of reasons, many of which are linked to their social status and discriminatory treatment. Congress recognized these disparities by enacting the Women's Health Equity Act of 1990 and establishing the Office of Women's Health.

- Differences between women and men in medical risks exist, yet insufficient research has been done to better understand these differences. Before 1990, heart disease and cancer, the leading causes of death for women, were treated as "male" diseases and few clinical studies included women as subjects. Even worse, some studies show that women today are still less likely to be treated for heart disease than men.

- Women experience health conditions that are unique to women or more prevalent among women than men:

  o more research is needed to prevent and treat breast cancer and osteoporosis;

  o maternal, prenatal, and child health services are essential to the health of both women and children;

  o poor women are especially vulnerable to inadequate nutrition and medical care during pregnancy;

  o AIDS/HIV has been growing at a faster rate for heterosexual women, especially poor women from inner cities or rural areas, than for heterosexual men, and has increased to alarming rates;

- o   women who use family planning services are more likely to have prenatal care and healthy babies, but access to family planning is still a problem for women and adolescent girls;

- o   sexual and domestic violence against women is a serious mortality and health risk for women;

- Age-based disparities also exist, some of which stem from greater vulnerability at various stages of human growth, such as infancy or old age; other disparities are caused by socioeconomic inequity and discrimination. Elder abuse is a good example of the latter.

- Children have the highest rates of chronic illness and, as they proceed from infancy to adolescence, are constantly vulnerable to new and changing health risks. Children depend on adults for their health and wellbeing, and are at risk of child abuse, neglect, and exposure to domestic violence. Poor children are particularly vulnerable.

- Adults aged over 65 are more vulnerable to life-threatening diseases (heart disease and cancer) and physical and mental disabilities. Older adults, like children, are at greater risk for poverty, which exacerbates the health problems and conditions of old age, particularly the need for long-term care.

- Societal stigma, discrimination, and oppression impact the health of the LGBTQ community, particularly in the areas of cancer, HIV/AIDS, alcohol and substance abuse, suicide, exposure to violence, and behavioral and mental health.

- Efforts to collect data about the health of the LGBTQ community as a separate group through surveys, reports, and research is needed to gain more information about disparities and needs.

WEBSITES TO OBTAIN UPDATED AND ADDITIONAL INFORMATION

The Commonwealth Fund:

www.commonwealthfund.org

Urban Institute Assessing the New Federalism:

www.urban.org

Maternal and Child Health Policy Research Center:

www.mchpolicy.org

Children's Defense Fund:

www.childrensdefense.org

Office of Women's Health, U.S. Department of Health and Human Services:

www.womenshealth.gov

National Center on Elderly Abuse, U.S. Department of Health and Human Services:

www.aoa.gov

Agency for Healthcare Research and Quality, U.S. Department of Health and Human Services:

www.ahrq.gov

Safe Start Center, Office of Juvenile Justice and Delinquency Prevention (OJJDP) Office of Justice Programs, U.S. Department of Justice:

www.safestartcenter.org/about

Mental Health America:

www.mentalhealthamerica.net/lgbt-mental-health

Centers for Disease Control and Prevention:

www.cdc.gov/healthyyouth/disparities/smy.htm

Gay, Lesbian, and Straight Education Alliance Network:

www.glsen.org/learn/research/national-school-climate-survey

Healthy People 2020:

www.healthypeople.gov

REFERENCED LEGAL CASES

Ledbetter v. Goodyear Tire & Rubber Co – see https://supreme.justia.com/cases/federal/us/550/618

Roe v. Wade 1973 – see www.britannica.com/event/Roe-v-Wad

REFERENCES

Agency for Health Care Policy and Research (AHCPR). (1999, April). *AHCPR Women's Health Highlights*, Fact Sheet, AHCPR Pub. No. 99-PO17. Retrieved from www.ahrq.gov/research/womenh1.htm

——. (2005). *Women's Health Highlights: Recent Findings*. Retrieved from www.ahrq.gov/research/womenh1.htm

Agency for Healthcare Research and Quality (AHRQ). (2000). *Performance Plans for FY 2000 and 2001 and Performance Report for FY 1999*. Retrieved from www.ahrq.gov/about/gpra2001/gpra01a.htm

Alan Guttmacher Institute. (2017, April 27). *Medicaid Continues to Account for Three-Quarters of U.S. Publicly Funded Family Planning Expenditures*. Retrieved from www.guttmacher.org/news-release/2017/medicaid-continues-account-three-quarters-us-publicly-funded-family-planning

American Geriatrics Society. (2001). *Position Statement on Ethnogeriatrics*. Retrieved from www.americangeriatrics.org

——. (2008). *Underrepresentation of Older Adults in Clinical Trials*. Retrieved from www.americangeriatrics.org/files/documents/Older_Adults_in_Clinical_Trials_FINAL.pdf

American Heart Association. (2003). *Tobacco Industry's Targeting of Youth, Minorities, and Women (Fact Sheet)*. Dallas, TX: American Heart Association.

American Psychiatric Association. (1998). Psychiatric Effects of Media Violence, APA Fact Sheet Series. Retrieved from www.psych.org/public_info/media_violence.html

Amnesty International. (2008, Spring). *Maze of Injustice: The Failure to Protect Indigenous Women from Sexual Violence in the USA, One Year Update*. Retrieved from www.amnestyusa.org/reports/maze-of-injustice

——. (2010). *Deadly Delivery: The Maternal Health Care Crisis in the USA*. Retrieved from www.amnestyusa.org/sites/default/files/pdfs/deadlydelivery.pdf

Annadale, E. and Hunt, K. (Eds.). (2000). *Gender Inequalities in Health*. Milton Keynes: Open University Press.

Austin, S. B., Pazaris, M. J., Nichols, L. P., Bowen, D., Wei, E. K., and Spiegelman, D. (2013). An Examination of Sexual Orientation Group Patterns in Mammographic and Colorectal Screening in a Cohort of U.S. Women. *Cancer Causes & Control*, 24: 539–547.

Balsanek, J. (1997). Addressing At-risk Pregnant Women's Issues through Community, Individual, and Corporate Grassroots Efforts. *Health and Social Work*, 22(1), 63–69.

Beeson, E. (2012, March 25). Long-term Care Insurance Market Shrinks as Prudential, Others Pull Back. *The Star Ledger*. Retrieved from www.nj.com/news/index.ssf/2012/03/insurers_including_njs_prudent.html

Bennetts, L. (2011, September 14). Women: The Invisible Poor. *The Daily Beast*. Retrieved from www.thedailybeast.com/articles/2011/09/14/u-s-women-hit-hardest-by-poverty-says-census-report.html

Bernstein, N. (2012, September 12). With Medicaid, Long-term Care of Elderly Looms as a Rising Cost. *New York Times*. Retrieved from www.nytimes.com/2012/09/07/health/policy/long-term-care-looms-as-rising-medicaid-cost.html?mtrref=undefined

Blosnich, J., Jarrett, T., and Horn, K. (2010). Disparities in Smoking and Acute Respiratory Illnesses among Sexual Minority Young Adults. *Lung* 188:401–407.

Boehmer, U. and Elk, R. (Eds.) (2015). *Cancer and the LGBT Community: Unique Perspectives from Risk to Survivorship*. Geneva: Springer International Publishing.

Boehmer, U., Cooley, T. P., and Clark, M. A. (2012). Cancer and Men Who have Sex with Men: A Systematic Review. *Lancet Oncology* 13: E545–E553.

Boehmer, U., Miao, X., Maxwell, N.I., and Ozonoff, A. (2014). Sexual minority population density and incidence of lung, colorectal and female breast cancer in California. *British Medical Journal* Open 4:e004461.

Bonnie, R. J. and Wallace, R. B. (Eds.). (2002). *Elder Mistreatment: Abuse, Neglect, and Exploitation in an Aging America*. Washington, DC: National Research Council of the National Academies Press.

Browne, A. (1987). *When Battered Women Kill*. New York: Free Press.

——. (1993). Violence against Women by Male Partners: Prevalence, Outcomes, and Policy Implications. *American Psychologist*, 48(10), 1077–1087.

Brush, L. D. (1990). Violent Acts and Injurious Outcomes in Married Couples: Methodological Issues in the National Survey of Families and Households. *Gender and Society*, 4(1), 56.

Burkhalter, J. E., Margolies, L., Sigurdsson, H. O., Walland, J., Radix, A., Rice, D., et al. (2016). *The National LGBT Cancer Action Plan*: A White Paper of the 2014 National Summit on Cancer in the LGBT Communities. Retrieved from https://cancer-network.org/wp-content/uploads/2017/02/White-paper.pdf

Cahill, S. (2017, April). LGBT Experiences With Health Care. *Health Affairs*. Retrieved from www.healthaffairs.org/doi/full/10.1377/hlthaff.2017.0277

Canto, J. G., Allison, J. J., Kiefe, C. I., Fincher, C., Farmer, R., Sekar, P., Person, S., and Weissman, W. N. (2000, April). Relationship of Race and Sex to the Use of Reperfusion Therapy in Medicare Beneficiaries with Acute Myocardial Infarction. *New England Journal of Medicine*, 15(342), 1094–1100.

Centers for Disease Control and Prevention. (2004, May 21). Youth Risk Behavior Surveillance: United States, 2003. *Morbidity and Mortality Weekly Report*, 53(SS-02).

——. (2008, June 6). Youth Risk Behavior Surveillance: United States, 2007. *Morbidity and Mortality Weekly Report*, 53(SS-04).

——. (2012a, May 14). *Cancer and Women*. Retrieved from www.cdc.gov/features/womenandcancer/

——. (2012b, September 7). National, State, and Local Area Vaccination Coverage Among Children Aged 19–35 Months: United States, 2011. *Morbidity and Mortality Weekly Report*, 61(35), 689–696.

——. (2012c, October 29). *Underage Drinking: Alcohol and Public Health*. Retrieved from www.cdc.gov/alcohol/fact-sheets/underage-drinking.htm

——. (2012d). *Youth Violence: Facts at a Glance*. Retrieved from www.cdc.gov/violence-prevention/pdf/yv-datasheet-a.pdf

——. (2013, January 11). *Adolescent Health*. Retrieved from www.cdc.gov/nchs/fastats/adolescent_health.htm

——. (2016, February 23). *Lifetime Risk of HIV Diagnosis*. Retrieved from www.cdc.gov/nchhstp/newsroom/2016/croi-press-release-risk.html

——. (2018a, June 4). *HIV among Women*. Retrieved from www.cdc.gov/hiv/group/gender/women/index.html

——. (2018b, January 2). *Infant Mortality*. Retrieved from www.cdc.gov/reproductivehealth/maternalinfanthealth/infantmortality.htm

——. (2018c, February 27). *HIV among Gay and Bisexual Men*. Retrieved from www.cdc.gov/hiv/group/msm/index.html

Chernof, B. (2013, January 23). Creating Realistic Long-term Solutions as Part of the Entitlement Reform Debate. *Health Affairs Blog*. Retrieved from http://healthaffairs.org/blog/2013/01/23/creating-realistic-long-term-care-solutions-as-part-of-the-entitlement-reform-debate

Cohen, S. A. (2007). Repeat Abortion, Repeat Unintended Pregnancy, Repeated and Misguided Government Policies. *Guttmacher Policy Review*, 10(2). Retrieved from www.guttmacher.org/pubs/gpr/10/2/gpr100208.html

Coleman, B. C. (1999, August 11). New Therapy Decreases Number of AIDS Babies. *Concord Monitor*, 3.

Congressional Budget Office. (1999, March). *Projections of Expenditures for Long-term Care Services for the Elderly*. Washington, DC: U.S. Printing Office.

de Anda, D. (1995). Adolescence Overview. In R. L. Edwards (Ed.), *Encyclopedia of Social Work*, 19th edn. (pp. 16–133). Washington, DC: National Association of Social Workers.

Deykin, E. Y., Levy, J. C., and Wells, V. (1987). Adolescent Depression, Alcohol and Drug Abuse. *American Journal of Public Health*, 77(2), 178–182.

———. (1992). Depressive Illness among Chemically Dependent Adolescents. *American Journal of Psychiatry*, 149(10), 1341–1347.

Dibble, V. and Straus, M. E. (1990). Some Structure Determinants of Inconsistency between Attitudes and Behaviors: The Case of Family Violence. In M. A. Straus and R. J. Gelles (Eds.), *Physical Violence in American Families* (pp. 167–180). New Brunswick, NJ: Transaction.

Dooren, J. C. (2012, December 19). Teen Smoking Keeps Falling. *Wall Street Journal*. Retrieved from http://online.wsj.com/article/SB100014241278873247313045781897503794502228.html

Duncan, D. T. and Hatzenbuehler, M. L. (2014, February). Lesbian, Gay, Bisexual, and Transgender Hate Crimes and Suicidality among a Population-based Sample of Sexual-minority Adolescents in Boston. *American Journal of Public Health*. Retrieved from https://ajph.aphapublications.org/doi/abs/10.2105/AJPH.2013.301424

Edelman, M. W. (1999). *The State of America's Children*. Boston, MA: Beacon Press.

Edwards, A., Bee, A., and Fox, L. (2017, September 12). *Outlying Older Americans: The Puzzle of Increasing Poverty among those 65 and Older*. U.S. Census Bureau. Retrieved from www.census.gov/newsroom/blogs/random-samplings/2017/09/outlying_older_ameri.html

Employee Benefit Research Institute. (2012, April). Time Trends in Poverty for Older Americans Between 2001 and 2009. *Notes*, 33(4). Retrieved from www.ebri.org/pdf/notespdf/EBRI_Notes_04_Apr-12.EldPovty.pdf

Epstein, H. (2013, March 21). Lead Poisoning: The Ignored Scandal. *New York Review of Books*. Retrieved from www.nybooks.com/articles/archives/2013/mar/21/lead-poisoning-ignored-scandal/?page=2

Falk, N. L., Baigis, J., and Kopak, C. (2012, September). Elder Mistreatment and the Elder Justice Act. *Online Journal of issues in Nursing*, 17(3). Retrieved from www.nursing-world.org/MainMenuCategories/ANAMarketplace/ANAPeriodicals/OJIN/Table-ofContents/Vol-17-2012/No3-Sept-2012/Articles-Previous-Topics/Elder-Mistreat-ment-and-Elder-Justice-Act.htm

Fallin, A., Lee, Y. O., Bennett, K., and Goodin, A. (2016). Smoking Cessation Awareness and Utilization Among Lesbian, Gay, Bisexual, and Transgender Adults: An Analysis of the 2009–2010 National Adult Tobacco Survey. *Nicotine & Tobacco Research*, 18(4):496–500.

FBI. (2014). *Hate Crime Statistics Summary*. Retrieved from https://ucr.fbi.gov/hate-crime/2014/resource-pages/hate-crime-2014-_summary

FBI. (2017). *Hate Crimes*. Washington, DC: U. S. Department of Justice. Retrieved from www.fbi.gov/about-us/investigate/civilrights/hate_crimes/overview

Fantuzzo, J. W. and Mohr, W. K. (1999). Prevalence and Effects of Child Exposure to Domestic Violence. *Future of Children*, 9(3), 21–32.

Farrelly, M. C., Healton, C. G., Davis, K., Messeri, P., Hersey, J., and Haviland, M. L. (2002, June). Getting to the Truth: Evaluating National Tobacco Countermarketing Campaigns. *American Journal Public Health*, 92(6), 901–907.

Feder, J., Komisar, H. L., and Niefeld, M. (2000). Long-term Care in the U.S.: An Overview. *Health Affairs*, 19(1), 40–56.

Federal Interagency Forum on Aging-Related Statistics. (2004). *Older Americans 2004: Key Indicators of Well-being*. Retrieved from www.agingstats.gov/chartbook2000.html

Felts, W. M., Chernier, T., and Barnes, R. (1992). Drug Use and Suicide Ideation and Behavior among North Carolina Public School Students. *American Journal of Public Health*, 82(6), 870–872.

Finkelhor, D., Turner, H. A., Shattuck, A., and Hamby, S. L. (2015). Prevalence of Childhood Exposure to Violence, Crime, and Abuse: Results from the National Survey of Children's Exposure to Violence. *JAMA Pediatrics*, 169(8), 746–754.

Finley, L. I. (2013, February 9). *Congress Must Act to Save Lives: Reauthorize VAWA*. Retrieved from www.zcommunications.org/congress-must-act-to-safe-lives-reauthorize-vawa-by-laura-l-finley

Fitzpatrick, C., Barnett, T., and Pagani, L. S. (2012, May). Early Exposure to Media Violence and Later Child Adjustment. *Journal of Developmental and Behavioral Pediatrics*, 33(4), 291–297.

Fletcher, M. (2011, November 7). Census Bureau Measures More Americans Living in Poverty. *Wall Street Journal*. Retrieved from http://articles.washingtonpost.com/2011-11-07/business/35284270_1_poverty-rate-poverty-picture-poverty-experts

Flores, A. R. (2014, November). *National Trends in Public Opinion on LGBT Rights in the United States*. Williams Institute. Retrieved from https://williamsinstitute.law.ucla.edu/wp-content/uploads/POP-natl-trends-nov-2014.pdf

Freed, G. L., Cowan, A. E., and Clark, S. J. (2008, December). Primary Care Physician Perspectives on Reimbursement for Childhood Immunizations. *Pediatrics*, 122(6), 1319–1324.

Fremstad, S. (2012, August 3). *The Supplemental Poverty Measure: Is Child Poverty Really Less of a Problem than We Thought?* Center for Economic and Policy Research. Retrieved from www.cepr.net/index.php/blogs/cepr-blog/the-supplemental-poverty-measure-does-it-paint-a-more-accurate-picture-of-poverty

Garrison, C. Z., McKeown, R. E., Valois, R. F., and Vincent, M. L. (1993). Aggression, Substance Use, and Suicidal Behaviors in High School Students. *American Journal of Public Health*, 83(2), 179–184.

Gates, G. J. (2013). Demographics and LGBT health. *Journal of Health and Social Behavior*. 54(1), 72–74.

Gates, G. J. (2017). *In U.S., more adults identifying as LGBT*. Retrieved from www.gallup.com/poll/201731/lgbt-identification-rises.aspx?version=print

Gelles, R. J. and Cornell, C. P. (1990). *Intimate Violence in Families*, 2nd edn. Newbury Park, CA: Sage.

Gergen, P. J., Fowler, J. A., and Mauter, K. R. (1998, February). The Burden of Environmental Tobacco Smoke Exposure on the Respiratory Health of Children 2 Months through 5 Years of Age in the U.S.: Third National Health and Nutrition Examination Survey, 1988–1994. *Pediatric Electronic Pages*, 101(2). Retrieved from www.pediatrics.org

Gerstenfeld, P. B. (2011). *Hate Crimes: Causes, Controls, and Controversies*. Thousand Oaks, CA: Sage.

Gilligan, J. (1996). *Violence: Our Deadly Epidemic and Its Causes*. New York: G. P. Putnam's Sons.

Glied, S. and Kofman, S. (1995). *Women and Mental Health: Issues for Health Reform*. New York: Commonwealth Fund.

Gonzales, G. and Henning-Smith, C. (2017, May). Health Disparities by Sexual Orientation: Results and Implications from the Behavioral Risk Factor Surveillance System. *Journal of Community Health*, 42(6), 1163–1172.

Graham-Bermann, S. and Seng, J. (2005). Violence Exposure and Traumatic Stress Symptoms as Additional Predictors of Health Problems in High-risk Children. *Journal of Pediatrics*, 146(3), 349–354.

Green, K. E. and Feinstein, B. A. (2012). Substance use in lesbian, gay, and bisexual populations: an update on empirical research and implications for treatment. *Psychology of Addictive Behaviors: Journal of the Society of Psychologists in Addictive Behaviors*: 26(2), 265–278.

Grinshteyn, E. and Hemenway, D. (2016). Violent Death Rates: The US Compared with Other High-income OECD Countries, 2010. *American Journal of Medicine*, 129, 266–273. Retrieved from www.amjmed.com/article/S0002-9343(15)01030-X/pdf

Gruber, J. and Zinman, J. (2000). *Youth Smoking in the U.S.: Evidence and Implications (Working Paper No. 7780)*. Cambridge, MA: National Bureau of Economic Research.

Guttmacher Institute. (2009). *Next Steps for America's Family Planning Program*. Retrieved from www.guttmacher.org/pubs/NextSteps.pdf

——. (2011, January 2011). *Long-term Decline in Abortions has Stalled: Medication Abortion Becoming More Common*. Retrieved from www.guttmacher.org/media/nr/2011/01/11/index.html

——. (2013, January 8). *Roe at 40: New Infographics Illustrate Key Facts About Abortion in the United States*. Retrieved from www.guttmacher.org/media/inthenews/2013/01/08/index.html

Hackl, K. I., Somlai, A. M., Kelly, J. A., and Kalichman, S. C. (1997). Women Living with AIDS: The Dual Challenge of Being a Patient and Caregiver. *Health & Social Work*, 22(1), 53–62.

Harvard Health. (2017, March 25, updated). *Gender Matters: Heart Disease Risk in Women*. Retrieved from www.health.harvard.edu/heart-health/gender-matters-heart-disease-risk-in-women

Harvard Maternal Health Task Force. (2018). *Maternal Health in the U.S.* Retrieved from www.mhtf.org/topics/maternal-health-in-the-united-states/

Harvard Medical School. (2011, May). *Women and Depression*. Retrieved from www.health.harvard.edu/womens-health/women-and-depression

Healthy People 2000. (1997, October 30). *Progress Review. People with Low Income*. Washington, DC: U.S. Department of Health and Human Services.

——. (1998a, July 9). *Progress Review. Adolescents and Young Adults*. Washington, DC: U.S. Department of Health and Human Services.

——. (1998b, May 20). *Progress Review. Women's Health*. Washington, DC: U.S. Department of Health and Human Services.

——. (1999a, March 3). *Progress Review. Family Planning*. Washington, DC: U.S. Department of Health and Human Services.

——. (1999b, May 5). *Progress Review. Maternal and Infant Health*. Washington, DC: U.S. Department of Health and Human Services.

Healthy People 2020 (2018, July 10). *Lesbian, Gay, Bisexual, and Transgender Health*. Retrieved from www.healthypeople.gov/2020/topics-objectives/topic/lesbian-gay-bisexual-and-transgender-health

Hinman, A. R., Orenstein, W. S., and Rodewald, L. (2004, May 15). Financing immunizations in the United States. *Clinical Infectious Diseases*, 38(10), 1440–1446. Retrieved from www.ncbi.nlm.nih.gov/pubmed/15156483

Hoffer, K. and Kerr, J. (2003). Women and Men with CVD and High Cholesterol May Receive Different Levels of Treatment. *General Internal Medicine*, 18, 854–863.

Holinger, P. C., Offer, D., Barter, J. T., and Bell, C. C. (1994). *Suicide and Homicide among Adolescents*. New York: Guilford Press.

Holley, L. C., Tavassoli, K. Y. and Stromwell, L. K. (2016). Mental Illness Discrimination in Mental Health Treatment Programs: Intersections of Race, Ethnicity, and Sexual Orientation. *Community Mental Health Journal*. 52(3), 311–322.

Homan, R. K. and Korenbrot, C. C. (1998). Explaining Variation in Birth Outcomes of Medicaid Eligible Women with Variation in the Adequacy of Prenatal Support. *Medical Care*, 36(2), 190–201.

Howard, J. (2018, February 28). 1 in 14 Women Still Smokes while Pregnant, CDC says. *CNN*. Retrieved from www.cnn.com/2018/02/28/health/pregnant-cigarettes-smoking-cdc-study/index.html

Huggins, A., Weist, M. D., McCall, M., Kloos, B., Miller, E., and George, M. W. (2016). Qualitative analysis of key informant interviews about adolescent stigma surrounding use of school mental health services. *International Journal of Mental Health Promotion*, 18(1), 21–32.

Iezzoni, L. I., Ash, A. S., Schwartz, M., and Mackierman, Y. D. (1997, February). Differences in Procedure Use, In-hospital Mortality, and Illness Severity by Gender for Acute Myocardial Infarction Patients: Are Answers Affected by Data Source and Severity? *Medical Care*, 35(2), 158–171.

Institute of Medicine. (2011). *The Health of Lesbian, Gay, Bisexual, and Transgender People: Building a Foundation for Better Understanding*. Washington, DC: The National Academies Press.

Jaros, K. J. and Evans, J. C. (1995). Maternal and Child Health. In R. L. Edwards (Ed.), *Encyclopedia of Social Work*, 19th edn. (pp. 1683–1689). Washington, DC: National Association of Social Workers.

Jogerst, G. J., Daly, J., Brinig, M., and Dawson, J. (2003). Domestic Elder Abuse and the Law. *American Journal of Public Health*, 93(12), 2131–2136.

Johnston, L. D., O'Malley, P. M., and Bachman, J. G. (1995). *National Survey Results on Drug Use from the Monitoring the Future Study, 1975–1998*: Vol. I, *Secondary School Students*. Bethesda, MD: National Institute on Drug Abuse.

——. (2000). *Monitoring the Future National Results on Alcohol Drug Abuse, Overview of the Findings, 1999*. Bethesda, MD: National Institute on Drug Abuse.

——. (2008). *Monitoring the Future National Survey Results on Drug Use, 1975–2007*. Vol. I, *Secondary School Students*. National Institute on Drug Abuse, Institute for Social Research, University of Michigan.

Johnston, L. D., O'Malley, P. M., Bachman, J. G., and Schulenberg, J. (2005). *Monitoring the Future, National Results on Alcohol Drug Abuse, Overview of the Findings, 2004*. Bethesda, MD: National Institute on Drug Abuse.

——. (2011). *Monitoring the Future, National Results on Alcohol Drug Abuse, Overview of the Findings, 2011*. Bethesda, MD: National Institute on Drug Abuse.

Kaiser Family Foundation. (2005, July). *Women and Health Care: A National Profile*. Washington, DC: The Foundation.

——. (2012, December). *Women and HIV/AIDS in the United States*. Retrieved from www.kff.org/hivaids/upload/6092-10.pdf

——. (2017, June 20). *Medicaid's Role in Nursing Home Care*. Kaiser Family Foundation. Retrieved from www.kff.org/infographic/medicaids-role-in-nursing-home-care

Kirby, D. (2001). *Emerging Answers: Research Findings on Programs to Reduce Teen Pregnancy*. Washington, DC: National Campaign to Prevent Teen Pregnancy.

Kindig, D. A. and Cheng, E. R. (2013, March). Even as Mortality Fell in Most US Counties, Female Mortality Nonetheless Rose in 42.8 Percent of Counties from 1992 to 2006. *Health Affairs*, 32(3), 451–467.

Kinkel, R. J., Bailey, C. W., and Josef, N. C. (1989). Correlates of Adolescent Suicide Attempts: Alienation, Drugs, and Social Background. *Journal of Alcohol and Drug Education*, 34(3), 85–96.

Kochanek, K. D., Murphy, S. L., Xu, J., and Arias, E. (2017, December). NCHS Data Brief, No. 293, *Mortality in the United States, 2016*. Retrieved from www.cdc.gov/nchs/data/databriefs/db293.pdf

Kracke, K. (2001, April). *Children's Exposure to Violence: The Safe Start Initiative*. Washington, DC: U.S. Department of Justice.

Kracke, K. and Cohen, E. (2008). The Safe Start Initiative: Building and Disseminating Knowledge to Support Children Exposed to Violence. *Journal of Emotional Abuse*, 8(1), 155–174.

Krehely, J. (2009). *How to close the LGBT Health Disparities Gap*. Center for American Progress. Retrieved from www.americanprogress.org/wp-content/uploads/issues/2009/12/pdf/lgbt_health_disparities.pdf

Kushner, M. G. and Sher, K. J. (1993). Comorbidity of Alcohol and Anxiety Disorders among College Students: Effects of Gender and Family History of Alcoholism. *Addictive Behaviors*, 18(5), 543–552.

Lachs, M. S. and Pillemer, K. (2004, October). Elder Abuse. *The Lancet*, 364(9441), 1192–1263.

Lambrew, J. M. (2001, August). *Diagnosing Disparities in Health Insurance for Women: A Prescription for Change*. New York: Commonwealth Fund.

Long, N., Brendtro, L., and Johnson, J. (1993). Alcohol and Kids: Facing Our Problem. *Journal of Emotional and Behavioral Problems*, 2(3), 2–4.

McQueen, A. (2001, July 29). Abuse in Nursing Homes Widespread. *Concord Monitor*, p. A1.

Macy, R. J., Ferron, J., and Crosby, C. (2009, January). Partner Violence and Survivors' Chronic Health Problems: Informing Social Work Practice. *Social Work*, 54(1), 29–44.

Maternal and Child Health Bureau. (2005). Maternal and Child Health Services Title V Block Grant. Retrieved from http://mchb.hrsa.gov/programs/blockgrant/overview.htm

Mathews, M. A. (1999). The Impact of Federal and State Laws on Children Exposed to Domestic Violence. In R. E. Behrman (Ed.), *The Future of Children* (pp. 50–66). Los Altos, CA: David and Lucile Packard Foundation.

Medley, G., Lipari, R., Bose, J., Cribb, D., Kroutil, L., and McHenry, G. (2016, October). *Sexual Orientation and Estimates of Adult Substance Use and Mental Health: Results from the 2015 National Survey on Drug Use and Health*. NSDUH Data Review. Retrieved from www.samhsa.gov/data/sites/default/files/NSDUH-SexualOrientation-2015/NSDUH-SexualOrientation-2015/NSDUH-SexualOrientation-2015.htm.

Meyer, H. H. (2003). Prejudice, Social Stress, and Mental Health in Lesbian, Gay, and Bisexual Populations: Conceptual Issues and Research Evidence. *Psychological Bulletin*. Retrieved from www.ncbi.nlm.nih.gov/pmc/articles/PMC2072932

Miech, R., Schulenberg, J., Johnston, L., Bachman, J., O'Malley, P., and Patrick, M. (2017). Monitoring the Future National Adolescent Drug Trends in 2017: Findings Released. Institute for Social Research, University of Michigan. Retrieved from www.monitoringthefuture.org//pressreleases/17drugpr.pdf

Mitka, M. (2003). Too Few Older Patients in Cancer Trials. *Journal of the American Medical Association*, 290(1), 27–28.

National Academy on an Aging Society. (2000, July). *Challenges for the 21st Century: Chronic and Disabling Conditions*, No. 9 *Depression*. Washington, DC: National Academy on an Aging Society.

National Alliance for Caregiving and AARP. (2004, April). *Caregiving in the U.S.* Retrieved from www.caregiving.org

National Association of Social Workers. (1999). *The Social Work Dictionary*. Washington, DC: The Association of Social Workers.

——. (2000a). Alcohol, Tobacco, and Other Substance Abuse. *Social Work Speaks*, 5th edn. Washington, DC: The Association.

——. (2000b). Child Abuse and Neglect. *Social Work Speaks*, 5th edn. Washington, DC: The Association.

——. (2000c). Family Planning and Reproductive Choice. *Social Work Speaks*, 5th edn. Washington, DC: The Association.

——. (2000d). Long-term Care. *Social Work Speaks*, 5th edn. Washington, DC: The Association.

——. (2000e). Women's Issues. *Social Work Speaks*, 5th edn. Washington, DC: The Association.

——. (2013). *Standards for Social Work Practice with Clients with Substance Use Disorders*. Retrieved from www.socialworkers.org/LinkClick.aspx?fileticket= ICxAggMy9CU%3D&portalid=0

National Center on Addiction and Substance Abuse. (2002). *Teen Tipplers: America's Underage Drinking Epidemic*. New York: Columbia University Press.

National Center for Children in Poverty. (2018, January 31). *America's Child Poverty Rate Remains Stubbornly High Despite Important Progress*. Columbia University's Mailman School of Public Health. Retrieved from https://medicalxpress.com/ news/2018-01-america-child-poverty-stubbornly-high.html

National Center on Elder Abuse. (1998, September). *National Elder Abuse Incidence Study*, Final Report. Retrieved from www.aoa.gov/abuse/report.html

——. (2003). *A Response to the Abuse of Vulnerable Adults: The 2000 Survey of State Adult Protective Services*. Washington, DC: U.S. Department of Health and Human Services.

——. (2004). *Abuse of Adults Aged 60+ 2004 Survey of Adult Protective Services*: Fact Sheet. Retrieved from www.ncea.aoa.gov/ncearoot/Main_Site/pdf/021406_ 60FACTSHEET.pdf

National Center for Health Statistics. (2008). *Health United States, 2007*. Hyattsville, MD: U.S. Department of Health and Human Services.

National Coalition Against Domestic Violence. (2015). *Domestic Violence National Statistics*. Retrieved from www.ncadv.org

National Institute of Child Health and Human Development. (2002). Workshop on Children Exposed to Violence: Current Status, Gaps, and Research Priorities. Retrieved December 5, 2005. Available at: www.nichd.gov/crmc/cdb/workshop_ on_childrenviolence.pdf

National Institute on Drug Abuse. (2017, December). *Monitoring the Future Survey: High School and Youth Trends*. Retrieved from www.drugabuse.gov/publications/drug-facts/monitoring-future-survey-high-school-youth-trends

National Institute for Health Care Management. (2007, February). *Reducing Health Disparities among Children: Strategies and Programs for Health Plans*. Retrieved from http://nihcm.org/pdf/HealthDisparitiesFinal.pdf

National Institute of Mental Health. (2005). *Depression: What Every Woman Should Know*. Retrieved from www.nimh.nih.gov/publicat/depwomenknows.cfm#ptdep3

National Women's Law Center. (2007). *Making the Grade on Women's Health: A National and State-by-State Report Card*. Retrieved from http://hrc.nwlc.org/Key-Findings.aspx

Newberger, E. H., Newberger, C. M., and Richmond, J. B. (1976). Child Health in America: Toward a Rational Public Policy. *Milbank Memorial Fund Quarterly/Health and Society*, 54(3), 249–298.

Office of Minority Health. (2000, May). *Healthy People 2010: Objectives for Older Adults*. Washington, DC: U.S. Department of Health and Human Services.

Office of Research on Women's Health. (2018). *Including Women and Minorities in Clinical Research*. Retrieved from https://orwh.od.nih.gov/research/clinical-research-trials/nih-inclusion-policy/including-women-and-minorities-clinical

Office on Women's Health. (2001). *Women's Health Issues: An Overview*. Washington, DC: U.S. Department of Health and Human Services.

Osberg, M. (2018, March 9). *States are Competing to pass the Country's Worst Anti-Abortion Laws*. Retrieved from https://splinternews.com/states-are-competing-to-pass-the-countrys-worst-anti-ab-1823902676

Osofsky, J. D. (1999). The Impact of Violence on Children. In R. E. Behrman (Ed.), *The Future of Children* (pp. 33–49). Los Altos, CA: David and Lucile Packard Foundation.

Ostlin, P., Eckermann, E., Shankar Mishra, U., Nkowane, M., and Wallstam, E. (2006). Gender and Health Promotion: A Multisectoral Policy Approach. *Health Promotion International*, 21(1), 25–35.

Oxendine, J. (2000, May). *Who Is Helping the Caregivers? Closing the Gap*. Washington, DC: Office of Minority Health, U.S. Department of Health and Human Services.

Ozawa, M. N, and Tseng, H. Y. (2000). Differences in Net Worth between Elderly Black People and Elderly White People. In S. Keigher, A. Fortune, and S. Witkin (Eds.), *Aging and Social Work* (pp. 67–82). Washington, DC: National Association of Social Workers.

Ozawa, M. N., Lum, Y. S., and Tseng, H. Y. (1999). Net Worth at Retirement and 10 Years Later. In S. S. Nager (Ed.), *The Substance of Public Policy* (pp. 245–275). New York: Nova Science.

Paradise, J., Rosenbaum, S., Markus, A., Sharac, J., Tran, C., Reynolds, D., and Shin, P. (2017). *Community Health Centers: Recent Growth and the Role of the ACA. Kaiser Family Foundation*. Retrieved from www.kff.org/report-section/community-health-centers-recent-growth-and-the-role-of-the-aca-issue-brief

Patel, J. (2018, February 15). After Sandy Hook, More Than 400 People Have Been Shot in Over 200 School Shootings. *New York Times*. Retrieved from www.nytimes.com/interactive/2018/02/15/us/school-shootings-sandy-hook-parkland.html

Paterson, J., Walters. M. A., Brown, R., and Fearn, H. (2018, January). *The Sussex Hate Crime Project*: Final Report. University of Sussex. Retrieved from www.sussex.ac.uk/webteam/gateway/file.php?name=sussex-hate-crime-project-report.pdf&site=430

Pillemer, K. A. and Finkelhor, D. (1988). The Prevalence of Elder Abuse: A Random Sample. *Gerontologist*, 28(1), 51–57.

Pollack, W. S. (2000). *Real Boys' Voices*. New York: Random House.

Powell, K. B. (1999). Correlates of Violent and Nonviolent Behavior among Vulnerable Inner-city Youth. In J. G. Sebastian and A. Bushy (Eds.), *Special Populations in the Community* (pp. 39–48). Gaithersburg, MD: Aspen Publishers.

Proctor, E. K. and Stiffman, A. R. (1998). Background of Services and Treatment Research. In J. B. W. Williams and K. Ell (Eds.), *Mental Health Research* (pp. 259–286). Washington, DC: National Association of Social Workers.

Prothrow-Stith, D. and Quaday, S. (1995). *Hidden Casualties: The Relationship between Violence and Learning.* Washington, DC: National Health and Education Consortium.

Quinn, G. P., Sanchez, J. A., Sutton, S. K., Vadaparampil, S. T., Nguyen, G. T., Green, B. L., et al. (2015). Cancer and lesbian, gay, bisexual, transgender/transsexual, and queer/questioning (LGBTQ) populations. *CA: A Cancer Journal for Clinicians,* 65(5):384–400.

Rau, J. (2017, June 24). Medicaid Cuts May Force Retirees out of Nursing Homes. *New York Times.* Retrieved from www.nytimes.com/2017/06/24/science/medicaid-cutbacks-elderly-nursing-homes.html

Reaves, E. L. and Musumeci, M. (2015, December 15). *Medicaid and Long-term Services and Supports: A Primer.* Kaiser Family Foundation. Retrieved from www.kff.org/medicaid/report/medicaid-and-long-term-services-and-supports-a-primer/

Saathoff, A. J. and Stoffel, E. A. (1999). Community-Based Domestic Violence Services. In R. E. Behrman (Ed.), *The Future of Children* (pp. 97–110). Los Altos, CA: David and Lucile Packard Foundation.

Sabin, J. A., Riskind, R. G., and Nosek, B. A. (2015). Health care providers' implicit and explicit attitudes toward lesbian women and gay men. *American Journal of Public Health* (online). Retrieved from www.ncbi.nlm.nih.gov/pmc/articles/PMC4539817/

Schoen, C., Davis, K., DesRoches, C., and Shekhdar, A. (1998, June). *The Health of Adolescent Boys: Commonwealth Fund Survey Findings.* New York: Commonwealth Fund.

Schulman, D., Berlin, J., William, H., Kerner, J., and Ayers, W. (1999). The Effects of Race and Sex on Physicians' Recommendations for Cardiac Catheterization. *New England Journal of Medicine,* 340(14), 618–627.

Schwartz, M. D. (1987). Gender and Injury in Spousal Assault. *Sociological Focus,* 20(1), 61–75.

Semega, J. L., Fontenot, K. R., and Kollar, M. A. (2017, September). *Income and Poverty in the United States: 2016.* Current Population Reports. U.S. Census Bureau. Retrieved from www.census.gov/content/dam/Census/library/publications/2017/demo/P60-259.pdf

Senreich, E. (2010). Are Specialized LGBT Program Components Helpful for Gay and Bisexual Men in Substance Abuse Treatment? *Substance Use Misuse,* 45(7–8):1077–1096.

Sherman, A. (1994). *Wasting America's Future, Children's Defense Fund Report on the Costs of Child Poverty.* Boston, MA: Beacon Press.

Shumaker, S. A. and Smith, T. R. (1999). The Politics of Women's Health. In K. Charmaz and D. A. Paterniti (Eds.), *Health, Illness, and Healing* (pp. 574–581). Los Angeles, CA: Roxbury Publishing.

SIECUS (Sexuality Information and Education Council of U.S.). (2005). *What the Research Says . . . (Abstinence-only Programs).* Retrieved from www.siecus.org/policy/research_says.pdf

Slifkin, R. T., Clark, S. J., Strandhoy, S. E., and Konrad, T. R. (1997, Fall). Public Sector Immunization Coverage in 11 States: The Status of Rural Areas. *Journal of Rural Health*, 13(4), 334–341.

Sly, D., Gary, G., and Ray, S. (2001). The Florida "Truth" Anti-tobacco Media Evaluation. *Tobacco Control*, 10(1), 9–15.

Sonfeld, A. and Gold, R. B. (2012, March). *Public Funding for Contraceptive, Sterilization, and Abortion Services*, FY 1980–2010. New York: Alan Guttmacher Institute.

Span, P. (2011, August 19). Clinical Trials Neglect the Elderly. *New York Times*. Retrieved from http://newoldage.blogs.nytimes.com/2011/08/19/clinical-trials-neglect-theelderly/

Spetz, J., Trupin, L., Bates, T., and Coffman, J. M. (2015, June). Future Demand For Long-term Care Workers will be Influenced by Demographic and Utilization Changes. *Health Affairs*. Retrieved from www.healthaffairs.org/doi/10.1377/hlthaff.2015.0005

Stop Street Harassment. (2018, February). *A National Study on Sexual Harassment and Assault*. Retrieved from www.stopstreetharassment.org/wp-content/uploads/2018/01/Full-Report-2018-National-Study-on-Sexual-Harassment-and-Assault.pdf

Strunin, L. and Hingson, R. (1992). Alcohol, Drugs, and Adolescent Sexual Behavior. *International Journal of the Addictions*, 27(2), 129–146.

Substance Abuse and Mental Health Services Administration. (2017, September 20). *Underage Drinking*. Retrieved from www.samhsa.gov/underage-drinking-topic

Tatara, T. (1995a). *An Analysis of State Laws Addressing Elder Abuse, Neglect, and Exploitation*. Washington, DC: National Center on Elder Abuse.

——. (1995b). Elder Abuse. In R. L. Edwards (Ed.), *Encyclopedia of Social Work*, 19th edn. (pp. 834–842). Washington, DC: National Association of Social Workers.

Tatara, T., Kuzmeskas, L., and Duckhorn, E. (1997). *Elder Abuse in Domestic Settings*. Informational Series. Washington, DC: National Center on Elder Abuse, American Public Welfare Association.

Thakrar, A. P., Forrest, A. D., Maltenfort, M. G., and Forrest, C. B. (January, 2018). *Child Mortality in the US and 19 OECD Comparator Nations: A 50-year Time-trend Analysis*. Retrieved from www.healthaffairs.org/doi/full/10.1377/hlthaff.2017.0767

Thomas, B. (2017, October 16). *Emergency Departments Often First Point of Care for Domestic Violence Trauma, Injury Cases*. Retrieved from www.acepnow.com/article/emergency-departments-often-first-point-care-domestic-violence-trauma-injury-cases

Trans People of Color Coalition, Human Rights Campaign. (2017). *A Time to Act: Fatal Violence Against Transgender People in America in 2017*. Retrieved from http://assets2.hrc.org/files/assets/resources/A_Time_To_Act_2017_REV3.pdf

UNICEF. (2012). *Measuring Child Poverty: New League Tables of Child Poverty in the World's Richest Countries*. Retrieved from www.unicef-irc.org/publications/pdf/rc10_eng.pdf

U.S. Census Bureau. (1976). *Current Population Report*. Retrieved from www.census.population.html

——. (2012). *March Demographic Profiles*. Current Population Surveys. Retrieved from www.census.gov/population/socdemo

U.S. Department of Agriculture. (2010). Final Report (Vol. I) *National and State-level Estimates of Special Supplemental Nutrition Program for Women, Infants, and Children (WIC) Eligibles and Program Reach*. Retrieved from www.fns.usda.gov/ora/MENU/Published/WIC/FILES/WICEligibles2010Vol1.pdf

_____. (2018, April 23). *WIC Program*. Retrieved from www.ers.usda.gov/topics/food-nutrition-assistance/wic-program

U.S. Department of Health and Human Services. (1999, December). *Mental Health: A Report of the Surgeon General*. Rockville, MD: U.S. Department of Health and Human Services Substance Abuse and Mental Health Services Administration, Center for Mental Health Services, National Institute of Mental Health.

——. (2008). *Ryan White HIV/AIDS Program Progress Report*. Retrieved from http://hab.hrsa.gov/publications/progressreport08/default.htm

——. (2010). *Healthy People 2010: Women's and Men's Health: A Comparison of Select Indicators*. Retrieved from www.womenshealth.gov/publications/federal-reports/healthy-people/healthypeople2010-report-070109.pdf

——. (2011). *Women's Health USA 2011*. Maternal and Child Health Bureau. Retrieved from http://mchb.hrsa.gov/whusa11/hstat/hshi/downloads/pdf/218vaw.pdf

——. (2012a). *Healthy People 2020: Maternal, Infant, and Child Health Objectives*. Retrieved from www.healthypeople.gov/2020/topicsobjectives2020/objectiveslist.aspx?topicid=26

——. (2012b). *Healthy People 2020*: Older Adults. Retrieved from www.healthypeople.gov/2020/topicsobjectives2020/overview.aspx?topicId=31

——. (2012c). *Title V State Abstinence Education Grant Program Fact Sheet*. Family and Youth Services Bureau. Retrieved from www.healthypeople.gov/2020/topicsobjectives2020/objectiveslist.aspx?topicid=26

_____. (2015). *The Health Consequences of Smoking: 50 Years of Progress*: A Report of the Surgeon General, 2014. Retrieved from www.surgeongeneral.gov/library/reports/50-years-of-progress/index.html

_____. (2017a). *Child Maltreatment*. Retrieved from www.acf.hhs.gov/sites/default/files/cb/cm2016.pdf#page=29

_____ (2017b, February). *State Abstinence Education Grant Program Fact Sheet*. Retrieved from www.acf.hhs.gov/sites/default/files/fysb/aegp_facts_20170217.pdf

_____. (2018a, January). *HRSA's Ryan White HIV/AIDS Program*. Program Overview. Retrieved from https://hab.hrsa.gov/sites/default/files/hab/Publications/factsheets/program-factsheet-program-overview.pdf

——. (2018b, June 10). *Healthy People 2020*: Maternal, Infant, and Child Health Objectives. Retrieved from www.healthypeople.gov/2020/topics-objectives/topic/maternal-infant-and-child-health/objectives

U.S. Department of Justice. (2006). *Biennial Report to Congress on the Effectiveness of Grant Programs under the Violence against Women Act*. Office on Violence against Women, 2006. Retrieved from www.ovw.usdoj.gov/docs/ovw-measuring-effectivenessreport.pdf

U.S. General Accounting Office. (2000a, March). *Community Health Centers: Adapting to Changing Health Care Environment Key to Continued Success* (HEHS-00-39). Washington, DC: U.S. Government Printing Office.

——. (2000b, May). *Women's Health: NIH Has Increased Its Efforts to Include Women in Research* (HEHS-00-96). Washington, DC: U.S. Government Printing Office.

——. (2000c, March). *HIV/AIDS: Use of Ryan White CARE Act and other Assistance Grant Funds* (HEHS-00-54). Washington, DC: U.S. Government Printing Office.

U.S. Health Resources and Services Administration. (2007). *Health Centers: America's Primary Care Safety Net Reflections on Success, 2002–2007*. Retrieved from http://bphc.hrsa.gov/success

Villarosa, L. (2017, June 6). America's Hidden H.I.V. Epidemic: Why do America's Black Gay and Bisexual Men have a Higher H.I.V. Rate than Any Country in the World? *New York Times*. Retrieved from www.nytimes.com/2017/06/06/magazine/americas-hidden-hiv-epidemic.html

Ward, B. W., Dahlhamer, J. M., Galinsky, A. M., and Joestl, S. S. (2014). *Sexual Orientation and Health Among U.S. Adults: National Health Interview Survey, 2013*. Hyattsville, MD: National Center for Health Statistics. Retrieved from www.cdc.gov/nchs/data/nhsr/nhsr077.pdf

WebMd. (2018). Major Depression (Clinical Depression). Retrieved from www.webmd.com/depression/guide/major-depression#1

White House. (2009, October 30). Remarks by the President at Signing of the Ryan White HIV/AIDS Treatment Extension Act of 2009. Retrieved from www.thebodypro.com/content/art54259.html

Williams, D. R. (1990). Socioeconomic Differentials in Health: A Review and Redirection. *Social Psychology Quarterly*, 53(2), 81–99.

Williams, V. (2012, March 20). Breast Cancer Toll among Black Women Fed in Part by Fear, Silence. *Washington Post*. Retrieved from http://articles.washingtonpost.com/2012-03-20/national/35449548_1_black-women-breast-cancer-white-women

Wolf, R. S. (2000, Fall). The Nature and Scope of Elder Abuse. *Journal of the American Society on Aging*, 24, 2.

Women's Heart Foundation (2007). Women and Heart Disease Facts. Retrieved from www.womensheart.org/content/heartdisease/heart_disease_facts.asp

World Health Organization. (2012). *Gender Equity in Health: Fact Sheet*. Retrieved from www.paho.org/english/hdp/hdw/GenderEquityinHealth.pdf

Yao, T. (2016). Key Changes of the Older Americans Act Reauthorization Act of 2016. *Bifocal. Journal of Commission on Law and Aging*. Retrieved from www.americanbar.org/groups/law_aging/publications/bifocal/vol_37/issue_6_august2016/older-americans-act-reauthorization-2016-overview.html

Zambrana, R. E. and Scrimshaw, S. C. (1997, May–June). Maternal Psychosocial Factors Associated with Substance Use in Mexican–American Origin and African American Low-income Pregnant Women. *Pediatric Nursing*, 23(3), 253–259, 274.

CHAPTER 12

Advocating for Policies that Improve Health

Models of Health and Health Policy

INTRODUCTION

IN THIS LAST CHAPTER, WE CONSIDER MODELS OF HEALTH and health policy. To do this, we consider the questions outlined in Chapter 8 for policy practice for the stage of developing policy goals and objectives (stage 4):

- What should health policy achieve?

- What are the options for achieving these goals?

- How can the problem of access to care best be alleviated or ameliorated using evidence-based solutions?

- What is achievable?

- What is the best fit with the target population?

- What values guide the policy options?

- What rights or benefits will be preserved or enhanced?

- Are disparities in equality, equity, and adequacy addressed?

Both health and health policy are complex; thus, this chapter includes theoretical frameworks for both heath and health policy. It concludes with implications for advocating for health policy in the U.S.

WHAT IS HEALTH?

Let us begin with health. Although the answer may seem obvious or something we know intuitively, defining health is a complex task. For many years, health was understood as the absence of illness or disease. One was either sick or not, in good health or poor health. This definition is misleading, however. First, it is too static and abstract; health is not an either/or phenomenon, but a relative, or quantitative, one (Rose, 1993). It is difficult to define precisely where health ends and illness begins; rather, health seems much more a matter of degree.

Second, the definition is too narrow. It focuses our attention on individuals, not the broader context in which they live and flourish. Today, however, we know that health is as much a social process as an individual or biological one (Berkman and Kawachi, 2000).

In 1946, the World Health Organization (WHO) advanced a broader definition of health. Challenging the static, either/or approach, WHO defined health as "a state of complete physical, mental and social well-being and not simply the absence of disease or infirmity" (WHO, 1958, as cited in Sagan, 1987, p. 8). Under this definition, individuals could be well physically, yet have serious psychological, social, or other problems. The WHO definition also grasped health as a goal, or moving target: an unfolding process that one does not necessarily achieve.

However, the WHO definition is somewhat abstract. If health encompasses every aspect of "physical, mental, and social" wellbeing, then anything and everything, including *all* social policy, is health related (Evans and Stoddart, 1994). Although this may be true in a broad sense, it leaves us with the question of how, or even whether, to consider specific *health* policies and issues. If everything is health related, health reform can take place only through fundamental social transformation. Although this may make sense from a theoretical perspective, it does little to address the practical problems of our society, such as infant mortality, lack of health care coverage, and the cost of health care. If the earlier definition was too narrow, the WHO definition seems too broad.

DETERMINANTS OF HEALTH: A BIOPSYCHOSOCIAL PERSPECTIVE

Social work has developed a more concrete approach to health, known as the *biopsychosocial* perspective (Berkman and Volland, 1997). The biopsychosocial perspective considers the impact on health and wellbeing of *biological* (genetics and the human aging process), *psychological* (perception, cognition, emotion), and *social* (lifestyle, culture, politics, race and ethnicity, class, gender) factors. Although these factors, or determinants, are distinct, they are also interrelated. In fact, the interaction among these factors has become the focus of recent frameworks of health (Evans and Stoddart, 1994).

Let us first briefly consider the role of biological, psychological, and social factors as distinct entities, or determinants. This will lay the foundation for analyzing the interactions among these influences and discussing the biopsychosocial framework.

Biological Factors

Longres (1990) identifies four basic ways in which biology underlies "individual functioning." First, human genetic structure, anatomy, and physiology impose fundamental limits on the species' behavior, growth, and development. Second, biological and genetic factors play a role in psychological wellbeing. For example, researchers have linked schizophrenia with the "lateral and third ventricles" and the temporal lobes of the brain (Farmer and Pandurangi, 1997, p. 110).

Bipolar disorder seems largely genetic, showing "a nearly 100 percent rate of concordance among identical twins" (Ratey and Johnson, 1998, p. 120). Third, "illness, injury, or disability" can change an individual's cognition, emotions, and behavior. Finally, "physical growth," from fertilization to old age, provides impetus for "personal change and development" (Longres, 1990, p. 24).

Psychological Factors

Longres (1990) also discusses three essential "subsystems" of the "psychological domain": Cognition, affect, and behavior. Cognition consists of "perception, sensation, memory, imagination, judgment, and language, as well as intelligence and other aspects of intellectual functioning such as knowledge, beliefs, and opinions" (Longres, 1990, p. 24). Cognitive processes enable the individual to interpret and grasp the external world. Affect involves feeling and emotion and an individual's "sense of well-being or ill-being" (Longres, 1990, p. 25). Behavior refers to "the ways individuals express themselves in action" and includes "mannerisms, habits, and . . . communication skills" (Longres, 1990, p. 25). Although humans express cognition and affect through behavior, the latter, unlike the former, directly involves what "people say and do" (Longres, 1990, p. 25).

Finally, as Longres points out, cognition, affect, and behavior "form increasingly larger and more complex systems within the individual" (Longres, 1990, p. 26). A good example of this is the development of attitudes, which includes a cognitive level (what an individual believes), an affective level (what an individual feels), and a behavioral level (a predisposition to behave in a certain way).

Social Factors

Individuals are also social beings who exist within physical and social environments. From a sociological perspective, both culture and social structure are essential to human behavior. Culture refers to the beliefs, values, language, traditions, and material objects shared by a people. Social structure refers to the social organization of society. Most sociologists identify increasingly complex levels of social organization, beginning with statuses and roles, including dyads, families, groups, organizations, communities, and complex social institutions. Belief systems and traditions shape human behavior. Social structures provide social norms (informal and formal social rules of conduct) and include social statuses (social ranking based on race, class, gender, and/or age) that play a significant role in shaping human behavior. Social institutions, including the health care system, include policies, programs, and services that exert enormous influence on individuals.

Biopsychosocial Dynamics

The Council on Social Work Education (CSWE, 1995) requires that social work programs "provide content about theories and knowledge of human biopsycho-social development" (CSWE, 1995, pp. 102, 140). (In 2002, CSWE introduced content on spiritual development as an additional requirement for social work curricula. Although we recognize what the term "spiritual" refers to, for the purposes of this discussion we are incorporating spirituality into our category of social factors, which includes belief systems and traditions.) This biopsychosocial approach is rooted in early holistic approaches to understanding human behavior. Theoretical foundations include Richmond's (1917) social diagnosis, Gordon's (1969) general systems approach, Bartlett and Saunder's (1970) common base of practice, Germain's (1973) ecological perspective, and Germain and Gitterman's (1980) life model of social work practice.

The National Association of Social Workers (NASW) funded the development of the PIE classification system in an effort to establish "uniform descriptions of a client's interpersonal, environmental, mental, and physical health problems" (Karls and Wandrei, 1995, p. 1818). The PIE (person in environment) approach to assessment and intervention focuses on the interaction between people and their environments (Karls and Wandrei, 1995). PIE conceptualizes practice in terms of processes—what Weick (1986) calls "fields of interaction between people and their multiple environments"—rather than "static, linear relationships" (Weick, 1986, p. 552). From this perspective, the client is less the individual than the individual within a system, which consists of interacting biological, psychological, and social factors. The generalist practitioner plans intervention on the basis of the clients' physical, emotional, social, and economic needs. This requires intervention at multiple levels to help change individual, familial, group, and organizational or community behavior. The biopsychosocial perspective captures these multiple levels, or dimensions, of human existence and activity.

Unfortunately, most discussions of the biopsychosocial perspective focus on the interaction that occurs among these dimensions. Yet, to understand and appreciate the biopsychosocial perspective fully, one must also acknowledge the relative, or partial, identity of these factors. By this we mean that, in addition to being separate, each factor also contains within it something of the others. This is not as complicated as it sounds.

Consider, for example, the age-old debate over nature and nurture. Is human behavior determined by biology or by the social environment? From a biopsychosocial perspective, the question itself is misleading. Nature and nurture are not only separate and distinct, but also interrelated. From a biopsychosocial perspective, human behavior is "100 percent hereditary" *and* "100 percent environmental" (Ferris, 1996, p. 26). How can this be?

Take the human brain. In recent years, our understanding of the growth and development of this organ has undergone dramatic change. At the 1997 White House Conference on Early Childhood Development and Learning, Hillary Rodham Clinton summarized the state of knowledge:

> Fifteen years ago, we thought . . . a baby's brain structure was virtually complete at birth. Now, we understand that it is a work in progress, and that everything we do with a child has . . . potential physical influence on that rapidly-forming brain. A child's earliest experiences, their relationships with parents and caregivers, the sights and sounds and smells and feelings they encounter, the challenges they meet determine how their brains are wired. And that brain shapes itself

through repeated experiences. . . . The brain is the last organ to become fully mature anatomically. Neurological circuitry for many emotions isn't completed until a child reaches 15.

(Clinton, 1997, pp. 1–2)

In short, the brain is not hardwired, or fixed, at birth, but in a continual state of change and development. This plasticity may even continue into adulthood. Researchers at UCLA have found that cognitive and behavioral modification can actually alter the brain and "genetic disposition" of individuals with obsessive–compulsive disorder (Schwartz, 1994).

Social factors have a profound impact on the development of the brain (Kotulak, 1997). McEwen (2012) noted that although, in the short term, chronic stress can "protect the body," over time, "the burden of chronic stress causes changes in the brain and body that can lead to disease" (McEwen, 2012, p. 17180). According to Siegel, social experience "selectively shapes genetic neuronal potential and thus directly influences the structure and function of the brain" (cited in Maté, 1999, p. 77). Emotional deprivation can "warp" an infant's "developing neural circuits" and irreversibly alter "the way an organism behaves and responds to the world around it" (Hotz, 1997, p. A2). Depriving a child of hugging, caressing, and other forms of caring touch can change the brain's biochemistry (Hotz, 1997). Emotional support—the ability to respond actively and positively to a child's needs—plays a central role in the development of intelligence as well (Greenspan with Benderly, 1997).

Not surprisingly, violence can have a particularly adverse impact on the chemistry of the brain and individual development. Children living in violent neighborhoods are at risk of developing a form of posttraumatic stress disorder that limits their capacity to learn and develop interpersonal relationships (Prothrow-Stith and Quaday, 1995). Many abused children grow up to become "antisocial" adults, as "violence begets violence" (Ferris, 1996, p. 23). Gilligan (1996), a former director of mental health in Massachusetts' prisons, found that in many cases adult violence was linked with feelings of shame originating in early abuse and neglect.

In short, the human brain is not only a *biological* phenomenon, but also a *social* (and *psychological*) one. As Levins (1998, p. 12) puts it:

As mammals, we are born partly formed. Our development depends on regularly occurring environmental factors that have become incorporated into our developmental biology. The development of vision requires light. The development of muscles and bone require[s] exercise. Brain development requires stimulation. Intellectual development needs challenge. Emotional and social development require[s] touch, attention and loving care.

From this perspective, the biological, psychological, and social dimensions of life are separate and interrelated. Although this may seem contradictory, it is a contradiction in real life, not theory. This is the true insight of the biopsychosocial perspective.

A BIOPSYCHOSOCIAL APPROACH TO HEALTH

In the mid-1980s, Weick (1986) developed a "health model" based on a biopsychosocial approach to health. She contrasted her perspective with the medical model, which focuses largely on the individual. According to Weick (1986), the medical model reduces the study of human health to the study and treatment of disease and seeks to uncover "specific, identifiable causes and antidotes for particular disease conditions" (Weick, 1986, p. 553). The traditional roles of doctor and patient are deeply rooted in this model. The physician is the trained expert and authority who diagnoses and treats the patient; the patient relies on the judgment of the doctor and cooperates with the prescribed treatment. The medical model has promoted research into the causes of disease and the development of new means of treatment. Few of the dollars spent on health care have been spent on health promotion or prevention (Weick, 1986).

In contrast with the medical model, the health model goes beyond linear explanations for health and disease, and focuses on the multiple influences that shape individual health. The complexity of interactions among these influences creates conditions that may have an even greater effect on individual health.

The health model also views treatment from this perspective. Weick (1986) argues that a central assumption of the health model is "the capacity of humans to heal themselves. . . . The human body contains innate, self-correcting mechanisms that respond to a continuously changing environment" (Weick, 1986, p. 556). Thus, treatment requires an active role on the part of patients in achieving health. In the health model, the goal is to empower individuals to use their capacities to heal themselves. However, Weick recognizes that, ultimately, individuals can be well only if society takes responsibility for the promotion of good health and access to resources.

Finally, Weick (1986) discusses the consistency between the health model and social work, both of which emphasize strengths, self-determination, and social context.

> At any given moment, an individual's state of health reflects the capacity of the individual and the capacity of the social–physical environments, both past and present, to provide the necessary raw materials and resources for healing to take place . . . rather than confining ourselves to questions about how growth and development fail to occur . . . a health perspective asks how we can create environments in which people have the best chance for maximum healing–health–wholeness . . . we ask how people can be helped to develop their strengths more fully.
>
> (Weick, 1986, p. 558)

Weick (1986) makes an important contribution to our understanding of health from a biopsychosocial perspective. She stresses that the environment determines the health of individuals. In the years since Weick's article, scholars have come closer to understanding *which* environmental factors are most important.

WHAT DETERMINES GOOD HEALTH? A SOCIAL DETERMINANTS MODEL OF HEALTH

Over the past 25 years, scholars from western Europe and North America have increasingly focused on the role of *social* factors in shaping the health of populations (Evans et al., 1994). This growing body of literature reinforces the biopsychosocial perspective and therefore has important implications for social work.

In a sense, the social determinants of health approach is not a new one. Speculation about the relationship between health and society has gone on for years. During the 1830s and 1840s, Villerme in France and Virchow in Germany argued that "social conditions," such as inadequate housing, malnutrition, and poor sanitation, contributed to high rates of disease and mortality among working and poor people (Amick et al., 1995). In 1842, Edwin Chadwick issued *Report on an Enquiry into the Sanitary Conditions of the Labouring Population of Great Britain* (Amick et al., 1995): "Chadwick called for organized public health, and he defined its mission as one of sanitary cleanup" (Garrett, 2000, p. 284).

There were similar developments in the U.S. In 1850, Lemuel Shattuck issued *Report of the Sanitary Commission of Massachusetts*, which led to the creation of the first state board of health in the nation and became a blueprint for public health in this country (Moroney, 1995). During the late 1880s, in response to developments in Europe, particularly the emergence of Pasteur's theory linking disease to germs, officials in New York City established "the nation's first public health laboratory" (Garrett, 2000, p. 293). By the turn of the century, public health leaders, armed with newly developed vaccines, "routinely deployed police officers and zealous nurses or physicians to the homes of those suspected of carrying disease. . . . In some cases, police officers pinned the arm of those who refused while a city nurse jabbed it with a vaccination needle" (Garrett, 2000, p. 299). The U.S. Public Health Service was created in 1902, and public health programs were established at major universities during the 1920s (Amick et al., 1995; Moroney, 1995).

During the 1950s, the World Health Organization (WHO, 1958) challenged the static notion of health as the absence of disease. One factor behind this shift was increased life expectancy. In the 1800s, only 3 out of 10 newborn infants lived beyond the age of 25 years (McKeown, 1994). Infant mortality was high, life expectancy short, and childhood diseases were often fatal. By 1992, in the U.S., the infant mortality rate (per 1000 live births) had risen to 8.52 and life expectancy to 72 years. Today in the U.S. few infants are victims of infectious disease, and infant death is most often associated with low birth weight and poverty (Turnock, 1997).

Social scientists have studied the declines in mortality for decades. Early studies emphasized the role of medicine and health care in improving health status. During the 1950s and 1960s, however, researchers began to call this view into question (McKinlay and McKinlay, 1994). In a seminal work, McKeown (1979) showed that medical care played a relatively limited role in reducing mortality in the west. Thus, in England and Canada, death rates from tuberculosis began to decline before the discovery of streptomycin. Extending this work to the U.S., McKinlay and McKinlay (1994) contended that "medical measures" could account for "at most 3.5 percent of the decline in mortality" between 1900 and 1973 (McKinlay and McKinlay, 1994, p. 21).

If health care does not explain the reduction in mortality, what does? McKeown (1994) argued that increased income, improved nutrition, and public health efforts played a far more important role than medical care in improving life expectancy. Building on this work, Reves (1985) suggested that family planning and smaller families were also central factors by improving conditions for women and children. Sagan (1987) developed this further, arguing that an "increased sense of psychological well-being," stimulated by economic growth, may have increased resistance to infection and reduced rates of mortality (Sagan, 1987, p. 126). Fogel (1994) emphasized the role of improved nutrition in reducing mortality.

INEQUALITY AND HEALTH

As researchers delved more deeply into the health of populations, they discovered that countries with the greatest wealth, as measured by per capita gross national product and median income, did not necessarily have the healthiest populations (Wilkinson, 1996). Although the U.S. is the wealthiest nation in the world and spends more per capita on health care than any other country, we have "poorer health than 20 developed countries, including all European Union (EU) nations" (Wilkinson, 2001, p. 30). Indeed, during the 1980s, males living in Bangladesh, one of the poorest nations in the world, had a greater chance of living until age 65 than males living in Harlem (McCord and Freeman, 1994).

This does not mean that economic growth has played no role in population health. For much of human history, material deprivation, or *absolute* poverty, limited the lives of most of the world's people. During the past few centuries, however, due to what Wilkinson (1997) and others have called the epidemiological transition, a dramatic change has taken place.

The epidemiological transition refers to changes in patterns of morbidity and mortality. Until around 1800, infectious diseases, such as smallpox, diphtheria, and measles, were the major cause of death (Tarlov, 1996). Since then, the death rate from these diseases has rapidly declined and life expectancy nearly doubled (Tarlov, 1996). Much of this change is attributable to economic growth and resulting improvements in material standards of living (Wilkinson, 1996). At the same time, mortality from chronic diseases, such as heart disease, cancer, and diabetes, has increased, and these diseases "now account" for three out of four deaths in the U.S. (Tarlov, 1996). This raises two important questions: First, why has economic growth failed to reduce the incidence of all disease (i.e., infectious as well as chronic)? Second, what explains the increasing importance of chronic disease? (As noted in Chapter 3, infectious disease has reemerged in recent years, due in large part to the growth of inequality and the collapse of public health systems [Garrett, 2000].)

The answer to the first question seems to be that the relationship between economic growth and population health, although real, is also limited (Duleep, 1995).

Wilkinson (1996) estimated that, as a country's per capita income approaches $5000, the returns to health of economic growth begin to diminish. At this point, the distribution of income becomes a more important determinant of health than the level of economic growth. As the distribution of income grows increasingly important, so too does the role of *relative* poverty, or inequality. Inequality helps explain why economic growth has a limited impact on mortality and chronic disease has replaced infectious disease as a major cause of death (Wilkinson, 1997).

Absolute versus Relative Poverty

What is relative poverty and why does it matter? Absolute poverty is a state of material deprivation. It implies a minimal standard of need, below which survival becomes difficult or impossible. Relative poverty, on the other hand, is not a state or condition, but a social relationship. One can be unequal only in a relative sense, i.e., in contrast or relation to others (DeLone, 1979); relative poverty is poverty in relation to "the standards of the mainstream community" (Barker, 1999, p. 407). At the same time, relative and absolute poverty often overlap. In the U.S., homelessness and hunger are forms of both material deprivation and extreme inequality.

Income Inequality and Health

Many researchers have found a relationship between income inequality and health status (Kawachi et al., 1999; Muennig et al., 2005; Wilkinson, 2005; Wilkinson and Pickett, 2010). After examining income distribution and infant mortality in 70 nations, Waldmann (1999, p. 14) concluded: "Comparing two countries in which the poor have equal real incomes, the one in which the rich are wealthier is likely to have a higher infant mortality rate." Wennemo (1993) also discovered a relationship between income inequality and infant mortality in wealthy nations. In a study of income distribution and life expectancy in several countries, Wilkinson (1999b) found a "strong relation" between a country's distribution of income and its "average life expectancy" (Wilkinson, 1999b, p. 32). He also noted that, if Britain had a distribution of income similar to that in the "most egalitarian European countries," it would add "about two years . . . to the population's life expectancy" (Wilkinson, 1999b, p. 33).

In the U.S., Kaplan et al. (1999) reported that, between 1980 and 1990, states with the widest income gaps (in 1980) had "smaller declines in mortality" than other states (Kaplan et al., 1999, p. 55). They also found a relationship between age-adjusted death rates and income (Kaplan et al., 1999). In another state-by-state study, Kennedy et al. (1999) found a correlation between income inequality and rates of mortality, infant mortality, heart disease, cancer, and murder. In an analysis of 273 metropolitan areas, Shi and Starfield (2001) also found a significant relationship between income inequality and mortality among blacks and whites.

Not everyone accepts that income inequality has a "direct effect" on health (Kawachi et al., 1999; Wolfson et al., 1999; Lynch et al., 2004a, 2004b).

Some critics argue that this research is subject to what sociologists call "the ecological fallacy," which assumes that what holds at a macro, or population, level necessarily holds at a micro, or individual, level (Macintyre and Ellaway, 2000). In this case, critics assert, researchers have not taken into account the well-known fact that people in poverty are usually in poorer health than other people (Kawachi et al., 1999). Thus, "the apparent impact of inequality on health" may reflect "the larger number of poor people in the areas being studied" (Kawachi and Kennedy, 2001, p. 20).

In response, Wilkinson (2005) and others vigorously defended the proposition that inequality has an impact independent, or "on top," of the composition of the population (Subramanian and Kawachi, 2003; Subramanian et al., 2003; Wilkinson and Pickett, 2006; Kim et al., 2008). According to Wilkinson (2005), a wide range of studies of the U.S., Britain, Canada, Russia, and several other countries has found "empirical relationships between inequality and various health measures" (Wilkinson, 2005, p. 121). In a literature review, Wilkinson and Pickett (2006, p. 1769) found that 78 percent of published "analyses . . . showed at least some statistically significant evidence of a tendency for health to be better in more equal societies" and "70 percent were wholly supportive."

Wilkinson (2005) identified several factors that explain studies that did not find a relationship between income inequality and health. For example, some focused on small geographic areas, although the relationship between inequality and population health "tends to be strongest when inequality is measured over large areas such as whole states or cities" (Wilkinson, 2005, p. 128). In addition, some studies introduced "potentially illegitimate control variables," which are themselves "patterned by social class" and therefore aspects of inequality (Wilkinson, 2005, pp. 141–142). The oft-noted link between individual "income and health" may "reflect," at least in part, a "relation" between inequality and health (Wilkinson, 1999a). To put it differently, "compositional" factors (the number of people in poverty) may be intertwined with "contextual" factors (inequality) (Wilkinson, 2005). It may also be that the impact of inequality on health is not "instantaneous" but unfolds over a period of years (Zheng, 2012).

Interestingly, from a policy perspective, supporters and opponents of the theory that income inequality determines health may not be as far apart as a reading of the literature might suggest; after all, the link between poverty and poor health is well established (Lynch et al., 2004a). The central issue is narrowing the gap between those at the bottom and those at the top. It matters little whether this is done in the name of increasing "the incomes of more disadvantaged people" or reducing inequality (Lynch et al., 2004a). In either instance, "redistributing income from rich to poor improves health" (Wilkinson, 2005, p. 143).

Status and Health

Both Wilkinson (2005) and Marmot (2004) have noted that the link between income inequality and health may reflect a more fundamental connection between status inequality and health. The Whitehall studies of British civil servants provide particularly detailed information on this issue (Marmot, 1994, 2005). The first series of studies (Whitehall I), which included only males, found that the mortality rate for lower-level workers (support staff) was three times higher than the rate for workers at the highest level (administrators). Obvious risk factors, such as blood pressure, cholesterol, and smoking, explained less than half this difference. Absolute poverty, or material deprivation, also had little to do with the difference in mortality. All the participants in the study belonged to the middle or upper class, worked in white-collar settings, and had job security (Marmot, 1994). Access to health care and differences in lifestyles were also not issues (Marmot, 2004).

Despite this, at every level, individuals in higher job grades had lower rates of mortality and morbidity than individuals directly beneath them (Marmot, 1994). Someone with a home and two automobiles enjoyed better health than someone who rented and owned one automobile; individuals in the "highest income group" had better health "than those only slightly less well-off" (Wilkinson, 1994, p. 70). The researchers even found these gradations in health status among smokers. After controlling for "pack-years . . . tar content" and other factors, administrators who smoked 20 cigarettes a day were less likely to die from lung cancer than were clerical and manual workers who smoked 20 a day (Marmot, 1994, p. 206). Although some studies have called into question the link between status and health, others have confirmed it (Redelmeier and Singh, 2001; Rablen and Oswald, 2007; Boyce and Oswald, 2008).

The Whitehall studies imply that merely living in a hierarchical, or stratified, society is a threat to one's health (Wilkinson, 2000). Wilkinson and Pickett (2010) suggested that income inequality may be a reflection or measure of levels of hierarchy or stratification within societies. According to Marmot (2004, p. 80): "A society that excludes high proportions of its population from full social participation is one that does not value all its people equally highly. Such a society is not likely to provide the conditions that favor good health." The inverse relationship between "socioeconomic position" and "morbidity and mortality" is called the health "gradient" (Marmot and Wilkinson, 2001). Wilkinson and Pickett (2010) found striking confirmation of this gradient in the U.S. by examining mortality rates by zip codes: almost uniformly, "zip code areas" with higher "typical household income" had "lower death rates" than areas with lower income (Wilkinson and Pickett, 2010, p. 12).

EXPLAINING THE HEALTH GRADIENT

For many years, researchers and policy makers had assumed that socioeconomic factors primarily influenced the health of people in poverty (Adler, 2001). The discovery of a far wider-reaching relation between *inequality* and health undermined this view. It now seemed that in developed countries *relative poverty* posed a greater threat to health than absolute poverty. This section examines four factors that researchers believe may explain this relationship: Psychosocial variables, social cohesion, childhood development, and material conditions (Smith and Egger, 1996).

Psychosocial Variables

Wilkinson (1996) and others have argued that psychosocial variables associated with living in a stratified society are a central cause of the relationship between inequality and health. Although these theorists do not deny the role of material factors, such as inadequate diet, poor housing, and pollution, they stress the importance of "social status, social networks and stress in early childhood" (Wilkinson and Pickett, 2010, p. 77). Brunner (1997) links psychosocial factors with "social position." He includes among these factors "perceived financial strain, job insecurity, low control and monotony at work, stressful life events and poor social networks" and "fatalism" (Brunner, 1997, p. 1473).

Psychosocial variables have both direct and indirect effects on health (Wilkinson, 1997). The direct effects are the "physiological" consequences "of chronic mental and emotional stress" (Wilkinson, 1997, p. 592). Chronic stress can increase one's chances of developing potentially deadly conditions (e.g., hypertension and heart disease), weaken immunity, and accelerate aging (Brunner, 1997). The indirect, or mediated, effects are the behavioral risks, such as smoking, overeating, and alcohol and drug abuse, which individuals engage in to manage or deaden stress (Wilkinson, 1997, 2005; Dallman et al., 2003). According to Wilkinson (2006), stress increases our vulnerability to so many diseases that it has been likened to more rapid ageing. It would be surprising if psychosocial factors did *not* play a central role in the health gradient. If, as the gradient suggests, inequality is an important determinant of health, psychosocial factors must be involved in some way; after all, relative poverty is fundamentally a social relationship. One is poor or deprived not in the abstract, but in relation, or comparison, to others. These evaluations affect how people think and feel about themselves (Burns, 1980; Beck, 1991; Ellis, 1996). Individuals who cannot live up to society's standards often develop a sense of shame or self-hatred (Gilligan, 1996). Conversely, "when everyone . . . becomes worse off," individuals' "life satisfaction remains pretty much the same" (Lyubomirsky, 2008, p. A19).

Shame is also a function of power and control. To shame people is to expose them, to catch them with their "pants down" (Erikson, 1963). When we reveal someone's secrets or inner being, we render that person powerless. Powerlessness, in turn, has well-documented effects on health (Wilkinson, 1996; Brunner, 1997). Researchers have "repeatedly" found that "health and well-being" depend on an individual's ability to influence the "forces" affecting his or her "life" (Syme, 1996, p. 85).

Whitehall II, a follow-up study of British civil servants, which, unlike Whitehall I, included women, revealed the importance of psychosocial factors (Marmor et al., 1994; Marmot and Wilkinson, 2001). Again, researchers found that workers in lower occupational categories were less healthy than workers in higher categories (Marmor et al., 1994). Lower-level workers also had less control over their jobs and fewer sources of social support (Marmot et al., 1995). This suggests that lack of control, or powerlessness, contributes to the development of the health gradient (Syme, 1996; Marmot and Wilkinson, 2001; Marmot, 2004). Studies from Sweden, the U.S., and Germany substantiate the findings of Whitehall II (Wilkinson, 1996).

Kawachi et al. (1994) have also addressed the issue of control. According to them, "frustrated aspirations," or "gaps between aspirations and rewards," can be "detrimental to health" (Kawachi et al., 1994, p. 11). They note that, even if the income of the entire population rises, individuals will feel deprived if their own incomes do not increase as quickly as they had expected or as quickly as the incomes of others. As people "evaluate their . . . well-being in relative terms," their frustration may increase even during periods of rapid economic growth (Kawachi et al., 1994, p. 11). An individual's failure to live up to community expectations can result in frustration and a wide range of mental and physical disorders.

Finally, animal studies have contributed to our understanding of the influence of social rank on health (Sapolsky, 2004). In extensive observations of wild baboons in Kenya, Sapolsky (1994) found that dominant animals were much healthier than subordinate ones. This does not necessarily prove that high social rank leads to better health. Indeed, it could be the other way around, i.e., healthier individuals may rise in the social hierarchy. In a study of captive monkeys, Shively and Clarkson (1994) discovered that manipulating an individual's status (i.e., making a dominant monkey subordinate and a subordinate one dominant) adversely affected the health of both animals. However, change in status had a far greater impact on previously dominant animals than on previously subordinate ones (Shively and Clarkson, 1994). This seems to indicate that social rank influences health status, rather than the other way around (Sapolsky, 1994).

Sapolsky also found a link between personality type and physiological health. Independent of social status, baboons that were best able to cope with stressful situations, and thus had some measure of control over their environment, were healthier than their counterparts. However, social relationships played a critical role as well. The most psychologically adjusted baboons were those "most capable of developing friendships," or social supports (Sapolsky, 1994, p. 264). (Petticrew and Davey Smith [2012] have questioned the applicability of nonhuman primate studies, including Sapolsky's, to humans.)

Smith (1996), a contributor to the Whitehall studies, has raised questions about the role of psychosocial factors. He notes that, although changes in inequality may explain mental and emotional "distress" and deaths from "accidents and violence," they seem to have minimal influence on "major causes of death," such as cardiovascular disease and cancer (Smith, 1996, p. 988). Lynch et al. (2000) also question the importance of psychosocial factors. Despite this, Wilkinson and Pickett (2010) argue that psychosocial factors can get "under our skin," as the "psyche affects the neural system and in turn the immune system," and increase an individual's likelihood of developing "heart disease, infections, and other bodily ills" (Wilkinson and Pickett, 2010, p. 85).

Social Cohesion

Researchers have also linked the health gradient to social cohesion. By social cohesion, scholars mean the level of interaction and cooperation between and among members of a society (Kawachi and Berkman, 2000). A century ago, Durkheim (1951), a French social theorist, found that rates of suicide varied according to the "degree" of cohesion, or "integration," within a community (Durkheim, 1951, p. 209). Catholic countries, where social ties were relatively strong, had lower suicide rates than Protestant countries, where social ties were weaker. The importance of this work was that it examined suicide as a social phenomenon and not "purely in terms of individual psychology and circumstances" (Wilkinson, 1996, p. 15).

Bruhn and Wolf (1979) addressed the relationship between social cohesion and health in their study of the town of Roseto, Pennsylvania. The population of Roseto largely descended from individuals who had emigrated from Italy during the 1880s. Although they had lifestyles similar to those of residents of neighboring towns, the citizens of Roseto had significantly lower rates of mortality from heart disease (Wilkinson, 1996). A central factor in Roseto's success seemed to be the town's "egalitarian ethos." Although Roseto had class differences, social pressure kept them muted. According to Bruhn and Wolf:

> The local priest emphasised [sic] that when the preoccupation with earning money exceeded the unmarked boundary it became the basis for social rejection, irrespective of the standing of the person. . . . Despite the affluence of many, there was no atmosphere of "keeping up with the Joneses."
>
> (cited in Wilkinson, 1996, p. 117)

During the 1960s, Roseto began to change. As the town grew more prosperous and the population more educated, social and class differences became more obvious. With increasing stratification and social division, Roseto lost its "health advantage" (Wilkinson, 1996). "[By] the 1980s, Roseto's new generation of adults had a heart attack rate above that of their neighbors in a nearby and demographically similar town" (Putnam, 2000, p. 329). These findings have been corroborated by other researchers (Egolf et al., 1992; Lasker et al., 1994).

Researchers have also explored the links among income equality, social cohesion, and health outcomes (Wilkinson, 1997). The inspiration for much of this work has come from Robert Putnam, a Harvard political scientist. In 1993, Putnam and two colleagues published a study of regional governments in Italy. They discovered that the "hallmarks of a successful region" were a tradition of citizen involvement through civil and "community organizations" and other "horizontal" networks (Putnam, 2000, p. 345). Putnam characterized these forms of association as "social capital" (cited in Kawachi and Kennedy, 1997). As specific examples of social capital, Putnam (2000) mentions extended families, bridge and Rotary clubs, "ethnic fraternal groups," civic organizations, parent–teacher organizations, and "the network of professional acquaintances recorded in your address book" (Putnam, 2000, pp. 20–22).

Social capital also includes people's feelings and attitudes about the nature and character of their fellow citizens and society. Individuals who belong to civic organizations and engage in community activity are likely to have positive feelings about their fellow citizens and society. Communities with a high degree of citizen participation and trust are thus rich in social capital. In Italy, the regions with the most social capital also had the least income inequality (Wilkinson, 1996).

Although Putnam and his colleagues did not specifically address health-related issues, they found an inverse correlation between the degree of civic engagement in a community and its rate of infant mortality (cited in Wilkinson, 1996).

Building on this work, Kawachi et al. (1997) examined the relationship among social capital, income inequality, and mortality in 39 states in the U.S. To measure social capital, they relied on survey data from the National Opinion Research Center, which includes questions on "social trust and organizational membership" (Kawachi et al., 1997, p. 1491). The authors found an inverse relationship between inequality and levels of social trust and citizen involvement in organized activity. At the same time, low levels of trust and involvement correlated with high rates of mortality. The authors concluded that a low level of social capital may be "one of the pathways through which growing income inequality exerts its effects on population-level mortality" (Kawachi et al., 1997, p. 1495).

This suggests that social capital plays a mediating role, linking a society's distribution of income with its rate of morbidity and mortality. The distribution of income is also a force for cohesion or division. A relatively equitable distribution of income promotes social cohesion, whereas a relatively inequitable distribution undermines cohesion and promotes social division.

Childhood Development

Childhood experiences also contribute to the relationship between inequality and health (Bartley et al., 1997; Hertzman, 2000; Marmot, 2004; Bartley, 2012). From infancy, environmental, and particularly socioeconomic, factors have a profound impact on the brain's growth and development (Hertzman, 1994). The brain, in turn, "influences" the development of "cardiovascular . . . immune," and other systems, as well as the "sensory, cognitive, and social skills necessary to guide the organism through life" (Cynader, 1994, pp. 155, 163).

Socioeconomic factors affect more than an infant's brain, however. Hertzman (1994, p. 169) notes that birth itself has a more adverse impact on "lower-class" children than on "upper-class children." Social rank even "buffers" upper-class children from the effects of "exposure to lead in the environment" (Hertzman, 1994, p. 170). Thus, the "quality" of early experiences can have a lasting impact on an "individual's social responsivity throughout life" (Cynader, 1994, p. 162).

In an effort to explain how childhood experiences influence health outcomes, researchers have developed two approaches. The "latency," or critical periods, model assumes that individuals go through critical biological and social periods (Hertzman, 1994). Thus, some researchers believe babies' brains are "open to experience of a particular kind only during narrow periods of opportunity" (Gopnik et al., 1999, p. 189). Distinct events, particularly in the early stages of life, can reverberate throughout the lifecycle (Hertzman, 1994).

The "pathways model," on the other hand, focuses on the "cumulative effects of life events and the ongoing importance of the conditions of life" (Hertzman, 1994, p. 174). This approach relies on studies showing that an accumulation of events influences health status (Bartley et al., 1997). The pathways model does not deny the importance of critical events. However, it stresses that "if appropriate stimulation is missed at a specific time in early childhood, the function can be developed through other forms of stimulation later in life" (Hertzman, 1994, p. 177).

Both perspectives acknowledge the importance of inequality. For example, Hertzman (1994, p. 171) notes that early education may prevent "a decline in mental function in late life." If children do not learn to read at a young age, their brains may fail to develop in crucial ways that could protect them later against the ravages of dementia (Hertzman, 1994). Not surprisingly, the risk of dementia is lower among high school graduates than among individuals with less than a secondary education (Hertzman, 1994). Lack of education has clear links with poverty and inequality.

In terms of the pathways model, Hertzman (1994) has discussed how events related to socioeconomic status can lead to adverse outcomes throughout the lifecycle. The disadvantages associated with being born into a poor or low-income family can trigger a chain of events that results in "failure in school" and "low levels of wellbeing in early adulthood" (Hertzman, 1994, p. 174). This, in turn, can push an individual into poorly paying jobs with "high" demands and "low levels of control," lead to "disability and absenteeism," and eventually to an early death (Hertzman, 1994, p. 174). Although it is possible to break this chain at any stage, it becomes harder and more unlikely as the lifecycle unfolds. Smith (1996) argues that illnesses with lengthy gestation periods are likely rooted in long-term "cumulative factors," such as "wealth, family assets," and "lifetime earnings" (Smith, 1996. p. 987). In short, as Irwin et al. (2007) point out, "Healthy early child development . . . strongly influences wellbeing, obesity/stunting, mental health, heart disease, competence in literacy and numeracy, criminality, and economic participation throughout life" (Irwin et al., 2007, p. 7).

Material Conditions

Material conditions also seem to play a role in the development of the health gradient. Lynch et al. (2000) have developed a "neo-material" interpretation, which stresses the "combination of negative exposures and lack of resources held by individuals, along with systematic underinvestment across a wide range of human, physical, health, and social infrastructure" (Lynch et al., 2000, p. 1201). According to them, an inequitable distribution of income is part of a wider "cluster of neo-material conditions," including education, health care, food, housing, and jobs, which "affect population health" (Lynch et al., 2000, p. 1201).

To illustrate the impact of "neo-material conditions" on health, they cite, as a "metaphor," the difference between first- and economy-class air travel. Individuals traveling first class receive benefits, such as good food and comfortable seats, that enable them to "arrive fresh and rested," which economy-class passengers, who "arrive feeling a bit rough," do not receive (Lynch et al., 2000, p. 1201).

Conclusion

Although the existence of the health gradient is widely accepted, the reasons for it remain in dispute (Tarlov, 1999). The social cohesion and psychosocial explanations are persuasive, but they have not convinced everyone (Smith and

Egger, 1996). Many studies suffer from methodological flaws and rely on inadequate data (Kawachi et al., 1994). Some scholars have noted the difficulty of defining and measuring social cohesion and social capital (Kaplan and Lynch, 1997; Kawachi et al., 1997). On the other hand, some observers deny the impact of social cohesion and psychosocial factors (Lynch et al., 2000). This view seems too extreme, however, and does not fit the evidence (Marmot and Wilkinson, 2001; Wilkinson and Pickett, 2010).

SOCIAL DETERMINANTS APPROACH TO HEALTH POLICY

In writing this book, we were influenced by the framework of Evans and Stoddart (1994), who developed a multidimensional, universal framework for health and health policy based on several social determinants of health. This framework identifies five stages in the development of western health care policy: (1) Disease and health care, (2) escalating costs, (3) a new concept of health, (4) a new framework for health policy, and (5) the costs and benefits of health policy.

Stage 1: Disease and Health Care

According to Evans and Stoddart (1994), traditional approaches to health policy have been based on a narrowly conceived "thermostat" model that defines illness as a deviation from a normal state of health. Just as cold weather encourages us to turn up the thermostat in our homes, medicine responds to illness by turning up the level of treatment and services. Medicine's traditional response takes the path shown in Figure 12.1.

In this model, the "level of health of a population is the negative or inverse of the burden of disease" and "professionally defined needs for care are themselves adjusted according to the capacity of the health care system and the pressures on it" (Evans and Stoddart, 1994, p. 21). More and more resources are expended for health care, rather than health: "As one need is met another is discovered" (Evans and Stoddart, 1994, p. 22).

DISEASE ⇨ Individual may/may not seek and may/may not have access to

MEDICAL CARE ⇨ NEED for care and RESPONSE determined by

HEALTH CARE SYSTEM ⇨ LEVEL OF CARE determined by

ACCESS ⇨ DISEASE reduced through CURE and CARE

FIGURE 12.1

Medicine's Traditional Path

Source: Evans and Stoddart (1994).

Stage 2: Escalating Costs

By the 1970s, with the exception of the U.S., all of the world's developed countries had established universal, comprehensive systems of health care delivery. In all these countries "ever-increasing needs" were in conflict with "increasingly restrained resources." In Evans and Stoddart's (1994) model, public concern is expressed as shown in Figure 12.2.

According to Evans and Stoddart (1994), there is little scientific evidence to support much of the health care that is provided; in fact, there is evidence that some health care leads to poor health outcomes. Consequently, there seems to be relatively little payoff to society for the ever-increasing resources expended on health care. In addition, variations in health care spending among countries do not lead to demonstrable differences in health.

Stage 3: A New Concept of Health

To "shift the focus of health policy from an exclusive concern with health care" (Evans and Stoddart, 1994, p. 25) to health, Evans and Stoddart proposed three categories for determinants of health: Lifestyles, environment, and human biology. From this perspective, the delivery of health care is viewed as only one of many ways that public policy can address health outcomes and raises larger questions for policy analysts and planners. What else can and should nations do? To what extent should government be involved? Are individuals responsible for their lifestyle behaviors? What are the obligations and responsibilities of government and the private corporate sector? To focus on health outcomes, Evans and Stoddart (1994) have offered a revision of the "thermostat model" of health (Figure 12.3).

Stage 4: A New Framework for Health Policy

Evans and Stoddart (1994) incorporated the findings of McKeown, Marmot, and others concerning the role of social relationships, social class, and hierarchy in determining health outcomes to establish a new framework. They included important findings that show currently relative poverty is a greater risk to health than is absolute poverty (Figure 12.4). Environmental factors, in the broadest sense of the term, are a health issue for *all* of us, not *some* of us. Evans and Stoddart's (1994) offerings are shown in Figures 12.4 and 12.5.

FIGURE 12.2

Medicine's Traditional Response to Needs

DISEASE ⇨ addressed by **HEALTH CARE SYSTEM**

INCREASED RESPONSE ⇨ has led to **GROWING HEALTH CARE COSTS**

Source: Evans and Stoddart (1994).

			FIGURE 12.3
LIFESTYLE ⇨	*ENVIRONMENT* ⇨	*HUMAN BIOLOGY*	*Determinants of Health*
⇩	⇩	⇩	

DISEASE ⇨ Individual may/may not seek and may/may not have access to

MEDICAL CARE ⇨ **NEED** for care and **RESPONSE** determined by

HEALTH CARE SYSTEM ⇨ **LEVEL OF CARE** determined by

ACCESS ⇨ **DISEASE** reduced through **CURE** and **CARE**

Source: Evans and Stoddart (1994).

FIGURE 12.4

Absolute versus Relative Poverty versus Income Inequality

ABSOLUTE POVERTY	**RELATIVE POVERTY**
The term *absolute poverty* refers to the fixed measure of poverty established by the federal government to determine the amount of income needed for subsistence living. The United States has established an official federal poverty level since 1964.	The term *relative poverty* refers to a relative measure of poverty that changes as the overall standard of living of a population changes. European countries often use a relative measure of poverty, such as a proportion of the national median income.

INCOME INEQUALITY

The term *income inequality* refers to a measure of income distribution in a society. A commonly used measure in the United States is the proportion of aggregate income received by families or households per quintile of the population (slices of the economic pie).	**Example**: Share (as percent) of aggregate income received by each 1/5 of families in the U.S., 2017 (U.S. Census Bureau, 2018). Top fifth: 50.1% Second fifth: 22.7% Third fifth: 14.7% Fourth fifth: 9% Bottom fifth: 3.5%

Source: Census Bureau (2017).

FIGURE 12.5

A New Framework for Health Policy

DISEASE ⇨ addressed by **HEALTH CARE SYSTEM**
HEALTH and **FUNCTION** ⇨ experienced by **INDIVIDUALS**
ILLNESS does not necessarily equal **DISEASE**
DISEASE, HEALTH CARE, and **HEALTH** ⇨ affected by **SOCIAL ENVIRONMENT,**
PHYSICAL ENVIRONMENT, and **GENETIC ENDOWMENT**
ULTIMATE GOAL OF HEALTH POLICY ⇨ **INDIVIDUAL, SOCIAL,** and **ECONOMIC**
WELLBEING PROSPERITY ⇨ affects **DISEASE, HEALTH CARE, HEALTH,** and **WELLBEING**

Source: Evans and Stoddart (1994).

From this perspective, whether individuals become "sick" depends on the *interactions* of their genetic endowments with the physical and social environment. At a societal level, the "relationship between the health care system and the health of the population becomes even more complex" (Evans and Stoddart, 1994, p. 29).

Stage 5: Costs and Benefits of Health Policy

A health *care* policy of "ever increasing needs" leads to escalating costs. In addition, the expansion of health care inevitably means that societal resources are reduced for other uses. Evans and Stoddart (1994, p. 32) suggest that the "positive effects of health care on health may be outweighed by its negative effects through competition for resources with other health-enhancing activities." To shift from a health *care* policy to a *health* policy requires an all-encompassing framework (Figure 12.6).

Ultimately, "[A] society that spends so much on health care that it cannot or will not spend adequately on other health-enhancing activities may actually be *reducing* the health of its population through increased health spending" (Evans and Stoddart, 1994, p. 32).

INTERNATIONAL EFFORTS TO APPLY SOCIAL DETERMINANTS APPROACH TO HEALTH POLICY

The social determinants perspective and framework outlined by Evans and Stoddart have had an impact on some government policies, primarily in Canada and the United Kingdom. In 1974, the Canadian government published *A New Perspective on the Health of Canadians* (Laonde, 1974), or the Lalonde Report. The Lalonde Report argued that genes, the environment, and individual behavior were more important than medical care in determining health status (Marmor et al., 1994). Although the Lalonde Report proved highly influential and helped transform thinking about determinants of health, its primary focus was still on individual habits (Rachlis and Kushner, 1989; Armstrong and Armstrong, 1996).

DISEASE ⇨ addressed by **HEALTH CARE SYSTEM**
HEALTH and FUNCTION ⇨ experienced by **INDIVIDUALS**
ILLNESS does not necessarily equal **DISEASE**
DISEASE, HEALTH CARE, and **HEALTH** ⇨ affected by **SOCIAL ENVIRONMENT, PHYSICAL ENVIRONMENT,** and **GENETIC ENDOWMENT**
ULTIMATE GOAL OF HEALTH POLICY ⇨ **INDIVIDUAL, SOCIAL,** and **ECONOMIC WELLBEING PROSPERITY** ⇨ affects **DISEASE, HEALTH CARE, HEALTH,** and **WELLBEING**

FIGURE 12.6

All-encompassing Health Policy

Source: Evans and Stoddart (1994).

In 1976, the British government appointed a commission, chaired by Sir Douglas Black, to investigate increasing mortality among people with low incomes (Wilkinson, 1996). The subsequent Black report, which the government of Margaret Thatcher attempted to suppress, offered "compelling evidence that poverty causes ill health" (Rachlis and Kushner, 1989, p. 179; Dean, 1994). This report ushered in a new era of research on the social causes of health and illness in the developed world, much of it under the leadership of Richard Wilkinson and Michael Marmot, two British researchers (Wilkinson, 1996, p. ix).

In 1997, in light of the research findings on social determinants of health, the government of Tony Blair appointed a commission chaired by Sir Donald Acheson to investigate inequality and health (Davey-Smith et al., 1998). The Acheson report summarized data on trends in health inequality and the socioeconomic determinants of health and recommended steps to reduce inequalities (Acheson, 1998).

Reaction to the report was mixed. In an editorial in the *British Medical Journal*, Davey-Smith et al. (1998, p. 1465) welcomed the report, but criticized it for being "too cautious and vague" in its recommendations. On the other hand, Tarlov (1999), a physician and leading health policy theorist in the U.S., praised the report as a "major accomplishment" and called it a possible "beacon guide for many nations" (Tarlov, 1999, p. 1466).

Social Determinants Approach and the ACA

In the U.S., the Affordable Care Act (ACA) takes steps to address the social determinants of health. This occurs in a variety of ways. First, as noted by Leonhardt (2010), the legislation reverses growing economic inequality by taxing upper-income individuals and distributing benefits to lower-income people. Extending health care coverage to a larger segment of the population will also reduce income inequality (Burtless and Svaton, 2010).

Second, and perhaps most directly, the ACA provides "unprecedented attention to and funding for public health." Only 3 percent of health care dollars in the U.S. are spent on prevention, whereas 75 percent of health care expenditures are related to preventable conditions (University of Minnesota, School of Public

Health, 2013). For the first time, the U.S. has legislated a national health care policy to improve public health. The ACA includes measures aimed at expanding preventive and health promotion efforts, including creation of the National Prevention, Health Promotion and Public Health Council and a Prevention and Public Health Fund (Stoto, 2013) and shifts the health care focus from illness to wellness (University of Minnesota, School of Public Health, 2013). In addition, the legislation requires hospitals to conduct a community health needs assessment and "implementation strategy" every three years, which has the "potential to transform population health" (Stoto, 2013, p. 4). Although limited, in that the ACA does not mandate full integration of health care and public health, these steps could mark the beginning of a broader effort to improve population health.

IMPLICATIONS FOR HEALTH AND HEALTH CARE POLICY IN THE U.S.: ADVOCATING FOR POLICIES THAT IMPROVE HEALTH

In considering the implications of these findings and models for policy practice in health, we return to the guiding questions offered at the beginning of the chapter:

- What should health policy achieve?

- What are the options for achieving these goals?

- How can the problem of access to care best be alleviated or ameliorated using evidence-based solutions?

- What is achievable?

- What is the best fit with the target population?

- What values guide the policy options?

- What rights or benefits will be preserved or enhanced?

- Are disparities in equality, equity, and adequacy addressed?

Social work and public health have long been in the forefront of the struggle for universal coverage, and should not rest until this goal is achieved. Social justice and advocacy have been an integral part of social work's mission as a profession, and it must continue to support legislative and community-based efforts to achieve universal access to health care. However, in light of the relationship between health and inequality, there is evidence that efforts to reduce inequality in the U.S. could contribute to the nation's health.

Social work and public health should also take note of the links between the health gradient and its biopsychosocial approach. In fact, the health gradient is a biopsychosocial relation. It is biological because humans are fundamentally biological beings, and morbidity and mortality are rooted in interruptions of biological processes. It is social because it is linked with distribution of income and relative deprivation, which are fundamentally social relationships.

Finally, the gradient is also a psychological phenomenon. The link, or pathway, between income inequality and the distribution of morbidity and mortality is, at least in part, the mental and emotional stress associated with relative deprivation. Even Smith (1996), who questions the immediate importance of psychosocial factors, acknowledges their link with violence, accidents, and similar phenomena, and their role throughout the lifespan.

The literature on the social determinants of health shows that health is essentially a biopsychosocial phenomenon. Social work and public health are both rooted in a biopsychosocial perspective. As the largest group of mental health providers and as professionals in a wide range of health settings, including public health, social workers have an important role to play in providing further insight into the psychosocial dimensions of health.

HIGHLIGHTS

- Individual and population health is a biopsychosocial process that encompasses biological (genetics and human aging process), psychological (perception, cognition, and emotion), and social (lifestyle, culture, politics, race and ethnicity, class, and gender) factors, which are both distinct and interrelated.

- Weick's (1986) health model, in contrast to the traditional medical model, focuses on multiple influences that shape health status. Ultimately, individuals and the population as a whole can be well only if society takes responsibility for health promotion.

- The discovery of a relationship between inequality and health has implications for national health care in the U.S. and for the professions of social work and public health.

- Evans and Stoddart (1994) developed a framework to conceptualize the role of inequality and incorporate research on social determinants of health. In the final stage of their framework, they argue that the expansion of health care may do little to improve *health*. Nations must allocate resources toward health-enhancing activities to achieve healthy populations.

- Canada and Britain have taken steps to apply this framework to health policy, but their efforts have been very limited.

- In the U.S., universal access to health care services is a basic need that should be, but has not yet been, met. Long-range efforts to go beyond *health care* and toward *health* require much broader socioeconomic reforms, particularly as relative poverty seems to pose a greater threat to health than absolute poverty. The Affordable Care Act (ACA) enacted in 2010 takes steps to address the social determinants of health and has the potential to impact population health.

- A growing body of research indicates that social factors are indeed critical determinants of health and begins to explain this phenomenon by identifying specific causal factors. Research shows that medical care has played a limited role in reducing mortality in western nations, whereas factors such as increased income, improved nutrition, and public health efforts have played a greater role in the extension of human life.

- However, Wilkinson (1996) discovered that countries with the greatest wealth do not necessarily have the healthiest populations in terms of mortality and morbidity. Thus, material standards of living (income and wealth) have a limited impact on mortality and morbidity.

- Inequality or the distribution of income in a population seems to play a more significant role in population health than absolute poverty. The wider the income gap within a nation, the higher the mortality and morbidity rate. In other words, after a certain point or threshold, economic growth has a diminished impact on population health.

- Relative poverty poses a greater threat to health than absolute poverty. Researchers have found four factors that help explain this relationship between inequality and health: (1) Psychosocial variables, (2) social cohesion, (3) childhood development, and (4) material conditions.

- Social work and public health have special roles to perform in efforts to achieve a healthy population. Both fields are rooted in a biopsychosocial perspective and can make significant contributions to the social determinants of health perspective through practice and research.

- The role of social work (and public health) in advocacy efforts to achieve social justice and equity may have implications for the nation's health.

WEBSITES TO OBTAIN UPDATED AND ADDITIONAL INFORMATION

Why More Equality/The Equality Trust (Wilkinson and Pickett):

www.equalitytrust.org.uk/why

Unnatural Causes: Is Inequality Making Us Sick?:

www.unnaturalcauses.org

World Health Organization (WHO) Commission on Social Determinants of Health:

www.who.int/social_determinants/thecommission/en

Population Health Forum: Advocating for Action Toward a Healthier Society University of Washington, School of Public Health http://depts.washington.edu/eqhlth/index.htm

County Health Calculator:

http://countyhealthcalculator.org

REFERENCES

Acheson, D., Chair (1998, November 26). *Independent Inquiry into Inequalities in Health Report*. London: The Stationery Office. Retrieved from www.official-documents.co.uk/document/doh/ih/ih.htm

Adler, N. E. (2001). A Consideration of Multiple Pathways from Socioeconomic Status to Health. In J. A. Auerbach and B. K. Krimgold (Eds.), *Income, Socioeconomic Status, and Health: Exploring the Relationships* (pp. 56–66). Washington, DC: National Policy Association.

Amick III, B. C., Levine, S., Tarlov, A. R., and Walsh, D. C. (1995). Introduction. In B. C. Amick III, S. Levine, A. R. Tarlov, and D. C. Walsh (Eds.), *Society and Health* (pp. 3–17). New York: Oxford University Press.

Armstrong, P. and Armstrong, H. (1996). *Wasting Away: The Undermining of Canadian Health Care*. Toronto: Oxford University Press.

Barker, R. (1999). *The Social Work Dictionary*, 4th edn. Washington, DC: National Association of Social Workers Press.

Bartlett, H. M. and Saunders, B. N. (1970). *The Common Base of Social Work Practice*. New York: National Association of Social Workers.

Bartley, M. (Ed.). (2012). *Life Gets Under Your Skin*. UCL Research Department of Epidemiology and Public Health. Retrieved from www.ucl.ac.uk/icls/publications/booklets/lguys.pdf

Bartley, M., Blane, D., and Montgomery, S. (1997, April 19). Socioeconomic Determinants of Health: Health and the Life Course: Why Safety Nets Matter. *British Medical Journal*, 314(7095), 1194–1198.

Beck, A. (1991). Cognitive Therapy: A 30-year Retrospective. *American Psychologist*, 46(4), 382–389.

Berkman, B., and Volland, P. (1997). Health Care Practice: Overview. In R. L. Edwards (Ed.), *Encyclopedia of Social Work*, 19th edn., Supplement (pp. 143–149). Washington, DC: National Association of Social Workers.

Berkman, L. F. and Kawachi, I. (Eds.). (2000). *Social Epidemiology*. New York: Oxford University Press.

Boyce, C. and Oswald, A. J. (2008, December). Do People Become Healthier after Being Promoted? Institute for the Study of Labor. Discussion Paper No. 3894. Retrieved from http://papers.ssrn.com/sol3/papers.cfm?abstract_id=1318853

Bruhn, J. and Wolf, S. (1979). *The Roseto Story*. Norman, OK: University of Oklahoma Press.

Brunner, E. (1997). Socioeconomic Determinants of Health: Stress and the Biology of Inequality. *British Medical Journal*, 314(7095), 1472–1478.

Burns, D. D. (1980). *Feeling Good—The New Mood Therapy*. New York: Signet.

Burtless, G. and Svaton, P. (2010). Health Care, Health Insurance, and the Distribution of American Incomes. *Forum for Health Economics & Policy*, 13(1). Retrieved from http://works.bepress.com/gary_burtless/1

Clinton, H. (1997, April 17). Remarks by the First Lady at the White House Conference on Early Childhood Development. Retrieved from www.clinton.nara.com.

Council on Social Work Education. (1995; 2002). *Curriculum Policy Statement for Baccalaureate/Master's Degree Programs in Social Work Education. Handbook of Accreditation Standards and Procedures*. Alexandria, VA: CSWE.

——. (2012). Educational Policy and Accreditation Standards. Retrieved from www.cswe. org/getattachment/Accreditation/Standards-and-Policies/2008-EPAS/2008EDUCATIO NALPOLICYANDACCREDITATIONSTANDARDS(EPAS)-08-24-2012.pdf.aspx

Cynader, M. S. (1994, Fall). Mechanisms of Brain Development and Their Role in Health and Well-Being. *Daedalus*, 123(4), 155–166.

Dallman, M. F., Pecoraro, N., Akana, S. F., la Fleur, S. E., Gomez, F., Houshyar, H., et al. (2003, September 15). Chronic Stress and Obesity: A New View of "Comfort Food." *Proceedings of the National Academy of Sciences of the United States of America*, 100(20), 11696–11701.

Davey-Smith, G., Morris, J. N., and Shaw, M. (1998, November 28). The Independent Inquiry into Inequalities in Health. *British Medical Journal*, 317, 1465–1466.

Dean, M. (1994). Beveridge Revisited and Restructured. *The Lancet*, 344(8932), 1285.

DeLone, R. (1979). *Small Futures: Children, Inequality, and the Limits of Liberal Reform*. New York: Harcourt Brace Jovanovich.

Duleep, H. C. (1995, Summer). Mortality and Income Inequality among Economically Developed Countries. *Social Security Bulletin*, 58(2), 34–50.

Durkheim, E. (1951). *Suicide: A Study in Sociology*. New York: Free Press.

Egolf, B., Lasker, J., Wolf, S., and Potvin, L. (1992). The Roseto Effect: A 50-year Comparison of Mortality Rates. *American Journal of Public Health*, 82(8), 1089–1092.

Ellis, A. (1996). *Better, Deeper, and More Enduring Brief Therapy: The Rational Emotive Behavior Therapy Approach*. New York: Brunner/Mazel.

Erikson, E. H. (1963). *Childhood and Society*, 2nd edn. New York: Norton.

Evans, R. G. and Stoddart, G. L. (1994). Producing Health, Consuming Health Care. In P. R. Lee and C. L. Estes (Eds.), *The Nation's Health*, 4th edn. (pp. 14–33). Boston, MA: Jones & Bartlett Publishers.

Evans, R. G., Barer, M. L., and Marmor, T. R. (1994). *Why Are Some People Healthy and Others Not?* New York: Aldine de Gruyter.

Farmer, R. L. and Pandurangi, A. K. (1997). Diversity in Schizophrenia: Toward a Richer Biopsychosocial Understanding for Social Work Practice. *Health & Social Work*, 22(2), 109–116.

Ferris, C. F. (1996). The Rage of Innocents. *The Sciences*, 36(2), 22–26.

Fogel, R. W. (1994, April). *Economic Growth, Population Theory, and Physiology: The Bearing of Long-Term Processes in the Making of Economic Theory*. Working Paper No. 4638. Cambridge, MA: National Bureau of Economic Research.

Garrett, L. (2000). *Betrayal of Trust: The Collapse of Global Public Health*. New York: Hyperion.

Germain, C. B. (1973). An Ecological Perspective in Casework Practice. *Social Casework*, 54(6), 323–330.

Germain, C. B. and Gitterman, A. (1980). *The Life Model of Social Work Practice*. New York: Columbia University Press.

Gilligan, J. (1996). *Violence, Our Deadly Epidemic and Its Causes*. New York: Grosset/ Putnam.

Gopnik, A., Meltzoff, A., and Kuhl, P. K. (1999). *The Scientist in the Crib: Minds, Brains, and How Children Learn*. New York: Morrow.

Gordon, W. E. (1969). Basic Constructs for an Integrative and Generative Conception of Social Work. In G. Hearn (Ed.), *The General Systems Approach: Contributions Toward an Holistic Conception of Social Work* (pp. 5–12). New York: Council on Social Work Education.

Greenspan, S. I. with Benderly, B. L. (1997). *The Growth of the Mind and the Endangered Origins of Intelligence*. Reading, MA: Addison-Wesley.

Hertzman, C. (1994, Fall). The Lifelong Impact of Childhood Experiences: A Population Health Perspective. *Daedalus*, 123(4), 167–180.

——. (2000, Autumn). The Case for an Early Childhood Development Strategy. *Isuma: Canadian Journal of Policy Research*. 1(2). Retrieved January 9, 2006, from www.isuma.net/v01n02/hertzman/hertzman_e.pdf

Hotz, R. L. (1997, October 28). Lack of Maternal Love Can Affect Brain Chemistry. *Concord Monitor*, p. A2.

Irwin, G., Siddiqi, A., and Hertzman, C. (2007, June). *Early Child Development: A Powerful Equalizer*. Final Report for the World Health Organization's Commission on Social Determinants of Health. Retrieved from www.earlylearning.ubc.ca/globalknowledgehub/documents/WHO_ECD_Final_Report.pdf

Kaplan, G. A. and Lynch, J. W. (1997). Whither Studies on the Socioeconomic Foundations of Population Health? *American Journal of Public Health*, 87(9), 1409–1413.

Kaplan, G. A., Pamuk, E., Lynch, J. W., Cohen, R. D., and Balfour, J. L. (1999). Income Inequality and Mortality in the United States. In I. Kawachi, B. P. Kennedy, and R. G. Wilkinson (Eds.), *The Society and Population Health Reader*. Vol. 1, *Income Inequality and Health* (pp. 50–59). New York: New Press.

Karls, J. M., and Wandrei, K. E. (1995). Person-in-environment. In R. L. Edwards (Ed.), *Encyclopedia of Social Work*, 19th edn. (pp. 1818–1827). Washington, DC: National Association of Social Workers.

Kawachi, I. and Berkman, L. (2000). Social Cohesion, Social Capital, and Health. In L. F. Berkman and I. Kawachi (Eds.), *Social Epidemiology* (pp. 174–190). New York: Oxford University Press.

Kawachi, I. and Kennedy, B. P. (1997, April 5). Health and Social Cohesion: Why Care about Income Inequality. *British Medical Journal*, 314(7083), 1037–1040.

Kawachi, I. and Kennedy, B. P. (2001). How Income Inequality Affects Health: Evidence from Research in the United States. In J. A. Auerbach and B. K. Krimgold (Eds.), *Income, Socioeconomic Status, and Health: Exploring the Relationships* (pp. 16–28). Washington, DC: National Policy Association.

Kawachi, I., Levine, S., Miller, M., Lasch, K., and Amick III, B. (1994). *Income Inequality and Life Expectancy—Theory, Research and Policy. Society and Health Working Group Paper Series No. 94–2*. Boston: Harvard School of Public Health.

Kawachi, I., Kennedy, B., Lochner, K., and Prothrow-Stith, D. (1997). Social Capital, Income Inequality, and Mortality. *American Journal of Public Health*, 87(9), 1491–1498.

Kawachi, I., Wilkinson, R. G., and Kennedy, B. P. (1999). Introduction. In I. Kawachi, B. P. Kennedy, and R. G. Wilkinson (Eds.), *The Society and Population Health Reader*. Vol. 1, *Income Inequality and Health* (pp. xi–xxxiv). New York: New Press.

Kennedy, B. P., Kawachi, I., and Prothrow-Stith, D. (1999). Income Distribution and Mortality: Cross Sectional Ecological Study of the Robin Hood Index in the United States. In I. Kawachi, B. P. Kennedy, and R. G. Wilkinson (Eds.), *The Society and Population Health Reader.* Vol. 1, *Income Inequality and Health* (pp. 60–68). New York: New Press.

Kim, D., Kawachi, I., Vander Hoorn, S., and Ezzati, M. (2008). Is Inequality at the Heart of it? Cross-country Associations of Income Inequality with Cardiovascular Diseases and Risk Factors. *Social Science & Medicine*, 66(8), 1719–1732.

Kotulak, R. (1997). *Inside the Brain: Revolutionary Discoveries of How the Mind Works.* Kansas City, MO: Andrews McMeel Publishing.

Lalonde, M. (1974) *A New Perspective on the Health of Canadians.* Retrieved from www. hc-sc.gc.ca/hcs-sss/alt_formats/hpb-dgps/pdf/pubs/1974-lalonde/lalonde-eng.pdf

Lasker, J., Egolf, B. P., and Wolf, S. (1994). Community Social Change and Mortality. *Social Science & Medicine*, 39(1), 53–62.

Leonhardt, D. (2010, March 23). In Health Bill, Obama Attacks Wealth Inequality. *New York Times.* Retrieved from www.nytimes.com/2010/03/24/business/24leonhardt.html

Levins, R. (1998). *Looking at the Whole: Toward a Social Ecology of Health. Robert H. Ebert Lecture.* Available from the Department of Population and International Health, Harvard School of Public Health, Cambridge, MA.

Longres, J. F. (1990). *Human Behavior and the Social Environment.* Itasca, IL: Peacock Publishers.

Lynch, J. W., Davey Smith, G., Kaplan, G. A., and House, J. S. (2000, April 29). Income Inequality and Mortality: Importance to Health of Individual Income, Psychosocial Environment, or Material Conditions. *British Medical Journal*, 320(7243), 1200–1204.

Lynch, J. W., Davey Smith, G., Harper, S., Hillemeier, M., Ross, N., Kaplan, G. A., and Wolfson, M. (2004a). Is Income Inequality a Determinant of Population Health? Part 1. A Systematic Review. *Milbank Quarterly*, 82(1), 5–99.

Lynch, J. W., Davey Smith, G., Harper, S., Hillemeier, M., Ross, N., and Kaplan, G. A. (2004b). Is Income Inequality a Determinant of Population Health? Part 2. U.S. National and Regional Trends in Income Inequality and Age- and Cause-Specific Mortality. *Milbank Quarterly*, 82(2), 355–400.

Lyubomirsky, S. (2008, December 27). Why We're Still Happy. *New York Times*, p. A19.

McCord, C. and Freeman, H. P. (1994). Excess Mortality in Harlem. In P. Conrad and R. Kern (Eds.), *The Sociology of Health and Illness: Critical Perspectives* (pp. 35–42). New York: St. Martin's.

McEwen, B. S. (2012, October 16). Brain on Stress: How the Social Environment Gets under the Skin. *Proceedings of the National Academy of Sciences of the United States of America*, 109(2), 17180–17185.

Macintyre, S. and Ellaway, A. (2000). Ecological Approaches: Rediscovering the Role of the Physical and Social Environment. In L. F. Berkman and I. Kawachi (Eds.), *Social Epidemiology* (pp. 332–348). New York: Oxford University Press.

McKeown, T. (1979). *The Role of Medicine: Dream, Mirage, or Nemesis?* Oxford: Basil Blackwell.

——. (1994). Determinants of Health. In P. R. Lee and C. L. Estes (Eds.), *Nation's Health*, 4th edn. (pp. 6–13). Boston: Jones and Bartlett.

McKinlay, J. and McKinlay, S. (1994). Medical Measures and the Decline of Mortality. In P. Conrad and R. Kern (Eds.), *The Sociology of Health and Illness: Critical Perspective* (pp. 10–23). New York: St. Martin's.

Marmor, T. R., Barer, M. L., and Evans, R. G. (1994). The Determinants of a Population's Health: What Can Be Done to Improve a Democratic Nation's Health Status? In R. G. Evans, M. L. Barer, and T. R. Marmor (Eds.), *Why Are Some People Healthy and Others Not?* (pp. 217–230). New York: Aldine de Gruyter.

Marmot, M. G. (1994, Fall). Social Differentials in Health within and between Populations. *Daedalus*, 123(4), 197–216.

——. (2004). *The Status Syndrome: How Social Standing Affects Our Health and Longevity.* New York: Times Books/Henry Holt & Co.

Marmot, M. G. and Wilkinson, R. G. (2001, May 19). Psychosocial and Material Pathways in the Relation between Income and Health: A Response to Lynch et al. *British Medical Journal*, 322(7296), 1233–1236.

Marmot, M. G., Bobak, M., and Smith, G. D. (1995). Explanations for Social Inequalities in Health. In B. C. Amick III, S. Levine, A. R. Tarlov, and D. C. Walsh (Eds.), *Society and Health* (pp. 172–210). New York: Oxford University Press.

Maté, G. (1999). *Scattered: How Attention Deficit Disorder Originates and What You Can Do About It.* New York: Dutton.

Moroney, R. (1995). Public Health Services. In R. L. Edwards (Ed.), *Encyclopedia of Social Work*, 19th edn. (pp. 1967–1973). Washington, DC: National Association of Social Workers.

Muennig, P., Franks, P., Jia, H., Lubetkin, E., and Gold, M. R. (2005). The Income-Associated Burden of Disease in the United States. *Social Science & Medicine*, 61(9), 2018–2026.

Petticrew, M. and Davey Smith, G. (2012, March 21). The Monkey Puzzle: A Systematic Review of Studies of Stress, Social Hierarchies, and Heart Disease in Monkeys. *PLoS ONE*, 7(3), e27939.

Prothrow-Stith, D. and Quaday, S. (1995). *Hidden Casualties: The Relationship between Violence and Learning.* Available from National Health and Education Consortium, c/o Institute for Educational Leadership, 1001 Connecticut Ave., NW, Suite 310, Washington, DC 20036.

Putnam, R. D. (2000). *Bowling Alone: The Collapse and Revival of American Community.* New York: Simon & Schuster.

Rablen, M. D. and Oswald, A. J. (2007, January). *Mortality and Immortality.* Retrieved from www.warwick.ac.uk/fac/soc/economics/staff/faculty/oswald/nobelsrable nos07.pdf

Rachlis, M. and Kushner, C. (1989). *Second Opinion: What's Wrong with Canada's Health Care System and How to Fix It.* Toronto: HarperCollins Publishers.

Ratey, J. J. and Johnson, C. J. (1998). *Shadow Syndromes: The Mild Forms of Major Mental Disorders that Sabotage Us.* New York: Bantam Books.

Redelmeier, D. A. and Singh, S. M. (2001, May 15). Survival in Academy Award-winning Actors and Actresses. *Annals of Internal Medicine*, 134(10), 955–962.

Reves, R. (1985). Declining fertility in England and Wales as a Major Cause of the 20th Century Decline in Mortality. *American Journal of Epidemiology*, 122(1), 112–126.

Richmond, M. E. (1917). *Social Diagnosis.* New York: Russell Sage Foundation.

Rose, G. (1993). *The Strategy of Preventive Medicine.* New York: Oxford University Press.

Sagan, L. A. (1987). *The Health of Nations: True Causes of Sickness and Well-Being.* New York: Basic Books.

Sapolsky, R. M. (1994). *Why Zebras Don't Get Ulcers: A Guide to Stress, Stress-related Diseases, and Coping.* New York: W. H. Freeman.

——. (2004, October). Social Status and Health in Humans and Other Animals. *Annual Review of Anthropology*, 33, 393–418.

Schwartz, L. L. (1994, April). *The Medicalization of Social Problems: America's Special Health Care Dilemma: Special Report*. Washington, DC: American Health System Institute.

Shi, L. and Starfield, B. (2001, August). The Effect of Primary Care Physician Supply and Income Equality on Mortality among Blacks and Whites in U.S. Metropolitan Areas. *American Journal of Public Health*, 91(8), 1246–1251.

Shively, C. A. and Clarkson, T. B. (1994). Social Status and Coronary Artery Atherosclerosis in Female Monkeys. *Arteriosclerosis and Thrombosis*, 14(5), 721–726.

Smith, G. D. (1996, April 20). Income Inequality and Mortality: Why Are They Related? *British Medical Journal*, 312(7243), 987–988.

Smith, G. D. and Egger, M. (1996). Unequal in Death, Commentary: Understanding It All: Health, Meta-theories, and Mortality Trends. *British Medical Journal*, 313(7072), 1584–1585.

Stoto, M. A. (2013, February 21). *Population Health in the Affordable Care Act Era*. Academy Health. Retrieved from www.academyhealth.org/files/AH2013pophealth.pdf

Subramanian, S. V. and Kawachi, I. (2003). The Association between State Income Inequality and Worse Health is not Confounded by Race. *International Journal of Epidemiology*, 32(6), 1022–1028.

Subramanian, S. V., Blakely, T., and Kawachi, I. (2003, February). Income Inequality as a Public Health Concern: Where Do We Stand? Commentary on "Is Exposure to Income Inequality a Public Health Concern?" *Health Services Research*, 38(1), 153–167.

Syme, S. L. (1996). To Prevent Disease: The Need for a New Approach. In D. Blane, E. Brunner, and R. Wilkinson (Eds.), *Health and Social Organization: Towards a Health Policy for the Twenty-First Century* (pp. 21–31). London and New York: Routledge.

Tarlov, A. R. (1996). Social Determinants of Health, the Sociobiological Translation. In D. Blane, E. Brunner, and R. Wilkinson (Eds.), *Health and Social Organization*. New York: Routledge.

——. (1999, March 3). Response to George D. Smith et al., The Independent Inquiry into Inequalities in Health (Letter). *British Medical Journal*, 317(7159), 1465–1466.

Turnock, B. J. (1997). *Public Health: What It Is and How It Works*. Gaithersburg, MD: Aspen Publishers.

University of Minnesota, School of Public Health. (2013, April 1). A Powerful Partnership: Public Health and the Affordable Care Act Join Forces. Advances. Retrieved from www.advances.umn.edu/2013/04/a-powerful-partnership-public-health-and-the-affordable-care-act-join-forces

U.S. Census Bureau. (2018, September). *Income and Poverty in the United States: 2017*. Retrieved from www.census.gov/library/publications/2018/demo/p60-263.html

Waldmann, R. J. (1999). Income Distribution and Infant Mortality. In I. Kawachi, B. P. Kennedy, and R. G. Wilkinson (Eds.), *The Society and Population Health Reader*. Vol. 1, *Income Inequality and Health* (pp. 14–27). New York: New Press.

Weick, A. (1986). The Philosophical Context of a Health Model of Social Work. *Social Casework*, 67(9), 551–559.

Wennemo, I. (1993). Infant Mortality, Public Policy and Inequality: A Comparison of 18 Industrialized Countries 1950–1985. *Sociology of Health and Illness*, 15(4), 429–446.

Wilkinson, R. G. (1994). The Epidemiological Transition: From Material Scarcity to Social Disadvantage? *Daedalus*, 123(4), 61–79.

——. (1996). *Unhealthy Societies: The Affliction of Inequality*. London and New York: Routledge.

——. (1997). Income, Inequality, and Social Cohesion (Comment). *American Journal of Public Health*, 87(9), 1504–1506.

——. (1999a). Two Pathways, but How Much Do They Diverge? *British Medical Journal*, 319, 953–957.

——. (1999b). Income Distribution and Life Expectancy. In I. Kawachi, B. P. Kennedy, and R. G. Wilkinson (Eds.), *The Society and Population Health Reader. Vol. 1, Income Inequality and Health* (pp. 28–35). New York: New Press.

——. (2000). *Mind the Gap: Hierarchies, Health and Human Evolution*. London: Weidenfeld & Nicolson.

——. (2001). Why is Inequality Bad for Health? In J. A. Auerbach and B. K. Krimgold (Eds.), *Income, Socioeconomic Status, and Health: Exploring the Relationships* (pp. 29–43). Washington, DC: National Policy Association.

——. (2005). *The Impact of Inequality: How to Make Sick Societies Healthier*. New York: New Press.

——. (2006, Summer). The Impact of Inequality. *Social Research*, 73(2), 711–732.

Wilkinson, R. G. and Pickett, K. E. (2006). Income Inequality and Population Health: A Review and Explanation of the Evidence. *Social Science & Medicine*, 62(7), 1768–1784.

——. (2010). *The Spirit Level: Why More Equal Societies Almost Always Do Better*. London: AllenLane (Penguin Books).

Wolfson, M., Kaplan, G., Lynch, J., Ross, N., and Backlund, E. (1999, October 9). Relation between Income Inequality and Mortality: Empirical Demonstration. *British Medical Journal*, 319(7215), 953–957.

World Health Organization. (1958). *The First Ten Years of the World Health Organization*. Geneva: WHO.

Zheng, H. (2012, July). Do People Die from Income Inequality from a Decade Ago? *Social Science & Medicine*, 75(1), 36–45. Retrieved from www.ncbi.nlm.nih.gov/pubmed/22503559

Glossary

access An individual's ability to obtain health care services. Barriers to access are often financial (insufficient resources), geographic (distance to services), organizational (insufficient providers and services), and social (cultural, lingual, discrimination).

activities of daily living (ADL) Self-care, including bathing, dressing, eating, and moving from one place to another. An index or scale is used to measure an individual's level of independence in these activities.

acute care Medical care for short-term or episodic illness or health problems.

age-adjusted rates Age-adjusting rates is a method used to make fairer comparisons between groups with different age distributions. The age-adjusted rates are rates that would have existed if the population under study had the same age distribution as a "standard" population.

behavioral health managed care Various strategies used to control mental health and substance abuse costs while maintaining quality and appropriate levels of care.

beneficiary An individual eligible for and enrolled in a health insurance plan.

capitation A prospective method of payment for health care services. Providers are typically paid a fixed amount for each enrolled member of a health care plan to provide a predetermined package of benefits and services over a specified period of time.

carve-out plans A managed care organization that specializes in the management or provision of mental health or substance abuse benefits.

catastrophic health insurance Health insurance that protects against high cost of treating severe or long-term illness or disability; usually these policies cover expenses beyond those covered by another insurance policy, up to a maximum limit.

catchment area A geographically defined area served by a health program, institution, or plan; the area is determined on the basis of factors such as population distribution, natural geographic boundaries, and access to transportation. Typically, all residents within the area are eligible for services.

categorically needy Individuals eligible for Medicaid based on family, age, or disability status (see Chapter 6 for full discussion of distinct population groups).

charity care Medical services provided to individuals who cannot afford to pay for services, especially those who are uninsured and underinsured.

chronic care Medical care for long-term illness or disability; often these conditions are permanent, leave residual disability, are nonreversible, require patient training for rehabilitation, or require lengthy periods of supervision, observation, or care.

coinsurance The beneficiary's share of a medical bill required by a health care plan after the deductible is paid. Typically, the health care plan pays 80 percent of the cost and the beneficiary pays 20 percent.

community-based care Medical and social services provided in an individual or family's community residence to promote health and minimize the effects of illness and disability.

community health center An outpatient or ambulatory health center that usually serves residents of a catchment area with scarce services or special needs; community or neighborhood health centers were established by the federal government during the 1960s to serve low-income families in medically underserved areas. Today, these centers primarily provide services to uninsured and Medicaid populations who are in worse health than the general population.

community mental health center A center that provides ambulatory mental health services to residents within a catchment area; these centers were also established by the federal government during the 1960s. Today, these centers continue to provide services primarily to the most vulnerable populations who are poor or low income.

copayment A fixed amount paid by a beneficiary when covered services are received. Beneficiaries typically pay copayments ranging from $5 to $15 each time they receive medical benefits or services.

cost sharing The portion of the medical expenses of a health insurance policy or plan that individual enrollees are required to pay; typically, these expenses are paid through deductibles, copayments, and coinsurance.

cost shifting This occurs when providers are not reimbursed or fully reimbursed for their services. Providers charge the balance or a portion of the balance of their costs to those who pay.

covered services Medical services eligible for payment by a health care plan.

current population survey (CPS) An annual national survey conducted by the U.S. Department of Commerce, Census Bureau, to gather annual statistics about the U.S. population. The CPS provides data on health status and insurance coverage.

deductible The fixed annual amount paid by a beneficiary for medical services before the health care plan covers expenses.

deinstitutionalization A policy to reduce treatment in hospital and institutional settings and provide community-based care; this occurred in mental health care in the 1960s and 1970s.

developmental disability A chronic, severe mental and/or physical disability that manifests before adulthood (by age 21), usually continues indefinitely, and creates functional limitations in daily living. The need for special care is typically life-long or extended.

diagnostic-related groups (DRGs) The classification system established by Medicare to pay hospitals a predetermined fee for patient care for specific diagnoses; each case is reimbursed at the same rate, regardless of the actual cost of patient care.

disability Any individual limitation of physical, mental, or social activity compared with individuals of similar age, sex, and occupation; usually refers to vocational limitations, but includes functional and learning disabilities. Disabilities vary in degree and duration.

disenrollment The procedures required to cancel membership in a health care plan.

dually eligible Individuals entitled to Medicare who are also eligible for Medicaid because of their income status.

durable medical equipment Prescribed medical equipment that can be used for long periods of time, such as wheelchairs.

enrolled population or enrollees Individuals covered by a particular health plan.

epidemiology The study of the causes and patterns of illness and/or disease in human populations. Epidemiologists' aim is to apply their findings for disease prevention and health promotion.

exclusions Health care plans do not cover all health services, such as cosmetic surgery, or all services under all circumstances, such as nonemergency care in an emergency room.

federal poverty level (FPL) The U.S. Census Bureau has established an absolute measure or definition of poverty that is based on a minimal standard of living and income threshold. The poverty index is updated annually to account for inflation and is proportional to family size and composition.

fee-for-service (FFS) A traditional payment method that pays providers for each service provided. Beneficiaries with traditional fee-for-service indemnity insurance would be reimbursed for all or part of the paid fee.

group practice A formal association of three or more providers; income is pooled and redistributed to the members according to a prearranged agreement.

health disparity A particular disparity in health outcomes that is closely linked with social or economic disadvantage.

health equity The absence of systematic, unfair disparities in health (or determinants of health) among population groups in a social hierarchy or society with different levels of social advantage or disadvantage.

heath inequity A difference or disparity in health outcomes that is systematic, unfair, and can be changed.

health insurance Financial protection against medical costs that are related to disease, illness, or disability; it usually covers all or some of the costs and can be obtained on an individual or group basis.

health maintenance organization (HMO) A health care plan that provides a comprehensive set of health care services to a group of beneficiaries, usually in a geographic area, for a predetermined, prepaid, fixed fee per enrollee. The payment is fixed without regard to actual services provided

(costs incurred). Beneficiaries are often restricted to care provided by the HMO's network of providers and hospitals.

health plan An organization that provides a defined set of benefits, usually structured like an HMO.

health promotion Education and related interventions designed to improve or protect individual or population health.

health status The state of health of an individual, group, or population measured by subjective assessments, indicators of population mortality or morbidity, or incidence or prevalence of disease or illness.

home health care Services provided in the home to elderly, disabled, ill, or convalescent individuals, rather than in an institutional setting, by visiting nurses, private duty nurses, home health agency, public health department, hospital, or other groups. Nursing care, occupational and physical therapy, homemaker services, and social services are typically provided.

hospice Palliative and supportive care for terminally ill individuals and their families; hospice workers' care and support for family members often extend through their mourning period.

hospital A medical institution that provides inpatient diagnostic and therapeutic services, both surgical and nonsurgical; it also typically provides outpatient and emergency services. Hospitals can be classified as short- or long-term stay, teaching (affiliated with a university medical school) or nonteaching, specialized (such as psychiatric), or for-profit or nonprofit.

incidence In epidemiology, the number of cases of disease, infection, or other health condition or event, such as morbidity, that occurs within a prescribed period of time.

indemnity plan A fee-for-service health insurance plan.

independent practice association (IPA) A group practice that provides services on a prepaid, capitated, or fee-for-service basis. The providers remain in their own office settings, but contract with health plans to provide services.

indigent care Health care services provided to poor individuals or those unable to pay. Typically, these individuals are ineligible for Medicaid.

inpatient An individual admitted at least overnight to a hospital or health facility.

intermediate care facility (ICF) An institution licensed by a state to provide care and services to individuals who do not require hospital or skilled nursing care.

Katie Beckett children Children with disabilities under age 18 who qualify for home health care coverage through a special Medicaid provision; Katie Beckett was a ventilator-dependent child who remained institutionalized in order to maintain her Medicaid eligibility.

license or licensure Permission granted to individuals or organizations by public authorities to engage in a practice or occupation. The licensing process typically requires completion of an appropriate education, examination, and achievement of other performance measures, such as continuing education or practice supervision.

lifetime limit The maximum dollar amount paid by a health care plan for a beneficiary over his or her lifetime. A single catastrophic illness can cause a beneficiary to reach the lifetime limit.

long-term care Long-term personal care and social services provided to individuals who cannot function independently, regardless of age; services can be provided in an institution or at home, but traditionally have been provided in nursing care facilities.

managed care A variety of clinical, financial, and organizational methods used to reduce health care costs and achieve cost efficiency.

Medicaid (Title XIX of the Social Security Act) A federal–state public insurance system that provides access to health care for certain low-income individuals who meet eligibility criteria. States determine benefits, eligibility, provider payment rates, and program administration (see Chapter 6).

medically necessary An insurance industry term used to define appropriate care and care provided according to general standards of practice. A proposed treatment plan may be reviewed to determine if it is medically necessary.

medically needy Individuals categorically eligible for Medicaid whose income, less accumulated medical expenses, is lower than state income eligibility limits. This determination of eligibility is referred to as "spending down."

medically underserved population A geographically or socially defined population that has a shortage of health services, such as Native Americans. The term is used to assess priority for federal assistance from certain programs.

Medicare (Title XVIII of the Social Security Act) A federal social insurance system that provides access to health care for retired workers over the age of 65, disabled workers eligible for Social Security disability benefits, and certain individuals who need kidney transplants or dialysis (see Chapter 6).

medigap policy A private health insurance policy, strictly regulated by the federal government, offered to Medicare beneficiaries to cover expenses not covered by Medicare.

morbidity In epidemiology, the extent (incidence or prevalence) of illness, injury, or disability in a defined population.

mortality In epidemiology, the rate of death in a defined population in a prescribed period of time. *Crude death rates* are the total number of deaths in relation to total population during a year; *specified death rates* are the total number of deaths for specific diseases during a given year, and can be further specified by age, race, gender, or other attributes.

network The health care providers, medical centers, clinics, and hospitals that have a contractual agreement with a health plan to provide services to its beneficiaries.

open enrollment A specific period each year when health plans must accept all who apply; this reduces the opportunity for insurance plans to exclude individuals who are considered poor health risks.

out-of-network The use of providers who are not part of the plan's provider network. HMO beneficiaries are typically prohibited from using out-of-network services except in an emergency. Members of preferred provider organizations and HMOs with point-of-service options can seek care out-of-network but are required to pay additional costs.

out-of-pocket limit The maximum dollar amount a health care plan requires a beneficiary to pay for deductibles, copayments, and coinsurance annually (excluding premiums).

outpatient An individual who receives ambulatory services without being admitted to the hospital.

point-of-service (POS) A health insurance benefits plan that gives beneficiaries the option to choose among different delivery systems (HMO, PPO, FFS), rather than selecting one option during open enrollment. Typically, this is a more expensive option for enrollees.

practice guidelines A set of guidelines developed by health care professionals to determine the most effective treatments.

preexisting condition A diagnosed condition or problem that existed before enrollment in a health plan or insurance policy. Under the Health Insurance Portability and Accountability Act of 1997, insurers can no longer deny coverage for preexisting conditions until beneficiaries meet waiting period requirements.

preferred provider organization (PPO) A formal organization that typically includes hospitals and providers who receive discounted rates in exchange for a market share of beneficiaries and expedited payments. Enrollees can receive services from PPO or non-PPO providers, but their cost sharing is lower if they stay within the PPO.

primary care Routine health care services provided by a physician trained in family medicine, internal medicine, or pediatrics, or a nurse practitioner or physician's assistant. Primary care physicians are considered the ideal point of entry into the medical system and should be responsible for overall coordination of patient care.

privatization The trend to shift functions traditionally performed by public entities to the private sector.

prospective payment Amounts or rates of payment determined in advance for a defined period; providers accept these amounts regardless of actual costs incurred.

prospective payment system The system established by Medicare to pay hospitals on a prospective basis using diagnostic-related groups (DRGs).

provider Hospital, facility, or licensed professional that provides health care services.

public health Organized health promotion activities, programs, and policies. Typical public health activities include immunizations, sanitation, health education, disease control, occupational health and safety programs, and air, food, and water quality.

quality of care Extent to which health care services meet professional standards and consumer satisfaction; providers, procedures, and outcomes can be measured.

risk An unpredictable level of need and associated costs for health care services; the potential difference between projected and actual costs.

risk-bearing entity An organization that assumes financial responsibility for the provision of a set of benefits by accepting prepayment for *some* (partial risk) or *all* (full risk) of the cost of care.

risk sharing An arrangement among parties to share the financial responsibility for the provision of services.

section 1115 Medicaid waiver Establishes authority to waive certain Medicaid regulations to encourage demonstration or experimental projects; states allowed to change Medicaid provisions.

section 1915(b) Medicaid waiver Allows states to establish mandatory enrollment in managed care plans in an effort to reduce costs; often referred to as "freedom-of-choice waiver."

seriously mentally ill Individuals defined by the community mental health services block grant as adults over age 18 who have been diagnosed with a mental illness that results in functional impairment and substantially limits activities of daily living.

skilled nursing facility (SNF) Nursing care facilities that meet specified regulations for services, staffing, and safety to participate in the Medicare and Medicaid programs.

social determinants of health (SDH) *(World Health Organization definition)* "The circumstances in which people are born, grow up, live, work, and age, as well as the systems put in place to deal with illness. These circumstances are in turn shaped by a wider set of forces: economics, social policies, and politics" (see www.who.int/social_determinants/thecommission/finalreport/key_concepts/en/index.html).

social determinants of health (SDH) *(U.S. Department of Health and Human Services [DHHS] definition)* "The complex, integrated, and overlapping social structures and economic systems that include the social environment, physical environment, and health services; structural and societal factors that are responsible for most health inequities. SDH are shaped by the distribution of money, power and resources at global, national, and local levels, which are themselves influenced by policy choices" (see www.cdc.gov/socialdeterminants/docs/SDH-White-Paper-2010.pdf).

underinsured Individuals with private or public insurance that does not cover all necessary health care services, resulting in out-of-pocket expenses that exceed ability to pay or represent a significant portion of income.

uninsured Individuals who lack private or public health insurance.

utilization review Evaluation of the use of health care services, procedures, and facilities, including necessity, appropriateness, and efficiency, conducted by a peer review group or a public agency. This process has been used to reduce unnecessary hospital admissions and reduce the length of hospital stays.

I n d e x